Integrative Assessment
of Adult Personality

Integrative Assessment of Adult Personality

Edited by
LARRY E. BEUTLER
MICHAEL R. BERREN

THE GUILFORD PRESS / New York   London

Library of Congress Cataloging-in-Publication Data

Integrative assessment of adult personality / edited by Larry E.
    Beutler, Michael R. Berren.
        p.   cm.
    Includes bibliographical references and index.
    ISBN 0-89862-281-6
    1. Personality assessment.   2. Personality tests.   3. Adulthood—
Psychological aspects.   I. Beutler, Larry E.   II. Berren, Michael
R.
    [DNLM: 1. Personality Tests.   2. Personality Assessment.   WM 145
I57 1994]
BF698.4.I58 1995
155.2'8—dc20
DNLM/DLC
for Library of Congress   94-19183
                                                              CIP

To my patients, clients, and students,
all of whom have been and are my teachers.
                                    —L. E. B.

To my family: my departed father;
my mother; the core of my joy, my children,
Melissa and Scott; and certainly the center
of my life, my wife, Esther.
                                    —M. R. B.

Contributors

Michael R. Berren, Ph.D., is a psychologist who resides in Tucson, Arizona. His work as a psychologist focuses primarily on assessment and rehabilitation of the seriously mentally ill. Dr. Berren is also Adjunct Associate Professor in the Department of Psychology at the University of Arizona, where he teaches the graduate clinical psychology assessment practicum. Dr. Berren obtained his Ph.D. from Texas Tech University. He has published numerous articles on issues related to systems of care for the seriously mentally ill. When not "being a psychologist," Dr. Berren is an accomplished artist and has had many gallery showings.

Larry E. Beutler, Ph.D., is Professor and Director of the Counseling/Clinical/School Psychology Program at the University of California, Santa Barbara. He is also the Editor of the *Journal of Consulting and Clinical Psychology*, a Diplomate (Clinical) of the American Board of Professional Psychology, and a Past President of the Society for Psychotherapy Research.

James N. Butcher, Ph.D., is Professor of Psychology in the Department of Psychology at the University of Minnesota. He obtained an M.A. in experimental psychology in 1962 and a Ph.D. in clinical psychology in 1964 from the University of North Carolina at Chapel Hill. In 1990 he was awarded an honorary doctorate from the Free University of Brussels. Dr. Butcher is a member of the University of Minnesota Press's MMPI Consultative Committee. He is the Editor of *Psychological Assessment* and serves as consulting editor for numerous other journals in psychology and psychiatry. He is a Fellow of the American Psychological Association and the Society for Personality Assessment.

John F. Clarkin, Ph.D., is Professor of Clinical Psychology in the Department of Psychiatry at Cornell University Medical College, and Director, Division of Psychology, at The New York Hospital. He obtained his Ph.D. from Fordham University in 1971. He is a consulting editor for the *Journal of Consulting and Clinical Psychology* and on the editorial boards of a number of other journals.

M. Anne Corbishley, Ph.D., is a Graduate Faculty Associate at the Simon Fraser University in British Columbia, Canada. She obtained her doctorate from the University of Arizona in 1987. Her research interests include sleep patterns and psychotherapy in aging adults, and cognitive therapy.

Roger Davis, Ph.D., is a University Fellow at the University of Miami. His recent publications include "The Five-Factor Model for Personality Disorders: Apt or Misguided," in *Psychological Inquiry*; "The Importance of Theory to a Taxonomy of Personality Disorders," a chapter in W. J. Livesley (Ed.), *The DSM-IV Personality Disorders*; and "Objective Assessment of Anxiety," a chapter in B. Wolman (Ed.), *Handbook of Anxiety*. He is a coauthor of the MCMI-III, MACI, and MIPS.

Kevin F. Gaw, Ph.D., is a staff psychologist at the University of Missouri, Rolla, providing psychotherapy and assessment services at UMR's Counseling and Career Development Center. He is a graduate of the Counseling Psychology Program at the University of California, Santa Barbara. His interests include psychotherapy research, the training of psychotherapists, student development, religion and psychology, cross-cultural psychology, and culture shock.

Stephen W. Hurt, Ph.D., is Associate Professor at Cornell University Medical College and Associate Attending Psychologist at The New York Hospital–Cornell Medical Center—Westchester Division in White Plains, New York. He obtained his Ph.D. from the University of Chicago in 1978; is a member of the editorial boards of the *Journal of Personality Disorders* and *Assessment*; and is the coauthor, with Marvin Reznikoff and John F. Clarkin, of *Psychological Assessment, Psychiatric Diagnosis and Treatment Planning*.

Theodore Millon, Ph.D., is Professor of Psychology at the University of Miami and Professor in Psychiatry at Harvard Medical School. He is Co-Editor-in-Chief of the *Journal of Personality Disorders* and a Past President of the International Society for the Study of Personality Disorders. A recent recipient of an honorary doctorate from the University of Brussels, Dr. Millon is the author of several self-report inventories (MCMI-III, MACI, MBHI), as well as the recently published *Millon Inventory of Personality Styles* (*MIPS*). His books include *Disorders of Personality* and *Toward a New Personology: An Evolutionary Model.*

Marvin Reznikoff, Ph.D., is Professor of Psychology at Fordham University, where he also served as Director of the Clinical Program and then Chair of the Psychology Department. He received his Ph.D. from New York University in 1953 and is a Diplomate in Clinical Psychology of the American Board of Professional Psychology. His principal research interests and publications are in the areas of personality assessment and health psychology.

Rita Rosner, Diplom-Psychologin, is a Scientific Collaborator at the Ludwig-Maximilians-Universität in Munich, Germany. She is concurrently teaching courses on psychotherapy research and completing her dissertation on emotional arousal in group psychotherapies.

Elizabeth B. Yost, Ph.D., is a lecturer in the Counseling/Clinical/School Psychology Program at the University of California, Santa Barbara. She received her Ph.D. in counseling psychology from the University of Oregon in 1973. Dr. Yost is a Diplomate of the American Board of Professional Psychology and was formerly Associate Professor and Research Associate in the Department of Psychiatry, University of Arizona Medical Center.

Heidi A. Zetzer, Ph.D., is Project Coordinator of the Psychotherapy Research Project in the Graduate School of Education at the University of California, Santa Barbara. She obtained a master's degree in counseling psychology from Ohio State University in 1986 and a Ph.D. in counseling psychology from the University of California, Santa Barbara, in 1990. Research and clinical areas of expertise include child sexual abuse, eating disorders, student development, and psychotherapy process and outcome.

Preface

Although it is common to judge individuals by the clothes they wear or by the way they appear (or, if you are a psychologist, by MMPI or MCMI profiles, or by Rorschach or WAIS-R scores, or by a clinical interview), this single-dimension approach is likely to result in invalid conclusions and incorrect predictions. The conclusions will be invalid not because of anything inherently faulty in the source of information used or in the accuracy of the observation, but because a single source or type of information, even if it is as sophisticated as the MMPI-2 or MCMI, is limited in how accurately it reflects real-world experience. Each piece of information about a patient—psychological test data, observation, history, or clinical interview—is only one piece of an assessment puzzle. Depending upon the complexity of the questions asked, the clinical issues that need to be addressed, and the amount of error that can be tolerated, more (or fewer) pieces of the puzzle will need to be obtained and integrated. For example, personality assessment that is done as part of an intake procedure in a university counseling center serving only students will probably require fewer pieces of information and less integration than an assessment done in a forensic setting, or an assessment that will be used as part of child custody determination.

Long before humorists identified the issue, we were all aware of the fable about the blind men who were trying to determine the nature of an elephant by touching it. The blind man who touched the long trunk concluded that the elephant was one thing; the blind man touching the leathery and wide leg of the elephant concluded that it was something else; and the blind man touching the tusks concluded that it must be something else again. Each of the blind men might have been quite accurate in describing what he had touched. None, however, were correct in *generalizing* from what they touched. They were not correct because they had obtained useful but insufficient data. The data we collect during the process of personality assessment are useful only to the extent that we can translate the "snapshots" derived from each instrument into an accurate "moving picture" of the patient. The data must be both useful and sufficient if we are to do so.

Personality assessment, as a general rule of thumb, is not based on either a single issue or observation. An individual's assessment should not be based solely on his/her responses to an MMPI or an MCMI. Similarly, although a clinical interview is extremely important, it may not yield an accurate picture of a patient unless it is supplemented by objective, normative data. In undertaking a comprehensive assessment of a patient, it is important to collect and utilize a variety of sources and types of information, including psychological testing data, observations, interviews, and collateral reports. It is just as important (or even more so) to integrate that information.

As you are reading this preface, you may already be asking yourself: "What are the questions that an assessment should address?" "What types of data are necessary to complete a personality assessment?" "How many data are sufficient to complete a personality assessment?" "How does one integrate the data once various types have been collected?" and "How does one utilize the integrated assessment in treatment planning?" It is with those questions in mind that we have prepared this textbook.

Many textbooks presently available are dedicated to various aspects of personality assessment. Some textbooks focus on clinical interviewing and direct observations, and others focus on the use of formal psychological tests. Those that focus on psychological tests can be further subdivided into two basic types: those that provide compendia of psychological instruments and descriptions, and those that focus on specific procedures, such as the MMPI or Rorschach.

Like the editors of many other textbooks, we began this book because of our belief that there was and is something missing in the array of textbooks available to our students. Because of the decision of previous authors and editors to focus either on one test, a variety of formal tests, or on clinical interviewing and observational methods, none of the textbooks currently available are well suited to constructing the "moving picture" of a complex personality. None focus on the integration of various observations and the use of the assessment in treatment planning. This narrow view has obscured the fact that personality assessment is not merely psychological testing or clinical interviewing.

Our recognition of the weaknesses in available textbooks has always been clearest when we have taught classes and practica in psychological assessment, as we have at two separate universities. Each of us teaches an assessment practicum in an integrated manner, attempting to lead the students to recognize that personality assessment is partly art and partly science. It is with our students in mind and a focus on teaching the scientific and artistic parts that are necessary and how to integrate those parts that we have organized this book. As we view it, personality assessment is a process that includes the administration, scoring, and interpretation of psychological tests; clinical interviewing, observation, and the gathering of historical and collateral information; and, finally, the integration of those unique pieces of information so that they can be used to predict the patient's functioning reliably and validly.

Being pragmatists, we believe that personality assessment should serve some purpose other than just academic interest. In most situations, that purpose is treatment planning. The more objective information we have about our patients (in terms of cognitive processing, likely responses to stress, defense mechanisms, etc.), the more likely it is that we will be able to work with the patients in deriving effective treatment plans. Given the reality of managed care and national health care, it is incumbent upon all of us to design the most effective treatment plans we can. Adequate assessment and treatment planning, which may have initial up-front costs, can save dollars and human suffering.

This is not a textbook of personality theory, and hence we do not devote time or space to espousing a particular definition or theory of personality. We have worked to make this approach to personality assessment appropriate and useful, regardless of particular theories about the nature and determinants of personality. Suffice it to say that our notions of personality assessment focus primarily on predictions of present and future behavior, based on the development of hypotheses about how individuals view the world, how they cope with stress, how they process information, and how they relate to other people.

As we undertook this task, we recognized that we could not (and did not want to) include a vast number of tests in this book, such as are often included in survey texts. We decided to sample the available tests and to include an in-depth presentation of those that are the most frequently used in the psychologist's tool kit. Certainly, however, we recognize that we have not included many important tests that psychologists use. We have employed three criteria for deciding which tests to consider. First, this text addresses assessment of adults; hence, any tests that focus primarily on children and adolescents were not considered. Second, since personality and related behaviors are our primary concern, tests and issues related to specific purposes in health and neuropsychological assessment are not included. Finally, we selected those for which empirical validation was most readily available. The authors of the individual chapters in this book were asked to write their chapters from the perspective that the information they were sharing was but one part of the assessment process. They were given the general model of assessment that we espouse, and kindly agreed to organize their presentations around the integrative purposes of this volume. We thank them for their willingness to accede to our views.

The chapters of this book are arranged to reflect a method of assessment and integration that proceeds from the definition of the referral question to the organization of treatment plans. The first chapter provides basic information on test development and validation. The second chapter provides our method of integrating information from disparate sources, and presents a model of report writing. The third chapter considers issues related to the selection of assessment instruments, and the following chapter describes the use of the clinical interview both for gathering information and for setting the stage for the rest of the assessment experience. Chapters 5, 6, 7, and 8 focus on specific assessment procedures—the WAIS-R, the Rorschach, the MMPI, and the MCMI, respectively. Chapter 9 is a description of how information can be applied to the task of making treatment recommendations, and the last chapter is a workbook that will assist the reader in learning the principles both of test interpretation and of integrative report writing.

We hope that as new tests evolve, and that even as our readers decide to include tests other than those described here in the process of assessment, the present guidelines will continue to be useful and helpful. The methods presented for integrating sources of information are designed to be portable and relatively simple to adapt to a variety of purposes. Whether a psychologist is using the MMPI, the MCMI, the TAT, or the Eating Disorders Inventory, the issues of integrating the test findings with other information for a comprehensive evaluation and treatment plan remain the same.

Although this textbook has been written primarily for graduate students taking an assessment practicum and for trainees doing initial assessment and treatment planning work, we hope that it will also be useful to practicing psychologists as a reference and guide.

Finally, we would hope that following the reading and studying of this book, it would be clear to the men feeling the elephant that in order to draw accurate conclusions, one needs to base opinions on observations of various and divergent types.

LARRY E. BEUTLER
MICHAEL R. BERREN

Contents

9. Integrating Treatment Recommendations   280
Kevin F. Gaw and Larry E. Beutler

10. Integrative Assessment: A Workbook   320
M. Anne Corbishley and Elizabeth B. Yost

Index   403

Introduction to Psychological Assessment

Larry E. Beutler
Rita Rosner

How would you describe the distinctive qualities of George Bush, Bill Clinton, and Ronald Reagan? In certain ways, these individuals are the same: They are males and they have all been elected president of the United States. However, in most ways, each of these men is different from the others. Which of the many differences among them are relevant enough to select as "distinctive"? Relevant for what? Which differences reflect variation in intellectual ability? Which are "personality" traits? Which reflect the influences of being in the role of "president"?

Psychological assessment is designed to answer such questions, as well as other questions that have clinical relevance. Psychological "assessment" or "measurement" is the application of classification or numbering systems to the description of individual differences. The objectives of psychological assessment in clinical settings are to answer questions that pertain to five clinically relevant domains of behavior: (1) diagnosis; (2) etiology, or causes of behavior; (3) prognosis, or anticipated course of the symptoms; (4) treatments that may ameliorate or alter that course; and (5) the degree of functional impairment in both routine and specialized life functions.

Although these objectives of clinical assessment all focus on questions relating to disordered or disruptive behavior, assessment, in order to address these questions, must also be able to identify the many varieties of normal or usual behaviors. Only by knowing what constitute "usual" behaviors and "normal" responses to life's situations will a clinician be able to identify the nature and severity of behavioral disturbance and to assess the relevance of the measured behaviors for the questions asked.

Since differences among people may occur in so many different ways, and the questions asked in psychological assessment are so diverse, psychological assessment has come to be identified by a variety of terms. Many of these terms reflect different subdivisions of human experience and functioning. "Mental status," "cognitive," "intellectual," "emotional," "social," and "personality" assessment reflect what are thought by some to be different and distinct domains of psychological performance. These distinctions are quite arbitrary, however, and all these types of assessment involve overlapping methods, albeit with somewhat different targets of functioning. Indeed, we believe that by implying that intelligence, mental state, and personality (for instance) are independent of one another, these different identifiers create a fractionated picture of a person. In the course of human functioning, "cognitive" and "intellectual" skills are not independent of one's "personality"; one's "mental status" is neither different nor dissociated from one's "emotional" or "behavioral" status; and so on.

Because these terms suggest that different domains of functioning are being addressed by differently labeled evaluations, it is not unusual for a client or patient to be referred to three or more different mental health professionals in order to obtain, variously, a "social history" evaluation by a social worker, an "intellectual" evaluation or "personality" evaluation by a psychologist, and a "mental status" examination by a psychiatrist. When disciplines are fragmented in this way, professionals within each discipline develop their own favored procedures; express opinions and formulate responses from a favored theoretical perspective; and (not surprisingly) make recommendations contradicting those of other professioinals who use different methods, language, and theories. In reading different reports from different professionals, one often cannot tell that they are describing the same person. This variability perpetuates the myth that different aspects or domains of functioning are being assessed by these different methods. However, Kopta, Newman, McGovern, and Sandrock (1986) have demonstrated the profound differences that various theoretical frameworks and procedures can make in the nature and cost of recommended treatment. One need not invoke the story of the blind men and the elephant (see the Preface) to see the problems in this picture.

A fragmented picture of the client also frequently emerges in another way among practitioners who report the results of psychological tests. This fragmentation is observed when clinicians report the findings from one test after another as if each provides a comprehensive view of the person. The inevitable contradictions in the findings of different tests are either presented and ignored, omitted in the report, or hastily excused in a summary paragraph. The failure to integrate and explain discrepancies in terms of *person* functions, rather than *test* functions, leaves the reader with a confused picture of the patient.

This book is written with a decided emphasis on integration. It is designed to address the need for both bringing together information from different domains of patient experience and, concurrently, making sense of the interpretative discrepancies that often exist among the sources of information available to the clinician. Although the means that conventionally are used to assess human experience are too varied to address within a single volume, we have undertaken two tasks in this book: (1) to outline a general method for integrating and organizing a divergent array of clinical methods and observations, in order to evaluate patterns and resolve contradictions among clinical procedures; and (2) to provide some representative and specific guidelines for extracting and integrating information from a few of the most frequently used and empirically defensible clinical assessment procedures. The method presented for organizing and integrating sources of information is sufficiently general and flexible to be applicable to as many types of referral questions and assessment methods as possible. Concomitantly, the specific procedures illustrated have been selected not only because of their frequency of use among clinicians, but because they can be adapted to address many of the questions that referrants are likely to have in mind when they request "cognitive" assessment, "personality" assessment, "mental status" evaluation, and "diagnostic" testing.

The Nature of Psychological Tests

The use of modern psychological tests is a contemporary representation of a process that is as long as the history of humankind—the effort to identify the nature of individual differences and to account for both the similarities and uniqueness of each human's experience. These efforts were and are imbedded in the perennial attempts of peoples worldwide to predict and control their lives. Throughout time, the speed at which people gained the abilities to predict and control events around them was governed by how well they overcame two major problems: (1) distinguishing among the situational and personal contributors to behavior, and (2) identifying the concepts that could best describe these similarities and differences. Psychological tests represent contemporary efforts to respond to the first of these problems, while contemporary theories of human development and psychopathology represent efforts to respond to the second.

Estimates of the situational and characterological ("state" vs. "trait") contributions to behavior and personal experience can be based on formal procecures (psychological tests) or informal procedures (intuitive or unspecified observations). The distinction between these methods is simply that formal procedures define the rules of logic that govern the process, standardize the contexts and methods of observation, and define the terms used for describing the differences observed. These processes are illustrated in Figure 1.1, which presents the responses of two different individuals to the Bender Visual Motor Gestalt Test (BVMGT; Bender, 1938). The BVMGT

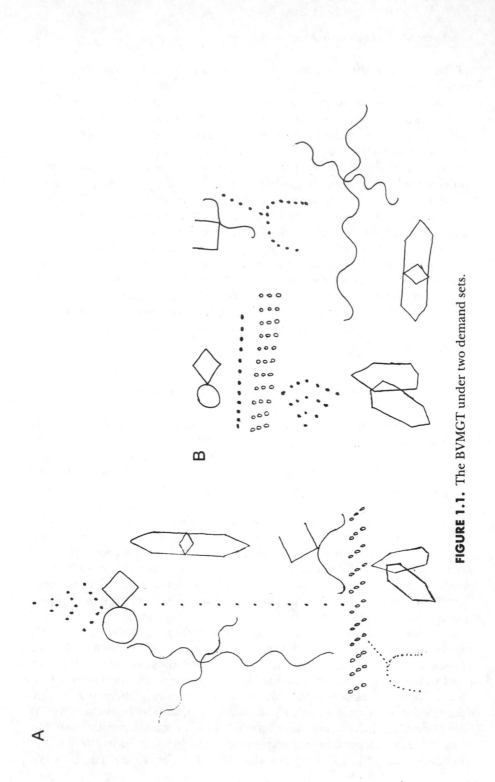

FIGURE 1.1. The BVMGT under two demand sets.

requires the subject to copy nine geometric figures, each of which is separately presented on a small card. As you inspect the differences, speculate about what these drawings indicate about the people who made them. Do they have different intellectual levels? Different personalities? Is one psychotic or emotionally disturbed?

Answers to these questions are not possible unless we know what the subjects were asked to do. Suppose that person A was told, "Copy these figures, placing them all in some pattern," whereas person B was told simply, "Copy the figures the best you can." Under these conditions, we cannot determine how much of the difference between the two sets of drawings can be attributed to the instructions and how much to differences in the characteristics (i.e., intellectual abilities, perceptual–motor skills, or personalities) of the respondents. To get around this problem, psychological tests attempt to provide a constant environment and a standard set of instructions, so that externally induced sources of variation in the two responses can be reduced or eliminated.

Instead of the respondents' having been given different instructions, let us suppose that (as in the standardized administration of the BVMGT) the two respondents were both given the instructions, "Copy each design the best you can." Knowing that the test was the same for each of the respondents, what can we infer about the relative conventionality of their problem-solving efforts and the integrity of their personalities? To make such inferences, tests are scored; that is, the responses are classified.

The results of psychological measurement, whether they be formal tests or informal clinical observations, are expressed as either a "categorical" or a "dimensional" classification. An example of a categorical classification is the application of a psychiatric diagnosis. A person is assigned to a diagnostic class or type on the basis of a simple dichotomy of "fit" or "no fit" with certain criteria. Dimensional assessment, on the other hand, assumes that certain qualities are best described as existing in some varying amount in most or all people. It is assumed, therefore, that qualities of this type are only roughly and inaccurately described by a categorical classification. Dimensional assessment is exemplified in quantitative estimates of the magnitude of such attributes as anger, depression, maladjustment, anxiety, neuroticism, extraversion, fear, and so forth.

Interpreting these scores forces us to grapple with the second problem in psychological measurement—translating the scores into concepts that have clinical meaning to others. Tests are administered and scored according to established rules and conventions. However, assigning an accurate meaning to the results of the tests depends on the nature, validity, and usefulness of the theoretical concepts that clinicians themselves use when they think about how and why people behave as they do. Such concepts as "problem-solving ability," "anxiety," "conflict," and "personality" are inferred, not observed directly. That is, they are hypothetical constructs whose existence can only be estimated from observed behaviors or reported experience. Their value is measured not only by how well they describe or predict behavior, but by how much consensual agreement exists in their meaning among those with whom clinicians communicate. As will be pointed out repeatedly in the following chapters, it is important for psychologists to learn the concepts and terms that are embodied in several different theories, and to communicate results in common as well as theory-specific language in order to maximize the value of communication. It is also necessary for clinicians to be aware of the theoretical concepts and models that they use as they think about why people behave as they do, since these will always be reflected in their reports.

Psychological tests can only help us as clinicians in the task of responding to consultation requests after we decide what concepts to use when we communicate our findings. The processes of integrating, ordering, and transmitting information from both informal and formal measurement procedures are considerably less systematic and technical than the tasks of administering and scoring psychological tests. In this volume, we prefer to use the term "psychological assessment" rather than "psychological testing" to capture this broader function of the clinician. Psychological assessment includes the use of clinical skills beyond the mechanical administration of tests and computation of scores. It recognizes that the measurement instrument of greatest value in the final analysis is the clinician, not the test. The clinician's skills in integrating sources of information, contemplating the meanings of discrepant cues, formulating opinions, and persuading others to listen constitute the focus of this book. The clinician who conducts a psychological assessment is a consultant, rather than a technician who administers a test; a consultant delivers opinions, not procedures.

The Nature of Psychological Assessment

The requirements of psychological assessment can be illustrated by addressing the four steps that constitute the process itself. These steps require an understanding of the social systems through which patients enter or seek assessment; an understanding of the nature of measurement, and familiarity with the measurement devices available; knowledge of methods of interpreting these observations; and familiarity with the process of communicating the findings and opinions to others. The four steps are as follows:

1. Identifying the problem to be addressed.
2. Selecting and implementing methods for extracting the information needed.
3. Integrating sources of information around the original purposes.
4. Reporting opinions and recommendations.

The first of these steps is basic to the psychologist's role in many contexts, and the second is the technical function of test selection, administration, and scoring. We assume that the advanced graduate students and professionals for whom this text is intended are familiar with basic psychometric principles and with the technical skills of responding to a referral, selecting instruments, administering these tests, and scoring them. Thus, in this chapter we review only the basic principles associated with the first two steps. Chapter 3 considers the selection of specific tests. The rest of the book is devoted to the third and fourth steps, the advanced principles of formulating, integrating, and communicating opinions—the activities of the consultant/psychologist.

Identifying the Problem

We have said that psychological testing is the application of measurement to the description of individual differences. However, in practice the nature of psychological assessment is more complex than this simple statement suggests. Good clinical assessment begins with translating requests for consultation into questions that can be meaningfully answered by clinical methods. Patients are referred to psychologists for many different reasons, not all of which are stated by the persons making the referrals. Moreover, not all of the ways in which people differ from one another are either likely to be of interest to a clinician or amenable to clinical assessment methods.

For example, let us return to the questions asked at the beginning of this chapter. To a political analyst, the most important distinctions among Bush, Reagan, and Clinton may be their political affiliations. Reagan and Bush are Republicans and Clinton is a Democrat. Although classifying these men by political affiliation represents a method of categorical measurement and scoring, the resultant classification provides little help in deriving an answer to clinical questions. A mental health clinician may find that questions such as "Do any of these men have a clinical disorder?", "Are they depressed?", or "Do any of them pose a danger to themselves or others?" are more relevant.

Before accepting a referral, a clinician must determine what question or questions are being asked, whether these questions are clinically relevant, and whether they can be answered within the time allotted and by the methods available. The determination of clinical relevance is particularly important. Clinically relevant referral questions are of five general types: (1) They ask for a description or formulation of the pattern of current behaviors; (2) they ask about the causes of the behaviors observed; (3) they ask about the changes that can be anticipated in these behaviors over time; (4) they ask for ways in which these patterns may be modified; or (5) they ask about patterns and areas of deficit. In other words, they address the objectives of determining diagnosis, etiology, prognosis, differential treatment, and degree of functional impairment, respectively, as outlined at the beginning of this chapter.

Diagnostic questions may be phrased as requests to rule in or rule out certain diagnoses, or they may ask how certain symptoms and behaviors are related to one another. Questions of etiology may take the form of inquiring about whether or not traumatic brain damage is present, or asking whether a patient's disturbed interpersonal relationships can be attributed to a recent loss or trauma. Both diagnostic and etiological questions seek to clarify the nature (e.g., interrelationship, severity, etc.) of problematic behaviors.

On the other hand, questions about whether a given condition is likely to dissipate with time, or whether a given person is at risk for a future problem, are ones of prognosis. At issue is the prediction of the normal course of change and development in various behaviors and symptoms. Questions of the fourth type, differential treatment planning, are related to prognosis questions and ask the clinician to anticipate what will happen with the patient's symptoms under certain imposed conditions (e.g., "Is this patient a good candidate for psychotherapy?", "Should antidepressant or antipsychotic medication be used?"). Some treatment questions are designed to prevent future problems (e.g., "Will education prevent this at-risk person from developing alcoholism?"). And finally, questions about functional impairment may include those that seek information about the patient's premorbid level of performance (e.g., "How much of this person's impairment predated the trauma?") and those that seek to estimate some future level of performance (e.g., "What is this patient's employment potential?" or "What level of achievement can we expect of this individual?"). Questions of these types derive either from a desire to determine what expectations others may reasonably have of patients after their acute symptoms dissipate, or from a desire to compute the cost factors associated with a disability.

When health care professionals seek consultation from other professionals, they frequently use shorthand communication methods, often without being fully aware that those with whom they are consulting must be familiar with these abbreviated communications in order to respond to them adequately. Hence, a responding clinician must learn to distinguish the stated reasons for referring a patient from the unstated ones. Stated requests are often either too general or too specific to allow the responding clinician to adequately address the covert or unstated needs.

For example, the most frequent requests from referring psychiatrists are couched in very broad terms such as "diagnostic testing" or "personality assessment," which are too general to be easily addressed. Such requests do not allow a psychologist to select an efficient way of responding. The request for "diagnostic testing," if taken literally, could include an 8-hour neuropsychological evaluation, the administration of 30 different projective tests, 15 hours of interviews and paper-and-pencil tests, and a two-night sleep and penile plethysmographic study if all diagnoses described by the fourth edition of the *Diagnostic and Statistical Manual of Mental Disorders* (DSM-IV; American Psychiatric Association, 1994) were to be systematically considered. These procedures not only are very expensive but constitute an inefficient use of time, because the referrant usually has a more narrow view of the most likely diagnostic options that he or she wishes to have considered.

Similarly, some overt requests are so specific that they do not allow the psychologist enough latitude to develop a reasoned response. A request for the "MMPI" or "projective testing" is usually a code phrase that indicates a request for assistance in making a differential diagnosis. But if such requests are taken at face value, their specificity prevents the responding psychologist from selecting the most useful measures for addressing this issue, and precludes consideration of the concomitant influence of characteristics that may be more reliably and validly obtained from other methods. For example, restricting an assessment either to the MMPI-2 or to a projective method like the Rorschach will be inadequate if the covert request is to find out how the patient functions in his/her family. These tests do not directly consider the family context. Moreover, under the best of circumstances, a request for a specific test or type of tests will be insufficient if test results are not considered in light of the patient's living circumstances and intellectual abilities, both of which must be ascertained through the use of other assessment methods. A given profile on the MMPI-2 will warrant very different interpretations if the patient has borderline intellectual abilities and is living in a group home than if the patient has superior intellectual resources and is living independently.

Reframing or translating the overt request into a question that reflects the actual problem facing the referrant simplifies the tasks of the consulting psychologist. Reframing a request either for "diagnostic testing" or for the "MMPI," for example, will probably result in an answerable question such as the following: "Is this person's depression of the unipolar or bipolar type?" Similarly, restating the request for "personality evaluation" or for "projective testing" as an answerable question will probably result in something like this: "Is this patient able to cope with the stress of job loss without becoming psychotic?"

The first task of the clinician upon receiving a request for evaluation, therefore, is to contact the referrant and to discuss the request in sufficient detail that an answerable question emerges or can be developed. An answerable question possesses the qualities of being specific, of addressing concepts and issues that are within the domain of psychological practice, and of suggesting concepts that possess the qualities of specificity and sensitivity. In order to translate overt requests into questions that possess these qualities, the clinician usually needs to obtain information concerning the patient's background, current and anticipated treatments, and the time frame in which the answers are needed. For example, the clinician might ask the referrant to elaborate on the patient's current problem, to detail why the referrant thinks psychological assessment will help, to specify what the clinician needs to find out, to describe how the information obtained will be used, and to indicate what decisions are pending or awaiting the results. Background courses in normal development, abnormal psychology, psychopathology, comparative treatments, and differential treatment efficacy will help the clinician frame questions to define the nature of the referral.

Selecting and Implementing the Assessment Tools

Fundamentally, psychological assessment boils down to the task of measuring and classifying observations. The processes of selecting and administering psychological tests are formalized extensions of what we all do in daily life. We meet a person at a cocktail party (identify the situational demands on behavior); observe the person as he/she interacts with us (observe samples of behavior); compare the person's response to that of others or to our prior experiences in similar situations (measure and compare); and conclude that the person is likely to be friendly or unfriendly, likable or unlikable (generalize to unobserved or future situations). We have observed, measured, and classified (i.e., diagnosed) the person; queried about his/her history (explored etiology); developed expectations of future responses (determined prognosis); predicted how the person would respond to certain information about us (assessed a differential response to treatment); and drawn conclusions about the person's strengths and weaknesses (identified functional impairments). In daily life, our safety and existence often depend on our ability to observe, measure, and classify accurately. If we perform these tasks poorly, we may be socially insensitive (inaccurate measurement), mistakenly assume that others will not hurt us (inaccurate prediction), or find ourselves becoming anxious when others' behavior changes abruptly (inaccurate generalization).

The distinctions between these day-to-day assessments and professional psychological assessment lie primarily in the degree of measurement precision used by clinicians and the theoretical origin of the constructs used to lend understanding, prediction, and control to the realm of behavioral events. Unlike a cocktail party observer, a psychologist uses concepts founded in formal psychological theories rather than in common-sense meanings. But, like the cocktail party observer, the clinician looks beyond each subject's responses to the nature of the situation in which the response occurs. Behaviors are judged within their context. All psychological assessment assumes that both the test environment and the associated behaviors constitute representative samples both of external environments and of concomitant responses in these environments. Hence, it is assumed that the relationship that exists between relevant test demands and resultant "scores" will be recapitulated on a magnified scale in an external environment. In other words, clinicians assume that the important elements of the testing environment correspond with similar elements of the real world, and that the symbolized meaning of test "scores" will be associated with a predictable set of behaviors within these real-world environments.

Because of the various ways they are structured, some tests are better suited than others to assess the domain of cognition; others are best suited to assess the domain of overt behavior; and still others are best suited to tap the domain of emotion. Although these domains of experience are not independent, they have some unique qualities and vary in importance from one environment to another. Hence, a psychologist must know both the domain of behavior that is best assessed by a given test, and the nature of the environment to which that response domain is best generalized.

Test environments are designed to vary along at least three dimensions. These dimensions parallel aspects of various external or real-world environments. Hence, observing how patients respond to tests that embody the characteristics of different points along each of these dimensions has value for predicting the nature of behavior. Their value in a comprehensive assessment procedure is discussed at greater length in Chapter 2. Suffice it to say at this point that test environments are designed to vary in the degree to which they (1) are structured or ambiguous, (2) attend to internal or external experience, and (3) place stress on the respondent.

Depending on the nature of the referral question, various aspects of these dimensions should be emphasized in the selection of tests. Ambiguity in an environment provides information about the respondent's ability to organize and interpret experience. Hence, tests that vary in ambiguity may suggest something about the patient's ability to use cognitive resources such as abstract and logical thought to integrate experience. Likewise, observing how the patient responds to methods that focus variously on internal and external experience may provide information about his/her coping styles, impulsivity, vulnerabilities to threat, and accessibility to experience. This information may be important in addressing questions about intellectual abilities, personality disorders, the diagnosis of mood disorders, and suitability for insight-oriented versus behavior-oriented psychotherapies.

Finally, observing whether the patient responds with compliance, defiance, resistance, or decompensation to various levels of stress imposed in the testing environment may provide information about his/her stress tolerance, adequacy of protective defenses, resistance potential, and impulse control. Of course, in most instances the questions asked are complex, and the patient's response requires making generalizations to environments that vary in several or all of these qualities. Hence, instruments are usually selected to permit the systematic observation of response variations at several points along each of these dimensions.

Methods of psychological assessment also differ in the sensitivity and accuracy with which they measure and predict behavior. Hence, the task of the clinician is not only to select systematic methods for sampling the aspects of situations to which he/she wants to generalize, but to ensure that the behaviors observed in these situations are measured reliably and validly. In order to accomplish this latter task, the clinician must be familiar with certain qualities of good measurement procedures, including (1) the scaling methods used, (2) measurement sensitivity, (3) measurement specificity, (4) availability of normative data, (5) reliability of observations, and (6) validity of the observations. Each of these six areas deserves some brief review.

Scaling Methods

Whether it is in assessing the nature of the clinical question being asked, defining the type of situation to which generalizations must occur, or measuring an attribute such as intelligence or anxiety, the first and most fundamental quality of measurement is "identity." Simply, the measurement instrument—a clinician's judgment or test score—must translate samples of observed behaviors into a form that fairly represents distinctive qualities of individuals. The failure to identify or classify observations prevents accurate inferences from being made about past, present, or future behavior.

Measurement applies numbers to individuals or attributes as a means of establishing identity among observations. In increasing order of sophistication, there are four methods of preserving identity: "nominal," "ordinal," "interval," and "ratio." These four methods are often described as "scaling" methods because they order and classify observations.

"Nominal scaling" is the assignment of individuals or behaviors to categories. The best example of this type of measurement as applied to people is the use of diagnoses. A DSM diagnosis of Major Depression identifies a cluster of related symptoms, differentiates those who have the condition from those who do not, and suggests a particular course of development and treatment. Diagnostic labels define discrete categories or "types" of people, and have general application to a wide range of individuals who seek assistance from mental health practitioners. Diagnostic labels are limited, however, both because they fail to make some important discriminations among those who meet the criteria for the diagnosis (i.e., those with Major Depression differ from one another in important, treatment-relevant ways), and because they give us no information about the large number of individuals who fail to meet the criteria for a diagnosis, but who still seek and can benefit from mental health services.

That is, nominal scaling methods such as diagnosis identify who has a condition, but do not allow us to compare individuals either within or across groups. Using a nominal, diagnostic scale, for example, we cannot say that depression is "more than schizophrenia" any more than we can say that apples are "more than oranges"—they are entirely different classes. We yearn to ask, "More what?" Neither can we say that one person has "more depression" than another—again because the scale does not identify magnitude, only the presence of the condition.

"Ordinal scaling," on the other hand, is a measurement method that identifies the relative *ranking* of observations. We can say that depression is "more prevalent" than schizophrenia, that one person has "more depressive symptoms" than another, or that there are "more apples than oranges in Washington state." This ordinal or ranking method preserves the hierarchy that exists among the observations, as well as the identity of them. It does not, however, tell us how *much* more frequently depression is observed than schizophrenia, how *much* more depressed one person is than another, or how *many* more apples than oranges are grown in Washington state. Doing any of the latter tasks requires either "interval" or "ratio" measurement. These latter scaling methods allow identity, ranking, and comparison because they are forms of *dimensional* measurement.

More specifically, in clinical assessment it is often important to determine both the diagnosis (nominal scale), and how much anxiety or depression is present or how severe the schizophrenia may be (dimensional scale), in absolute rather than simply relative terms. To do so, we must construct instruments that apply continuous ratings to our observations in the form of numbers. If we can assume that the differences between numbers are the same all along the continuum (the principle of equal intervals), then we can compare one score against another and conclude something about both the presence and the magnitude of observed difference.

Again, both interval scaling and ratio scaling methods allow this latter type of magnitude comparison. The distinction between these two forms of measurement is that ratio measures can only be applied to characteristics that both exist in a continuous quantity and cannot exist at all (i.e., the scale has an absolute zero). Most psychological qualities of people do not possess both of these qualities at once. It is difficult to envision zero levels of anxiety or depression, for example. Unlike physical distance measures, where "0" means that no distance exists between two points, measures of most psychological properties are not possible by a ratio scale. Psychological characteristics are more similar to temperature than to physical distance; in the measurement of psychological qualities, as in that of temperature, a score of "0" is only one point along a scale in which lower scores are also possible. It is conceivable for someone to become even less depressed than a person who scores "0" on a test, much as temperatures can be measured below 0.

Sensitivity, Specificity, and Normative Value

Although necessary, identity as a property of a measurement scale is not sufficient for adequate assessment. If we reflect back on the question of how to describe the three presidents, we can see that the categorical (nominal) identification of political alliance is of little help in assessing clinical referral questions, because it is not sufficiently sensitive to individual variations and is a poor predictor of the degree to which the clinically relevant concepts of emotions and behaviors may depart from normal expectations. Both Democrats and Republicans can be emotionally healthy, disordered, or dangerous; not all Democrats are like Clinton, and not all Republicans are like Bush.

Using the example of the three presidents, we can illustrate three other important concepts in measurement: "sensitivity," "specificity," and "normative value." In a way, we have already discussed the concept of sensitivity. A measurement is sensitive if it has identity—if it can classify a person's uniqueness. That is, a sensitive measure is one that correctly identifies an individual as having a given characteristic or as being a member of a given group. Sensitivity is best understood when applied to categorical measurement, and in this case is simply the percentage of "true positives." We will describe a related estimate of sensitivity as applied to dimensional measurement when we discuss measurement reliability, and at that point it will be possible to see how the concepts of reliability and sensitivity are related.

To illustrate the concept of sensitivity, let us first suppose that we construct a self-report test consisting of a single question: "Are you now or have you ever been president of the United States?" If this test is then administered to Reagan, Bush, and Clinton, we may expect that all three will answer affirmatively. By checking their responses against public records, we can then determine that we have successfully identified all three of these individuals accurately. They are "true positives" in that they not only have responded positively to the question, but actually belong to the class of people defined by our historical criterion. Hence, we can conclude that our test has high (even perfect) sensitivity.

The more politically minded, however, may point out that though all three men were indeed elected to the office of President, each can claim unique accomplishments. With a series of subsidiary questions cross-referenced against historical records, therefore, we can develop three subscales for our test. Bush, but neither Reagan nor Clinton, can be identified with a subscale that asks whether he "Directed the invasion of Panama";

Reagan, but neither Bush nor Clinton, can be identified with a subscale that asks whether he "Negotiated an arms reduction agreement with the USSR"; Clinton, but neither Bush nor Reagan, can be identified with a subscale that asks whether he "Proposed an educational indenture program for college students." Thus, a measurement system made up of these categories will still possess 100% sensitivity, in that all three presidents can be accurately classified and distinguished from one another.

Although this designation system possesses impeccable sensitivity, in that it accurately assigns each of the presidents to a categorical class of which he is the only member, psychological assessment requires that the measurement used also be capable of identifying those who do *not* belong to the targeted group. The ability to accurately identify those who do not have a certain quality or group membership is called the scale's "specificity." Making a determination of our test's specificity is impossible at this point, however, because we have not yet tried it out on people who have not been president of the United States, have not waged war, have not negotiated arms reduction agreements, or have not publicly advanced indenture programs for higher education.

If we ask 1,000,000 randomly selected people the four questions posed to the three presidents, we will find that all (or most) will say "no" to all of them. In checking the public records (our criteria), we will probably find that, in fact, none have actually been president of the United States, none have directed troops to invade Panama, none have negotiated an arms reduction treaty with the USSR, and none have proposed an educational indenture program to Congress. Hence, we can conclude that our test possesses the quality of specificity—it has successfully identified nearly 100% of those in our sample who have not been president of the United States— as well as sensitivity.

Because we have administered our test to such a large group, it now also has some "normative value." If we assume that the million people we have asked are representative of those in the United States, we can infer that most people will answer "no" to the questions and that those who say "yes" will be unusual. But because there is so little variability in responses to our scale (1,000,000 people say "no" and only 3 people say "yes" to our questions), our scale does not allow us to say much of anything about the large number of people who have not been presidents. As this example illustrates, in order for the meaning of responses to be assessed, there must be both "response variability" and a normative value.

To illustrate the importance of these concepts in a different way, consider the following: If we hold up a piece of chalk and ask a classroom full of graduate students to identify what it is (a categorical rating), the characteristics of chalk are so constant and well known that there will be little variation among students' answers. Because all or most of the responses will be the same, we are able to conclude little about these students beyond the probability that they are sensitive to their environments and familiar with chalk. However, suppose one student says, "That is a prince who has been enchanted by a wicked witch." It is the departure of this student's response from the usual or normative response that will allow us to draw conclusions about how realistic his/her perceptions are. If the student comes from an unusual cultural background in which witches and demons are believed to inhabit all objects, then his/her response may be seen as normal or usual within that particular culture, and our ability to interpret its unique meaning is lost. This illustration underlines the need to consider the meanings of responses in terms of the respondent's social norms and history. Perhaps it is an unfortunate characteristic of psychological assessment that deviation from the "norm" is more informative than compliance with the usual.

If we can rule out the possibility that this student's response is usual or normal within the cultural or religious environment in which he/she lives by assessing a large number of people who are from the same culture, we can then conclude that the student's unique response represents some unusual characteristic of this person. The more unusual the response, compared to the norm that represents the culture with whom the student identifies and lives, the more clearly we can conclude that a variant response indicates some form of clinical abnormality. For example, suppose that our student looks frightened, jumps up, and runs out of the room when we hold up the chalk. We may infer, with some degree of confidence, that the student is fearful of and has negative attitudes toward wicked witches, above and beyond his/her beliefs about chalk. If he/she shares with the majority culture a primitive, animistic religion and background, then the unusual nature of this response may be assumed to reflect a deficit in the ability to objectively analyze, interpret, and respond to routine events. However, we can see that it is the deviation or variation of the response that gives us this ability, since we still can say little about the large number of students who have given the expected response, "chalk." Even with perfect sensitivity and specificity, in other words, our "Chalk Test" may have very limited value, because it only tells us something about those who *deviate* from the norm.

Since no one can be expected to be "average" in everything, we usually construct tests on which there are many ways to deviate from the average or norm. For example, in our illustration of the "President's Test," the 1,000,000 randomly selected individuals represent a normative sample because their characteristics are likely to be similar to those of the larger population. As in the case of the students in the "Chalk Test" example, however, their responses do not distinguish them from one another. In response to the question about having been elected president of the United States, almost all of them have said "no." To be able to draw conclusions about individuals within this group, we must find ways in which their individuality is manifest. If we add an item to our test that asks, "How many people have financially benefited from your decisions during the past year?," we will now obtain a number (i.e., a "score") from each of them that will manifest response variability. The arithmetic mean of these responses will provide a normative value against which we can compare our three presidents and all others in the group, even without knowing the accuracy of their estimates. Moreover, the scores (i.e., the number of people benefited) among our sample of 1,000,003 people will probably fall within a bell-shaped or normal distribution. Some people, like our presidents, will identify a large number of people as having benefited from their actions, whereas others will indicate that few or none have so benefited. Because our sample is both large and randomly selected from the entire population, the distribution of scores is likely to be representative of the general population. That is, the mean and distribution of the sample is likely to be a close approximation of what we would find if we were to ask this question of everyone in the United States.

After first computing the "standard deviation" of our sample, which is an estimate of how the responses are distributed (assuming that the scale measures a normally distributed characteristic), we can describe each individual within our sample by computing an "effect size" score. This score simply describes, in decimal form, the number of standard deviations separating the individual from the mean of the sample. Because of their visibility and positions of power, it is likely that all three of the presidents in our example will be at wide variance with most of the rest of our sample. They will have highly positive effect size scores (i.e., they will be several standard deviations above the mean) in the number of people who have financially benefited from their decisions. By inspecting these scores, we can compare the self-rated influence of any of the three presidents and that of any other person in our group.

Comparing individuals to normative standards based upon large numbers of randomly selected (i.e., representative) individuals, however, does not help us to understand either what caused any particular observed deviation, or the accuracy of the scores given. The questions we still face include a determination of whether or not scores obtained in this way are likely to be accurate. Alternatively, do these scores vary as a function of some still unknown quality of the environment? To what degree is their accuracy influenced by momentary distraction? Do these scores indicate a stable aspect of the respondent's personality or intelligence? Are they likely to be influenced by current distress levels or such impediments as a recent bad night's sleep? In reference to our presidents, for example, are their estimates of the numbers of people affected by their decisions a product of their need to feel important, or do these give an accurate indication of their influence? In other words, the measurement must be both reliable and valid.

Reliability and Validity

A measurement provides identity and sensitivity if it reflects the unique features of the patient's experience; it possesses specificity and normative value if it identifies the degree of similarity between an individual and others. The central purpose of psychological assessment, however, is to generalize to situations that we cannot observe directly or that have not yet occurred.

We know that behavior does not occur in a vacuum; it arises in response both to an environmental quality and to the individual qualities and characteristics of the person. Hence, if we are able to provide a constant (i.e., identical) environment for every person who completes our test, the resulting differences in behavior are likely to reflect individual qualities of personality, intellect, and expectations. Psychological tests attempt to provide such a constant environment for individuals, in order to permit us (1) to observe the variations among their responses, and (2) to infer the nature of each of their unique characteristics. We formalize the procedures of observation; study and standardize the environments from which a patient's behavior is sampled; and work to ensure that our instruments for observing and measuring are sensitive, are specific, and have normative value. Thereby, our observations can be judged to represent samples of how individuals differ in their responses to environments.

The next task that faces us as clinicians is to distinguish between transient and enduring characteristics of people's behavior. To the degree that a behavior characteristic changes in synchrony with time or events, it is said to be a "state" and is judged to be an attribute that is influenced by the environment. To the degree that a characteristic remains constant over time and across situations, it is said to be a "trait" and is judged to be a "personality" quality that is nonreactive to the environment. Situational anxiety is a state; eye color is a trait; and in between lie a host of qualities that have both state and trait properties—they change at various rates in response to environments.

Without knowing whether the observations are likely to be enduring or situational, we do not know the limits to which the observations or meanings of the scores obtained in our tests can be generalized. The methods of classifying and measuring, in other words, must also possess the ability to be replicated. This is the quality of "reliability." Reliability is an index of consistency or purity of measurement; it is usually expressed in the form of a correlation. Yet, because personal qualities vary in how much they are influenced and changed by the nature of the situation, different types of consistency or reliability are important for different measures. "Test–retest reliability" is indicated by high correspondence or similarity of responses on two different occasions. If our students say "chalk" every time they are asked, we can infer that their familiarity with the object derives from enduring knowledge—a base of knowledge that supersedes changes occurring in the environment. Conversely, if their responses are strikingly different in two different situations or at two different times, we can conclude that whatever their responses are measuring is a temporary or passing state in their experience.

If our measurement device has response variability, we can estimate the likelihood that a given response will be repeated if the test is administered over and over again on several different occasions. This is done by computing the "standard error of measurement" and is derived from a knowledge of the reliability of the test responses. The higher the correlation between scores on the test on two separate occasions, the higher the reliability, and the smaller the error of measurement—there are fewer unintended influences affecting the scores. The standard error of measurement is expressed as a standard deviation that is estimated to be likely to characterize the scores of a single individual if he/she took the test on many different occasions. It is used to estimate the possibility that the variation we observe in each of this individual's responses is an accidental occurrence. We can see in this example how test–retest reliability as applied to dimensional measurement is similar to the concept of sensitivity as applied to categorical measurement. It is an estimate of how sensitive the test is to variations in the condition being assessed.

Another form of reliability is applied to a test when we want to assure ourselves that an entire test or subtest is measuring the same thing. For this purpose, we compute the test's "internal consistency." This is simply an estimate of the degree to which each item or subpart of the test measures the same thing as the rest of the test items or subparts. Internal consistency is usually expressed as a correlation between the items and the total score. With tests that are designed to measure several different attributes by way of subtests, of course, internal consistency is estimated by the relationship of the items to the subtest scores rather than to a total score. It is expected that these part–whole correlations will be higher than the correlations between items and total scores on subtests that are designed to measure an attribute differing from one to be measured by an individual item.

"Equivalent-forms reliability" is a method of assessing consistency that combines some of the principles of test–retest and internal-consistency reliabilities. In this method, we may construct two forms of the test and compute the degree to which they measure the same thing, either when administered at the same time or when administered on two separate occasions. This form of reliability is used when there is some reason to believe that the act of responding to the test on one occasion will determine how a person responds on the second occasion. This concern arises when the response is affected either by memory or by corrective knowledge that is gained while the person is taking the test. For example, a subtest from the Wechsler Memory Scale—Revised (Wechsler, 1987) presents paired words and then asks the subject or client to recall the second word of each pair when the first is repeated to him/her. This paired learning task is repeated three times in each administration, and it is likely that the learning that takes place will be carried over to another occasion. Thus, a different but comparable list of words (an alternate form of the test) is used when the test is repeated, in order to avoid this problem.

Sometimes the test scores are quite subjective, as in the case where a clinician must make ratings of clients' drawings or of the meaning of behaviors. We want to assure ourselves that different raters make similar ratings (i.e., see things in a similar way). Thus, we may ask the raters to judge the amount of similarity and then compare the judges' ratings for agreement, to be sure that the same thing is being measured by each judge's rating. In such instances, the type of reliability that is desired is called "interrater reliability."

Although high reliability estimates tell us that something is being measured, and although comparisons of different types of reliability indicate whether the quality measured is a stable quality of the person, the test, the situation, and the rater, they do not tell us what it is that we are measuring. The accuracy with which a test measures the thing we want it to measure is called "validity." Validity is the most basic and yet the most difficult criterion to meet in test construction. Because the concept or attribute we are addressing is usually fuzzy and abstract, there are generally no direct measures of the essence of what we are assessing. Thus, it is almost impossible to completely establish a test's validity. But by first identifying the particular type of validity that is of principal concern, and then applying some established procedures to the task of measuring this type of validity, we can obtain an estimate of a test's validity that is sufficient for our purposes. The nature of validity, like that of reliability, varies because of the different purposes to which we want our test to apply. The main types are called "content," "construct," "criterion," and "incremental" validity.

In clinical appraisal, our desire to identify and distinguish between those behaviors that are situationally governed and those that are constant across situations is often made more difficult because the words and labels we use to define characteristics have various meanings to different people. In order to be useful, the terms we employ must have the same meaning across situations and cultures. The behaviors and acts that are called "aggression" in one culture must also be identifiable as "aggression" in another, even though both the normative levels and the acceptability of these behaviors may differ with the cultural values and norms. The political designations that define the presidents in our earlier example do not have these qualities; they are culture-specific, and whatever attributes may be legitimately associated with them do not translate across cultures. The political platforms of the "Christian Democrats" in Italy, for example, may carry little similarity to the collective beliefs of a U.S. Democrat who is also a Christian.

The task of establishing the meaningfulness of the content is central to the derivation of "content validity" of an assessment device. This form of validity deals with the subject of the test and is an effort to define the relevant aspects of the characteristic or construct that is being measured. To the degree that the items appear to the common observer to be related to the quality that is targeted for measurement, we may say that the test has "face validity." Not all content validity relies on its apparent similarity to the targeted construct or quality, however. Sometimes the quality that we are measuring cannot be measured by obvious items alone. Thus, in order to help us keep the definition of various words constant and to ensure that the content is accurate to our needs, we often define the meanings that we want for different terms by referring to a formal psychological theory.

Once the terms used in our test items are defined through either their face validity or their theoretical content, their meaning must be "operationalized." That is, their meaning must be identified in terms of something that is observable to others. Since these terms are often derived from formal theories in the field, their translation into observable behaviors often relies on the ratings of experts who are familiar with the theory from which the definitions and terms are being extracted. The importance of this point can be illustrated by our "President's Test." Let us assume that one of our items asks individuals to rate their "success." The meaning of this term among our presidents may be judged very differently if the term is extracted from economic theory and judged by economists; if it is drawn from a particular political party's platform and judged by the presidents themselves; or if it is borrowed from communication theory and judged by news correspondents. Thus, the theoretical as well as the practical meanings of terms must be considered in assessing content validity.

Another form of validity that bears even more directly on the theoretical meaning of the qualities being assessed is called "construct validity." Construct validity refers to the degree to which the measurement device accurately identifies the presence of a quality or construct. Since constructs are theoretical rather than observable entities, however, construct validity is usually established by demonstrating that the measured trait or state bears the expected relationships to members of a network of other constructs within our chosen theory. The nature of these relationships is defined by the theory from which the construct has been defined. If our theory defines a president's success by how closely he/she follows a conservative agenda, for example, then one measure of the construct validity of our test is how well it correlates with a measure of political conservatism. As is often true in the establishment of construct validity, scores on an established test are often used as a criterion in order to determine whether the same abstract constructs are also present in the new test. Sometimes this is referred to as "convergent validity," in that it is a demonstration that two tests converge or measure similar properties.

More than convergent validity is needed, however, in order to establish that a test has construct validity. In addition to demonstrating that the new test correlates with other tests that measure the same theoretically derived construct, a demonstration of construct validity also requires evidence that the new test does *not* correlate highly with tests that are designed to measure different constructs. This demonstration is called "discriminant validity." A person may score high on our test, for example, because he/ she is concerned with being conservative in an environment that is politically conservative. In that case, a portion of the test score may reflect the desire to fit in with others, or social desirability, rather than either "success" or "conservatism." If we demonstrate that our test does *not* correlate with a measure of social desirability, however, we have demonstrated its discriminant validity and provided more support for its construct validity.

To illustrate with a clinical example, scores on a test of depression should correlate highly with scores on other tests of depression, but should not correlate with a test of some other, supposedly different quality (e.g., anxiety). Unfortunately, this is a poor but important example of discriminant validity, because although depression and anxiety are theoretically distinctive concepts, few types of psychological measurement (including the ratings of clinical judges) can distinguish them. This fact illustrates an important "Catch-22" problem in demonstrating the validity of measurement: All of these validation estimates assume that it is already possible to measure the construct or concept under investigation. If we can already measure it, why develop the test in the first place? If we cannot measure it now, the new test cannot be shown to be valid.

Looking at this problem has led some to suggest that only conceptual or face validity is necessary under most conditions. That is, the test is valid if it appears to be valid and if it is reliable. Alternatively, this problem points to the need for still another type of validity based upon some external criterion. "Criterion validity" is usually subdivided into two types, "concurrent validity" and "predictive validity," depending on whether the test is expected to relate to external criteria that are present at the time the test is administered or to those that are expected to occur at sometime in the future. If our test of "success," founded as it is upon a conservative political theory, correlates with party affiliation, it may be said to have concurrent validity. If, on the other hand, it correlates with who wins the next presidential election, it may be said to have predictive validity.

The concepts of specificity and sensitivity are related to criterion validity. If a test of diagnosis is sensitive, it accurately identifies those who have the qualities that define the diagnosis—an external criterion. If it possesses specificity, it accurately identifies those who do *not* have the qualities that define the diagnosis—also an external criterion. Both of these examples of criterion validity are also examples of concurrent validity. A test that is able to predict the likelihood that a person will develop a set of symptoms meeting diagnostic criteria at some time in the future has predictive validity. More specifically, if a test of recurrent depression successfully predicts future depression, it may be said to have predictive validity. In clinical practice, the assessment of the course or differential treatment response of a patient relies on predictive validity. Indeed, predictive validity may be the most important but perhaps the most difficult type of validity to demonstrate.

Finally, "incremental validity" is the demonstration that the test provides more substantial knowledge of, greater ability to predict the behavior of, or more accurate identification of individuals than is possible by using more easily obtained information. Whereas most forms of validity are expressed as correlations or accuracy ratings, incremental validity is usually expressed as a partial correlation—a correlation expressing the relationship that exists between the test and a criterion while the influence of other variables or of prior knowledge is held constant statistically.

Summary

In this chapter, we have briefly reviewed the nature of psychological tests and addressed two of the four tasks required of those who conduct psychological assessment: defining the referral question and selecting the measurement device. This latter issue has only been addressed in term of the qualities that are needed in order to measure accurately what we seek to measure. We have pointed out the difficulty of translating the shorthand requests for consultation that are frequently received into meaningful questions. We have also pointed out that psychological tests and measures must possess the qualities of scaling identity, sensitivity, specificity, normative value, reliability, and validity. Each of these concepts has been described and illustrated.

Although we have pointed out some of the considerations that are necessary in the selection of test procedures for answering referral questions, we have said little about the usefulness of specific tests. This is because their usefulness depends on the questions being asked. Specifically, we have pointed to the need to select tests that represent, in some significant and meaningful way, the environment to which generalizations are to be made, and that evoke behaviors that are also representative of the behaviors likely to occur in these environments. The remainder of this book addresses the use and usefulness of several specific measures, the interpretative integration of these measures, and the communication of findings. It begins by providing a conceptual description of the dimensions of the environment that must be considered in the selection of specific tests, and a system for organizing observations in preparation for rendering an integrated summary of findings from different sources and methods. It then proceeds to a description of several specific measures and their integrative interpretation. We wish only to alert the reader that interpretations must be selected to address the referral questions asked. Because these questions are so varied, the thoughtful clinician must use discretion and judgment in extracting and using the information on specific tests for the purposes of responding to any given consultation request.

References

American Psychiatric Association. (1994). *Diagnostic and statistical manual of mental disorders* (4th ed.). Washington, DC: Author.

Bender, L. (1938). *A visual motor gestalt test and its clinical uses* (Research Monograph No. 3). New York: American Orthopsychiatric Association.

Kopta, S. M., Newman, F. L., McGovern, M. P., & Sandrock, D. (1986). Psychotherapeutic orientations: A comparison of conceptualizations, interventions, and treatment plan costs. *Journal of Consulting and Clinical Psychology, 54,* 369–374.

Wechsler, D. (1987). *Wechsler Memory Scale—Revised manual.* New York: Psychological Corporation.

2

Integrating and Communicating Findings

Larry E. Beutler

In the sequence of activities comprising psychological assessment, the role played by the consulting clinician shifts at several critical points. Making these shifts smoothly and effectively requires clear communication, informed intuition, and educated clinical judgment at each point. The clinician begins the process of psychological assessment by defining the nature of the question being asked. For this task, the clinician's role is one of consultant. Once the question has been defined and framed in an answerable fashion, however, the clinician's role shifts and becomes one of measurement expert. In this latter role, the clinician matches the requirements of the task with those of available measurement procedures, and develops a plan for sampling the environments of interest.

For the tasks of applying the measures and scoring them, the role of the clinician becomes (at least momentarily) that of a psychological technician, whose behavior is controlled by external standardization, performance guidelines, and rules. Once the clinician has completed these technical tasks, however, the role adopted reverts to that of measurement expert. Clinical judgment, experience, intuition, and formal training all have a place in the performance of this role, as the clinician makes sense of and organizes a formal response to the referral question(s). Responses are interpreted, and then dissonant findings are resolved. The observations and their assigned meanings are integrated; in this process, the clinician relies heavily upon knowledge of the psychometric qualities of the measurement procedures. Finally, the clinician returns to the role of consultant as he/she communicates the findings to the referring clinician.

This chapter outlines a model by which data from multiple assessment sources can be organized and integrated in order to address the questions asked of the psychological expert. In providing guidelines for integrating sources of data, I do not intend to imply either that the role of clinical intuition and judgment can be circumvented, or that only the clinical methods and tests presented in this volume are appropriate to answering the many questions asked of clinicians. Nor do I intend to convey the impression that the clinical methods described are suited to answer all the questions that a clinician may be asked. The model of integration to be presented is sufficiently broad to accommodate different referral questions, other assessment instruments, and different theoretical viewpoints. Likewise, the clinical methods to be reviewed in the following chapters are presented as representative of methods used in clinical practice, and illustrate how integration across procedures may facilitate efforts to answer questions about pathological functioning, personality development, and diagnosis.

Before the model is set forth, however, it may well be useful to describe in some detail the ways in which testing can be varied in order to obtain answers to particular questions of interest. To do so, it is necessary to consider tests as analogues to real-world environments.

Tests as Analogue Environments

Some of the names and labels that are conventionally applied to descriptions of people identify hypothesized internal qualities that are assumed to be consistent and constant for a given person across occasions. Others describe more transitory qualities and are assumed to differ for a given individual from occasion to occasion. As noted in Chapter 1, psychologists frequently find it useful to differentiate between psychological "traits" and "states." Traits are people's enduring qualities or response tendencies; they are generalizable across situations and transcend varying situational demands. States, on the other hand, are situationally induced reactions. Although state reactions may be affected by one's traits, they are less stable and change in response to changing environments.

Most qualities that are identified as describing human experience have both state- and trait-like qualities. Terms such as "personality" and "intelligence" are used to describe attributes that are primarily trait-like, whereas terms such as "acute," "distress," and "resistance" are used to describe attributes that are primarily state-like. Thus, when clinicians discuss differences between baseline and current functioning, they are usually talking about state responses. Likewise, when clinicians discuss differences between a patient's level of performance and normative values, they are usually discussing trait concepts. One task of the behavioral scientist is to determine which qualities of a patient are trait-like and which are state-like. Another task is to determine how to define both states and traits in "operational" (i.e., observable and replicable) ways, so that they will be useful for answering the questions related to diagnosis, etiology, prognosis, treatment, and functional impairment that comprise the task of psychological assessment.

As Chapter 1 has described, psychological assessment consists of constructing representative but analogue environments called "tests" and systematically measuring the resultant behavior. To the degree that the characteristics of our contrived environments bear a resemblance to those of our patients' actual living environment, we can logically assume that the responses to our "tests" are also similar to some aspect of patients' behaviors in their own environments. No single contrived environment or test procedure, however, can logically represent the varied aspects of any real-world environment in which a patient lives. For this reason, we must select different procedures to represent various targeted, discrete qualities or aspects of those environments to which we want to generalize most directly.

Likewise, no response is totally unitary. Like any real-world environment, any response or behavior consists of many qualities that come together in a pattern. An integrative interpretation and communication of psychological assessment, therefore, must account for the variations of patient behavior that are observed (1) within the different analogue environments that we have constructed as our "procedures," and (2) across the diverse aspects of behavior that constitute "test responses."

Again, each test environment can be considered to be analogous to a real-world environment. Analogue environments have an advantage over real-world environments, however, in that they can be constructed and maintained in a relatively constant way through the use of standard materials and standardized administration procedures. Hence, when responses to them differ both among people and from one time and situation to another, these difference can logically be attributed to the presence of different personal traits and states.

Characteristics of Analogue Environments

To respond most effectively to a referral question, a clinician selects a variety of analogue environments to be presented to the patient. The instructions that establish the nature of each of these selected environments are designed to limit the patient's response in various ways. These limits are referred to as the "demand characteristics" of the test. In other words, a test's demand characteristics are the rules that govern what the respondent must do. Because the clinician systematically manipulates these analogue environments by altering the instructional qualities, the demand characteristics of a test are conceptually similar to the manipulation of an independent variable in an experiment.

Concomitantly, the various constructed demand characteristics of an analogue environment are designed to evoke different classes of response. Some demand characteristics require an individual to think, thus providing information about thought processes. Other demand characteristics evoke information about emotional and interpersonal behaviors. The forms that these behaviors take are referred to as the "response characteristics" of the evoking environment. The response characteristics indicate the domain or area of experience that is targeted for observation by the demand characteristics of the environment. Although the domains of functioning that distinguish different responses must be identifiable when different demand characteristics are encountered, the variations in the client's responses within each response domain and to each analogue environment are what are observed and interpreted. Hence, the observations and measurement of the patient's behavior and experience serve the same functions as the dependent variable in an experiment.

Two cardinal assumptions are made by the clinician in order to generalize from the observations within the analogue environments of the consulting room to the environments of interest in the external world: (1) The variations that exist in the demand characteristics of the test environments are similar to critical aspects of the everyday environments of patients; and (2) the response characteristics that are observed are diminutive or symbolic representations of behaviors likely to be exhibited in real-world environments. Stated another way, in order to make accurate interpretations, the clinician counts on the ability to accurately predict the parameters of both stimulus generalization and response generalization.

"Stimulus generalization" is the basis for predicting the likelihood (i.e., probability or frequency) that a response that has been observed in a test environment will also be exhibited in a real-world environment. In contrast, "response generalization" is the basis for predicting the nature and form that a real-world behavior will take. Whereas stimulus generalization is a function of the similarity that exists between the demand characteristics of the analogue and the real-world environments, response generalization is a function of the similarity of the responses that occur in these two types of environments.

The value of clinical assessment relies on the ability of the clinician, first, to identify relevant similarities between the real-world and analogue environments, and second, to construct a testing environment that evokes generalizable and relevant behaviors. Hence, it is important to give some consideration both to the dimensions that clinicians alter in order to construct a generalizable testing environment, and to the domains of human experience and performance to which test responses are generalized. The former are discussed below; the latter are discussed in a later section.

Dimensions of Variation in Analogue Environments

In order to make accurate generalizations from the testing environment to the real world, analogue and actual environments must share some qualities. As noted in Chapter 1, testing environments consist of presenting respondents with problems that vary along three bipolar dimensions. These stimulus properties are designed to parallel variations in real-world environments. Hence, the demand characteristics (the requirements that are placed on the respondent) of each of these dimensions are relatively specific.

Structured versus Ambiguous Environments

Assessment procedures vary in the degree of structure provided to the respondent. High levels of structure are maintained by test instructions (i.e., demand characteristics) that either limit the number of responses available to the patient or identify responses as either "correct" or "incorrect." The truc–false format of the Minnesota Multiphasic Personality Inventory (MMPI; Dahlstrom, Welsh, & Dahlstrom, 1972) and the open-ended format of the Wechsler Adult Intelligence Scale—Revised (WAIS-R; Wechsler, 1981) are examples of the two ways by which high structure levels are provided.

Structure relieves the individual's need to impose order and organization on, or to attribute meaning to, the stimulus material or task. Asking a person to draw the designs of the Bender Visual Motor Gestalt Test (BVMGT; Bender, 1938) "the best you can" is a structured task, as is the request to define the vocabulary words in the WAIS-R. There is little ambiguity in what the clinician wants. Both of these tasks require (i.e, they have the demand characteristic of) accuracy. With minor modifications, an additional demand characteristic may be imposed—speed. The response characteristics evoked by structured tasks include efficiency of information access, accuracy of factual knowledge, observation skills, and selective response bias or disposition. The structured subtests of the WAIS-R are reliable and valid measures of knowledge; they tap cognitive content and assess observational accuracy. The true–false format of the MMPI provides reliable and valid measures based on self-observations, attributions, and decisiveness.

In contrast, in ambiguous tasks, tests require (i.e., they have the demand characteristics of) construction and selection of responses in the relative absence of information. The methods used for inducing ambiguity in an assessment environment include reducing cues that indicate the number or nature of acceptable responses, and introducing instructions that lack specificity. The most salient and measurable characteristics of a person's response to these demands include accuracy and quality of problem-solving organization. Another response quality that is assumed to occur when an individual is faced with ambiguous stimuli is projection. "Projection," in this context, is a hypothetical process, not one that is directly measured. Projection is inferred to have occurred whenever meaning is attributed to an ambiguous event. The meaning ascribed is assumed to reflect the internal qualities of the respondent rather than a quality of the external world. Projective theory maintains that when structure is removed, the respondent attributes either his/her own private meanings or aspects of his/her own internal experiences to the ambiguous stimuli.

The "Scrud Test" is an example of an unstructured test.[1] In this test, respondents are asked to draw a "scrud," to take their time, and to do the best they can. This test embodies, by the inference that some "scruds" are better than others, the demand characteristic of response accuracy. However, in order to maintain ambiguity, neither the stimuli nor the clinician provide cues by which accuracy can be inferred. In the absence of prior experience with a "scrud" (a nonsense word), the respondent is forced to associate or attribute a private meaning to the term. The resulting response is taken as an indication of the degree to which the respondent's private world allows an organized and structured response to be imposed on the task.

The Rorschach Inkblot Test (Rorschach, 1921/1942) is a standardized example of an analogue environment that uses visual and instructional ambiguity and an implied demand for accuracy to evoke organizational and projective responses. Once again, the demand characteristic of accuracy, when there is no consensual standard by which to assess compliance with this requirement, evokes information about the organizing qualities of a patient's internal processes. The content ascribed to the nonsense visual material is considered to represent an example of how the patient may be able to find order in external situations in which ambiguity is a characteristic. From the response characteristics and content, the clinician infers the presence of such defining traits as conventionality, order, and a selective bias toward making external or internal causal attributions. The imposition of order on the stimuli serves as an index of the patient's ability to organize disparate elements in problem tasks; the degree of conventionality (assessed by normative criteria) serves as an index of social compliance; and the failure to discard unusual percepts serves as an indication of sensitivity to social convention.

Obviously, the assumption that projection is invoked by ambiguous stimuli is central for some interpretations of a person's responses to ambiguous environments. However, responses can also be seen more parsimoniously as representative of the person's efforts to solve ambiguous problems. In this latter case, a clinician can explore "empirical relationships" between various response characteristics and both concomitant and future behaviors, or the clinician can observe aspects of the patient's general problem-solving skills and assume that these observations reflect qualities of the patient's response to situations in which answers and implications

---

[1] I describe this fictitious test further in Chapter 3, in order to illustrate the role of normative values in test interpretation.

are not clear. Thus, the response characteristics of speed, accuracy, and problem-solving efficiency remain relevant even when the validity of the projective hypothesis is suspect.

Attending to Internal versus External Experience

A second way in which test environments vary is in the nature of the experience on which respondents are asked to focus. A clinician either may request a patient to disclose (or behave in such a way as to disclose) internal experience, or may directly observe external events. Thus, tests arc variously adept at drawing forth subjective versus objective behavioral samples. Overt behaviors that can be directly observed constitute objective experience, whereas internal behaviors that can only be inferred from what a respondent says or does are classes of subjective responses. Direct observations of behaviors that occur in response to the instruction are the most usual methods of sampling objective behavior. Reports of behavior or of the environment are other methods of sampling objective experience, although these are positioned more toward the subjective end of the continuum than are direct observations. Procedures such as direct behavioral observations and the MMPI-2 (Butcher, Dahlstrom, Graham, Tellegen, & Kaemmer, 1989) also embody demand characteristics that evoke responses from which generalizations to the domain of overt behavior may be made. The first of these methods samples overt behavior directly, and the second does so by asking questions to which a behavioral reference point is applied.

On the other hand, assessment of subjective behavior must rely on self-reports of some kind or on observations of behaviors that are considered to be symbolic expressions of internal experience. Both the WAIS-R and the Rorschach, for example, embody demand characteristics that are designed to evoke samples of subjective experience. These latter methods vary in the degree of structure imposed by the environment. Hence, eliciting responses regarding subjective experiences on instruments such as these may be useful in answering diagnostic questions associated with the degree and nature of cognitive impairment, occurring in circumstances that vary in structure.

Most procedures that purport to assess "personality" evoke responses that represent several points along the dimension of subjective–objective experience. This is done because "personality traits" are thought not only to be operative in a variety of environments, but to be causally related to how subjective experiences become enacted in objective behaviors. The MMPI-2, for example, includes some questions that require self-observations of overt behavior (e.g., "I have used alcohol excessively," "I have very few quarrels with members of my family") and others that require awareness of internal states (e.g., "Parts of my body often have feelings like burning, tingling, crawling, or like 'going to sleep,'" "I am worried about sex"). Likewise, clinical interviews ask respondents to report on both subjective experience (e.g., "How often do you feel depressed?") and observable behaviors (e.g., "How many times have you been in trouble with the law?").

The relationship between subjective and objective responses is not always clear or predictable. Hence, it is useful to ensure that both of these types of responses are sampled when most referral questions are being evaluated. With some questions, however, the responses evoked by the demand requirements of the procedure are sufficiently clear and reliable as to weight the scales toward one or the other when a clinician is selecting assessment procedures. Specifically, procedures are available that reliably sample such internal experiences as informational accuracy, thought content, and imagination. Other assessment procedures are quite discrete in sampling such objective behaviors as the use and abuse of chemicals, suicidal actions, and social introversion. Sampling overt behaviors that are related to these latter ones may reveal aspects of experience that may be particularly relevant to answering prognostic questions.

Finally, comparing the results of procedures that variously sample subjective and objective experiences may be especially helpful in addressing questions of differential diagnosis and treatment. Comparisons of a patient's sensitivity and ability to report subjective and objective experience, for example, may reflect the degree to which the patient's coping style is internally focused or externally focused. Reports of subjective anxiety in the absence of observed or reported behavioral disturbances suggest that a given individual internalizes experience; reports of drinking, hostile interactions, and legal difficulties without concomitant reports or observed indications of internal distress, suggest that an individual acts out (i.e., externalizes) conflicts. If both external behavior disruption and internal distress are present, it may indicate that an individual uses both types of coping strategies.

Information about the relative use of internalizing and externalizing coping styles has also been found to be predictive of an individual's response to different treatments. The identification of an internalizing coping style may serve as an indicator for the use of insight-oriented therapies, while an externalizing coping style may serve as an indicator for the use of behavior-focused, skill-building, and cognitive therapies (Beutler & Clarkin, 1990; Kadden, Cooney, Getter, & Litt, 1990). These points are discussed at greater length later.

Variations in Stress

A third dimension along which test environments vary is in the level of stress induced. The nature of the stress imposed by analogue assessment environments is of several types. It is necessary for a clinician to keep in mind the nature of the stress induction procedures, in order to provide an adequate interpretation of the resultant or corollary response.

One method that the clinician uses to induce stress is the imposition of directives. This method is defined by the relative distribution of control, between the clinician and the patient, over the nature of the respondent's subsequent action. The level of stress that is assumed to evolve from this method is reflected in the amount of direction exerted or the demand made by the clinician on the respondent's behavior. The demand characteristics of clinician control evoke the response characteristics of compliance and defiance. In many assessment environments, the clinician has a great deal of control—he/she gives directives and requires responses. However, some procedures are more controlling of the patient's responses than others are. Relatively noncontrolling procedures include unstructured interviews and requests for free associations; in these, the nature of the respondent's alternatives is not greatly limited. On the other hand, directive procedures impose limitations on the respondent's choices and limit perceived freedom. As this description indicates, the demand characteristics of a structured and controlling environment are not always easily distinguished. Although there are procedures that have relatively low levels of structure, they may be quite highly directive nonetheless; the Rorschach test is an example of this type of procedure. Other procedures are highly structured but impose relatively little direction; incomplete sentences are an example of such a procedure.

Observations of the patient's responses to environments that vary in the degree of imposed direction may provide an index of the patient's willingness to comply with treatment demands, or, conversely, the patient's potential to resist directive treatments. Low tolerance for external control may be manifested as various forms of defiance and rebellion; high levels of tolerance may be manifested in consistent efforts to please the clinician. The clinician can assess the strength of the patient's propensity to respond in a defiant or compliant fashion by systematically increasing the strength of the directives offered and observing the consequences.

The directive control of the clinician can be increased by two methods. Both of these methods overlap with methods of imposing structure. One method imposes the demand for precision (accuracy), and the other imposes a demand for speed. For example, the BVMGT is usually introduced by suggesting that the respondent "draw each design the best you can." The clinician can increase the directiveness of this procedure by introducing frequent reminders to attend to quality—"Remember, do the best you can." A different type of stress can be introduced by imposing a requirement for speed. This type of clinician control is usually imposed and increased by varying the frequency of the reminder ("Do it as fast as you can") and by varying the extent of making an obvious show of tracking performance time (holding a stopwatch in a visible position). Responses to these two approaches to inducing stress may yield different interpretations: one regarding the patient's ability to override impulses by cognitive controls, and the other regarding the patient's ability to override cognitive demands for precision in order to accommodate to the demand for speed.

Yet another type of stress is imposed by selecting assessment procedures that vary in the nature of the interpersonal environment used. Placing stress on the respondent by varying the interpersonal context pulls for behaviors that reflect interpersonal sensitivity, the ability to engage with others, and thresholds of compliance and defiance. Procedures that have written instructions and can be completed in a room alone are likely to induce less acute distress than ones that are individually administered. Sentence completion tasks, personality questionnaires, group forms of intellectual tests, and the like impose little interpersonal stress. Individual intelligence tests, most individually administered projective tests, and interviews all include a component of interpersonal stress. A patient who is reactive to interpersonal relationships is likely, therefore, to produce different and contradictory responses when confronted with these two types of environments.

A third method for introducing stress into an analogue assessment environment is to present an irreconcilable conflict. The demand quality of contradiction calls on the respondent to make choices. The instructions are typically contradictory and require that a person modulate between impulses and constraints. The responses observed under these conditions are interpreted as reflecting on the propensity of the respondent's cognitive organizational skills to decompensate. Environments that embody this type of stress are of particular help in determining whether an individual can utilize cognitive strengths to override frustration without any negative effect on the quality or organization of problem-solving output. For example, in pitting instructional demands for precision against those for speed, a clinician may require a patient both to be maximally accurate and to utilize maximal speed in reproducing the BVMGT designs (i.e., "Do it as well and as fast as you can"). Under the joint pressures of interpersonal stress and directiveness, the clinician can observe the respondent's ability to find a compromise between tendencies to over- and undercontrol behaviors.

Clinicians must remain sensitive to the varying demand characteristics inherent in the three methods for inducing stress that have been illustrated here. At one level, all have a common demand characteristic of tolerating stress. In all, that is, a clinician is interested in making a generalized interpretation about how well a respondent is able to maintain baseline levels of performance in the face of stress. A qualitative decline in the number of conventional responses; an increase in the number of regressive, unusual, or immature responses; the emergence of impulsive responses; and a relative increase in the number of affect-laden responses all suggest that the respondent has difficulty maintaining perspective in the face of strong emotions.

An additional area of functioning that may be sampled by introducing environmental stress, and one that particularly arises in environments that vary clinician control, is the ability of the respondent to comply with the demands of treatments. All treatments require at least some sacrifice of personal freedom, along with a willingness to accept the validity of external authorities. Although treatments may vary in these qualities, the patient's willingness to sacrifice control to the clinician during assessment may indicate the patient's ability to subjugate himself/herself to treatment in the interest of experiencing long-term gains.

Domains of Human Experience Assessed

Figure 2.1 provides a suggested outline of a psychological report, and Figure 2.2 provides an example of a brief report that follows this outline. On first glance, the sample report (Figure 2.2) looks quite standard, very much like a dozen other psychological reports that readers may have seen. However, there are some important distinctions between this and many reports written by psychologists in clinical settings. First, aside from identifying the assessment methods used, the sample report does not discuss the meaning of the separate procedures used. This stands in contrast to the frequent practice of separately identifying and interpreting each procedure or test.

Second, in the sample report, there is no special section that describes behavior observations. This is a variance with the tendency to include a section that describes the patient's appearance and test-taking behaviors.

Third, in the sample report, there is no reference to the test scores themselves. This stands in contrast to the tendency sometimes observed to report elaborately on scores from each of the tests, either in prelude to the report narrative itself or as part of the narrative.

These distinguishing features of the sample report illustrate the distinction between the roles of "testing" and "assessing" as described in Chapter 1. These features also illustrate two fundamental beliefs about the reporting of psychological findings: (1) Assessment is a consultative rather than a technical function, and includes, but is not limited to, the technical activities of testing and scoring observations; and (2) tests or sets of test scores cannot be adequately interpreted either independently of one another or in the absence of knowledge of context, norms, standard errors, and other psychometric properties.

The implication of the first of these valuative beliefs is that reports should summarize characteristics of the patient rather than reporting qualities of the test responses; the tests themselves are not discussed. The implication of the second belief is that clinicians should eschew the impulse to report either separate test scores or behavior observations as if they either are more important than other sources of data or can be interpreted independently from the other methods of gathering data. These points can be best illustrated by describing the contents of the report itself.

FIGURE 2.1. Outline of psychological report.

I. Identifying information
   A. Name of patient
   B. Sex
   C. Age
   D. Ethnicity
   E. Date of evaluation
   F. Referring clinician

II. Referral question

III. Assessment procedures

IV. Background
   A. Information relevant to clarifying the referral question
   B. A statement of the probable reliability/validity of conclusions

V. Summary of impressions and findings
   A. Cognitive level
      • Current intellectual and cognitive functioning (e.g., ideation, intelligence, memory, perception)
      • Degree (amount of) impairment compared to premorbid level
      • Probable cause of impairment
      (By end of this subsection, referrer should know whether the patient has a thought disorder, mental retardation, organicity.)

   B. Affective and mood levels
      • Mood, affect at present—compare this with premorbid levels
      • Degree of disturbance (mild, moderate, severe)
      • Chronic vs. acute nature of disturbance
      • Lability—how well can the person modulate, control affect with his/her cognitive resources?
      (By end of this subsection, referrer should know whether there is a mood disturbance, what the patient's affects are, and how well controlled his/her emotions are.)

   C. Interpersonal–intrapersonal level
      • Primary interpersonal and intrapersonal conflicts, and their significance
      • Interpersonal and intrapersonal coping strategies (including major defenses)
      • Formulation of personality

VI. Diagnostic impressions
   A. Series of impressions about cognitive and affective functioning, *or*
   B. The most probable diagnoses

VII. Recommendations
   A. Assessment of risk, need for confinement, medication
   B. Duration, modality, frequency of treatment

FIGURE 2.2. Sample psychological report.

Psychological Evaluation

I. *Identifying information*

Name:	Gladys Davis
Sex:	Female
Age:	49
Ethnicity:	European American
Date:	May 6, 1994
Referring clinician:	Henry J. Dorfman, M.D.

II. *Referral question*

This woman was admitted to the hospital because of recurrent muscular weakness and fatigue. Dr. Dorfman referred her for psychological evaluation, in order to determine the significance of psychological components of these symptoms and to provide a screening evaluation of central nervous system dysfunction.

III. *Assessment procedures*

May 3–4, 1994
MMPI-2
Sentence completion
Draw-a-Person
BVMGT
BVMGT, Stress Form
Rorschach
WAIS-R
Benton Visual Retention Test
Wechsler Memory Scale
Tapping Test
Clinical interview

IV. *Background*

This slim, 49-year-old, white female complains of numerous physical symptoms. She gives the appearance of being worn, tired, and somewhat older than her age. She reports an 11-year history of muscular weakness and fatigue, for which she has sought treatment at numerous medical facilities. Since September or October of 1993, her symptoms of weakness and fatigue have become exacerbated, but medical evaluation has failed to reveal definitive evidence for organic pathology.

This woman's personal history reveals that she has few friends. She was the second in a family of eight children, and was the oldest girl. She was raised in a "good Catholic" environment, in which her family was rather strict and conscientious. She describes her childhood as "quite happy." The patient reports that she is much less devoted to religion than her family was, but she continues to attend Mass at least once per week. She also reports that her marriage of 31 years is "good" and relatively trouble-free. She has given birth to three children, but has suffered two miscarriages and one stillbirth. Sexual relationships in her marriage are described as having been satisfactory until the present illness necessitated her sexual withdrawal.

(continued)

FIGURE 2.2. (Continued)

This woman's husband works for the U.S. Army, and his job often requires that he be away for extended periods. Especially during these periods, this woman's mother is described as "overbearing" and "controlling." The woman denies this as a problem, however. Throughout this evaluation session, this woman was cooperative and invested her time and energy in the test materials. Her responses were consistent and generally well organized. Hence, the results can be considered to be accurate reflections of her current functioning.

V. *Summary of impressions and findings*
This woman is currently functioning in the "bright normal" to "superior" range of intelligence (Verbal IQ = 128, Performance IQ = 109, Full Scale IQ = 121). Verbal comprehension skills are well developed, as are skills calling for concentration and attention. However, perceptual organization abilities show mild to moderate impairment relative to verbal skills, although still being within the average range of expectancy. Language and memory are well intact. Perceptual–motor performance, on the other hand, is suggestive of mild impairment. There is no indication of unusual ideation, and associative processes are within normal limits.

The foregoing data are suggestive of a mild but unspecified central nervous system disorder and are relatively consistent with a generalized impairment. It is notable that there are somewhat more pronounced negative effects on tasks that are typically associated with right-hemisphere or parieto-occiptal involvement than with left-hemisphere involvement. The nature and etiology of this condition is uncertain, but further neurological evaluation is indicated. Because of this woman's highly developed intellectual functions, however, one should be aware that the psychological impairments attendant upon this damage are likely to be masked during normal social interactions. Even though she is deficient in perceptual organizational skills, she is still able to perform tasks involving intellectual and perceptual functions at a level consistent with that of the average person her age.

From a personality perspective, several significant things become apparent. First, this woman appears to be mildly to moderately depressed and anxious. She is frightened for her well-being, and experiences a sense of hopelessness. Her anxiety and depression seem related both to her current hospitalization, and more generally to a long-standing morbid anticipation of harm or impending doom. She experiences many nebulous, undefined fears that seem in part to be a function of intense fear of affect eruption, and in part exaggerated needs for security, structure, and dependence. Consistent with her mood, the patient presents with depressed affect and mild motoric retardation at the present time. This mood disturbance appears to be exaggerated by her physical condition and seems to be of moderate severity.

Second, this woman exhibits a personality style that is likely to compound the symptomatic effects of physical conditions. Specifically, she has a difficult time divesting her own emotional state from external situations sufficiently to evaluate them realistically. She tends to personalize and overreact to even minute matters, and allows her emotions to color her perceptions severely. Her efforts to distance herself from frightening, indefinable things, or to

(*continued*)

FIGURE 2.2. (Continued)

escape her internal state, seem to be inadequate and ineffective. She represents a personality style that is characterized by defensive strategies designed to avoid expression of negative affect, to avoid confrontation with others' hostility, and to maintain rigid control over her own unwanted impulses. Because these defenses are unstable, however, her emotional expression or affect is likely to be variable. She is probably prone to be self-dramatizing and attention-seeking, and then to pull back and become overcontrolled.

Third, this patient's sense of overwhelming negative affect leads her to seek security and dependence excessively and malignantly. She has a morbid anticipation of dying and of losing love objects, particularly her husband, children, and mother. She exhibits a hunger for attention and reassurance, and her inability to satisfy these intense desires exacerbates her already poor self-esteem and low self-worth.

In view of this woman's excessive dependence, her ungratified need for reassurance and attention, and her morbid fear of expressing hostility, the likelihood of a secondary escalation of physical symptoms seems very high. Physical symptoms may provoke reassurance from others, as well as other secondary gains. Moreover, physical illness and her fear of being debilitatively ill may provoke or exaggerate ambivalent feelings regarding significant others, and morbid anticipation of losing the love of her husband and children.

Collectively, the patient presents with an active–dependent psychological orientation that exaggerates the significance of physical problems. The principal psychological needs revolve around the maintenance of closeness and reassurance from others. She attempts to obtain relief from her fear through active means, including somatization and emotional exaggeration. When relief is not forthcoming from others, she tends to become depressed and either to develop physical complaints or to exaggerate physiological responses to events. Emotional lability and depression are likely consequences of this coping pattern. Her general coping style is externalized in nature, being focused upon developing attachments to and obtaining gratifications from others. The problems appear to be relatively complex and are well embedded in a long-standing depressive personality configuration. At the present time, the subjective severity is moderate, but she has a low propensity to resist professional efforts to correct or treat her condition.

VI. *Diagnostic impression*

The relative contributions of biochemical/central nervous system dysfunction and of psychological conflicts to the current symptom picture are difficult to assess. The current data suggest the possibility of mild to moderate central nervous system impairment; they are also generally consistent with chronic fatigue syndrome, with a secondary mood disorder. Although physical and organic conditions may be implicated, these factors alone do not seem sufficient to account for the extensive physical history. Hence, the rather striking personality pattern that involves histrionic and depressive features probably carries the burden for understanding the exacerbation of the symptoms. The diagnostic impressions are as follows:

(continued)

FIGURE 2.2. (Continued)

Axis I
296.3, Major Depression
300.4, Dysthymia

Axis II
Rule out 301.5, Histrionic Personality Disorder

Axis III
Rule out central nervous system dysfunction of unknown etiology, and chronic fatigue syndrome. [*Note*: Some months later, this patient was diagnosed with multiple sclerosis.]

Axis IV
0—Inadequate information regarding recent stressors. Husband's absence appears to represent only a mild to moderate stressor.

Axis V
Global Assessment of Functioning: current = 55; within past year = 70

VII. *Recommendations*
This woman appears to be of sufficient intellectual ability and capacity for insight to benefit from treatment. The presence of mild to moderate psychological distress and disturbance, coupled with evidence of psychosocial contributors to her current symptomatic complaints, suggests both the motivation and need for psychological intervention. In planning for her psychosocial needs, the assignment of treatment should include the following considerations:

1. She does not present a level of either distress or danger sufficient to warrant a restrictive setting. Outpatient psychotherapy and pharmacotherapy are suggested.

2. The patient's problems are relatively complex and suggest the need for a psychotherapeutic intervention designed to have an impact on a life theme comprised of dependence strivings, active ambivalence, and inability to derive lasting security from others' expressions of emotional closeness or support.

3. The patient currently presents with an externalized coping style, suggesting the need for interventions at both the behavioral and cognitive levels. Explorations of schematic assumptions regarding the nature of self-sacrifice and external nurturance are particularly indicated. Procedures that confront unrealistic assumptions and that provide some direct assurance and means of validating and exploring these assumptions might prove to be useful, both in the relief of immediate symptoms and in the alleviation of more long-standing interpersonal patterns. In developing treatment programs, particular attention might be devoted to this woman's relationship with her mother and with other immediate family members. Extending her social contacts outside of the family into group therapy or into social activities might also be useful in diluting the impact of her symptoms.

4. The patient currently presents with a cooperative and generally compliant orientation to health care providers. She is likely to be able to establish a working alliance and to find directive interventions useful. The therapist does not need to exert excessive caution in the use of direct guidance,

(continued)

FIGURE 2.2. (Continued)

interpretive injunctions, or other confrontive interventions. Although the client may have some initial resistance to these procedures, it is likely to be temporary, and she ordinarily appears to be able to benefit from such interventions and to move toward self-exploration.

Overall, the patient's prognosis is moderate to good for the relief of depression. She does not appear to represent a major risk to self or others and appears able to benefit from insight oriented interventions. Continued monitoring and treatment of her medical condition are urged, however.

John Doe, Ph.D.
Psychologist

Contextual Information (Sections I–IV)

The psychological report is divided into seven sections. These sections usually are identified by separate headings, but not necessarily by the numbers used in Figures 2.1 and 2.2. The corresponding sections of Figures 2.1 and 2.2 are identified by the same roman numeral codes in order to facilitate discussion of the contents of psychological reports. The first four sections (I–IV) of the report constitute a compilation of contextual information—that is, the environmental and background information needed in order to understand the report. Section I, for example, provides identifying information about the patient and the details of when and where the assessment was conducted. This information is needed for the maintenance of records and patient tracking. Section II identifies the question that formed the focus of the evaluation. The question posed in this section is a refinement of the one originally asked by the referring clinician. It is framed in a way that is answerable by the methods of psychological assessment, relevant to the referring clinician's needs, and collaborative (in that the refinements reflect an interaction exchange between the assessing and the referring clinicians).

Section III identifies the procedures used in the assessment. It lists the tests, interview procedures, location, and dates during which observations were made. It usually also includes a list of the records reviewed, any ancillary persons contacted, and even the unstandardized procedures employed in the service of answering the question(s) posed. This section allows others who may also be asked to consult on the case, either concomitantly or at some time in the future, to identify the location, time, place, and methods that served the needs of the evaluation and informed their judgment. These others are then in a position to decide independently whether sufficient similarity exists between the previous and the current situation to warrant generalization.

Section IV provides a narrative background review that identifies the reason for the question being asked. This section places the patient and the evaluation itself in a relevant historical context. This section is designed specifically to clarify the history and concomitant reasons for raising the referral questions. In some ways, this section is similar to that which often contains a social history in other types of reports, except for two features: (1) The historical information itself is not interpreted in this section; and (2) the material reported may come from several different sources (e.g., interviews with informants, reviews of records, and parts of the clinical interview), rather than from the clinical interview alone.

The material used to develop this fourth section is organized in order to address three questions: (1) *Why* is the patient here? (2) Why is the patient *here*? (3) Why is the patient here *now*?

As the foregoing information will convey, my colleagues and I do not distinguish between interview-derived assessment data and test-derived data, as many clinicians do. This is because we believe that all of these methods entail the same processes of observing, scoring, and interpreting selected samples of behavior under controlled circumstances. The clinical interview, like any and all psychological tests, is an analogue environment that embodies the demand characteristics discussed in the preceding section. The interviewer uses the same process of observing, codifying, and rating observations as a clinician uses for all test responses, in order to reach conclusions about the question(s) raised. To separate conclusions and interpretations that arise from a loosely structured interview gives exaggerated importance to a single method that has dubious or unknown psychometric properties, and at the same time diminishes the importance of less arbitrary and more methodologically sound methods.

Although the information provided in Section IV is descriptive rather than interpretive, we do recommend including a short interpretive paragraph at the end of this section. Before the findings are summarized, a statement that indicates the degree to which faith in the report is justified. This statement may say something like the following:

> The consistency and detail of this patient's responses suggest that he was invested in the procedure, was able to organize his observations in a reliable fashion, and was candid and forthright in responding to the assessment tasks. Hence, the results to be reported here must be considered to be reasonably reliable and valid indicators of the patient's functioning.

Or:

> This patient presented with inconsistent levels of motivation, frequently became uncooperative, and often seemed uninvested in matters requiring accuracy, self-reflection, and candor during the evaluation process.

Hence, the results of this evaluation should be considered with moderate caution.

These descriptive interpretations are not derived simply from the observations made of test-taking behavior. They represent summary interpretations of the degree to which the patient was cooperative, honest, invested, consistent, and able to participate in providing the information needed.

Impressions and Findings (Section V)

Use of the Worksheet

A worksheet for deriving an integrated summary of observations from multiple sources of data is presented in Figure 2.3. This worksheet forms the basis for the integrative interpretation of psychological assessment procedures to be discussed in later sections of this chapter. Figure 2.3 is a modified version of a worksheet that was originally developed by Klopfer (1960); it has since been modified and found useful by several authors of texts on psychological assessment (e.g., Choca, 1980; Groth-Marnat, 1990). Our particular modification is designed to parallel the topics presented in Sections IV–VII of the psychological report as outlined in Figure 2.1.

To use the worksheet, a clinician first enters the name of each assessment device (e.g., WAIS-R, projective drawings, Rorschach, clinical interview, etc.) along the top row, so that the name of each device serves as a column heading. A brief interpretive summary of each device is then entered in the boxes below each one for each of the topics listed in the left-most column. In this step, the clinician independently analyzes (as much as possible) each procedure and formulates hypotheses regarding the patient's functioning in each domain of experience represented in the left-most column.

To illustrate, the reader will note that the first row on the worksheet is identified as "Approach and Reliability/Validity." This row is used to enter hypotheses about the degree to which the patient's approach to the assessment process warrants faith in the results. The clinician using the worksheet begins with one assessment device (e.g., the interview), extracts some hypotheses about the patient's approach, and enters these hypotheses in the box below the heading "Interview." Then the clinician proceeds down the column, focusing only on what the interview has suggested about each domain of functioning in turn—cognitive functioning, emotional functioning, conflict areas, interpersonal–intrapersonal coping styles, diagnosis, and treatment planning. This process is repeated for each assessment device, with an effort to ignore what has been previously entered. In this way, each assessment procedure can be independently inspected, analyzed, and interpreted.

	Procedures							Summary
Approach and Reliability/Validity								
Cognitive Functioning and Ideation								
Affect/Mood/ Emotional Control								
Conflict Areas								
Intra- and Interpersonal Coping Strategies								
Diagnostic Impression								
Recommendations								

FIGURE 2.3. Worksheet for integrative assessment of personality.

When each device has been thus inspected, the last column (labeled "Summary") is used to organize a set of summary hypotheses that now focuses on each domain of patient functioning rather than on the separate instruments. That is, now the clinician begins to summarize across rows rather than down the columns. The summary judgments in the last column both highlight the hypotheses that are consistent across different instruments as a form of cross-validation, and help the clinician to formulate new hypotheses in instances where different methods have yielded different conclusions about the domain under scrutiny.

The process of resolving discrepancies among data sources follows three steps. First, the clinician identifies the instruments that have given rise to contradictory hypotheses. Let us suppose, for example, that during both the interview and the administration of the Rorschach, the clinician suspected that the patient was not disclosing important information and suffered from more serious pathology than was obvious. The clinician has thus concluded that the validity of these parts of the evaluation was suspect. Let us further suppose, however, that the scores on the validity scales of both the MMPI-2 and the Millon Clinical Multiaxial Inventory—II (MCMI-II; Millon, 1987) were within normal limits and suggested a fair degree of openness and candor. The clinician has thus concluded that the results of these instruments were reasonably valid.

Once the clinician identifies the contradictory sources of information (e.g., the MMPI-2 and MCMI-II on the one hand, and the interview and the Rorschach on the other), the next step is to assign a priority to each of these instruments, with the highest priority being given to the instrument whose value for assessing the validity and honesty of a patient's response is most clearly established. In this example, the MCMI-II and the MMPI-2 should be given a higher priority than the clinical interview, since both of these instruments have empirically derived validity scales that reflect a patient's candor and openness, whereas the interview does not. The Rorschach does include some indices of defensiveness, but these indices are probably not as sensitive as those provided by the more structured tests. Thus, the interpretations arising from the MMPI-2 and the MCMI-II are likely to be better indicators of the overall validity of the findings than are those arising from the interview and the Rorschach.

If the distinctions among instruments are as clear-cut as in this example, in which the empirically validated instruments all provided one hypothesis and the other hypothesis arose solely from rationally derived or unvalidated instruments, the task of resolving contradictions is easy. However, in the more usual case, there are contradictions either between two equally well-validated tests or between a single well-validated test and consensual information from several less well-validated tests. In such instances, a clinician must attempt to make some conceptual sense of the differences. Hence, the third step in assessing contradictions is to cross-tabulate the hypotheses derived with the varying demand requirements of the tests. For example, it may be hypothesized that the patient in the example above is open and candid in inspecting her interpersonal patterns of behavior when the environment is reasonably well structured, but becomes guarded when structure is removed and expectations are unclear (unstructured demand characteristics).

By applying a similar approach for cross-validating hypotheses and resolving contradictions among instruments, a clinician can summarize each of the domains of experience identified in the left-most column of the worksheet. The result is a coherent, person-centered report that follows the outline emerging in the right-most column ("Summary"). This type of interpretation may contrast with a more test-oriented interpretative report, but it has the advantage of keeping the referral question in focus and the patient as the topic of discussion.

Organizing the Report

The body of the psychological report is incorporated under Section V. Although, as indicated above, my colleagues and I eschew the tendency to fractionate patients unnecessarily, it is both convenient and useful to distinguish among various conventionally accepted domains of human functioning in order to clarify the interrelationships and contradictions that characterize a given patient. Accordingly, Section V of the model report outline (Figure 2.1) is subdivided into three basic, albeit somewhat arbitrarily differentiated, functional domains: cognitive functioning, emotional functioning, and interpersonal–intrapersonal functioning. There is a minor variation between Figures 2.1 and 2.3, in that the latter figure, purely to enhance the convenience of coding and interpreting the data, provides a special row for identifying the patient's dominant conflict areas. Conflict areas are subsumed under the more general domain of interpersonal–intrapersonal functioning in the report outline presented in Figure 2.1. (Note also that the three domains of experience are not usually set off by separate paragraph headings in this section of the actual report; see Figure 2.2.)

Each assessment device and observation is assumed to be capable of contributing some understanding of the patient's functioning in each of the domains of functioning identified in the outline and the worksheet. For any given referral question, one or another of these areas of patient functioning may be more or less emphasized, but information within all three areas is necessary in order to provide a comprehensive picture of the patient in the report. For example, conclusions about cognitive functioning must take into account the several aspects comprising this domain of experience; these include the patient's intellectual ability, problem-solving efficiency, memory, thought processes, and thought content. The cognitive domain will warrant the greatest attention from the clinician when the questions asked are of this nature: "Does this patient's dementia reflect neurological impairment?" or "Is the patient able to benefit from partial care placement?" Ignoring secondary effects on mood, affect, and interpersonal–intrapsychic life, however, will result in an incomplete picture and may result in the development of an inappropriate treatment plan. The same concerns will arise in a different form if a clinician concentrates on the domain of emotional functioning in assessing a patient's level of depression, while ignoring either its interpersonal meanings or the presence of related suicidal ideation (a cognitive function).

Each of the three experience domains in Section V calls for formulating a response to six questions: (1) What areas of functioning are impaired? (2) How impaired are these functions, compared to a normative standard? (3) How severe are the impairments, compared to the patient's baseline or premorbid level of performance? (4) What is the nature of the relationships that exist among these functional areas? (5) What is the probable cause of the impairments? (6) What is the likely course of each impairment, including the likelihood that baseline functioning will be recovered?

The varying ways in which these six questions are addressed can best be illustrated by giving examples of the nature of the material to be presented under each of the three domains. For further illustrative purposes, the report outline presented in Figure 2.1 illustrates how data of specific types are interpreted and integrated with other information.

Cognitive Functioning. In the section on cognitive functioning, it is important to discuss such varied but related aspects of the individual as functional intelligence level, conceptual ability, ability to organize experience and concepts, ability to solve abstract problems, content of perceptual experience, integrative capacities, and memory. Many of these concepts are captured under the general theme of "intelligence," but some are more closely related to conventionality, cognitive integrity, and distractibility. To address these concepts adequately in terms of the six questions that are to be addressed to the domain of cognitive functioning, a clinician may first identify areas of strength and weakness. Let us suppose that assessment has revealed strong cognitive organizational skills but poor memory in an individual with average intelligence and no evidence of impaired emotional functioning. These two cognitive attributes should be noted, followed by a statement of the basis for normative comparison:

> The patient is functioning within the average range of intelligence, but the variability of intellectual performance indicates relatively low levels of cognitive efficiency. The patient's memory functions are moderately lower than expected on the basis of the patient's age and gender, but cognitive organizational abilities are considerably above average (within the superior range).

Then the question of the degree of impairment from baseline functioning may be addressed:

> The patient's memory impairment appears to be an acute feature of his performance, and is significantly reduced below the level of his usual functioning. Cognitive organizational skills, on the other hand, appear to reflect the level of his premorbid performance more closely.

In order to address the question of the interrelationship among these impairments, a statement such as this may follow:

> The deficits in memory may preclude the emergence or expression of the patient's strength in organizing his experience in interpersonal settings, resulting in his appearing to have more impairment in social situations than is actually evident.

A statement addressing the cause of impairment may come next:

> The uneven pattern of cognitive deficits and the relative differences in levels of performance suggest that the memory deficits cannot be easily attributed either to environmental circumstances or to a comorbid condition. Instead, the pattern suggests the presence of a rapidly developing, space-occupying, central nervous system lesion.

The final statement addresses the expected course of the impairment:

> Without active intervention, a continuing decline in the patient's mental functioning is probable. Overall, the outlook for recovery without treatment is poor.

Note that throughout these statements, the patient's functioning is being described, not the tests or test scores. The grammatical subject of each sentence is either the patient or a functional ability of the patient. In the role of consultant, the clinician's opinion is being expressed about the *patient*, not the tests; at each point, this opinion derives from compiling evidence from all the assessment procedures used. Although the clinician must be able to justify his/her opinion if called upon to do so, it is the consultant's, not the referring clinician's, prerogative to provide an interpretation of the data. We assume that the clinician has more familiarity with the assessment materials and more expertise in interpreting this data than does the referrer. Hence, the consultant tries to avoid leaving the referrer with an uninterpreted observation or an uninterpreted array of test scores.

Parenthetically, when assessing children for school placement or in custody deliberations, legal requirements imposed to protect against bias may affect how reports are written. Scores from intelligence and achievement tests are the ones that come under these rules most often, and are treated by the courts or service systems quite mechanistically. If such requirements occur with adult assessments, we present the scores parenthetically within the interpretation, rather than to give them a status that suggests that they can be considered independently of the clinician's interpretation. For example, we might write: "The patient is functioning within the average range of intelligence (WISC-III Full Scale IQ = 107)." Another but less desirable option, because it suggests that the scores can be interpreted rather mechanistically, is to present a listing of scores at the beginning of the report, along with the list of assessment procedures (Section III of the report).

Emotional Functioning. Emotional functioning is typically divided into two aspects—mood and affect. A third aspect of emotional functioning, the relationship between the cognitive and emotional domains, is also included. Specifically, the part of the interpretive report pertaining to this third aspect may define the degree to which a patient employs cognitive resources to control and manage emotional life, the degree to which the patient can maintain objectivity in the face of emotional stress, or the degree to which the patient is emotionally accessible.

"Mood" refers to the patient's subjective emotional experience. In describing this aspect of functioning, the patient's dominant (trait) and current (state) moods are usually separately indicated first, followed by a statement about the relative importance of the various moods identified:

> The patient's mood is dominated by depression and anger. These two qualities of emotional experience seem to characterize his response to a wide variety of situations. That is, resentment and dysphoria appear to be chronic conditions that override any direct awareness of fear, anxiety, or euthymia.

Conventional clinical terminology, as applied to identifying moods, usually begins with a simple tripartite differentiation of "euphoria," "euthymia," and "dysphoria." A refinement of this distinction might draw from efforts to differentiate between primary and secondary emotions or moods. Primary moods or emotions are those that are most basic, universal, and pure. Conventionally, love, joy, surprise, sadness, rage, and fear are thought to constitute the primary emotions and are assumedly evoked by situations that have direct relevance to survival; variations and permutations of these experiences represent secondary emotions.

For example, "euphoria" may be recognized by its identity with positive primary emotions and their permutations—love, joy, and surprise. In clinical terms, euphoric moods are described as unrealistically strong feelings of excitement or well-being. These moods contrast with "euthymia," which refers to a lack of emotional intensity. "Dysthymia" is a term that refers to the more uncomfortable and unwanted emotions of sadness, anger, and fear; clinically, these experiences are usually described as "depression," "hostility," and "anxiety," respectively.

"Affect," in contrast to "mood," describes a patient's observable response to situational contexts. The same classification of emotions as that used in describing moods can be helpful in describing the nature of the affect. Hence, the clinician can observe the correspondence between subjective mood and overt expression. In addition, the clinician can make a social comparative assessment of the "appropriateness" of the patient's affect. This judgment indicates the degree to which the patient's affect departs from that normally expected in various situations. Assessment of appropriateness thus requires the presence of an established normative base for judging situational responses. By varying the demand characteristics represented by various psychological assessment procedures, a clinician can directly observe both the responsivity and range of a patient's affect.

In a related fashion, assessment of emotional functioning requires an evaluation of how adequately the patient is able to tolerate stress without becoming overwhelmed by emotions and experiencing either a deterioration of problem-solving skills or increased behavioral instability. Assessment of this domain derives directly from observations made when psychological assessment procedures are constructed to vary in the degree of structure and stress.

Putting these three components of emotional functioning together, and responding to the six questions to be addressed, result in a series of statements. The first may simply specify the dominant moods and affects, placing them in a context of relative impairment. The following statements define the interrelationship among the moods and affects, and specify the level of control the patient is able to maintain over them when responding to a variety of stressful conditions:

> The patient presents a moderately depressed mood and mild to moderate levels of subjective anxiety. She does not appear to experience excessive levels of anger or hostility, however, and her affective responses are generally consistent with her mood. Though expansive and exaggerated, her affective presentation indicates that her mood is responsive to the demands of different situations. That is, her depression and anxiety both appear to be reactive in nature.
>
> Interpersonal demands, time pressures, and reduced environmental structure all induce considerable distress and correspondent deterioration of both cognitive efficiency and behavioral stability. Under these stress-evoking conditions, the patient's thought processes become more rigid, her problem-solving efforts become significantly less flexible, her

affect becomes labile, and her behavior becomes unstable. Hence, she is likely to become tearful, disorganized, and impulsive under these stress-provoking situations. Although decompensating cognitive skills are apparent at these times, they do not achieve psychotic levels. She continues to be realistic in her perceptions, but is nonetheless unable to establish the emotional distance needed to approach problems objectively. Overall, these latter patterns appear to be long-standing characteristics, but are acutely exacerbated by the current marital distress.

By the end of this subsection, any questions about either a thought disorder or a mood disorder should be clearly answered. Moreover, the degree to which mood and affect are successfully controlled by the patient's cognitive resources should be apparent to the referrer. Conversely, the degree to which cognitive skills and qualities are altered by strong emotional experiences should also be clear.

Interpersonal–Intrapersonal Functioning. Cognitive and emotional functioning do not occur in a vacuum. The description of interpersonal and intrapersonal conflicts and coping patterns is presented in the psychological report as a brief formulation of how behaviors, thoughts, and feelings are expressed and interrelated both to one another and to situational/interpersonal contexts. Recurrent patterns that exist among these features of person and environment represent what is often referred to as the "personality" of the patient. That is, "personality" consists of the enduring response patterns that distinguish individuals from one another.

However, not all clinicians are comfortable either with this term or with the task of identifying recurrent patterns. Some believe that descriptions of any "pattern" necessarily occlude important differences that exist in responses and evoking environments. These clinicians prefer to describe each problematic behavior in discrete terms. Other clinicians, on the other hand (and my colleagues and I include ourselves in this latter group), believe that constructing individualized catalogues of each patient's problematic behaviors—as if these responses were unrelated to one another—not only is inefficient, but underrepresents the significance of the many patterns that are important to and descriptive of a patient's life. We believe that psychological assessment must first represent an effort to determine the degree to which the problems resulting in the search for help can be best understood as isolated, situational responses or as reflections of more enduring and recurrent patterns that interfere with effective functioning.

A decision about whether behavior is best understood in one or the other of these frameworks cannot be made *a priori*, on the basis of theoretical preferences alone. Hence, psychological assessment entails an observation of behaviors within contexts whose demand characteristics are known, and results in a description of the degree to which multiple situations evoke similar and problem-related responses. An estimate of the "pervasiveness" of a given pattern of behavior across situations is an indication of the degree to which personality, as opposed to situational, characteristics may be involved in a patient's difficulty. To the degree that a patient's pattern of response either fails to accommodate to the changing demands of different situations, or changes capriciously (i.e., independently of the situational demands), a clinician may conclude that disturbances of personality are present.

The Usefulness of Theoretical Constructs

Although it is well to say that psychological assessment is a process of systematically observing behavioral patterns and changes that occur in juxtaposition with changing contextual demands, it is equally clear that not all behaviors and not all contexts can be systematically observed. The assumption underlying psychological assessment is that there are a finite number of discernible dimensions or continua within which people can fruitfully be described and compared. Yet different theories use different types of constructs and prioritize various concepts differently in their efforts to describe individual differences. The question then arises as to what theoretical framework the clinician should or can best use in order to formulate the importance of a patient's behavior and to communicate with other professionals.

There are major advantages to communicating the results of psychological assessment through an integrated theory. A consistent conceptual scheme reduces the redundancy and confusion that may result when a clinician attempts to invoke concepts from several theories, each of which may represent an alternative and often competing view of humankind. Moreover, using an internally consistent conceptual system simplifies the task of communicating by specifying the relative importance of various conflicts and associated coping behaviors. Because of the diversity that may also characterize the theories of those who read or use a report, it is helpful if the system used is sufficiently flexible and closely enough tied to observations that it can be transported across theoretical models.

The "Conflict Areas" and "Interpersonal–Intrapersonal Coping Strategies" sections of the worksheet (Figure 2.3) represent an attempt to provide guidelines for organizing material in a way that will facilitate communication across theoretical lines. Here, I present three basic systems or theoretical models whose explanatory constructs represent three different levels of abstraction, varying from psychodynamic to descriptive. The models are selected to illustrate how theoretical systems that vary in the levels of inference required to invoke their explanatory concepts can each provide the breadth needed to organize a written formulation of a patient's conflicts and coping methods. Other systems may also be adaptable to these needs, and, in fact, the systems presented here may not be useful for all questions. Questions regarding neuropsychological performance, for example, may be less applicable to the concepts illustrated in these models. The clinician's choice of these or other systems, therefore, is likely to be dependent upon his/her own theoretical preferences. When a system of theoretical constructs is selected to serve as the basis for formulating a picture of a patient, I urge only that flexibility, transportability across theoretical frameworks, and the communication value of the system to the referent be kept in mind as selection criteria.

Contemporary Psychodynamic Formulations.   Psychoanalytic theories and concepts provide explanatory formulations that constitute the most abstract of the three models to be presented here. They differentiate between causal and respondent factors, and generally view behaviors as symbols of internal states. Thus problems are usually attributed to unseen, internal processes rather than to situational demands. In turn, these internal causal variables can only be inferred from an integration of theoretical principles with the behaviors that are evoked by the assessment material. That is, in its classical rendition, intrapsychic or intrapersonal conflicts are distinguished from interpersonal ones in psychodynamic formulations. Increasingly, however, this distinction is considered to be less essential, as it has become clear that internal struggles recapitulate and are interdependent with interpersonal ones. Accordingly, the most systematic contemporary methods of formulating the interplay among intrapsychic conflicts emphasize the role of interpersonal wishes over intrapsychic impulses.

Though current methods differ somewhat, Luborsky (1984) and Strupp and Binder (1984) have each provided systematic methods for assessing conflicts from a psychoanalytic perspective. Both systems formulate behaviors and symptoms in terms of the needs or wishes that are seeking to be met, the anticipated responses from others, and the resultant actions taken or the introjects adopted by the patient. Moreover, in both systems, the pervasiveness of a similar set of needs, wishes, expectations, and responses across important relationships serves as an index of the degree to which the patient's presenting complaints represent part of a core pattern or focal conflictual theme. The more pervasive a single pattern across relationships, the more the patient's problems are thought to represent life adjustment problems as opposed to situational, transitory, or "state" reactions.

Though they have arisen from a largely psychoanalytic perspective, the methods and concepts used by Luborsky (1984) and by Strupp and Binder (1984) are adaptable to a variety of perspectives. In the case of the Luborsky method, a systematic measurement procedure has been developed that is likely to become available for the purposes of clinical assessment. This procedure is called the Core Conflictual Relationship Theme method; it entails a systematic clinical review of the patient's relationship history with key individuals. From this review, the clinician identifies three basic characteristics in each of the targeted relationships: wishes or impulses, expected actions from others, and resultant patient behaviors. Recently, standard lists of the most usual elements within each of these three relationship domains have been developed in order to help clinicians to identify and compare the basic patterns represented, and thereby to determine whether there are common themes across relationships. The list of wishes and impulses includes assertion, submission, sexual gratification, acceptance, being cared for, competence, inflicting hurt, and exercising control. The list of anticipated responses from others includes domination, support, exploitation, respect, acceptance, insensitivity, uncooperativeness, compliance, withdrawal, affection, understanding, dependence, and misunderstanding, among others. Likewise, the list of potential patient behaviors or introjects includes submission, assertion, dependence, helplessness, low self-esteem, feeling obligated, anger, happiness, guilt, anxiety, depression, jealousy, confusion, and frustration (Barber, Crits-Christoph, & Luborsky, 1990).

Using this system, a clinician can easily write a formulation of conflicts and coping strategies following the outline presented in Figure 2.1. Such a written formulation may appear as follows:

> The data suggest that the patient's presenting complaints of depression are representative of a long-standing and recurrent theme that characterizes many of his interpersonal relationships. This problematic theme is typically enacted with persons on whom the patient is dependent for intimacy. In these instances, a conflict exists between the patient's strong desire to be nurtured and protected, and his anticipation that those on whom he depends are more needy of affection and attention than he. Thus, he responds by suppressing his needs, endeavoring instead to provide to others the degree and type of nurturance that he desires for himself. He subsequently blames himself for being inadequate if these others deny having these needs or if they fail to thrive under his attentions. Although anger and resentment may be hidden in this self-blame, these feelings are seldom recognized or recognizable, and in fact may serve only to exacerbate his already high levels of guilt and sense of insufficiency.
>
> The patient's current depression appears to derive from an iteration, within his marriage, of the foregoing pattern. Thus, his many needs for nurturance are largely unexpressed in his haste to provide the nurturance and support that he believes are needed for his wife to achieve her goal of completing her education. He perceives her as very needy, uncertain, fragile, and demanding, thus leaving him with a sense of despair about his own gratification. With little hope of earning her nurturant support, he is left with a sense of hopelessness.

In less intimate relationships, the patient's conflicts take on a slightly different aspect. In work and peer relationships, for example, the patient has stronger needs for acknowledgment and recognition than for nurturance. Conflicts arise when these needs go unmet in his work and peer contacts. Under these circumstances, the patient may feel victimized rather than deprived, with the correspondent anger and resentment being more accessible to his awareness than when these feelings arise in his relationships with intimate others.

According to a clinician's preferences, more or less emphasis may be placed upon impulses rather than wishes, or on internal sanctions rather than the reactions or anticipated reactions of others, or on developmental stages and fixations. The important elements in this formulation method are as follows: The dominant conflicts are identified; the relative strength of these conflicts is specified; and a rationale is proposed that both accounts for the patient's presenting problems and specifies the conditions under which behaviors may depart from the dominant theme.

Biosocial Formulations. Biosocial theories interpret symptoms, problems, and behaviors as reflections of interactions among dispositions and environments. Although they attribute events and patterns to indwelling and inferred needs or drives, the recurrent patterns that they identify are more often descriptive than they are inferential. Therefore, their descriptions require less agreement with and understanding of the theoretical underpinnings. Millon, for example, suggests that personality differences can be conceptualized as an interplay among several polarities. An in-depth consideration of this theory is presented later in this volume in connection with the MCMI (Chapter 8). A simplified version (Millon, 1981; Millon & Everly, 1985) of this elaborate theory is used here, however, to illustrate the use of theory in psychological assessment and report writing.

In this simplified model, Millon conceptualizes personality patterns as an interplay between two major dimensions. The first dimension is a categorical description of what a person finds reinforcing, ostensibly as a joint function of inherent disposition and exposure to the forces of socialization. Assignment to one of four categories in this dimension is defined by the relative weight the person places upon dependence and autonomy. The second dimension is descriptive and is based upon a determination of whether the person is passive or active in seeking gratification of these needs. Desires for both dependence and autonomy are considered to be universal, but people are assumed to vary in the degree to which one or the other of these needs or strivings is dominant. Hence, a person may be said to be oriented toward the need for dependence (dependent type) or the need for autonomy (independent type), or toward the gratification of both needs equally (ambivalent type), or toward avoidance of either dependence or autonomy (detached type).

The assignment of an individual to one of these four categories describes the driving force behind his/her interpersonal theme, in much the same way as psychodynamic theories describe the more broadly defined interpersonal need or impulse. Conflicts are thought to be interpersonal and social. A person who is defined as having a need for attachment to others, for example, may experience a conflict either because the strength of his/her need is self-judged to be excessive (intrapersonal conflict), or because the family or social environment does not provide the degree of attachment sought (interpersonal conflict). Parallel distinctions can be found for each of the other three personality types.

Descriptively, the second dimension of this model reflects the degree to which a person passively or actively seeks reinforcement from others. Whereas dependence–autonomy reflects a source of either internal or interpersonal conflict, the passive–active distinction reflects one's coping style. The cross-tabulations of the reinforcement type and the activity level result in eight basic personality types that correspond (with varying levels of fit) to the Axis II categories of DSM-III-R, DSM-IV, and their derivatives: passive–detached (schizoid personality), active–detached (avoidant personality), passive–dependent (dependent personality), active–dependent (histrionic personality), passive–independent (narcissistic personality), active–independent (antisocial personality), passive–ambivalent (compulsive personality), and active–ambivalent (negativistic or passive–aggressive personality). These personality types are reflected in the personality subscales of the MCMI-II, to be discussed in Chapter 8.[2]

In formulating a description of the patient using a model that applies this medium level of abstraction, the clinician may express the findings of intrapersonal–interpersonal assessment in language such as this:

> This patient presents an active–ambivalent style of personality organization. That is, he struggles between equally dominant needs for closeness and separation. On the one hand, his needs for dependence remain ungratified, because his investment in achieving independence is so strong as to preclude tolerance for closeness. On the other hand, his needs for independence are also ungratified, because of the pull of his efforts to remain protected and dependent on others.
>
> The patient's current problems with depression reflect the futility of this personality organization. His needs for dependence on his wife for approval and nurturance preclude the expression of his own needs for power, and undermine his efforts to achieve a sense of self-efficacy.

[2]The reader will note in Chapter 8 that the MCMI-III has been updated to bring it into consistency with the changes introduced in DSM-IV. This has included a finer distinction among personality types and the addition of other polar dimensions. The reader should take careful note of the differences among the MCMI versions, since they reflect and are responsive to the evolution of the *Diagnostic and Statistical Manual*.

The reader will note that this description misses both an indication of the pervasiveness of the pattern relative to the current problems and a representation of the nature of any secondary or ancillary patterns that may be present. It is also not readily adaptable to a discussion of developmental levels or phases. Information about these factors requires supplementation from additional theories and associated assessment procedures. The MCMI is designed to provide some information on the relative salience of other reinforcement or personality types. However, this method is better suited to describing trait-like differences than to describing situationally induced states.

Empirical/Descriptive Formulations. Descriptive formulations are typically tied closely with a method of assessment. Behavioral assessment, for example, describes overt behavior, whereas personality descriptions assess relative standing on empirically derived descriptive dimensions. The concepts described may be internal or inferred (e.g., extraversion), but this latter method offers little interpretation of the driving forces or motivations behind behaviors.

In the past decade, personality theorists have come to some degree of consensus in identifying the trait-like qualities on which people differ. There is emerging agreement that permutations within and among five descriptive factors, called the "Big Five," capture most of the differences that exist among people (see Goldberg, 1992). The qualities associated with high and low values on these factors are worth reviewing here.

"Intellect" describes a person's level of cognitive ability. Those who are seen as having strengths in this area tend to be perceptive, analytical, reflective, curious, imaginative, and creative. Those for whom this is an area of weakness may be seen as lacking in intelligence, imperceptive, nonanalytic, unreflective, uninquisitive, lacking in imagination, and rigid or uncreative.

"Surgency" is a factor that corresponds with concepts such as extraversion, energy level, talkativeness, spontaneity, assertiveness, sociability, and adventurousness. In clinical literature, "surgency" defines a style of coping that is frequently defined as ranging from "internalizing" to "externalizing." Low-surgency or internalizing individuals tend to be introverted, self-reflective, nonassertive, and emotionally constricted, and to rely on defense mechanisms such as compartmentalization of affect, intellectualization, self-punishment, and reaction formation. High-surgency or externalizing individuals, on the other hand, are likely to employ such defensive maneuvers as direct avoidance, extrapunitiveness, projection, acting out, and denial of responsibility.

"Agreeableness" is related to an interpersonal affiliation or resistance dimension. At the high end, it corresponds with such dimensional traits as interpersonal warmth, cooperativeness, unselfishness, politeness, and generosity. Individuals who have low levels of this quality may be quite defensive and resistant when they are forced to give up control to others. They may become interpersonally cool, demeaning, uncooperative, undermining, rude, and even stingy with their time and possessions.

"Conscientiousness" is a quality that requires the ability to override emotional pressures with cognitive skills. Individuals with high levels of conscientiousness are adept at organizing and following through with problem-solving efforts. Clinically, they may be described as being responsible, reliable, practical, thorough, serious, and hard-working. Alternatively, those who are low on this dimension may be seen as disorganized, irresponsible, undependable, impractical, careless, lazy, and perhaps frivolous.

"Emotional stability" is conceptually similar to such clinical dimensions as severity of emotional distress or tolerance for stress. Those who are high on this dimension possess such correlated qualities as calmness and ability to relax; they are at ease with things, and are seen as emotionally secure and stable. At the other end of the dimension are individuals with significant levels of emotional distress, who tend to be emotionally changeable, angry, tense, nervous, envious, and insecure.

Drawing from this empirical taxonomy of personality characteristics, a clinician may provide a descriptive formulation as follows:

> The patient presents with moderate levels of surgency, but with relatively lower levels of both emotional stability and intellect. This pattern is likely to be reflected in social gregariousness, high energy levels, and general spontaneity, but also in poorly formulated plans for action and inconsistent organization. High levels of emotional instability are likely to be reflected in variable interpersonal behaviors. Variations in agreeableness or cooperation with others, dependability, and levels of trust or security are likely to be noted, for example. Moreover, the level of emotional instability suggests that responses in any given situation may be overdetermined and exaggerated, or even punctuated by unreasonable interpersonal demands and volatility.
>
> The patient's current depression is likely to reflect generalized emotional inconsistency, a degree of insensitivity to others in his environment, and a poor grasp of the situational demands or social nuances in current interpersonal relationships. These qualities all appear to reflect trait-like qualities, and therefore are not expected to be substantially alleviated if levels of environmental stress are reduced.

Such descriptions of the "Big Five" traits may be supplemented by descriptions of symptoms or states in order to make the formulation more complete. These descriptions may provide a more complete picture of the relationship between traits and states and between persona and environment.

Diagnosis and Recommendations (Sections VI and VII)

The sections of the assessment report that address diagnosis and treatment planning (Sections VI and VII) are probably the most frequently read of any in the report. Indeed, in many cases the answers to the referring clinician's questions are in one or both of these sections. Although the descriptions contained in the other sections add to the complexity and detail of the descriptions, diagnosis is frequently a shorthand description of many aspects of cognitive, emotional, and interpersonal–intrapersonal functioning. Similarly, treatment planning is the ultimate objective of all other descriptions. Of what value is diagnosis, an understanding of cognitive resources, or a description of emotional responsivity or interpersonal–intrapersonal functioning if it is not reflected in the way the patient is treated?

Because they are so central to the entire process of assessment, aspects of summarizing diagnostic and treatment implications are illustrated throughout the rest of this volume. The consideration of each test includes a section on the implications for diagnosis and for treatment planning. A few general principles bear attention at this point, however.

First, as is true of other sections of the report, the presentation of the patient's diagnosis should be framed in language that is conventional and accepted within the field. The DSM-IV (American Psychiatric Association, 1994) and the *International Classification of Diseases* (ICD-9; World Health Organization, 1977) provide the bases for this common descriptive language. Familiarity with and use of one of these systems facilitate communication among professionals, even though many mental health professionals disagree with some of the labels, concepts, and processes that have resulted in the development of these systems.

Second, although a patient's diagnosis is often informative and sought by a referrer, its relevance is suspect when it comes to planning nonmedical interventions (Beutler, 1989). Numerous nondiagnostic qualities and dimensions are more closely related to predicting and assigning treatments than descriptive diagnoses per se. Clarkin and I (Beutler & Clarkin, 1990), for example, point out the importance of a treatment selection model that includes but is not limited to formal diagnostic variables. We suggest that such "predisposing patient variables" as environmental stressors and resources, situational response traits, expectations, coping styles, resistance potential, level of distress, problem severity, and problem complexity serve as indicators for designing a treatment that is of the complexity needed for most patients.

Third, treatment plans must consider the interactive effects of these predisposing variables with at least three levels of treatment decision making: selecting contexts, developing helpful relationships, and applying specific procedures. Contexts that may be selected vary in the nature of the settings, the types of modalities used (psychosocial vs. medical/somatic), the format through which they are applied, and the duration and frequency of application. Likewise, selecting the type of relationship that will be most productive must take into account the contextual aspects of treatment assignments. Depending upon the context, the clinician who plans treatment must identify the nature of the patient's expectations of the relationship to the nature of the recommended treatment, and must outline plans for both preparing the patient and adjusting the environment either to meet or to alter these expectations.

Only when the clinician has some perspective on the type of treatment contexts available, and the nature of the relationships that are possible within these settings and modalities, can he/she define the nature of the specific psychosocial interventions to be used. It is at this level that the results of psychological assessment are invoked to define at least five variables that have implication for selecting specific psychotherapeutic interventions: (1) problem complexity, (2) problem severity, (3) level of motivational distress, (4) type of coping style, and (5) level of resistance potential. The implications of these variables in the development of treatment plans have been discussed extensively elsewhere (Beutler, 1983; Beutler & Clarkin, 1990), as have methods for their measurement (Beutler, Wakefield, & Williams, 1994). Their definitions and treatment implications are briefly summarized here; they are discussed at further length both in the chapters devoted to specific measures and in Chapter 9, where treatment planning is discussed in detail.

"Problem complexity" is the degree to which the patient's difficulty is associated with a pervasive pattern or theme, as opposed to being a transitory situational response. Complex or pervasive themes suggest the need for conflict-focused interventions, whereas nonpervasive, reactive, or simple problems suggest that a symptom-oriented intervention may be sufficient.

"Problem severity" reflects the degree of impairment the patient experiences in social functioning. An analysis of symptoms, of environmental resources, and of the chronicity of the disturbance is used to assess severity. The severity of the problem, taking into account the degree to which support systems are available in the community, is used in decisions regarding the degree of confinement needed, the intensity of treatment, and the mode and format of treatment. Severe problems often require medications, multiple treatment, enhancement of social ties, and careful monitoring.

"Motivational distress" is a concept that is closely related to problem severity, but reflects the extent to which the patient's subjective discomfort propels him/her to engage in treatment. It is indexed by a combination of subjective distress and the presence of an identified set of interpersonal problems that can serve as targets for change. The level of motivational distress is used in two ways to plan treatment: (1) as an indicator of progress, and (2) as an indicator of whether the procedures invoked are aimed at increasing or decreasing the level of interpersonal distress to achieve or maintain high levels of motivation. Patient motivation has long been speculated to be dependent upon the presence of subjective distress. Recent research (e.g., Mohr, Shoham-Salomon, Engle, & Beutler, 1991) suggests that both subjective distress and the presence of identifiable interpersonal problems are predictive of the likelihood of a positive versus a negative outcome. Hence, procedures that direct attention to or away from sources of interpersonal conflict, and that increase or decrease distress levels, may be differentially indicated by patient distress or symptom severity level.

"Coping styles" of patients vary along the dimensions outlined in previous sections of this chapter. Coping styles reflected in externalizing behaviors, such as social gregariousness, surgency, activity, acting out, projection, and so forth, may be particularly amenable to interventions that give high priority to making behavior change. Conversely, coping styles characterized by self-blame, inactivity, passivity, and introversion appear to be relatively more responsive to insight-oriented than to behavior-oriented interventions (Beutler, 1991; Beutler, Engle, Mohr, Daldrup, Bergan, Meredith, & Merry, 1991; Beutler, Machado, Engle, & Mohr, 1993; Beutler, Mohr, Grawe, Engle, & MacDonald, 1991; Calvert, Beutler, & Crago, 1988; Cooney, Kadden, Litt, & Getter, 1991; Kadden et al., 1990).

"Resistance potential" is defined as the patient's state-like or trait-like propensity to be oppositional toward and uncooperative with treatment demands. Those who are judged to have high levels of or high likelihood of resisting therapist suggestions may best be recommended either for nondirective procedures (i.e., self-directed; Beutler, Engle, et al., 1991; Beutler et al., 1993; Beutler, Mohr, et al., 1991) or for procedures that paradoxically proscribe change or prescribe symptom exaggeration (Shoham-Salomon, 1990; Shoham-Salomon & Hannah, 1991; Shoham-Salomon & Rosenthal, 1987). Conversely, those patients who are relatively agreeable and cooperative with the demands of treatment may be receptive to directive guidance and therapist-controlled interventions.

The foregoing variables are discussed at greater length in Chapter 9, which provides more detailed coverage of the implications of these patient qualities for making treatment recommendations.

Summary

In this chapter, I have attempted both to specify the dimensions that can be varied in the process of assessment and to provide a model by which aspects of patient functioning, as sampled by the assessment procedures employed by the psychologist, can be integrated, organized, and reported. In the process of describing the integrative model, I have illustrated several conceptual systems that differ in degree of abstractness, in order to demonstrate how theoretical concepts that vary in level of inference may be used for the purposes of communicating to referring professionals and others. I have described only three of many possible ways in which conflicts and coping styles can be conceptualized. By whatever system, it is useful for the clinician to use and develop a consistent framework and scheme for identifying and conceptually discriminating among various types of conflicts, so that he/she may describe them meaningfully to the referrer.

It should be apparent from the sample methods and reports illustrated here that answering appropriate referral questions requires that clinicians have a firmly grounded understanding in the development of behavior, the normal course of behavioral and symptom change, descriptive psychopathology, and the effects of different treatment settings and types on problematic behaviors. Without such knowledge, even relevant questions cannot be satisfactorily answered. Educating the reader in these latter knowledge areas is beyond the scope of this book. However, the reader is well advised to become familiar with both theoretical and empirical literature on normal behavior, behavioral deviations, and treatments. Later descriptions of patients and illustrations of integrative interpretation, diagnosis, and treatment planning will assume the presence of such background knowledge.

References

American Psychiatric Association. (1987). *Diagnostic and statistical manual of mental disorders* (3rd ed., rev.). Washington, DC: Author.

American Psychiatric Association. (1994). *Diagnostic and statistical manual of mental disorders* (4th ed.). Washington, DC: Author.

Barber, J. P., Crits-Christoph, P., & Luborsky, L. (1990). A guide to the CCRT standard categories and their classification. In L. Luborsky & P. Crits-Christoph (Eds.), *The core conflictual relationship theme* (pp. 35–49). New York: Basic Books.

Bender, L. (1938). *A visual motor gestalt test and its clinical uses* (Research Monograph No. 3). New York: American Orthopsychiatric Association.

Beutler, L. E. (1983). *Eclectic psychotherapy: A systematic approach*. Elmsford, NY: Pergamon Press.

Beutler, L. E. (1989). Differential treatment selection: The role of diagnosis in psychotherapy. *Psychotherapy, 26,* 271–281.

Beutler, L. E. (1991). Have all won and must all have prizes? Revisiting Luborsky et al.'s verdict. *Journal of Consulting and Clinical Psychology, 59,* 226–232.

Beutler, L. E., & Clarkin, J. (1990). *Systematic treatment selection: Toward targeted therapeutic interventions*. New York: Brunner/Mazel.

Beutler, L. E., Engle, D., Mohr, D., Daldrup, R. J., Bergan, J., Meredith, K., & Merry, W. (1991). Predictors of differential and self-directed psychotherapeutic procedures. *Journal of Consulting and Clinical Psychology, 59,* 333–340.

Beutler, L. E., Machado, P. P. P., Engle, D., & Mohr, D. (1993). Differential patient × treatment maintenance among cognitive, experiential, and self-directed psychotherapies. *Journal of Psychotherapy Integration, 3*, 15–31.

Beutler, L. E., Mohr, D. C., Grawe, K., Engle, D., & MacDonald, R. (1991). Looking for differential effects: Cross-cultural predictors of differential psychotherapy efficacy. *Journal of Psychotherapy Integration, 1*, 121–142.

Beutler, L. E., Wakefield, P., & Williams, R. E. (1994). Use of psychological tests/ instruments for treatment planning. In M. Maruish (Ed.), *Use of psychological testing for treatment planning and outcome assessment* (pp. 55–74). Hillsdale, NJ: Erlbaum.

Butcher, J. N., Dahlstrom, W. G., Graham, J. R., Tellegen, A. M., & Kaemmer, B. (1989). *Minnesota Multiphasic Personality Inventory–2 (MMPI-2): Manual for administration and scoring.* Minneapolis: University of Minnesota Press.

Calvert, S. J., Beutler, L. E., & Crago, M. (1988). Psychotherapy outcome as a function of therapist–patient matching on selected variables. *Journal of Social and Clinical Psychology, 6*, 104–117.

Choca, J. (1980). *Manual for clinical psychology practicums.* New York: Brunner/Mazel.

Cooney, N. L., Kadden, R. M., Litt, M. D., & Getter, H. (1991). Matching alcoholics to coping skills or interactional therapies: Two-year follow-up results. *Journal of Consulting and Clinical Psychology, 59*, 598–601.

Dahlstrom, W. G., Welsh, G. S., & Dahlstrom, L. E. (1972). *An MMPI handbook: A guide to use in clinical practice and research.* Minneapolis: University of Minnesota Press.

Goldberg, L. R. (1992). The development of markers for the Big-Five factor structure. *Psychological Assessment, 4*, 26–42.

Groth-Marnat, G. (1990). *Handbook of psychological assessment* (2nd ed.). New York: Wiley.

Kadden, R. M., Cooney, N. L., Getter, H., & Litt, M. D. (1990). Matching alcoholics to coping skills or interactional therapies: Posttreatment results. *Journal of Consulting and Clinical Psychology, 57*, 698–704.

Klopfer, W. G. (1960). *The psychological report.* New York: Grune & Stratton.

Luborsky, L. (1984). *Principles of psychoanalytic psychotherapy: A manual for supportive-expressive treatment.* New York: Basic Books.

Millon, T. (1981). *Disorders of personality: DSM-III, Axis II.* New York: Wiley–Interscience.

Millon, T. (1987). *Millon Clinical Multiaxial Inventory–II (MCMI-II manual).* Minneapolis: National Computer Systems.

Millon, T., & Everly, G. S. (1985). *Personality and its disorders.* New York: Wiley.

Mohr, D. C., Shoham-Salomon, V., Engle, D., & Beutler, L. E. (1991). The expression of anger in psychotherapy for depression: Its role and measurement. *Psychotherapy Research, 1*, 125–135.

Rorschach, H. (1942). *Psychodiagnostics.* Bern: Bircher. (Original work published 1921)

Shoham-Salomon, V. (1990). Interrelating research processes of process research. *Journal of Consulting and Clinical Psychology, 58*, 295–303.

Shoham-Salomon, V., & Hannah, M. T. (1991). Client–treatment interactions in the study of differential change processes. *Journal of Consulting and Clinical Psychology, 59*, 217–225.

Shoham-Salomon, V., & Rosenthal, R. (1987). Paradoxical interventions: A meta-analysis. *Journal of Consulting and Clinical Psychology, 55,* 22–27.

Strupp, H. H., & Binder, J. L. (1984). *Psychotherapy in a new key.* New York: Basic Books.

Wechsler, D. A. (1981). *Manual for the Wechsler Adult Intelligence Scale—Revised.* New York: Psychological Corporation.

World Health Organization. (1977). *International classification of diseases* (9th rev.). Geneva: Author.

3

Issues in Selecting an Assessment Battery

Larry E. Beutler

Although the preceding chapter has addressed, in general terms, the test characteristics and qualities that should be considered in selecting a set of instruments with which to address defined referral questions, it is important to give greater attention to the availability and selection of specific instruments. Accordingly, this chapter addresses two major contemporary issues that must be considered in this process of selecting assessment procedures. The first of these is the issue of the relative merits of a standard battery of tests, as opposed to those of a battery of instruments selected to address only the specific questions raised by a referring clinician about a given patient.

The second issue is that of the relative merits of qualitative versus quantitative methods of assessing human functioning. This is a particularly salient issue on the contemporary scene, and one that is emerging in many fields of behavioral science. In recent years, a good deal of attention has been given to the development of new paradigms and methods for deepening our understanding of human experience. In clinical practice, the debate between the relative merits of qualitative and quantitative methods arises from a concern that quantitative procedures, arising as they do from group or nomothetic studies, fail to capture the idiosyncrasies that characterize individual motivation and response. Qualitative methods, based on intensive individual analysis of process, promise a new view of individual behavior.

Standard versus Problem-Focused Assessment

Standard Batteries: Content, Advantages, and Disadvantages

Ever since the work of Rapaport, Gill, and Schafer (1946), most clinical treatment programs have advocated and employed a standard set of assessment devices as part of the intake procedure (Sweeney, Clarkin, & Fitzgibbon, 1987). Although the same instruments are administered to all incoming patients, with little or no modification, the interpretation itself is usually modified according to patients' ethnic background, sex, and referral problems. This "standard battery" approach to assessment is designed to provide a broad base of similar and reliable information from which to compare patients, make diagnoses, evaluate areas of patients' strength and weakness, determine prognoses, and plan treatment.

At times, the selection of these standard tests places a premium on brevity. Thus, "screening batteries" are largely comprised of paper-and-pencil instruments that collectively require little clinician time. At other times, especially in long-term inpatient care settings, the standard battery is much more extensive and includes a variety of time-intensive, individual assessment devices (Sweeney et al., 1987). In either case, the instruments selected for a standard battery are chosen in order to ensure the ability to observe a broad array of response domains, and to provide stimulus materials whose demand characteristics represent both simple and complex environments (see Lubin, Larsen, & Matarazzo, 1984; Sweeney et al., 1987).

The kind of test most frequently selected in the modal standard battery is an omnibus personality test of "trait-like" qualities. One or two instruments of this type are often included, in order to obtain behavioral samples from both subjective and objective experience domains. The next most frequently selected instrument type consists of intellectual and cognitive tests designed to determine level of abstract reasoning, problem-solving efficiency, and the nature of cognitive organization. Symptom and other state measures, though high on the list, are less frequently selected in the standard battery than tests of either global personality or general cognitive functioning. When symptom measures are included, however, tests that evaluate several different problem domains and that provide both an estimate of the objective level of social dysfunction and an indication of patient subjective distress are favored.

In terms of specific instruments, the Minnesota Multiphasic Personality Inventory (MMPI), the Wechsler Adult Intelligence Scale—Revised (WAIS-R), and the Rorschach are the most frequently selected devices. The Wechsler Memory Scale (WMS), the Shipley Institute of Living Scale (which yields similar information on intellectual level and efficiency), and the Bender

Visual Motor Gestalt Test (BVMGT) are also frequently included in screening batteries. Specific symptom measures, such as the Beck Depression Inventory (BDI), the Brief Symptom Inventory (BSI), and the BSI's longer counterpart, the Symptom Checklist 90—Revised (SCL-90-R), complete the list of most used instruments (Sweeney et al., 1987).

When an institution or clinical facility places more emphasis on obtaining a comprehensive picture of each patient than on the amount of time required, the intake battery is also likely to include tests that tap the domains of interpersonal functioning. The Thematic Apperception Test (TAT) and some form of sentence completion test are frequently used to assess interpersonal needs and responses in the extended and screening evaluations, respectively. Likewise, projective drawings are among the most frequently selected devices in extended batteries (Sweeney et al., 1987).

Approaching assessment through the use of a general or "core" battery of devices has several advantages over individualized assessment procedures. For example, through the consistent and repeated use of the instruments from a core battery, a clinician may develop a set of explicit expectations about the characteristics of those patients who seek services at a given clinical institution. By referencing setting-specific norms and by observing the patient characteristics that are associated with a good response to the treatment in a particular setting, the clinician develops the ability to extract very individualized interpretations from the test materials. Thus, a core battery may allow highly individualized interpretations because of the increased expertise resulting from an in-depth familiarity with the instruments used.

In addition, a core battery permits the accumulation of a data base that will allow a clinician to review the changes over time in patients applying for service at a given site (and, where applicable, the changes within individuals from one admission to another). Even the overall efficacy of various treatment programs in a facility can be determined if postdischarge follow-up evaluations are included in the standard battery. In contrast, if each entering patient receives a different set of tests based upon his/her particular presentation, it is difficult either to compare patients entering the facility at different times or to estimate the efficacy of the treatment programs established.

On the other hand, there are drawbacks to using a core battery that is applied to everyone. The primary drawback is the lack of flexibility for addressing the unique needs of individual patients. That is, there are questions that a single, all-purpose test battery is simply unable to answer. Because of the insensitivity of omnibus tests to specific neuropathologies, for example, neuropsychological assessments were developed. The modal battery consisting of the MMPI, the Rorschach, the SCL-90-R, the BVMGT, and the WAIS-R simply is ill suited for either identifying the nature of such impairments or localizing neuropathology.

The Problem-Focused Approach

Adapting the neuropsychology model to functional mental health issues, some authors (Sweeney et al., 1987; Clarkin & Hurt, 1988) argue for a more focused or problem-specific form of evaluation as an alternative to the use of a "core" battery. This type of assessment battery is comprised of instruments that are intensely focused on the most salient issues for the patient's diagnosis and treatment; it may be very different for different individuals, depending upon the nature of the questions asked by referring professionals. The advantages of this "individualized" approach lie in its ability to respond specifically to presenting issues and referral questions. Problem-focused assessment allows a more in-depth analysis of a given patient's problems than the usual core battery, because it acknowledges that some tests are better for addressing certain problems than are others.

The prevalence, in practice, of using a core battery approach rather than individualized assessment suggests that many clinicians believe that a problem-focused approach (1) is too expensive or (2) does not provide enough of an increment in knowledge to justify its use over the simpler core battery. This belief is supported by the suggestion that the overwhelmingly large number of patient variables that are important in diagnosis and treatment planning can be reduced to a relatively small number of dimensions (Beutler, 1991; Goldberg, 1992). Under most circumstances, this finite number of patient dimensions is of sufficient specificity to allow extrapolation to the planning needs of most settings and most referral questions.

Of course, the use of a core battery does not by any means preclude the additional use of specific instruments. Indeed, there may be decided advantages to combining these approaches. Two methods are possible. A clinician may use several different core batteries in a given setting, each tailored to particular problems typically presented by patients who come to that setting. For example, many clinics have specialized treatment programs for anxiety disorders, depression, and eating disorders. Depending on a patient's initial complaints, as assessed by the first telephone contact or interview, one of several core batteries may be administered to address these complaints separately.

Alternatively, and perhaps more advantageously, a clinician may use a core battery of a few basic instruments and supplement this battery with individualized tests that reflect the needs of specific patients. Thus, for a person with initial complaints of depression, a standard battery consisting of an omnibus personality test, a symptom checklist, an assessment of social background, and a test of interpersonal relationships may be augmented with tests that are sensitive to mood and affect, memory, and suicidality. The supplemental tests allow desirable individualization in assessing those functional areas that are presented in the referral question, whereas the core tests allow comparisons to be made across patients and time. Using this approach, a clinician not only can evaluate each of the areas of functioning discussed in Chapter 2, but can tap special needs and deficits that address the specific referral question.

Recommended Instruments for Various Response Domains

As discussed in Chapter 2, within some set of boundary conditions, the behaviors sampled by a given test can generate hypotheses about behaviors that reflect several different response domains. Six such domains are the most central ones to most referral questions: (1) historical background, (2) cognitive functioning, (3) emotional functioning, (4) interpersonal–intrapersonal functioning, (5) diagnostic status, and (6) prognosis and treatment response. (These are the domains covered in Sections IV–VII of the psychological report outline presented in Figure 2.1.) The consultant/clinician who is able to integrate disparate information from multiple sources of information, whether derived from a core or a problem-specific test battery, is in a position to provide accurate information about the meaning and nature of present and future behaviors as they relate to these areas (see Lovitt, 1988). The limits of any test for sampling from and generalizing to these several domains are found in each instrument's reliability, sensitivity, and specificity. Each instrument may be more adept and reliable for assessing some areas of functioning than for assessing others.

Clarkin and Hurt (1988) have identified a number of areas in which reliable and sensitive instruments exist for specific purposes. Adapting their suggestions, Table 3.1 identifies the instruments whose focus and content are most useful for each of the six response domains listed above and presented in Chapter 2. Two points should be noted in reference to Table 3.1. First, the list of tests is only representative, not comprehensive; it does little justice to the very large number of available measures that may be used to assess each area. Indeed, there are instruments that may be better suited for specific purposes than those presented here. This list of instruments represents an effort to balance the adequacy of the information obtained with the time cost of each instrument.

Second, the table does not account for the fact that omnibus, trait-oriented instruments (e.g., the Millon Clinical Multiaxial Inventory [MCMI], the MMPI-2, and the Rorschach) also include special scales and procedures that can be extracted and used for more specific purposes, such as assessing risk for depression, severity of alcohol abuse, and anger control. The reader will find more information about some of these special scales and their uses in the chapters of this book devoted to these tests.

To aid in the selection of instruments to use in either a core or a problem-focused battery, I now describe the instruments presented in Table 3.1. This introduction should provide an initial familiarization for the reader.

TABLE 3.1. Recommended Instruments for Various Response Domains

Domain/instrument(s)	Rater
Historical background	
Life Experiences Survey	Patient
Social Support Questionnaire (SSQ)	Patient
Cognitive functioning	
General functioning	
Mini-Mental State Examination (MMSE)	Clinician
Intellectual functioning	
Wechsler Adult Intelligence Scale—Revised (WAIS-R)	Patient
Shipley Institute of Living Scale	Patient
Memory functions	
Wechsler Memory Scale (WMS)	Patient
Cognitive process/content	
Rorschach	Clinician
Perceptual–motor functioning	
Bender Visual Motor Gestalt Test (BVMGT)	Clinician
Emotional functioning	
General severity and pattern	
Symptom Checklist 90—Revised (SCL-90-R)	Patient
Brief Symptom Inventory (BSI)	Patient
Client Emotional Configuration Scale	Clinician
Depression	
Hamilton Rating Scale for Depression (HRSD)	Clinician
Beck Depression Inventory (BDI)	Patient
Anxiety	
State–Trait Anxiety Inventory (STAI)	Patient
Anger/hostility	
Buss–Durkee Hostility Scale	Patient
Interpersonal–intrapersonal functioning	
Coping style	
Minnesota Multiphasic Personality Inventory—2 (MMPI-2)	Patient
Inventory of Interpersonal Problems	Patient
Structural Analysis of Social Behavior	Clinician
Sexual disturbance	
Derogatis Sexual Functioning Inventory	Patient
Child Abuse Potential Inventory	Patient
Marital/family disturbance	
Dyadic Adjustment Scale	Patient
Family Environment Scale	Patient
Marital Satisfaction Inventory	Patient
Social adjustment	
Social Adjustment Scale—Self-Report	Patient
Michigan Alcoholism Screening Test	Patient
Diagnosis	
Structured Clinical Interview for DSM-III-R (SCID)	Clinician
Structured Interview for DSM-III Personality (SIDP)	Clinician
Anxiety Disorders Interview Schedule (ADIS)	Clinician
Millon Clinical Multiaxial Inventory (MCMI)	Patient

(*continued*)

TABLE 3.1. (Continued)

Domain/instrument(s)	Rater
Prognosis and risk	
Suicide potential	
Scale of Suicide Ideation	Clinician
Beck Hopelessness Scale (BHS)	Patient
Alcohol abuse potential	
Alcohol Use Inventory	Patient
Schizophrenia prognosis	
Camberwell Family Interview	Clinician

Some of these instruments, especially the Structured Clinical Interview for DSM-III-R (SCID), the Mini-Mental State Examination (MMSE), the BVMGT, the MMPI-2, the MCMI, the Rorschach, and the WAIS-R, will be given additional and more intensive consideration in later chapters.

Historical Background

Details about a patient's history can best be obtained with the interview procedures to be discussed in Chapter 4. It is not sufficient simply to know what has happened to an individual, however; a clinician also needs to have an understanding of the impact of these events and the resources that are available to support change.

The objective measurement of life changes and their impacts is very complex. In order to accomplish the task in the most complete fashion, a very extensive, multidimensional assessment procedure is required (Monroe, 1982; Schulz & Tompkins, 1990; Zimmerman, 1983). A less intensive approach to this problem may focus on two related dimensions: life changes and social support systems. The information provided in assessments of these two dimensions will ordinarily be supplemented by the historical information available from diagnostic interviews and procedures, which are discussed somewhat later in this chapter.

The Life Experiences Survey (Sarason, Johnson, & Siegel, 1978) is a 57-item self-report instrument that requires patients to report the subjective impact of change events over the prior year. The scale consists of two parts. The first part refers to life changes that are common to individuals in a variety of situations; to this list, patients are allowed to add events that have been significant and peculiar to them. The second part lists 10 events that are particular to students, and this part is excluded when one is evaluating nonstudents. In both parts, patients first indicate whether the events occurred in the past year and then rate (separately) the desirability and impact of the event along a series of 7-point scales. Scores for positive change, negative change, and total change are obtained.

The Social Support Questionnaire (SSQ; Sarason, Levine, Basham, & Sarason, 1983) is a 27-item self-report inventory designed to assess both perceived number of social supports and satisfaction with these social support systems. Responses to the SSQ have been found to be negatively related to level of subjective discomfort, especially among women; they are also related to subsequent persistence in a difficult or frustrating task. This test provides a relatively efficient method of determining the source and strength of supportive family and social relationships.

Cognitive Functioning

Cognitive functioning is a multidimensional domain. The aspects of functioning that are most salient for most patients include problem-solving level, abstract reasoning abilities, memory, perceptual content and accuracy, and perceptual–motor integration. Cognitive functioning (including these several subareas) is the domain that is given the greatest attention in the assessment of organic and intellectual impairment. The numerous neuropsychological procedures that are used for very specific purposes are not reviewed here. Instead, a few instruments that together provide a range of information within and across the various subareas of cognitive functioning are surveyed.

General Functioning. The Mini-Mental State Examination (MMSE; Folstein, Folstein, & McHugh, 1975) consists of a brief standardized interview administered by a clinical rater. It has demonstrated good reliability and is sensitive to different pathologies. In particular, it quite adequately distinguishes patients suffering from organic dementia from those with functional disturbances. The MMSE taps the subareas of cognitive control, abstract reasoning, orientation (time, place, and person), memory, and thought processes. It usually serves as a screening device to supplement or replace more intensive and time-consuming assessment procedures that focus on separate aspects of mental state.

Intellectual Functioning. The Wechsler Adult Intelligence Scale– Revised (WAIS-R; Wechsler, 1981) is a standardized, individual assessment device that yields three global scores (Performance IQ, Verbal IQ, and Full Scale IQ) and 11 subscales reflecting more specific aspects of cognitive processing. These various aspects of cognitive functioning are most directly represented by two stable factors, expressing performance in the areas of Verbal Comprehension and Perceptual Organization (Silverstein, 1982). The WAIS-R is discussed in detail in Chapter 5.

The Shipley Institute of Living Scale (Shipley, 1940) is a self-administered device comprised of two subscales designed to assess verbal recognition/comprehension and abstract reasoning. These scores are combined to provide an index of cognitive efficiency and an estimated full-scale IQ that is comparable to that obtained with the longer WAIS-R (Paulson & Tien-Tih, 1970; Zachary, Crumpton, & Spiegel, 1985). The Shipley Institute of Living Scale frequently serves as a screening device when the depth of knowledge available from the WAIS-R is not considered necessary to answer the referral question being asked.

Memory Functions. The Wechsler Memory Scale (WMS; Wechsler, 1945, 1987) is a standardized measure of verbal, perceptual, remote, recent, rote, and logical memory. Visual and auditory stimuli are presented to provide a general estimate of information retrieval and storage. The instrument provides a standard comparison to the levels of functioning that can be expected on the basis of general intelligence, and has become a standard device for most assessment batteries that evaluate cognitive impairments (Cattell & Johnson, 1986).

Cognitive Process/Content. The famous Rorschach Inkblot Test (Rorschach, 1921/1942) is comprised of 10 standard cards. The test is administered in two phases—a free association phase and an inquiry phase. In the first phase, respondents are asked to indicate what the inkblots on the cards appear to be. In the second, they describe the characteristics and qualities of the blots themselves that led them to their responses. The Rorschach provides an avenue by which to observe a patient's thought processes. Unusual cognitive organization and mental content are readily observed in the nature of the patient's response. Recent developments in the standardization of scoring have led to improved reliability and to an increasing array of studies on validity (Exner, 1974). The Rorschach is discussed at greater length in Chapter 6.

Perceptual–Motor Functioning. The Bender Visual Motor Gestalt Test (BVMGT; Bender, 1938) is a brief screening device that was originally designed for detecting brain damage. Its use has been extended to the assessment of other cognitive and personality functions, however (Hutt, 1985; Koppitz, 1975). The BVMGT consists of nine designs presented to a patient in a constant order, with instructions to draw the figures "the best you can." Structural inaccuracies and distortions are scored to assess perceptual–motor integrity and problem-solving organization, with some patterns being used as projective indicators for the presence of interpersonal needs, conflicts, and cognitive integration. To facilitate the use of this instrument in this latter way, variations of the standard administration procedure have frequently been used (see Groth-Marnat, 1990). Although these procedures are promising, the greatest strength of the BVMGT continues to be in its assessment of perceptual–motor and organizational ability.

Emotional Functioning

The domain of emotional functioning, as outlined in Chapter 2, includes the assessment of both mood and affect; estimates of the chronicity of dysphoria, when present; evaluation of emotional stability; and a determination of the level of emotional control that the patient exhibits. The instruments described here and listed in Table 3.1 are designed to allow the assessment of general emotional qualities; symptoms of emotional dysphoria and disturbances; and specific aspects of behavior that are related to depression, anxiety, and anger. These latter areas of disturbance are the most likely ones in which mood and affect will be noted.

General Severity and Pattern. The Symptom Checklist 90—Revised (SCL-90-R; Derogatis, 1977; Derogatis, Rickels, & Rock, 1976) is a 90-item self-report instrument that yields nine symptom scores and three global summary scores. The symptom dimensions include somatization, obsessive--compulsive behaviors, interpersonal sensitivity, depression, anxiety, hostility, phobic anxiety, paranoid ideation, and psychoticism (this last score is usually interpreted as reflecting social alienation in nonpsychotic populations). The summary scores reflect overall subjective distress, symptom specificity or spread, and the intensity of presenting symptoms.

The Brief Symptom Inventory (BSI; Derogatis, 1992) is a brief form of the SCL-90-R. Like the parent instrument, this 53-item self-report form yields nine symptom scores and three global summary scores. These scales are the same as those on the longer version. The brevity of the BSI is especially useful in situations requiring rapid assessment, and it has been normalized on older populations (Hale, Cochran, & Hedgepeth, 1984).

The Client Emotional Configuration Scale (Daldrup, Beutler, Engle, & Greenberg, 1988) assesses the mode of emotional expression exhibited by the client. These expressive modes are based upon theoretical descriptions of boundary disturbances as derived from gestalt therapy literature, and include retroflection, introjection, confluence, projection, and deflection. Ratings are made by an experienced clinician using a Likert scale.

Depression. The Hamilton Rating Scale for Depression (HRSD; Hamilton, 1967) provides an independent rating of patient dysphoria. The scale taps such areas as sleep disturbances, libido and sexual functioning disturbance, diffuse somatic complaints, suicide ideation, guilt, and anergia. The clinical utility and reliability of the HRSD have been well documented, and it has been used widely in both research and clinical practice (Endicott, Cohen, Nee, Fleiss, & Sarantakos, 1981).

The Beck Depression Inventory (BDI; Beck, 1978) is an easily administered self-report device for assessing severity of depressive symptoms. It is readily applied in a repeated administrations and reliably assesses depression level (Beutler & Crago, 1983). Its value lies in the ease with which it is administered and the ecological or face validity of patient responses. Because it is not tied to specific diagnostic criteria, it is not easily used either for establishing a diagnosis or for differentiating between depressed and nondepressed individuals. However, it does provide a stable indicator of depressed mood in clinical, medical, and normal populations.

Anxiety. The State–Trait Anxiety Inventory (STAI; Spielberger, Gorsuch, Lushene, Vagg, & Jacobs, 1983) is a 40-item, multiple-choice, self-report inventory. This is a revised version of the original scale by Spielberger, Gorsuch, and Lushene (1970). It is a quickly administered method of assessing anxiety in two domains. "State anxiety" reflects a patient's stress level in specified situations and can often be taken as an index of how well the patient is presently coping with current anxiety-evoking environments. On the other hand, "trait anxiety" reflects stable individual differences and a general propensity to perceive stressful situations as dangerous. Compared to state anxiety, trait anxiety reflects the adequacy with which a patient is likely to cope with distressing events over time.

Anger/Hostility. The Buss–Durkee Hostility Scale (Buss & Durkee, 1957) assesses the degree of interpersonal anger and associated diminished functioning in four areas. The subscale scores indicate level of experienced anger, the nature of its expression, and the degree to which a respondent internalizes or externalizes blame. Of particular importance for predicting a patient's response to external environments, the test provides an estimate of the degree to which the patient can express anger directly to offending persons in the environment.

Interpersonal–Intrapersonal Functioning

Chapter 2 has outlined some of the dimensions of symptomatic and interpersonal functioning that have been proposed as being among the most relevant for making treatment decisions (see also Beutler & Clarkin, 1990). Of particular concern to the present discussion are patient conflict areas, coping styles, and potential for resisting the influence of others. Chapter 2 has also noted that interpersonal–intrapersonal functioning includes both trait-like and state-like qualities, which must be taken into account during assessment. The trait-like aspects are typically described as aspects of personality, whereas the state-like aspects often reflect levels of distress and reactivity to stress. Thus, to some degree, these latter concepts overlap with the more general concepts considered in connection with emotional functioning. The instruments presented here include both state and trait components.

Coping Style. The Minnesota Multiphasic Personality Inventory—2 (MMPI-2; Butcher, Dahlstrom, Graham, Tellegen, & Kaemmer, 1989) is a 567-item revision of the well-known MMPI (Dahlstrom, Welsh, & Dahlstrom, 1972). It is an empirically derived self-report test on which patients' responses are compared to those of individuals presenting with defined symptoms and disorders. The MMPI-2 is scored on 13 scales, 3 of which are designed to assess the validity and conventionality of a person's responses, and 10 of which reflect various clinical patterns and symptoms. In addition, a very large number of special scales and scale combinations have been developed to apply to specific aspects of coping style, symptom manifestation, type and severity of conflict, authority relationships, and response dispositions. Although most scales of the MMPI-2 reflect trait-like qualities, some are also sensitive to transitory changes and disturbances.

The revision of the MMPI has updated the language of the original version, eliminated questionable items, restandardized the responses based on census-based samples, and introduced some new items that may contribute to the development of promising new scales. The MMPI-2 is discussed at length in Chapter 7.

The Inventory of Interpersonal Problems (Horowitz, Rosenberg, Baer, Ureno, & Villasenor, 1988) uses a self-report format to assess levels of distress arising from interpersonal relationships. Interpersonal problems are organized into the categories that are thought to represent the types of complaints patients most often bring to psychotherapy. The scale yields six subscales: H. Assertive, H. Sociable, H. Intimate, H. Submissive, T. Responsible, and T. Controlling. These subscales reflect two types of problems: those about which a patient indicates that he/she finds it "hard to" do or be (prefixes of "H"), and those about which the respondent indicates that he/she does or is "too much" (prefixes of "T"). The scale is sensitive to changes induced in short-term psychotherapy, and it has been successfully applied both to studies of psychodynamic psychotherapy processes (Horowitz, 1986) and to predicting the likelihood of negative outcomes in psychotherapy (Mohr et al., 1991).

The Structural Analysis of Social Behavior (Benjamin, 1974) assesses a patient's perceptions of interpersonal events along three dimensions: (1) focus on self or other; (2) affiliation (love–hate and friendliness–hostility); and (3) interdependence (control–autonomy giving). This instrument is based upon a circumplex conceptual system and defines interpersonal exchanges among participants as permutations of the three underlying dimensions (e.g., McLemore & Benjamin, 1979). It describes the tendency of the patient to respond in kind to the friendly or hostile behaviors of others, and in a complementary way to behaviors that occur along the control dimension.

Sexual Disturbance. The Derogatis Sexual Functioning Inventory (Derogatis, 1975) is a self-report, multidimensional instrument made up of

247 items. It assesses functioning in seven primary, sex-defined domains: information, experience, drive, attitudes, affects, gender role definition, and fantasy. In addition, however, it both includes a global rating of sexual satisfaction and totally encompasses 53 items from the SCL-90-R. This latter scale allows the screening evaluation of the presence of general psychiatric symptoms. This scale can be separately scored to yield the same dimensions as the SCL-90-R; hence, individual symptoms as well as global distress can be evaluated.

The Child Abuse Potential Inventory (Milner, 1980) is comprised of 10 subscales. The test is in self-report format, and the six clinical subscales are derived from 77 items reflecting aspects of self–other relationships and impulse control. These subscales are designed to evaluate personal rigidity, unhappiness, and general distress. In addition, they tap three domains of interpersonal and family unhappiness. The nonclinical scales are designed to evaluate the patient's consistency of response, random response sets, and willingness to admit to problems (lie scale) in a manner reminiscent of that used with the MMPI. The inventory has been used both descriptively (Milner, 1989) and predictively (Milner & Robertson, 1989), with impressive results.

Marital/Family Disturbance. The Dyadic Adjustment Scale (Spanier, 1976) is the most widely used self-report instrument in the clinical and nonclinical research literature for assessing marital satisfaction and adjustment. The instrument is reported to have excellent psychometric properties both for evaluating the presence of marital disturbance and for highlighting some specific areas of concern, such as sexual, financial, and communication difficulties (Jacob & Tennenbaum, 1988).

The Family Environment Scale (Moos & Moos, 1976, 1981) is a self-report measure that is completed by both the subject and a significant other of the subject's choosing. It is designed to assess 10 domains of family environment: cohesion, expressiveness, conflict, independence, achievement orientation, intellectual/cultural orientation, active/recreational orientation, moral/religious emphasis, organization, and control. Validity and reliability studies have shown the instrument to be statistically sound and meaningful.

The Marital Satisfaction Inventory (Snyder, 1979) is a 280-item self-report instrument presented in a true–false format. The content covers marital relations, with a separate section adapted for use among couples with children. Eleven areas are covered: conventionalization, global distress, affective communication, problem-solving communication, time together, disagreement about finances, sexual dissatisfaction, role orientation, family history of distress, dissatisfaction with children, and conflict over childbearing. Internal-consistency coefficients and test–retest reliabilities average about .90, and research has supported the discriminant validity of the scales (Snyder, Wills, & Keiser, 1981).

Social Adjustment. The Social Adjustment Scale–Self-Report (Weissman & Bothwell, 1976) is comprised of 42 questions relating to everyday adjustment and performance. The questions cover such areas as impairment and adequacy in social role perfomance at work and home, leisure activities, relationships with significant others, integrity of the family unit, and economic self-support. Available norms allow comparisons to be made both to nonpatient and various patient samples.

The Michigan Alcoholism Screening Test (Selzer, 1971) is a brief screening procedure for the detection of excessive alcohol consumption. It is frequently used for the classification of drinking patterns, as well as for determining the clinical significance of changes in alcohol consumption. It is frequently used in clinical practice for obtaining an indication of drinking severity based upon patient self-report.

Diagnosis

Determination of a patient's diagnosis is one of the primary reasons for referral. Although the instruments described up to this point variously assess symptom severity and patterns of interpersonal behaviors, they do not assess diagnostic syndromes. "Syndromes" are clusters of symptoms and signs that are consensually believed to represent distinctive and frequently occurring patterns. Because diagnoses are criteria-based patterns of related symptoms, they can efficiently be determined only with instruments whose structure parallels the current edition of the DSM or ICD.

The unstructured clinical interview is the most frequently used diagnostic device, but has not been found historically to be particularly reliable for this purpose (see Chapter 4). There are instruments that are better suited and more efficient for establishing a diagnosis, however; a few of these are reviewed here.

The Structured Clinical Interview for DSM-III-R (SCID; Spitzer, Williams, & Gibbon, 1986) has modules for assessing both Axis I and Axis II disorders. The interview format is determined strictly by the DSM-III-R criteria (American Psychiatric Association, 1987), and the authors report acceptable reliability scores. Raters are trained on criteria-based videotape samples to ensure comparability.

The Structured Interview for DSM-III Personality (SIDP; Pfohl, Stangl, & Zimmerman, 1983) is a semistructured, independently rated interview assessing the criteria for personality disorders as described in DSM-III. Its format and structure parallel those of the SCID, and its validity is assessed against the criteria of DSM Axis II disorders.

The Anxiety Disorders Interview Schedule (ADIS; DiNardo, O'Brien, Barlow, Waddell, & Blanchard, 1983) is an interview-based assessment of the anxiety symptoms presented in DSM-III. It yields a diagnosis of both type of anxiety disorder and severity; it is thus useful for responding to diagnostic questions as well as descriptive ones, and is closely linked to the implementation of treatment strategies for specific symptoms as well.

The Millon Clinical Multiaxial Inventory—II (MCMI-II; Millon, 1987) is a revision of the original 175-item MCMI-I (Millon, 1983). It is a multidimensional self-report instrument that yields scales designed to reflect syndromes that parallel DSM-III-R diagnostic criteria. Three basic clusters of scores are obtained—one reflecting patterns that define basic personality styles corresponding with eight of the Axis II disorders, one that assesses more severe personality patterns corresponding with Schizotypal, Borderline, and Paranoid Personality Disorders; and one that assesses patterns corresponding with more circumscribed or transient clinical syndromes. This last cluster includes the spectrum of anxiety syndromes, somatoform disorder, hypomanic disorders, substance abuse disorders, severe depression, and psychotic thinking processes. The MCMI has frequently been proposed as a shorter alternative to the MMPI (Gynther & Gynther, 1983), but current research suggests that the two instruments differ, particularly on the dimension of diagnostic specificity (McCann, 1991). Chapter 8 of this volume discusses the development and use of the MCMI (including that of the latest version, the MCMI-III) in greater detail.

Prognosis and Risk

Most, if not all, of the instruments discussed in the preceding paragraphs have been used to assess prognosis and to explore ways of matching treatments to patient needs. Combinations of scales from the MMPI, for example, have been found to predict differential responses to insight- and symptom-focused treatments and to directive and nondirective treatments (Beutler et al., 1990; Beutler & Mitchell, 1981); the ADIS has been used to determine the probable value of cognitive and exposure therapies (Barlow, 1985); and the SCL-90-R is a frequently used measure of clinical effectiveness (Beutler & Crago, 1983). This section, however, describes several instruments whose purpose is specifically to assess risk and prognosis in selective areas of functioning.

Suicide Potential. The Scale of Suicide Ideation (Beck, Kovacs, & Weissman, 1979) is an interview-based instrument that is administered by a trained clinician. It is designed to quantify clinical indicators of suicide potential. It focuses on the intensity of current conscious suicidal intent by tapping the presence of self-destructive thoughts and wishes, suicidal threats, overt suicidal plans, and depressive cognitions. It employs a flexible format in order to allow the clinician to elicit as much information as possible in each area, in order to accurately determine the presence of suicidal behaviors and to estimate the probability of future suicidal acts.

The Beck Hopelessness Scale (BHS; Beck, Weissman, Lester, & Trexler,

1974) is a 20-item, self-report, true–false questionnaire that assesses the aspect of clinical depression that most closely relates to suicidal behavior. A patient's sense of futility and hopelessness has been found to be more predictive than depressed mood of risk for suicidality. Accordingly, the BHS has good internal consistency and concurrent validity, and is sensitive to relatively small changes in depression and suicidal thoughts over time.

Alcohol Abuse Potential. The Alcohol Use Inventory (Horn, Wanberg, & Foster, 1974; Wanberg, Horn, & Foster, 1977) was developed to provide an assessment of the nature and range of alcohol-related problems. The 147 items of the instrument are grouped into 22 scales and organized around a three-factor structure: styles of alcohol use, symptoms and consequences of alcohol use, and perceived benefits of drinking. It appears to yield quite reliable and consensually valid responses (Wanberg et al., 1977; Wanberg & Horn, 1983).

Schizophrenia Prognosis. The Camberwell Family Interview (Brown & Rutter, 1966) is a semistructured interview designed for administration to a significant family member of a patient with schizophrenia. It yields information about "expressed emotion," based upon ratings of criticality, hostility, and overinvolvement. This interview requires extensive training and experience for reliable adminstration, but does appear to be a significant predictor of prognosis. For example, not only does the level of expressed emotion predict rehospitalization, but treatments that modify patterns of expressed emotion are successful in reducing rehospitalization rates.

Comment

It should be reiterateed that the list and descriptions of psychological tests provided in the foregoing pages and in Table 3.1 are far from complete; the most notable omissions are instruments specifically assessing neuropsychological functions. Nonetheless, the clinician who is armed with an understanding of these tests will be able to address most of the questions that form the basis for referral. With this in mind, let us now turn to a consideration of the other major issue to be addressed in this chapter—seeking a balance between qualitative and quantitative assessment and interpretative methods.

Qualitative versus Quantitative Assessment

Dissatisfaction with Quantitative Methods

In Chapter 1, the descriptions of measurement procedures have emphasized the role of normative comparisons, reliability estimates, and validity demonstrations. All of these properties of measurement involve numbers and numerical concepts. Sensitivity and specificity are expressed as percentages; validity and reliability are expressed as correlations between numbers; norms reflect means and standard deviations of numbers. Within this quantitative perspective, important information about the value of different measures is obtained when observations can be transformed into numbers, compared through numerical manipulations, and then translated back to descriptive language.

Preferences for quantitative measurement and methodologies have characterized the fields of psychology and measurement theory for several decades, especially in academic circles. This preference for numbers—which are explicit in meaning, replicable, and comparable from person to person—may account for the rise and success of "empirical" tests like the MMPI and MCMI, as well as for the relative demise of "rational" tests like the Rorschach and TAT in academic circles.

"Empirical" tests are those based upon the demonstration that the scores (numbers) are different among patients with different, known characteristics (i.e., normative and criteria-group comparisons). These empirical demonstrations are at the very foundation of quantitative assessment, and, of necessity, rely on the demonstration of *group* differences in numerical scores. However, some professionals in the field have become disillusioned with quantitative methods and have criticized academic psychology and measurement theorists for the failure to attend to individual idiosyncrasies. These individuals attach far less importance to subgroup norms as the basis for assessing the value of clinical methods. They maintain that comparing a given individual to a standard based upon small criteria groups, as a means of determining the meaning of that individual's behavior, obscures clinically relevant uniqueness. They favor, instead, an "ipsative" description of the person, in which each individual serves as his/her own reference point for describing relative strengths and weaknesses.

The latter approach has been particularly favored by clinicians. Not surprisingly, practitioners who work daily with people are often less persuaded by demonstrations that an individual's test scores are either different from or similar to those of various reference groups than are academic psychologists, who are more familiar and comfortable with numerical concepts. Hence, although academic psychologists frequently criticize and even eschew tests like the Rorschach, clinicians continue to use such tests as a basis for developing clinical impressions. Many clinicians hold the belief that in comparison to empirically derived tests, "rationally" constructed and interpreted ones capture more of the complexity of human behavior. Tests like the Rorschach and projective figure drawings, for example, derive from theoretical concepts rather than empirical demonstrations, and their interpretation involves a process of synthisizing abstract concepts from nonnumerical productions. These procedures purport to offer a method for conceptualizing and assessing the complexity of intrapsychic needs and conflicts.

Efforts to Bridge the Gap

Exner's (1974) and others' translations of Rorschach narratives into numbers represent efforts to bridge the gap between the empirical and rational viewpoints by reconstructing qualitative narratives into a numerical scoring system to which quantitative methods can be empirically applied. As these efforts demonstrate, nothing in narrative productions inherently precludes clinicians from describing individuals by the use of quantitative scores; respondents can easily be described by reference to deviations from group mean values. Yet the emergence of non-numerical methods in contemporary psychological research belies the assertion that quantitative measurement procedures are well adapted to the verbal narrations and artistic productions widely used by clinicians. The complex and multidimensional relationships described in clinical formulations of personality functioning are difficult to distill into numbers. Even if procedures such as those developed by Exner are used, and numbers that capture some degree of the complexity represented in these clinical formulations (e.g., ratios of Rorschach determinants) can be constructed, many clinicians are concerned that these numbers fail to preserve the character of the phenomena being observed. They ask such questions as these: Do ratios and combinations of numbers adequately capture the essence of love? Do they adequately distinguish among different kinds of nonobservable experiences (love, anger, lust, etc.)? Do numbers adequately allow us to compare the amount that people love their wives or husbands with the amount that they love their mothers? Can numbers capture the variations in love-driven behaviors that occur when a child's life is threatened or when a spouse or lover is unfaithful?

It is equally hard to place other concepts—for instance, "conflicts," "ego," "anger," and "impulse"—within a numerical framework. These concepts often emerge in narrative form in the rationally derived clinical methods. These narratives are thought to represent the interplay of numerous complex forces and to allow a unique picture of individual, rather than group, behavior to emerge. Consider, for example, a patient's narrative response to a Rorschach card (card VIII):

> This is the face of a rooster. He has been killed. Oops! He's wearing sunglasses and has an extra eye on top of his comb. His insides are rotting, and here is where his spine is breaking through the skin and poking out.

Does a score that identifies the location of the percept, the use of form, and the content—"rooster," "sunglasses," and "anatomy"—adequately capture the essence of this narrative response? Advocates of the methods of "narrative assessment" and "hermeneutics" represent increasingly persuasive forces within contemporary measurement theory. These qualitative methods, attending as they do to the wholistic structure and content of natural language, have a particular affinity for clinicians for whom quantitative methods do not appear to be adaptable to describing the complexities and color of individual differences.

My colleagues and I believe that qualitative methods do offer an additional perspective in the measurement of human experience. However, we also believe that quantitative and qualitative methods are not inherently in opposition to each other; in fact, they are potentially synergistic (i.e., they can complement and add to each other). Qualitative methods of interpretation emphasize idiographic (i.e., idiosyncratic) patterns, whereas quantitative methods are distinguished by their nomothetic (i.e., normative) basis of deriving meanings from patient productions. The former methods rely on an ipsative comparison, in which various qualities of the patient himself/herself serve as a standard of relative comparison; the latter methods emphasize a normative or group comparison, in which the patient is compared to an outside norm reflective of others' responses. Narrative descriptions can enliven and deepen an understanding of test scores, while test scores can be used both to ensure the objectivity of narratives and allow a normative interpretation.

Cautions about Qualitative Interpretations

At their current level of development, qualitative interpretations of test materials are subject to several sources of error. The interpretations may not be accurate; they may not be replicable or constant; they may reflect a rater's mood or diet rather than actual characteristics of the patient; and they may have no heuristic value for predicting and planning treatment. Thus, even qualitative interpretive methods must come to grips with issues of reliability and validity. In order to be useful, non-numerical concepts (such as those complex verbal ones that characterize narrative descriptions) must be capable of reliable classification, and each category must be distinguishable from others. That is, a clinician must be able to assert that a conflict with a mother is manifestly different from a conflict with a wife; that two ego states are different; that aggressive impulses are different from sexual ones; or that two dynamic intrapsychic patterns differ from each other.

Fundamentally, qualitative interpretations encounter the same problems of measurement as traditional quantitative methods, because they must be assured of at least construct validity (Hogan & Nicholson, 1988), if not of sensitivity, specificity, and reliability. Measurement, at least at the nominal level, is needed in order to establish the value of these procedures. Nominal measurement allows narratives to be subject to assessments of interrater reliability, and thereby helps to assure that the qualities observed are not simply a reflection of irrelevant qualities of the clinical interpreter.

The "Scrud Test" as an Example

Let us further consider the interrelationships of normative and ipsative interpretation by reflecting on some of the examples used to illustrate the concepts of response variability, reliability, and validity in previous chapters. Contrast, for example, the limited response variabilities to both the "President's Test" and the "Chalk Test" (see Chapter 1) with what would happen if we asked students to draw a "scrud," a meaningless term in the English language (see Chapter 2).[1] In the first two tests, some consistency is expected among the responses of different people; in the "Scrud Test," no two individuals' responses will be the same, because everyone will have his/her own idea of a "scrud." Since the test environment that we have constructed with our instructions is held constant—it is the same for everyone—we must assume that the variability among responses reveals something unique about each of the respondents. Thus, each response is a unique production that should provide us with an avenue into the idiosyncratic nature of each individual's internal experience.

But what does each unique response mean? Here is where the test's "normative value" is necessary for an accurate interpretation. We must keep in mind that all responses are unique, but that they also have qualities similar to those of others' responses. Hence, we can begin our analysis by first looking at ways in which the responses of different people are similar. This will allow us to define what constitutes a "usual" response to the instructions. If we know what constitute the usual and the unusual aspects of an individual's response to the test environment we have created, we can begin to assess what qualities of people are associated with making these various responses. Our "normative" reasoning follows the logic that normatively unusual responses, which are nonetheless similar to one another, may indicate that the people who produced them are also similar to one another in some ways.

This point can can be illustrated by reference to Figure 3.1. This figure presents four drawings made by a college student who was asked to draw, in a randomized order, the following things: (1) two lines that love each other, (2) two lines that hate each other, (3) a happy line, and (4) an angry

[1]In spite of some obvious similarities, the "Scrud Test" described here and the "Blivet Test" described by McIvor (1979) as a parody on projective methods were independently developed.

FIGURE 3.1. Emotional qualities of lines.

line. Most of us can probably classify which lines are which at a rate of accuracy that exceeds chance (chance = 25%). We can do this because most people respond in a similar way. The two entwined and curving lines represent "loving lines"; the two angulated and heavy lines represent "hateful lines"; the soft, curved line is a "happy line"; and the jagged, heavy line is an "angry line." When we know these expected responses, we can determine whether a particular person's responses are unusual.

To extrapolate this example to our "Scrud Test," if we observe that there are striking similarities among all of those who draw "scruds," we may infer that "scrudness" is a frequently occurring quality among people. Likewise, we may inspect the internal consistency of the "scrud" by assessing the similarities of different aspects of the same drawing. For example, we may measure the degree to which each quadrant of a respondent's "scrud" is composed of the same types of "loving," "hateful," "happy," or "angry" lines. Furthermore, we may infer qualities of the person by comparing a given drawing to some standard of "usual" shape, pencil pressure, and organization. We may even augment our drawing task by giving the person an equivalent form of the test. We may ask him/her, for example, to draw a "brump." If the person's "brump" is "scrud"-like, we can conclude that both drawings reflect the same qualities of the person. If a similar figure is produced at a much later time, when the same person is asked to draw a "brump," we may conclude that "scrudness" is a stable quality that does not erode with time. All of these conclusions require a normative basis of comparison.

Alternatively, using a rational approach to interpreting a person's artistic productions, we can apply the normative qualities of line drawing in order to look at the idiosyncratic or unique aspects of the person. For example, armed with a theoretical formulation that people "project" their unwanted inner feelings onto unstructured environments, we *may* be justified in inferring that if the person has a propensity for drawing a "scrud" whose lines resemble "angry" ones, he/she may be angry, or that if the person has a predilection for drawing lines that resemble "loving" ones, he/she may be affiliative and caring. Thus, we may look at the structure of a given person's "scrud" and conclude that the uniqueness of this person is captured in (1) intolerance for ambiguity—the person has a need to impose order on his/her environment (the "scrud" is an object with a defined form, rather than an abstract figure), (2) a tendency to avoid self-exposure (the "scrud" is a smaller figure than usual), and (3) hidden anger and resentment (the "scrud" is drawn with heavy lines and has many sharp corners).

However, caution is necessary. Although it may be justified on theoretical grounds to infer that because a person's "scrud" and "brump" are composed entirely of soft, curved lines, he/she has the characteristics of being happy and loving, we can only do so if we have demonstrated the validity of these conclusions on some conceptual basis. A quantitative standard would argue that such an interpretation is warranted only if those who draw such lines exhibit behaviors or score on other tests that are known to indicate these other qualities. This is "construct validity." The logic of such an approach is that if a person makes drawings like those of loving and contented people, he/she is probably also loving and contented; however, this quantitative approach requires a reduction of drawings to a comparison of numbers. Because, as duly noted above, number reduction is not always in keeping with the effort to retain the richness of global productions, contemporary qualitative measurement emphasizes other criteria of "validity." These criteria are used both in selecting procedures that rely on qualitative interpretation and in the actual use of interpretive analytic procedures.

Criteria for the Use of Qualitative Methods

The following is a tentative list of evaluative criteria for judging the validity of procedures that are reliant on the analysis of narrative productions. This list represents an adaptation of guidelines provided to the review board members of the *Journal of Consulting and Clinical Psychology*, in order to assist them in evaluating the adequacy of qualitative research.[2] In the current context, these guidelines are considered to be useful when a clinician either selects instruments that are based on qualitative methods or undertakes to depart from or supplement a quantitative interpretation of patient productions.

1. *Method appropriateness.* A preliminary test of the usefulness and appropriateness of selecting qualitative assessment procedures is based on an initial determination that more economical procedures are either unavailable or inappropriate to the referral question. This concern with the appropriateness of the method accepts the proposition that quantitative methods are more clearly developed than qualitative ones and should be given preference whenever possible. The use of qualitative analysis must be clearly more appropriate than quantitative analytic methods to the subject matter, questions, and goals of the referral question. Moreover, when used, qualitative methods should be supplemented by quantitative ones whenever possible.

2. *Openness.* Qualitative analyses of test productions should clearly be framed within an explicit statement of the theoretical orientation that underlies it. Where appropriate, the internal processes and relevant reactions of those who interpret the data should be made explicit.

3. *Theoretical sensitivity.* Accepted theory, rather than personal adaptations, should be used to inform and guide the selection and interpretation of qualitative methods. This requires that a clinician be well informed as to current theoretical developments and protect, as much as possible, the interpretation from his/her idiosyncratic adaptations of theory.

4. *Bracketing of expectations.* If a clinician's interpretations of test productions depart from consensual theoretical formulations, this should be stated explicitly, in order to make the referring professional aware of the potential influence of the clinician's implicit expectations or biases. Where possible, the clinican should make use of checks against possible bias (e.g., having another clinician review his/her analysis).

5. *Responsibility.* In order to allow others to judge their conclusions, clinicians who select and interpret qualitative assessment procedures should clearly describe the nature of the procedures used and the conditions under which they are administered, as well as any efforts to achieve a consensual interpretation.

6. *Saturation/generalizability.* Where interpretations are intended to

---

[2]These criteria do not represent my own original ideas. They are adapted from the suggestions of Robert Elliot, who produced them upon the recommendation of Fredrick Newman, an associate editor of the journal. They also reflect the input of Judith Green, who served as a reviewer of the guidelines before they were submitted to the review board. I thank Drs. Elliot, Newman, and Green for their contributions; at the same time, I would like to acknowledge that these latter authors are not responsible for my own interpretation of their work.

indicate the presence of trait-like qualities, clinicians should make efforts to ensure that they have sampled an appropriate number and range of situations and methods to provide a thorough description of the phenomenon they have targeted. Where interpretations are meant to suggest the presence of situational responses, on the other hand, clinicians should ensure that these criteria samples of behavior have been studied thoroughly and comprehensively. Clinicians should be aware of the nature and limitations of their behavior samples.

7. *Verification methods.* The strongest test of the validity of qualitative procedures is the assurance that the interpretive categories, descriptions, themes, and interpretations are cross-validated. The most systematic methods for verification include the following:

a. *External verification.* The categories and themes that are extracted from the presentations are demonstrably related to some other variables (e.g., outcome).

b. *Testimonial/informant validity.* The interpretations are consistent with the reports of informants.

c. *Analytic "auditing" procedures.* Multiple qualitative analyses are undertaken. This may include either using an outside "auditor," or adding a same-analyst "verification step" for checking the interpretations for discrepancies.

d. *Triangulation.* Evidence of agreement is checked among multiple and varied perspectives, in order to identify the common or fundamental processes that underlie these different perspectives.

8. *Grounding.* The clinician who reports qualitative data does well to provide some examples of responses in the resulting report to illustrate the interpretations. The clinician should also take care to avoid departing substantially from the data in making the accompanying interpretations.

9. *Coherence.* The categories and constructs that arise in the interpretation of qualitative productions should be checked for how well they fit together to form a coherent story, narrative, "map," or framework for the phenomena or domain.

10. *Believability/helpfulness to readers.* When described in the report to the referring professional, the interpretations must be integrated with other data and presented in a believable narrative that enables the referrer or other readers to understand the patient's experience and presentation more explicitly and more fully than they would without this report.

11. *Intelligibility.* The resulting written report should be presented in a clear, accessible fashion, free of unnecessary jargon.

Conclusions

This chapter has addressed two dimensions on which the clinician must seek balance in the selection of psychological assessment methods. The first of these is the balance between the advantages of using an all-purpose core battery and those of using procedures that vary from individual to individual, depending upon the nature of the referral question presented. I have argued in favor of a combination of standard instruments, which allow the accumulation both of clinician familiarity and of setting-specific normative data, and individualized instruments, which are selected because they have the power to extract information that is relevant to the referral questions being asked.

This recommendation is based upon my colleagues' and my observations that different procedures are more or less effective for deriving valid information, depending upon the domain of experience and functioning being targeted for assessment. Hence, the use of specialized instruments makes sense, and I have discussed a number of instruments in terms of the areas of their special strengths. However, all instruments contain information concerning a common core of functional abilities, and most questions asked of clinicians can be answered by addressing a relatively small number of functional domains to which patients may be exposed in everyday experience. Thus, applying a small number of well-established core instruments, which tap the most common domains of functioning in a reliable and valid way, may allow the clinician to develop a high level of skill and to acquire a setting-specific internal norm with which to refine the interpretation of findings.

The second type of balancing required is that between the use of qualitative and quantitative data collection methods. As I have noted, reducing observations to numbers for quantitative analysis may fail to capture some subtle and representative patterns that exist in complex behaviors—patterns that may be maximally helpful in responding to referral questions about cognitive processing and personality. Accordingly, qualitative methods are recommended if quantitative ones are either unavailable or inappropriate to the question(s) raised. However, interpretations and life-changing decisions based upon qualitative methods must be protected against clinician bias. Thus, cross-validation with quantitative methods, reliance on theory-consistent interpretations, explicit descriptions of how procedures are used, and the establishment of consensual checks are often necessary to enhance and ensure the validity of these procedures. Ultimately, a combination of procedures may serve to be most useful in responding to the needs of most referring professionals.

References

American Psychiatric Association. (1987). *Diagnostic and statistical manual of mental disorders* (3rd ed., rev.). Washington, DC: Author.

Barlow, D. H. (Ed.). (1985). *Clinical handbook of psychological disorders: A step-by-step treatment manual*. New York: Guilford Press.

Beck, A. T. (1978). *Depression Inventory*. Philadelphia: Center for Cognitive Therapy.

Beck, A. T., Kovacs, M., & Weissman, A. (1979). Assessment of suicidal intention: The Scale of Suicide Ideation. *Journal of Consulting and Clinical Psychology*, *47*, 343–352.

Beck, A. T., Weissman, A., Lester, D., & Trexler, L. (1974). The measurement of pessimism: The Hopelessness Scale. *Journal of Consulting and Clinical Psychology*, *42*, 861–865.

Bender, L. (1938). *A visual motor gestalt test and its clinical uses* (Research Monograph No. 3). New York: American Orthopsychiatric Association.

Benjamin, L. S. (1974). Structural Analysis of Social Behavior. *Psychological Review*, *81*, 392–445.

Beutler, L. E. (1991). Have all won and must all have prizes? Revisiting Luborsky et al.'s verdict. *Journal of Consulting and Clinical Psychology*, *59*, 226–232.

Beutler, L. E., & Clarkin, J. (1990). *Systematic treatment selection: Toward targeted therapeutic interventions*. New York: Brunner/Mazel.

Beutler, L. E., & Crago, M. (1983). Self-report instruments. In M. J. Lambert, E. R. Christensen, & S. DeJulio (Eds.), *The assessment of psychotherapy outcome* (pp. 453–497). New York: Brunner/Mazel.

Beutler, L. E., Engle, D., Mohr, D., Daldrup, R. J., Bergan, J., Meredith, K., & Merry, W. (1990, June). *Predictors of differential response to therapeutic procedures*. Paper presented at the annual meeting of the Society for Psychotherapy Research, Toronto.

Beutler, L. E., & Mitchell, R. (1981). Psychotherapy outcome in depressed and impulsive patients as a function of analytic and experiential treatment procedures. *Psychiatry*, *44*, 297–306.

Brown, G. W., & Rutter, M. L. (1966). The measurement of family activities and relationships. *Human Relations*, *19*, 241–263.

Buss, A. H., & Durkee, A. (1957). An inventory for assessing different kinds of hostility. *Journal of Consulting Psychology*, *21*, 343–349.

Butcher, J. N., Dahlstrom, W. G., Graham, J. R., Tellegen, A. M., & Kaemmer, B. (1989). *Minnesota Multiphasic Personality Inventory—2 (MMPI-2): Manual for administration and scoring*. Minneapolis: University of Minnesota Press.

Cattell, R. B., & Johnson, R. C. (1986). *Functional psychological testing*. New York: Brunner/Mazel.

Clarkin, J. F., & Hurt, S. W. (1988). Psychological assessment: Tests and rating scales. In J. A. Talbott, R. E. Hales, & S. C. Yodofsky (Eds.), *The American Psychiatric Press textbook of psychiatry* (pp. 225–246). Washington, DC: American Psychiatric Press.

Dahlstrom, W. G., Welsh, G. S., & Dahlstrom, L. E. (1972). *An MMPI handbook: A guide to use in clinical practice and research*. Minneapolis: University of Minnesota Press.

Daldrup, R. J., Beutler, L. E., Engle, D., & Greenberg, L. S. (1988). *Focused expressive psychotherapy: Freeing the overcontrolled patient*. New York: Guilford Press.

Derogatis, L. R. (1975). *Derogatis Sexual Functioning Inventory*. Baltimore: Johns Hopkins University Press.

Derogatis, L. R. (1977). *The SCL-90 manual I: Scoring, administration and procedures*. Baltimore: Johns Hopkins University School of Medicine, Clinical Psychometrics Unit.

Derogatis, L. R. (1992). *BSI: Administration, scoring and procedures manual—II* (2nd ed.). Baltimore: Clinical Psychometric Research.

Derogatis, L. R., Rickels, K., & Rock, A. F. (1976). The new SCL-90 and the MMPI: A step in the validation of a new self-report scale. *British Journal of Psychiatry, 128,* 280–289.

DiNardo, P. A., O'Brien, G. T., Barlow, D. H., Waddell, M. T., & Blanchard, E. B. (1983). Reliability of DSM-III anxiety disorder categories using a new structured interview. *Archives of General Psychiatry, 40,* 1070–1075.

Endicott, J., Cohen, J., Nee, J., Fleiss, J., & Sarantakos, S. (1981). Hamilton Depression Rating Scale. *Archives of General Psychiatry, 38,* 98–103.

Exner, J. E., Jr. (1974). *The Rorschach: A comprehensive system.* New York: Wiley.

Folstein, M. F., Folstein, S. E., & McHugh, P. R. (1975). "Mini-Mental State": A practical method for grading the cognitive state of patients for the clinician. *Journal of Psychiatric Research, 12,* 189–198.

Goldberg, L. R. (1992). The development of markers for the Big-Five factor structure. *Psychological Assessment, 4,* 26–42.

Groth-Marnat, G. (1990). *Handbook of psychological assessment* (2nd ed.). New York: Wiley.

Gynther, M. D., & Gynther, R. A. (1983). Personality inventories. In I. B. Weiner (Ed.), *Clinical methods in psychology* (2nd ed., pp. 152–232). New York: Wiley.

Hale, W. D., Cochran, C. D., & Hedgepeth, B. E. (1984). Norms for the elderly on the Brief Symptom Inventory. *Journal of Consulting and Clinical Psychology, 52,* 231–232.

Hamilton, M. (1967). Development of a rating scale for primary depressive illness. *British Journal of Social and Clinical Psychology, 6,* 278–296.

Hogan, R., & Nicholson, R. A. (1988). The meaning of personality test scores. *American Psychologist, 43,* 621–626.

Horn, J. L., Wanberg, K. W., Foster, F. M. (1974). *The Alcohol Use Inventory.* Denver: Center for Alcohol Abuse Research and Evaluation.

Horowitz, L. M. (1986, June). *Interpersonal problems and dynamic case formulations.* Paper presented at the annual meeting of the Society for Psychotherapy Research, Wellesley, MA.

Horowitz, L. M., Rosenberg, S. E., Baer, B. A., Ureno, G. & Villasenor, V. S. (1988). Inventory of Interpersonal Problems: Psychometric properties and clinical applications. *Journal of Consulting and Clinical Psychology, 56,* 885–892.

Hutt, M. L. (1985). *The Hutt adaptation of the Bender–Gestalt test* (4th ed.). New York: Grune & Stratton.

Jacob, T., & Tennenbaum, D. (1988). *Family assessment: Rationale, methods and future directions.* New York: Plenum Press.

Koppitz, E. M. (1975). *The Bender–Gestalt Test for young children: Vol. 2. Research applications 1963–1973.* New York: Grune & Stratton.

Lovitt, R. (1988). Current practice of psychological assessment: Response to Sweeney, Clarkin, and Fitzgibbon. *Professional Psychology: Research and Practice, 19,* 516–521.

Lubin, B., Larsen, R. M., & Matarazzo, J. D. (1984). Patterns of psychological test usage in the United States: 1935–1982. *American Psychologist, 39,* 451–454.

McCann, J. T. (1991). Convergent and discriminant validity of the MCMI-II and MMPI personality disorder scales. *Psychological Assessment, 3,* 9–18.

McIvor, D. (1979). The Rorschach–Bender–McIvor Blivet Test. *Journal of Irreproducible Results,* 25, 3–5.

McLemore, C., & Benjamin, L. S. (1979). Whatever happened to interpersonal diagnosis?: A psychosocial alternative to DSM-III. *American Psychologist, 34,* 17–34.

Millon, T. (1983). *Millon Clinical Multiaxial Inventory manual* (3rd ed.). Minneapolis: National Computer Systems.

Millon, T. (1987). *Millon Clinical Multiaxial Inventory—II (MCMI-II) manual.* Minneapolis: National Computer Systems.

Milner, J. S. (1980). *The Child Abuse Potential Inventory: Manual.* Webster, NC: Psytec.

Milner, J. S. (1989). Additional cross-validation of the Child Abuse Potential Inventory. *Psychological Assessment, 1,* 219–223.

Milner, J. S., & Robertson, K. R. (1989). Inconsistent response patterns and the prediction of child maltreatment. *Child Abuse and Neglect, 13,* 59–64.

Mohr, D. C., Beutler, L. E., Engle, D., Shoham-Salomon, V., Bergan, J., Kaszniak, A. W., & Yost, E. (1990). Identification of patients at risk for non-response and negative outcome in psychotherapy. *Journal of Consulting and Clinical Psychology, 58,* 622–628.

Monroe, S. M. (1982). Life events assessment: Current practices, emerging trends. *Clinical Psychology Review, 2,* 435–453.

Moos, R., & Moos, B. (1976). A typology of family social environments. *Family Process, 15,* 357–372.

Moos, R., & Moos, B. (1981). *The process of recovery from alcoholism: III. Comparing family functioning in alcohol and matched control families.* Palo Alto, CA: Social Ecology Laboratory, Stanford University, and Veterans Administration Medical Center.

Paulson, M. J., & Tien-Teh, L. (1970). Predicting WAIS IQ from Shipley–Hartford scores. *Journal of Clinical Psychology, 26,* 453–461.

Pfohl, B., Stangl, D., & Zimmerman, M. (1983). The implications of the DSM-III personality disorders for patients with major depressions. *Journal of Affective Disorders, 7,* 309–318.

Rapaport, D., Gill, M., & Schafer, R. (1946). *Diagnostic psychological testing* (Vol. 1). Chicago: Year Book Medical.

Rorschach, H. (1942). *Psychodiagnostics.* Bern: Bircher. (Original work published 1921)

Sarason, I. G., Johnson, J. H., & Siegel, J. M. (1978). Assessing the impact of life changes: Development of the Life Experiences Survey. *Journal of Consulting and Clinical Psychology, 46,* 932–946.

Sarason, I. G., Levine, H. M., Basham, R. B., & Sarason, B. R. (1983). Assessing social support: The Social Support Questionnaire. *Journal of Personality and Social Psychology, 44,* 127–139.

Schulz, R., & Tompkins, C. A. (1990). Life events and changes in social relationships: Examples, mechanisms, and measurement. *Journal of Social and Clinical Psychology, 9,* 69–77.

Selzer, M. L. (1971). The Michigan Alcoholism Screening Test: The quest for a new diagnostic instrument. *American Journal of Psychiatry, 127,* 1653–1658.

Shipley, W. C. (1940). A self-administered scale for measuring intellectual impairment and deterioration. *Journal of Psychology, 9,* 371–377.

Silverstein, A. B. (1982). Factor structure of the Wechsler Adult Intelligence Scale—Revised. *Journal of Consulting and Clinical Psychology, 50,* 661–664.

Snyder, D. (1979). Multidimensional assessment of marital satisfaction. *Journal of Marital and Family Therapy, 11,* 813–823.

Snyder, D., Wills, R. M., & Keiser, T. W. (1981). Empirical validation of the Marital Satisfaction Inventory: An actuarial approach. *Journal of Consulting and clinical Psychology, 49,* 262–268.

Spanier, G. B. (1976). Measuring dyadic adjustment: New scales for assessing the quality of marriage and similar dyads. *Journal of Marriage and the Family, 38*(1), 15–30.

Spielberger, C. D., Gorsuch, R. L., & Lushene, R. E. (1970). *The State–Trait Anxiety Inventory (STAI) test manual for form X.* Palo Alto, CA: Consulting Psychologists Press.

Spielberger, C. D., Gorsuch, R. L., Lushene, R., Vagg, P. R., & Jacobs, G. A. (1983). *Manual for the State–Trait Anxiety Inventory.* Palo Alto, CA: Consulting Psychologists Press.

Spitzer, R. L., Williams, J. B. W., & Gibbon, M. (1986). *The Structured Clinical Interview for DSM III-R—Patient version.* New York: Biometrics Research Department, New York State Psychiatric Institute.

Sweeney, J. A., Clarkin, J. F., & Fitzgibbon, M. L. (1987). Current practice of psychological assessment. *Professional Psychology: Research and Practice, 18,* 377–380.

Wanberg, K. W., & Horn, J. L. (1983). Assessment of alcohol use with multidimensional concepts and measures. *American Psychologist, 38,* 1055–1069.

Wanberg, K. W., Horn, J. & Foster, F. (1977). A differential assessment model of alcoholism: The scales of the Alcohol Use Inventory. *Journal of Studies on Alcohol, 38,* 512–543.

Wechsler, D. A. (1945). A standardized memory scale for clinical use. *Journal of Psychology, 19,* 87–96.

Wechsler, D. A. (1981). *Manual for the Wechsler Adult Intelligence Scale—Revised.* New York: Psychological Corporation.

Wechsler, D. (1987). *Wechsler Memory Scale—Revised manual.* New York: Psychological Corporation.

Weissman, M. M., & Bothwell, S. (1976). Assessment of social adjustment by patient self-report. *Archives of General Psychiatry, 33,* 111–115.

Zachary, R. A., Crumpton, E., & Spiegel, D. E. (1985). Estimating WAIS-R IQ from the Shipley Institute of Living Scale. *Journal of Clinical Psychology, 41,* 532–540.

Zimmerman, M. (1983). Methodological issues in the assessment of life events: A review of issues and research. *Clinical Psychology Review, 3,* 339–370.

4

The Clinical Interview

Larry E. Beutler

The interview is the evaluation procedure most frequently used in clinical practice. As usually conducted, the interview follows a sequence that is developed and modified by the individual clinician. It is thus easy to administer; it is tailored to the patient's presenting problem; it requires no special materials; and it capitalizes upon the clinician's personal creativity and skill. However, precisely because it is so dependent upon the individual clinician's judgment and competence, and because these qualities vary widely among clinicians, the typical or "unstructured" clinical interview is also among the least reliable and potentially the least valid measure used in psychological assessment. To overcome some of the problems of varied and varying clinician abilities, "structured" and "semistructured" interview formats have been developed.

Structured Interviews

Structured interviews consist of a predetermined set of questions that are presented in a defined order. This standardized administration enhances the reliability of the presentation among interviewers and allows the development of normative values to aid in interpretation. Structured interviews are typically of two types, based upon their objectives and the nature of the format used. One type is designed to provide omnibus diagnostic information; in such an interview, the clinician relies both on the content of the responses and on his/her observations of the patient to form a diagnostic impression. The Diagnostic Interview Schedule (DIS; Robins, Helzer, Croughan, & Ratcliff, 1981) and the Structured Clinical Interview for DSM-III-R (SCID; Spitzer, Williams, & Gibbon, 1986), for example, direct the clinician through a sequence of choice points or a "decision tree." In the case of the SCID, the patient is systematically queried about critical symptoms associated with the syndromes represented in DSM-III-R (American

Psychiatric Association, 1987).[1] The result of this approach is a list of formal and consensually accepted diagnoses for which the patient is likely to qualify. The questions are designed to elicit information about symptom clusters, symptom duration, correspondence of symptoms with syndrome criteria, and severity of impairment.

Structured interviews of the second type are not so closely tied to contemporary diagnostic nomenclature and tend to take a more general approach to assessing severity of symptomatology. These interviews may be broadly focused upon an array of symptoms, or may be very specific to the signs of a single closely knit symptom cluster. Structured versions of the Mental Status Examination (MSE; Amchin, 1991) and the Hamilton Rating Scale for Depression (HRSD; Hamilton, 1967) typify broadly and narrowly focused interview-based assessments, respectively. Structured interviews such as these are not formulated in a decision tree format or centered around particular, formal diagnostic criteria. These procedures focus instead upon a particular area of functioning or set of related symptoms. The HRSD, for example, focuses on the severity of symptoms associated with depression, but does not indicate the degree to which a patient's symptom pattern is consistent with one or another of the syndromes within the depression spectrum. Similarly, but more broadly, the MSE provides information on the severity of impairment within a wide array of functional areas comprising the overall integration of cognitive, affect, mood, and personality functioning. It is left to the clinician's judgment, however, to decide how the assessed symptoms are to be translated into diagnostic impressions or treatment recommendations.

Broadly focused structured interviews, such as those designed to determine a patient's fit with a diagnostic syndrome or his/her general mental status, are usually designed as free-standing, comprehensive assessment procedures. Indeed, if the interview is to be the only assessment method used, then a broadly based structured interview provides the most valid and reliable information available. However, such interviews require extensive training and instruction in order for clinicians to develop the skill and consistency necessary to make them useful. The SCID, for example, not only requires clinicians to undergo an initial training period of 20 or more hours in order to administer it reliably, but also requires periodic retraining to prevent decay or drift in clinician reliability. Moreover, in covering a broad array of behaviors, omnibus sturctured interviews are quite lengthy and reduce the flexibility that is allowed to a clinician. They require such an investment of time to learn and administer that many clinicians find the process to be inhibiting and unpleasant.

---

[1]DSM-IV was released just as this volume was going to press. Concomitantly, a SCID based on DSM-IV will be forthcoming. The comments about the SCID iterated here will apply equally to this new version.

These problems are reduced only slightly by the use of more narrowly focused instruments such as the HRSD. Learning to administer these focused instruments, too, requires a considerable time investment; periodic retraining is also needed, as it is with the more broadly focused interviews, in order to maintain criteria-related validity. Without periodic retraining, even the ratings of skilled interviewers who learn these instruments tend to drift and change with time, becoming less valid when assessed against a standard criterion.

Because the time investment and inhibition of clinician initiative are so extensive, structured interviews that require extensive training and retraining are likely to be more frequently used for research purposes than in actual clinical practice. Clinical practitioners have continued to rely most strongly on unstructured or semistructured interview formats. Yet an effort has been made to preserve the advantages of structured interviews, either by modifying the use of the procedures themselves or by adapting them to specific and limited needs. Thus, for example, in their application to clinical practice, such structured interviews as the MSE and the HRSD are used primarily to provide some guidance to the clinician regarding the areas of functioning to be explored. The specific content and ordering of questions are left to the discretion of the clinician; the structured interview procedures serve only as a map of the content areas and the domains of information within each that are to be covered.

From a practical perspective, since modifying the procedures in this way is likely to compromise their reliability and validity, these methods should be supplemented by procedures that augment the information obtained while preserving reliability and validity. In some applications, for example, brief and focused structured interviews supplement a semistructured interview, in order to assess some specific symptom or quality that is of special interest to the referral question. The HRSD, for example, may be used as a supplement to a semistructured interview in order to assess the severity of depression. The semistructured interview focuses on target areas of needed inquiry; the structured interview, often along with other reliable psychological assessment devices, serves the function of focusing the information obtained on the referral question and diagnostic issues. Because of their limited objectives and time efficiency, brief but focused structured interviews like the HRSD are more likely to be used in clinical practice than more extensive, omnibus interview procedures like the SCID.

For some purposes, however, broadly focused structured interviews have been abbreviated in order to facilitate their use as adjuncts to other psychological assessment procedures in formulating diagnoses or assessing general functioning. The Mini-Mental State Examination (MMSE; Folstein, Folstein, & McHugh, 1975), for example, is a brief mental status examination that taps levels of impairment in thought content, thought process, mood and affect, verbal expression, memory, orientation, and perceptual conventionality. The MMSE is an abbreviated version of the more extensive format from which the mental status examination was developed, but covers each of the content areas of the longer procedure. Although it is less reliable than the longer instruments for assessing mental status, its brevity enhances its usefulness as a part of a multipurpose or multimethod evaluation.

In another application, structured interviews are retained intact, but applied in clinical practice in forms that minimize clinician time investment. Examples of this latter use include the computer-interactive Child Diagnostic System (Yokley & Reuter, 1989) and various computer-interactive versions of the SCID for Axis I (First, Gibbon, Williams, & Spitzer, 1990, 1991) and Axis II (First, Williams, & Spitzer, 1989) disorders of the DSM-III-R. Computer applications are also available for teaching the logic of the diagnostic system, and this software complements the computer-interactive system with a clinician-prompted diagnostic interview (First, Williams, & Spitzer, 1988).

Rather than focusing attention on the specific desirable and undesirable qualities of one or more structured interviews, this chapter emphasizes ways in which clinicians can organize and develop their own preferred interview methods in order to gather relevant assessment data. My colleagues and I believe that this approach complies closely with what clinicians are likely to find most useful. However, we also assume that the interview will be but one of several integrated methods of formulating hypotheses that are tailored to the referral questions being asked. When an interview is integrated with other, more easily validated, and more reliable measurement methods, the inherent potential for unreliability in using this procedure is balanced against its unique ability to gather certain types of information.

Viewed in this way, the interview occupies a central role in evaluation, but does not carry the burden of being the only or even the primary tool for deriving and testing hypotheses about behavior. This approach allows the clinician to balance the desirability of improving the interview's psychometric properties through the use of structure, with the flexibility obtained by adapting the interview to the peculiarities of the environment to which he/she is attempting to generalize. This conception of the interview as part of a comprehensive clinical evaluation invites the clinician to incorporate the semistructured interview into an integrative battery of assessment procedures.

The Integrative, Semistructured Interview

The semistructured interview offers three major advantages over omnibus, structured interview procedures such as the SCID, DIS, or MMSE. First, when viewed as an instrument that complements but does not replace other measurement devices, the semistructured nature of the interview allows maximal flexibility on the part of the clinician, as noted above. The interview may be modified at the clinician's discretion to fit the demand characteristics that are desired for the assessment environment. Moreover, it can be adapted in order to compensate for any weaknesses that may be encountered in or imposed upon the overall assessment process because of the unavailability of certain procedures.

For example, the clinician may choose to alter the level of structure employed, if other methods of assessing the patient's response to structure are deemed to be unusable with this patient or inadequate for the question being asked. Similarly, the clinician may alter the stress level imposed on the client during the interview, in order to assess the patient's likely response to external demands and his/her ability to collaborate with treatment. In doing so, the clinician can also selectively draw attention to type of experience (i.e., sensitivity to internal or external events), in order to generate hypotheses about the patient's response to these domains of experience.

A second strength of the semistructured clinical interview is in its use as a direct measure of the content of recalled experience. Thus, it is very helpful for identifying the external experiences and events associated with the patient's living contexts, and for taking a personal history. Although formal tests and computer-interactive software have often been used to gather social and developmental history, the semistructured interview allows a degree of follow-up that can provide a fuller description of the unique experiences and events affecting a given individual's behavior.

The semistructured clinical interview provides a third advantage over computer-administered or paper-and-pencil measures: It allows the clinician to observe the development of an interpersonal relationship at first hand, and to adapt his/her responses to the changing nature of the patient–clinician interactions. In this way, the semistructured interview elicits behaviors that are very similar to those likely to occur in the treatment relationship itself. Thus, the responses observed may form the foundation for hypotheses about a patient's ability to establish rapport and to cooperate with treatment demands.

To capitalize on these advantages of flexible semistructured interviews over both structured interviews and other assessment methods, it is desirable to impose at least a modest amount of standardization on an interview whenever circumstances will permit. Obviously, in institutional settings such as prisons, jails, and hospitals, the clinician does not always have the luxury of defining either the circumstances under which the assessment will take place or the information that is provided to the client in advance of the assessment. However, to the degree that the clinician can establish some control over three aspects of the assessment environment—the context in which the interview is conducted, the format of administration, and the content of the interview itself—use of the resulting information will be maximized. I discuss these three aspects as reflected in the ideal situation. The reader should keep in mind throughout that various settings will require flexibility on the part of the clinician, and correspondingly that lack of control in any of these domains potentially reduces the reliability and validity of the findings.

Interview Context

The "interview context" refers to the environmental structure in which the interview is conducted. The primary concern of the clinician in establishing the interview context is to ensure that the desired expectations and mind set are developed by the patient. Hence, the patient should be interviewed in a quiet, protected environment designed to provide reassurance that the information obtained will be treated responsibly and confidentially. Moreover, the environment should convey a sense of order and management, so that the patient can feel assured that the clinician is able to protect the safety of the material or information. Disorder in the contextual arrangements of the interview may create the expectation that the clinician may either become overwhelmed by the stress of the patient's problems or be unable to maintain confidentiality in protecting the patient's disclosures.

In addition to any explanations that might be offered by telephone at the time the patient schedules a visit, it is good practice to follow the initial phone call by mailing some written materials to the patient. These materials may consist of such things as the directions for finding the office and a map of parking facilities, if deemed necessary. It is also wise to include some descriptions of all the services available through the clinician's practice or clinic, as well as of the specific types of services to be provided on this occasion. In addition, the material should address the limits of confidentiality, outline the fee structures, and confirm the appointment time.

These efforts to enhance the patient's sense of safety and comfort should be continued and enhanced by the atmosphere provided by the staff and setting when the patient arrives for the session. A good deal of research has been devoted to discovering the nature of environments that promote disclosure, facilitate a sense of safety, and lead to the development of confidence in the clinician (see Wohlwill & Carson, 1972). By and large, this literature suggests the importance of open spaces, light, and friendly reception personnel in order to enhance the sense of personal freedom and comfort in the waiting area.

Moreover, because patients vary widely in their ability to read and understand material presented in written form, the interview itself must also reinforce and support the preinterview atmosphere. The office in which the interview is conducted should be a pleasantly appointed environment that allows the patient some choice in the selection of seating. The atmosphere of safety and relaxation can also be conveyed by the provision of soft light and comfortable furniture. In order to facilitate the development of a relationship that encourages disclosure, the arrangement of seats should be such as to allow but not to force eye contact with the interviewer.

It should be pointed out that this softly relaxing office atmosphere, though advantageous for the interview, may not be the most desirable for all aspects of the clinical evaluation. The environment in which many of the test materials are administered may need to be more flexible than the office in which the interview is conducted. Testing rooms must be conducive to constructing the analogue situations that provide the variable demand characteristics needed in the assessment environment. Firm desk chairs, lighting that is adequate for reading, and tables that have stable writing surfaces are required for the administration of psychological tests. The variability required of the interview and testing environments usually means that different rooms are used for these purposes. The clinician must ensure smoothly conducted but relatively few transitions among these settings, however, in order to maintain the sense of orderliness.

Interview Format

The format of the interview is interwoven with the nature and content of the preparatory material provided to the patient before the session, in order to emphasize even further the safety and confidentiality of the assessment process. It is often necessary for the patient to complete a registration form and to provide financial information prior to the initiation of the evaluation itself. Written materials may again assure the patient of confidentiality, outline appointment and emergency procedures, and describe financial arrangements. Written materials presented in the primary language of a patient whose first language is not English may signal the clinician's willingness to discuss topics that may be uncomfortable to the patient, although such materials are not adequate for ensuring the patient's informed consent.

Though establishing the patient's disposition toward the clinician begins prior to the first meeting, it should be carefully supported at the point the clinician and patient first meet. Ordinarily there are a few registration and insurance forms that can be completed immediately prior to the actual appointment time, but it is inadvisable for the patient to be left to fill out extensive forms before he/she meets the clinician and the interview begins. Preliminary activities should be kept to a minimum once the patient arrives at the office, and if possible, the clinician should meet briefly with the patient before leaving him/her to complete these tasks. During a brief meeting before the initiation of admission and registration procedures, the clinician should reassure the patient of confidentiality and of the right to refuse the evaluation itself. This reassurance can reinforce and clarify any written descriptions of services that may be made available prior to or at the time of his/her arrival for the appointment.

When initiating the interview itself, the clinician is well advised to be on time and to be ready to attend to the patient's presentation. Hence, the clinician should greet the patient in the waiting room, introduce himself/herself if they have not met earlier, and escort the patient to the examining room or office. If the subsequent adminstration of the tests is to be carried out by an assistant or someone other than the interviewer, it is helpful if the assistant is introduced before the procedures are begun and remains with the patient and clinician throughout the initial interview.

The interview is usually the first assessment procedure administered, because it is the easiest method of facilitating the patient's cooperation and is readily adapted to providing a context in which the other instruments can be selected and interpreted. As noted above, when the patient is invited into the office he/she should be given a choice of seating accommodations, varying both in distance from the clinician and in comfort level of the chairs. This is done not only because it provides an opportunity to construct hypotheses about personality functioning and interpersonal relatedness, but because it reinforces the patient's sense of control and self-governance.

The actual interview usually begins by reiterating major points presented in the standard, preappointment preparation materials. Hence, the clinician indicates the purpose of the evaluation, identifies what questions are being addressed, and reviews their anticipated consequences. At this point, it is useful for the clinician both to seek to know the patient's impression and to provide his/her own impression of how the results may be used. This latter information is especially important to provide to the patient whenever the referral questions to be addressed involve social consequences in the form of employability, insurance coverage, prescription of medication, recommendations for hospitalization, and/or social stigma. Assurance of the right to refuse evaluation and treatment is particularly important when the evaluation may result in the loss of freedom or in a major life change. Forensic evaluations dealing with questions of guilt, insanity, competence, disability, and sentencing are examples of such situations, as are custody evaluations and assessments of dangerousness.

Before ending these preliminaries, the clinician should invite the patient to ask questions about what has been presented. Moreover, the patient is reminded about the time limits of the evaluation, and the procedures to be used are briefly described.

All of this information is designed to provide reassurance to the patient and to emphasize the freedom that he/she has in the situation. This reassurance is of the same consequence in self-referred evaluations as in forensic examinations (when the patient is under court order) and in mental health examinations (when the patient may be incoherent), though in these latter circumstances it is often more difficult to provide these assurances. As a practical matter, the clinician should err in the direction of providing more information than the patient can adequately understand. It is wise not to take the risk of having failed to provide information that is later deemed to have been important to the client's ability to grant informed consent to the procedure.

From this point on, the format of the interview is organized around the desired content, but the clinician attempts to adjust the order of the content of material discussed in order to maintain a smooth flow from topic to topic. That is, the clinician should avoid moving mechanically from question to question and topic to topic. The approach should be conversational in tone, with each new topic being introduced as smoothly as possible, flowing naturally from what the patient has just reported. This smooth conversational flow is enhanced by placing more emphasis on open-ended than on closed-ended questions, by the judicious use of silence, by encouragement to expand upon relevant topics, and by progressing from general to specific topics (rather than vice versa).

Note that a clinician who begins with closed-ended questions is likely to obtain relatively flat and unrevealing answers, as in this example:

THERAPIST: What did your father do?

PATIENT: He was a carpenter.

T: How did you get along with him?

P: Oh, pretty well, most of the time.

T: And what did your mother do?

Contrast this with the use of more open-ended questions:

T: Tell me about your parents.

P: Well, they were poor people; my father was a carpenter and my mother was a housewife.

T: What was it like living with them?

P: Oh, it was okay most of the time, but my father was very strict and my mother often felt like she had to protect us kids from him.

T: Tell me more about how that happened.

Note that I am not suggesting that closed-ended questions should not be asked. Indeed, unlike the therapy session, the evaluation interview requires a clinician to obtain information that is often best requested with specific and structured questions. However, information is best obtained by beginning with open-ended queries and proceeding to more closed-ended questions as the need for more specific detail becomes apparent. All material elicited must be received with a matter-of-fact attitude. Indeed, in asking about sensitive subjects, it is a good idea to phrase the questions positively—it is assumed that everyone has done everything. Thus, for example, "How old were you when you began masturbating?" is generally preferable to "Have you ever masturbated?"

Similarly, the flow of questions best proceeds from general topics to specific areas of interest. The open-ended and general questions illustrated in the previous examples tend to pull for more general and complete answers than do closed-ended and specific questions. It is easier to proceed from these general questions to specific ones than vice versa. Moreover, by proceeding from general to specific and from open-ended to closed-ended questions, the clinician gathers the information within a smoothly flowing and topical conversation, seeking additional information as it is needed, without losing the focus or appearing overly rehearsed.

When it is necessary to change topics, it is worthwhile to keep the difference between interrogative/mechanistic and conversational styles in mind. A clinician using the first, mechanistic interviewing style may go from one topic to another as follows:

T: And was there anything else about your brothers and sisters?

P: No.

T: How has your health been?

A clinician using a more conversational style may proceed thus:

T: What else can you tell me about the relationship between you and your brothers and sisters?

P: Well, there's really not much to tell. They . . . [concludes the thought].

T: What kind of health problems did they have?.

P: Oh, they were all healthy, but my mother . . . [continues].

T: What similar kinds of problems have you had?

Note that the lead-in question in the second example is more open-ended than the one in the first example, and that the clinician introduces the patient's health as a topic within the context of a discussion about the family. Thus, the change in topic flows smoothly from a discussion of the siblings, and avoids an abrupt transition from talking about the brothers and sisters to again talking about the patient.

At the conclusion of the interview, the clinician is advised to invite comments and additional information that the patient might think is important:

T: What have I missed that you think might be important for me to know?

P: Well, I don't know. Did I tell you that my uncle committed suicide?

After processing new information that is highlighted in this way, and before moving to employ other assessment procedures, the clinician should again invite questions and comments. Moreover, before terminating the session at the end of the testing period, the clinician typically provides some limited feedback to the patient. If the patient has been with an assistant for the test administration, the clinician and the assistant provide this feedback together, after a brief private meeting to share and organize their thoughts. After feedback, another appointment is scheduled—either for completion of the assessment procedures, for more detailed feedback following the scoring and analysis of results, or for the beginning of treatment. Even if the end-of-session feedback seems satisfactory, it is wise to plan for at least one additional feedback session to be conducted after all materials are analyzed and before the final report has been sent to the referring clinician. This allows the clinician to incorporate, in the final report, any relevant new material that the feedback session itself elicits.

In this feedback session, it is wise to reiterate the purpose of the evaluation and to summarize the findings and recommendations. Even if the recommendations are not likely to be pleasing to the patient, this summary should take place frankly and openly, so that nothing provided by the referring clinician to the patient following receipt of the report will come as a surprise. For many purposes, especially in the case of court-ordered, forensic, and custody evaluations, the patient may usefully be invited to read a penultimate draft of the report and to comment on its content. Since these records will become available to the patient, allowing input may alleviate some of the potential negative effects attendant upon the patient's being confronted with some of the critical or controversial material in court. Certainly, under these conditions, the language and description should be provided in a way that minimizes the potential for harming the patient.

Interview Content

The content of the interview includes both verbal and nonverbal elements. Whereas the verbal content is adapted to the referral questions being addressed, behavioral observations that arise in response to the context and format of the interview are blended with the verbal content to provide the basis for making inferences and drawing conclusions about the areas of functioning to be described in the report. The areas of functioning to be addressed in the report have been described in Chapter 2, and are weighted in importance during the interview by both the nature of the referral question and the confidence that the clinician can legitimately place in his/her observations.

In integrating verbal and nonverbal observations, the clinician pays close attention to any discrepancies that may exist between observed behaviors and the verbal content of the patient's responses. These discrepancies are used to infer qualities of involvement or investment in the evaluation, and provide the basis for making inferences about aspects of cognitive, emotional, and interpersonal–intrapersonal functioning. In addition, the clinician attempts to extract information directly that will bear on diagnostic decisions, and observes patterns of interaction that will bear on treatment prognostications. Since some of the particular strengths of the interview procedure reside in the verbal content provided, this aspect of the interview bears particular consideration. Figure 4.1 provides an outline of the verbal content areas that are usually explored in the clinical interview, and in regard to which behavioral discrepancies and consistencies are observed.

Chief Complaint/Problem

One of the first statements obtained in the interview is the patient's description of the major problem or difficulty for which he/she is seeking help. This description of the problem is usually noted succinctly in the client's own words, along with notations of any relevant nonverbal indicators of distress. The clinician attempts to distill the patient's verbal response into one or two sentences that best describe how the patient identifies the purpose of the referral and evaluation. This verbatim patient description is important, because it must be contrasted against both the clinician's and the referring clinician's impressions of the problem and the purpose of the evaluation. Along with the patient's manner as he/she presents a description of the problem, any discrepancies observed between verbal reports and behaviors provide initial indications of the patient's investment in and willingness to change. Moreover, by succinctly paraphrasing the problem in a way that is acceptable to the patient, the treating clinician can periodically refer to this description when assessing the significance and relevance of changes that are observed later in the treatment process.

As previously described, it is at this early point in the context of describing the patient's problem that the clinician can easily interweave an effort both to explore misunderstandings that may exist about the evaluation process, and to explain how the results of the evaluation are actually to be used. The interviewer should be concerned at this juncture with the discrepancies that may exist among the informed opinions of interested others (significant others, the referring clinician, the interviewing clinician, etc.), as well as with obtaining the patient's informed consent to undertake the procedures. Obtaining informed consent is imperative not only from an ethical and legal perspective, but also from a practical one. A patient who feels free and informed is likely to be more cooperative than one who feels coerced and controlled. Thus, before going into depth about the nature of the problem itself, the clinician must be assured that the patient has a clear understanding of the purpose and use of the procedures.

FIGURE 4.1. Verbal content of clinical interview.

I. Chief complaint/problem (this is usually presented in the client's words)

II. History of problem
  A. This section reports how long the problem has been occurring, what initiated it, how severe it is, and the pattern of recurrence and change.
  B. It also covers how the problem has affected the patient's normal life routines, as well as how he/she copes with the symptoms.
  C. The roles played by others in the patient's problem should be discussed.
  D. Finally, the history of previous treatment should be covered.

III. Social and family history
  A. This section presents the client's developmental social history. It describes the structure of the early family and indicates changes in important family relationships over time.
  B. It also includes information about friendships, ability to relate to peers in school, problems with the law or with authorities, educational achievements, work history, and the ability to develop close relationships. Current and past attachment levels should be compared.
  C. Finally, sexual history should be covered here (including any history of sexual abuse, marriages, pattern of sexual dysfunctions, etc.).

IV. Medical history
  A. This section includes a review of medical problems, associated treatments, and both current and past medications.
  B. It also includes a description of illicit drug and alcohol use.

V. Mental status
  A. Appearance
  B. Cognitive functioning
  C. Affect and mood
  D. Interpersonal style
  E. Special behaviors or needs

T: It would help if you would tell me your understanding of why Dr. Jones referred you here.

P: Well, um, he just said that he wanted to have me tested.

T: What do you suppose he wants to find out?

P: I guess he wants to know if I'm crazy (*laughs*). [This response is noted as a possible concern of the patient regarding her own stability, for subsequent follow-up.]

T: What do you suppose he plans to do with the information that I give him?

P: Well, he said that he wanted to see if I needed to be put on medication for my anxiety.

T: Anxiety?

P: Well, yes, that's why I went to see Dr. Jones.

T: How does that anxiety affect you?

P: Well, I haven't been sleeping, and I've had trouble at work for the past few months. Dr. Jones thinks that I have something called "panic attacks."

T: So, if what we do here confirms that impression, then what?

P: Well, I think he wants me to take some kind of medication to make it better.

T: And if we conclude that you don't have panic attacks, then what?

P: Then, I guess—I don't know. Maybe there's nothing that can be done, then.

T: It sounds like you think your best chance for getting better is if you do have panic attacks.

P: Yeh, I guess that's true. We—Dr. Jones and I—we never talked about what would happen if I don't have panic attacks.

T: Well, perhaps it would help if I told you what my understanding of this process is.

P: Yes, it probably would.

T: Well, first, it is my understanding that Dr. Jones is working out a treatment program for you and is trying to decide if medication should be a part of that program. He asked if I would help him find out if you are experiencing panic attacks or some other kind of anxiety. How much did he tell you about "panic attacks"?

P: Well, actually, nothing. I just get this headache and feelings of dizziness sometimes, where I can't seem to breathe and my heart starts pounding. Is that it?

T: That's a good description of how you experience it, but there is a little more to it when it comes to treatment. For example, for treatment, it is important to know how the symptoms first started and under what circumstances they keep coming back. Some people have these symptoms only in certain situations, and others can have them almost anywhere and any time. Also, it is usually the case that when people begin to have these uncomfortable and frightening symptoms, they try to protect themselves, usually by anticipating and avoiding situations that might give rise to them. Thus, it will be helpful if we can come to know how these symptoms started, or their "onset," and also how you cope with and manage them. Treatment will be a bit different, depending upon the patterns that we find. Sometimes medication is useful, and at other times, what is required is learning a better way to protect yourself from having anxiety. Does that make sense to you?

P: Well, yes. I think he said something like that.

T: So is it all right with you if we go ahead with things today, trying to find out what the symptoms are, how they started, and how you have tried to cope with them in the past?

P: Yes.

Note that during an assessment interview, unlike the usual therapy interview, the clinical interviewer is willing to provide direct information to the client at this juncture in order to clarify the purposes and uses of the assessment procedure. The tasks of setting the patient at ease, creating a conducive mind set, and obtaining informed consent are best accomplished by this flexible style. In this way, the interview becomes an integral part of the assessment procedure and suitably sets the stage for the entire process. Only when this stage is set should the clinician narrow the focus to the task of adapting the interview content to the referral questions at hand. It is in this latter process that historical and factual information becomes critical.

History of Problem

After finding out how the patient conceptualizes the problem, the clinician begins to seek information about symptom onset, pattern, and treatment. Once again, the clinician is interested both in the verbal content of the patient's impressions and in the more subtle indicators of stress and coping that emanate from the accompanying nonverbal behaviors. Although overall assessment is not always concerned with the consensual accuracy of the patient's verbal report, cross-validating evidence is often sought to support the reliability of the interview content and to observe discrepancies that may exist among three interrelated aspects of the verbal presentation of history: (1) the developmental course of the condition, (2) its effects on life adjustment, and (3) the patient's efforts to cope with or prevent the problem.

Obtaining information on symptom course requires a detailed consideration both of the events that were present when the symptom patterns or presenting problems were first noticed, and of how the patterns or problems came to the patient's attention. This effort at discovery is extended into an exploration of the pattern of problem recurrence and change that has been noticed by the patient. This information may be compared with the reports that are available or that can be conveniently obtained from significant others, from prior treatment records, and from the referring professional. Specifically, in the interview the patient is asked to report on the circumstances under which he/she or someone else first noticed the problems; how he/she and significant others initially explained them; the frequency and nature of the circumstances in which the problems have recurred; and the changes that have been noted over time in both the problems and the circumstances.

It is particularly important to determine both the degree to which each pattern of symptoms is accepted as a "problem" and where the patient places its causal locus. This determination entails explorations of how the patient explains the problem to others and how others have accepted or altered this interpretation. It also entails an assessment of how serious the patient considers each problem to be, how he/she has coped with it, and the nature of the interpersonal and affective functioning that appears to result from these efforts. All possible permutations of self-assessed seriousness and attributed internal or external locus of cause are possible, and these carry different implications for formulations of the patient's personality, diagnosis, and differential treatment receptivity. It is one thing if the patient is distressed by the presence of the problem itself, and quite another if the source of distress is the reaction of others either to the patient's behavior or to his/her causal explanations. From a psychodynamic perspective, these two interrelated dimensions of the symptom and problem pattern are used to determine whether the problem is ego-dystonic (uncomfortable and unwanted) or ego-syntonic (not distressing or part of one's self-view). Determinations of this type are correlated with habitual internalizing or externalizing coping styles, respectively, and are correspondingly associated with the patient's capacity for insight and willingness to change.

The second major aspect of symptom or problem evaluation is a determination of how the problem or symptom has affected the patient's normal life routines. This aspect of the problem reflects problem severity as well as patterns of coping, social support, and interpersonal functioning. Indications of problem severity are inferred from how such activities as work, school, and interpersonal relationships have been affected. Here, multiple perspectives are often needed in order to determine the degree to which the patient is prone to cope by either exaggerating or minimizing his/her response. Hence, to the degree possible, it is a good idea for the historical information presented by the patient to be cross-validated by sources of information that are external to the patient. Although other assessment procedures can serve as cross-validating indicators of various coping styles and patterns, the validation of factual information requires information from either significant others, treatment records, or the referrer.

There are many clinical instances in which discrepancies between the patient's and external observers' assessments of impairment serve as differential diagnostic or etiological indicators. For example, patients with dementias of the Alzheimer type are often distinguished from those with dementia associated with depression by the latter group's tendencies to overestimate the degree of actual impairment of functions, as well as by their excessive concern with loss of memory or verbal fluency. Similarly, delusional disorders are frequently indicated by the degree to which the problem is attributed to self or to others. Thus, if the patient attributes the significance of the problem to the exaggeration of events by others, the clinician may infer the presence of a projective or externalizing coping style. However, the criteria for "exaggeration" are frequently elusive, and reviewing the observations of those who have viewed the patient in real-world settings may help clarify the matter.

Of course, whenever the patient's reports, the interviewer's own observations, and the reports of significant others are being compared, the interviewer must keep in mind that family members and friends may have vested interests that lead them either to minimize or to exaggerate the significance of the problems being addressed. When discrepancies are significant and the likely consequences are severe, the clinician should take particular care to complement the interview procedures with both indirect and direct observations of the patient and with interviews with disinterested parties, in order to derive reliable hypotheses about the roles of denial, minimization, and exaggeration among the parties involved. For example, work records, school reports, and sometimes even bank or spending records may be requested as supplements to the clinician's other assessments of performance, in order to determine what patterns and changes are occurring.

The third aspect of the symptom history consists of the patient's descriptions of how he/she copes with the symptoms. The clinician particularly wants to determine whether the recurrence and exacerbation of the symptoms or problems can be predicted by the patient or others in his/her environment. The clinician seeks the patient's report of what cognitive patterns are used and how helpful these are in warding off or reducing the symptoms, what behaviors are used in the service of self-protection, and what roles others play in altering the problem manifestation and severity of impairment. When taken together with observations of nonverbal behaviors and with information from other assessment devices, the resulting pattern of observations can be used to identify the nature of the patient's interpersonal–intrapersonal conflicts and coping styles. As always, discrepancies among these sources are interpreted (1) in terms of the relative reliabilities and validities of the assessment procedures, and (2) in terms of the nature of the demand characteristics represented. The reader is reminded and cautioned that the clinician's confidence in interview-based observations is almost always excessive; many aspects of coping and conflict are not reliably assessed by interview methods. The strength of the interview is in the verbal content obtained, not in the validity of the inferred coping styles and interpersonal patterns, although these inferences cannot and should not be ignored.

The reliability of inferences about interpersonal functioning may be increased by knowing the roles that others play in the patient's problem. The roles performed by others may be judged by the clinician, both from the patient's report and from whatever ancillary information is available regarding how these others support the patient, impede problem resolution, or contribute to problem development and maintenance. As the clinician seeks information about how and under what circumstances others in the patient's environment become involved in the problem, the clinician may come to infer the presence of certain patterns in the patient's manner of coping with interpersonal closeness and aggression.

In short, in the assessment process the clinician seeks to determine what the patient is attempting to avoid; how he/she is doing so; and what social events either trigger, enhance, or ameliorate the problem. These issues are relevant even when the condition is judged to be organic in nature, since they bear directly upon adaptation and compliance. Moreover, the sources through which the patient has sought help also comes into play in assessing how the patient copes. Hence, in the interview it is helpful to review the nature, the chronology, and the perceived helpfulness of previous treatments. If the patient has taken medication or been hospitalized, for example, queries should be initiated regarding the patient's response to the treatments, the nature of the medications used, and/or the nature of the hospital treatment. Likewise, if previous treatment has included group, individual, or family psychotherapy, the clinician should attempt to discover who the therapist was, what was discussed and not discussed, and the patient's overall response, and to obtain a description of those things that were both helpful and not helpful in the process. In this way, the clinician can begin to narrow down potential treatment recommendations and to formulate suggestions for treatment that will capitalize on the patient's prior responses. If time permits, the clinician should request a release-of-information form and subsequently seek to obtain treatment summaries from prior treatment sources, in order to supplement the patient's reports.

Social and Family History

Of course, the patient's problem history cannot be well understood without knowing something about the nature of the patient's current and developmental social conditioning experiences. Direct questioning during the interview may provide the most direct access to this information, since correspondent sources of data are frequently unavailable among adult patients. Thus, the clinician must elicit information from the patient about the structure of the family, the patient's roles within that structure, significant formative events, patterns of reinforcement and punishment to which the patient was subjected, progress in reaching key developmental milestones, and changes that have occurred in important family relationships over time. The effort here is to determine the nature of both past and present roles and allegiances within the family structure. Such questions as the following may initiate leads that can fruitfully be followed:

"As you were growing up, who in your family were you the most like?"
"To whom were you the closest?"
"How did you find out when there were problems between your father and mother?"
"What did other members of your family do when there were problems?"
"What were your most and least favorite family traditions?"

Special care should be taken to elicit any experiences of early abuse or deprivation, as well as any instances of drug, alcohol, or sexual difficulties that may have been experienced by the patient or by other members of the family. Examples that will inform the clinician about family attitudes toward aggression, sexual expression, and achievement should be requested. Such questions as the following may be helpful in initiating these topics:

"How did members of your family feel when you got angry?"
"What was the worst experience you had growing up in your family?"
"What did members of your family do when you discovered sex?"
"What would people in your family do when you got very angry?"
"How did members of your family teach you about sex?"
"How did the various members of your family show it when they were angry? Sad? Hurt? Happy?"
"Who in your family got into the most trouble because of drinking or drug use?"
"What attitudes did your parents have about sex? How did they convey these to you?"
"What role did religion play in your family?"

This information about the family should be supplemented by the patient's description of friendships and social development. The concern here is to evaluate the patient's capacity for both intimacy and autonomy. Hence, for most content areas, the subjectivity of these data is as relevant as their factuality. Thus, the patient's subjective responses to early friendships, love relationships, and sexual attachments are specifically sought. In eliciting such information, the clinician is not only seeking to determine past and present patterns in the way the patient deals with others, but also to form an impression about his/her capacity for forming a therapeutic or treatment alliance. Patients who report having had few friendships, or who do not recall having lasting friendships and love relationships, are at greater risk for failure to develop the therapeutic attachment that is often necessary for supporting change.

Whether social skills are conceptualized as "object relationships" or "social development," inferences about them are made from the factual information reported about adolescent group behavior, legal difficulties, postadolescent love relationships, sexual experiences, and relationships to school and work authorities. Special attention is frequently given to key points in time during which the patient went through social changes. Such questions as the following may provide leads for further exploration:

"What happened to the best friends you had as a child and adolescent?"
"What is the worst trouble you got into as a young person?"
"What was your first sexual experience like?"
"What kind of homosexual experiences have you had?"
"What was the worst trouble you got into with teachers at school?"
"What kind of trouble have you had with the law?"

These questions often invoke sensitive topics. Again, it is important both to treat the responses in a matter-of-fact way and to phrase the questions in a way that assumes that every behavior is "normal" or "expected."

When a clinician is evaluating patterns of social relationships, it is helpful to begin with a conceptual scheme that will guide him/her in seeking information. Strupp and Binder (1984) have proposed that four components of interpersonal relationship patterns can be reliably assessed: (1) the wish, fear, or desire that initiated a relationship; (2) the expected response from the other person; (3) the behavior of the patient in order to achieve or avoid the expected response; and (4) the effects or consequences of this behavior, especially within the relationship in question. These four aspects of relationships can be assessed both as interacting variables in the dominant patterns characterizing any relationship and as markers of changes occurring over time.

When information about interpersonal patterns is being obtained, Luborsky and Crits-Christoph (1990) have suggested that several key relationships should be explored, in order to determine the nature of the various social roles that others are perceived to play. The key relationships explored should include those with parents or parental figures, siblings, relatives of significance in the patient's life, and major love interests. To the degree that similar needs and expectations are found to be working across the different relationships described, the clinician can infer that the pattern observed is pervasive and ritualistic. That is, the patient's relationships are more dominated by his/her fixed needs than by the nature of the person to whom the patient is relating. Alternatively, if different needs and expectations are found to be expressed in different relationships, it may be inferred that the patient has the ability to be discriminating, flexible, and realistic in social interactions.

Patient descriptions of sexual history are particularly important, although it is not often possible to cross-validate these descriptions. These reports should encompass the areas of sexual or physical abuse, patterns of sexual difficulty and dysfunction, marital disruptions, and both extramarital and premarital sexual problems. The patient's social and sexual evolution should be sufficiently explored to provide the clinician with an informed opinion of how disruptions to social relationships have been handled, both in current and in past attachments.

Medical History

Nearly as important as developmental background is obtaining a description of the patient's significant medical history. Here, however, factual rather than subjective information is at a premium, and cross-validation of the patient's reports should be actively sought. Available sources of information should be reviewed to determine the nature of past and current medical problems, associated treatments, and lists of drugs that have been and are currently being taken. This section should also include obtaining a description of any illicit drug and alcohol use, along with its perceived benefits, drawbacks, and side effects. Questions that open up these areas in the interview may include the following:

"What have you been hospitalized for in your life?"
"What illnesses have you had for which you consulted a doctor?"
"What street drugs did you use as a young person?"
"What alcoholic beverages do you prefer?"
"Has anyone ever said that alcohol was a problem for you?"
"How often have you gotten into trouble because of your use of drugs or alcohol?"

When information is elicited about prior medical treatment, some pointed inquiry is often helpful in order to determine the degree to which emotional problems might have been implicated in the problem for which the patient was being treated. Questions about symptoms, nature of treatments, the treatment site, and the specialty of the caregiver are areas for exploration. In order to cross-check information about mental health history, especially when the patient has denied previous professional treatment, special questions may be directed at determining what contact the patient has had with nonphysician therapists:

"How often have you consulted a psychologist or social worker for a problem or concern that you've had?"
"What other kinds of healers and caregivers have you consulted?"

Attention to the types of medications will also often unobtrusively reveal concerns that the treating physician may have had with the role of emotional factors in prior conditions and complaints. Disclosure of having used medication for "nerves," "tension," "stress," or "depression," for example, are suggestive of prior emotional disturbances that may have not been recognized as such by the patient. The clinician cannot assume that the patient either knows or is willing to disclose the purpose of various medications, however. Furthermore, patients often keep old medications around for later use. It is helpful to ask what medications (both prescriptive and nonprescriptive) the patient keeps at home, and even to request that he/she bring in the medication bottles for inspection. Not only is a knowledge of medication usage helpful for determining the degree to which treatment has been focused on emotional difficulties or symptoms; it is imperative that the clinician take account both of possible misuse of prescriptive medications and of their potential iatrogenic effects before reporting information to the referrer that may result in additional prescriptions' being offered.

Mental Status

As I have reiterated from time to time, the semistructured interview is not well suited to deriving reliable and valid inferences about cognitive, emotional, and affective functioning. However, its importance for generating hypotheses about these areas of functioning should not be discounted. The assessment of mental status invokes the inclusive inferences of observed and reported information. To assist in the distillation of the several sources of information deriving from the interview, the clinician should note observations within the following areas of functioning.

Appearance. The clinician should make note of how appropriately the patient is dressed and how well he/she is groomed, as well as any evidence of inadequate self-help skills. Deficiencies in appearance may indicate deterioration of coping ability, inadequate cognitive resources or efficiency when planning and anticipating the consequences of behavior, inadequate fiscal resources, and/or the absence of caring social support systems. Decline of appearance may also indicate lack of social judgment, and is most often associated with cognitive disturbances that are in turn indicators of depressed mood, schizophreniform intrusions, or emerging manic behaviors.

Cognitive Functioning. Although intellectual level, memory, perception, and visual–motor organization are most reliably evaluated by standardized cognitive assessment procedures, the degree of verbal fluency and coherence observed during the interview is a supplemental avenue into the nature of some cognitive processes. For example, the clinician should note the degree to which verbal output is impeded (sluggish) or exaggerated (pressured) as a potential diagnostic indicator of cognitive efficiency, mood, and problem severity. The abilities both to retain a topical focus and to associate logically when moving from topic to topic are especially important to note as diagnostic indicators. Thought intrusions are indicated by spontaneous and usually momentary changes of verbal content, especially if these interuptions contain unusual or unconventional ideas. Thought content impairments and lowered cognitive efficiency are reflected in this pattern.

Circumstantial logic and tangential associations are other indicators of a thought process disturbance. In the former case, details and extraneous topics provide momentary distractions from topical focus, but the patient retains a general and contextually logical framework. Frequently, the patient reports information in excruciating detail, and develops expanded but loosely related side stories while attempting to make and emphasize a point. In contrast, tangential associations are revealed in the inability to stay on the same topic and within a single framework of logic. Often, however, the distinction between circumstantial and tangential associations lies only in how conventional the association between the main and the adjunctive topics is. Tangential logic is characterized by very loosely associated topics and unusual patterns of logic. Thus, the patient is unable to complete a story in even fractured detail because of the apparent competition of other, unrelated, and frequently unusual or morbid story lines.

Thought content disturbances are also to be noted whenever the patient inserts topics at inappropriate times and in inappropriate amounts. A tendency to insert contents and words associated with sexuality, aggression, potential victimization, or religious activities and figures into discourse are the most usual and indicative patterns. Fixed beliefs, delusions, and obsessions may be revealed in these preoccupations. In their extreme, the presence of unusual thought content is apparent; however, in less extreme forms, the nature of thought content disturbances may be difficult to delineate without special sensitivity to their subtle indicators. There is no substitute either for prior experience with people who present serious cognitive disturbances, or for the comparisons possible through the use of standard and criteria-related norms.

Affect and Mood.   Under ideal circumstances, a person's recall of emotionally trying events is balanced among appropriateness, empathic resonance, and congruence of affect and mood. That is, the feeling the person recalls having is one that would be expected to characterize most people in similar circumstances: He/she is sad at loss, happy when desired events occur, and angry when frustrated in his/her goals. Likewise, when the person recalls the emotional event, some of the same feelings are reactivated in the present momemt. This is the process of "empathic resonance," and may be either reflected in the recall of the person's own experience or activated by another person's experience. And finally, there is general congruence between the feeling that is experienced or reported and the one conveyed through facial, verbal, and postural expressions.

Accordingly, the clinician should note both the patient's behaviors and the terms and labels that the patient uses to describe his/her experiences. These notations will remind the clinician of the patient's reported mood, as well as of observed or apparent discrepancies. Queries about what the patient is feeling may well be inserted periodically either when potentially difficult material is being discussed or when significant affect is displayed; such questions will help the clinician identify the presence of empathic resonance. To assist in the evaluation of mood (subjective feelings) and affect (expressed or observed feeling qualities), the clinician notes changes in the expressed emotion or affect of the patient as different topics are discussed. He/she particularly observes the points at which there is an absence of correspondence between the nature of the emotion expressed and the topic given consideration.

As a final distillation of these observations, the clinician notes the degree to which the patient is able to keep feelings and emotions in check without restricting or overcontrolling affect. From observations of the variations in the range of available affect and associated nonverbal behavior, the clinician attempts to determine whether the patient can identify and re-experience the feelings that were present at a previous time without becoming impaired by their recurrence.

Incongruence between mood and affect may be of three types. First, the failure to show emotion when discussing a topic that would usually evoke sadness, anger, or pleasure may suggest that the range of emotions is constricted and that excessive control is being exerted to keep emotions in check. Second, exaggerated displays of the very emotions being discussed suggest the inability to step back from experience in order to retain objectivity. Third, the display of emotions that are at variance with those that would be normally evoked by the topic under discussion may indicate either an ineffective effort to reject and distance the self from the emotional experience, or a lack of capacity for empathic resonance.

Interpersonal Style.   Finally, the clinician observes the patient's pattern of response to the clinician himself/herself. Under the best of circumstances, the requirement of revealing oneself to a stranger is difficult. It is made even more difficult by the frequent fear that the clinician has special powers and can see things that even the patient himself/herself does not know are there. Hence, the interview is an ideal opportunity to observe interpersonal patterns of defense and expression, and further supplements the more indirect but standardized assessments of personality.

In order to capitalize on the opportunity available, the interviewer notes the efforts the patient makes to establish a relationship with the clinician. These include efforts to solicit reassurance about accuracy, normality, or acceptability, as well as any verbal and behavioral rejections of the assessment procedures by the patient. These observations are noted as representing the patient's effort to balance needs for acceptance with needs for autonomy. Hence, special tendencies either to comply or to reject and abandon the effort are noted. These directly observed patterns are considered along with the factual data and descriptions reported by the patient and others, in order to derive hypotheses about coping style, patterns or levels of resistance, social judgment, and level of distress.

Special Behaviors or Needs.   Other observations made directly by the clinician include any special behaviors or needs of the patient that will have a bearing on the need for special treatment settings, extra consultations, and other unusual arrangements for treatment. These include physical limitations and challenges, language fluency, availability of current support systems, and current medical or educational needs. With different patients, treatment settings must be selected to include wheelchair accessibility; a reference or support group of a given ethnic background or age range; staff members who can speak and understand the patient's primary language; or materials for teaching learning-disabled, deaf, or blind patients.

Summary

This chapter has emphasized the general functions, strengths, and limitations of structured and semistructured interviews. The strengths of the semistructured procedure include its flexibility and its unique adaptability to the quest for factual and historical information. Its weaknesses include its uncertain reliability and validity, and the tendency of clinicians to place more confidence in its results than may be warranted. Structured interviews can be used as adjuncts to the semistructured interview format that is preferred by most clinicians, in order to enhance the reliability of the diagnostic and symptomatic information obtained.

I have outlined the general topics to be included in a semistructured interview, in order to reach a reasonable balance between interview flexibility and comprehensiveness. Again, however, it is not wise to use such an interview as a stand-alone assessment device. Indeed, it should be considered to be no more or less valuable than other instruments, although because of its flexibility, it often provides the context and mind set for conducting the rest of the assessment. That is, a clinician can emphasize and capitalize on the qualitative strengths of the interview by using it as an entree to the assessment process, and by structuring it in such a way as to facilitate the establishment of cooperative and realistic expectations on the part of the patient. Moreover, providing adequate preassessment information within a facilitating setting can enhance the patient's cooperation and disclosure, both within the interview and in the other assessment procedures.

The content of the interview capitalizes on its strength at extracting factual information from the patient's recollection. However, the clinician's qualitative observations—particularly as related to discrepancies between the factual content provided by patients and that provided by others, between verbal content and nonverbal indicators of affect, and between judged affect and mood—can be helpful as means of constructing hypotheses about functioning to supplement those obtained in more structured and standardized ways. Moreover, direct observations of the methods used by the patient to establish and maintain the interviewer–interviewee relationship can form the basis for inferences about the nature of habitual coping strategies and self-presentation efforts. Although interview-derived observations are no more important and sometimes less valid than observations made through less direct psychological assessment devices, they add a valuable dimension to the overall effort to distill the meanings of current behaviors and to predict future ones.

References

Amchin, J. (1991). *Psychiatric diagnosis: A biopsychosocial approach using DSM-III-R.* Washington, DC: American Psychiatric Press.

American Psychiatric Association. (1987). *Diagnostic and statistical manual of mental disorders* (3rd ed., rev.). Washington, DC: Author.

First, M. B., Gibbon, M., Williams, J. B. W., & Spitzer, R. L. (1990). *Mini-SCID: Structured Clinical Interview for DSM-III-R.* North Tonawanda, NY: Multi-Health Systems.

First, M. B., Gibbon, M., Williams, J. B. W., & Spitzer, R. L. (1991). *AutoSCID II: Structured Clinical Interview for DSM-III-R.* North Tonawanda, NY: Multi-Health Systems.

First, M. B., Williams, J. B. W., & Spitzer, R. L. (1988). *DTREE: The electronic DSM-III-R (Axis II).* North Tonawanda, NY: Multi-Health Systems.

First, M. B., Williams, J. B. W., & Spitzer, R. L. (1989). *DTREE II: The electronic DSM-III-R (Axis II).* North Tonawanda, NY: Multi-Health Systems.

Folstein, M. F., Folstein, S. E., & McHugh, P. R. (1975). "Mini-Mental State": A practical method for grading the cognitive state of patients for the clinician. *Journal of Psychiatric Research, 12,* 189–198.

Hamilton, M. (1967). Development of a rating scale for primary depressive illness. *British Journal of Social and Clinical Psychology, 6,* 278–296.

Luborsky, L., & Crits-Christoph, P. (Eds.). (1990). *The core conflictual relationship theme.* New York: Basic Books.

Strupp, H. H., & Binder, J. L. (1984). *Psychotherapy in a new key.* New York: Basic Books.

Robins, L. N., Helzer, J. E., Croughan, J., & Ratcliff, K. S. (1981). National Institute of Mental Health Diagnostic Interview Schedule: Its history, characteristics, and validity. *Archives of General Psychiatry, 38,* 381–389.

Spitzer, R. L., Williams, J. B. W., & Gibbon, M. (1986). *The Structured Clinical Interview for DSM III-R—Patient version.* New York: Biometrics Research Department, New York State Psychiatric Institute.

Wohlwill, J., & Carson, D. (Eds.). (1972). *Environment and the social sciences.* Washington, DC: American Psychological Association.

Yokley, J. M., & Reuter, J. M. (1989). The computer-assisted Child Diagnostic System: A research and development project. *Computers in Human Development, 5,* 277–295.

5

The Assessment of Cognitive Functioning and the WAIS-R

Heidi A. Zetzer

Larry E. Beutler

The Wechsler Adult Intelligence Scale—Revised (WAIS-R; Wechsler, 1981) is a popular instrument for the assessment of a patient's cognitive functioning (Lubin, Larsen, Matarazzo, & Seever, 1985; Piotrowski & Keller, 1989). It is often the first approach taken when a clinician suspects that a patient suffers from organic brain dysfunction (Lezak, 1983; Zillmer & Ball, 1987), learning disabilities, or an intellectual deficit. In addition to its obvious utility as a source for generating hypotheses about cognitive functioning, the WAIS-R can provide information about the patient's psychopathology (Blatt & Allison, 1981; Matarazzo, 1972; Rapaport, Gill, & Schafer, 1968), affective and emotional control, conflict areas, coping strategies (Kaufman, 1990), and probable resistance to treatment. In sum, the WAIS-R is a valuable addition to an integrated approach to clinical assessment, diagnosis, and treatment formulation.

The purpose of this chapter is to describe how the WAIS-R can be used as part of the integrated approach to assessment described in Chapter 2. Consequently, the expanse of this chapter goes beyond the perimeter set by traditional discourses on the WAIS-R (e.g., Groth-Marnat, 1990; Kaufman, 1990; Sattler, 1992). We use common empirical and qualitative approaches to the interpretation of WAIS-R results as the foundation for our own description of the use of this instrument as part of an integrative assessment of adult personality.

Chapter 2 develops a useful metaphor for the conduct of psychological assessment, which is integrated into the organization of this chapter. In Chapter 2, a parallel has been drawn between the selection and administration of psychological assessments and the design and implementation of scientific research. A clinician manipulates the testing environment much as an experimenter manipulates the independent variable in a psychological experiment. In both situations, the subject's responses constitute the dependent variable. Like the experimenter, it is the clinician's responsibility to understand the demand characteristics of the independent variable well enough to predict the generalizability of the subject's responses to similar nonexperimental or nontesting situations. Thus, a major part of this chapter is devoted to describing the nature of the test demands of the WAIS-R as an independent variable. An even larger part of this chapter describes the generating of hypotheses about how the patient's testing behavior reflects behavior in nontesting situations. The patient's responses to the WAIS-R's demand characteristics are used to select treatment settings, goals, and methods.

The chapter is divided into seven major sections. First, we present background information on the development of the WAIS-R. This section includes a discussion of the test's psychometric properties, as well as a description of some of the merits and problems of the WAIS-R short forms. Second, we provide an overview of administration and scoring procedures. Third, we analyze the demand characteristics of the WAIS-R. Fourth, we present a synopsis of traditional methods for interpreting the response characteristics of the WAIS-R and conducting profile analyses. Fifth, we describe how the traditional empirical approaches we have reviewed can serve as the basis for forming hypotheses about diagnosis and treatment—and, more specifically, about a patient's intellectual, emotional, and interpersonal–intrapersonal functioning. The external validity of these observations is a topic of specific focus in this section. Sixth, we present case examples of how this assessment process can be used to make differential diagnoses and guide treatment planning. Finally, we discuss some of the limitations of using the WAIS-R with diverse populations.

Foundations of the WAIS-R

Origins and Development

The WAIS-R (Wechsler, 1981) made its debut as the Wechsler–Bellevue Intelligence Test (W-B; Wechsler, 1939). The W-B was drawn from existing assessments—namely, the Stanford–Binet (Terman, 1916; Terman & Merrill, 1937), the Army Alpha Test, the National Intelligence Tests, the Army Beta Test, the Kohs Block Design, and many others (Sprandel, 1985). The W-B contained six Verbal subtests and five Performance subtests.

Wechsler designed the W-B to redress two significant problems with the Stanford–Binet. First, Wechsler argued that the accurate assessment of a person's intelligence requires the measurement of both verbal *and* nonverbal abilities (Sprandel, 1985). The original Stanford–Binet (Terman, 1916) lacked this attribute for testing persons over 5 years of age. The 1937 revision by Terman and Merrill offered some improvement, but still provoked concern with its sensitivity among older age groups (Sattler, 1992). Second, both of these versions of the Stanford–Binet used ratio IQs as a means of standardization (IQ = mental age divided by chronological age times 100) (Maloney & Ward, 1976; Wechsler, 1958). Logically, as an examinee increases in age, the denominator also increases. At some point, the numerator will reach an asymptote, and increases in chronological age will give the appearance of decreases in IQ. This phenomenon is an artifact of the use of mental age in the derivation of the IQ. This use of the ratio IQ prohibited the testing of intellectually mature individuals and prevented the comparison of IQs across varying age levels (Wechsler, 1958).

To correct the problems of computing IQs based on mental age, Wechsler introduced the concept of the "deviation IQ" (Maloney & Ward, 1976). Deviation IQs represent an advantage over ratio IQs because the figure is not influenced by changes in the rate of intellectual development across the lifespan. The deviation IQ is based on the assumption that intelligence is distributed normally throughout the population (Maloney & Ward, 1976). Deviation IQs provide professionals and consumers with information about an examinee's level of intelligence *relative* to his/her age peers. An added assumption is that an examinee's relative position does not change over time (Maloney & Ward, 1976).

Unfortunately, deviation IQs are imperfect measures of intelligence, because they provide no information about the quality or components of an examinee's IQ. Two persons with the same IQ score may have very different intellectual talents. In addition, this measure is based on an ordinal scale, and scores cannot be compared directly. Someone who has an IQ of 130 is not twice as intelligent as someone with a score of 65 (Maloney & Ward, 1976).

Deviation IQs (Wechsler, 1981) are computed by converting the patient's raw subtest scores into scaled scores that are based on a normative reference group. The WAIS-R reference group consists of 500 persons between the ages of 20 and 34. Table 19 of the WAIS-R manual (Wechsler, 1981) is used to convert raw scale scores into scaled scores with $M = 10$ and $SD = 3$. In turn, a patient's Verbal IQ (VIQ), Performance IQ (PIQ), and Full Scale IQ (FSIQ) scores are generated by summing the relevant scaled scores and locating the deviation IQs in Table 20 of the WAIS-R manual (Wechsler, 1981). By following this procedure, the examiner effectively standardizes the examinee's scores ($M = 100$, $SD = 15$) and accounts for the differential effects of age. The VIQ, PIQ, and FSIQ can be used to compare a person's scores with those of others from his/her own age group. Since each score is normalized for age, scaled scores can also be used to compare the examinee's performance on the subtests with that of people in all other age groups. Age-corrected scale scores can be computed for each subtest to permit comparisons across subtests and within each age group (use Table 21, Wechsler, 1981). The reader should be aware that age-corrected scale scores are *not* used to compute the VIQ, PIQ, and FSIQ.

Wechsler published a revision of the W-B, called the Wechsler Adult Intelligence Scale (WAIS), in 1955. The WAIS-R followed in 1981; it retained approximately 80% of the items from the WAIS. Wechsler's (1981) comparisons of the WAIS and WAIS-R subtests revealed significant correlations that ranged from .66 to .71. Correlations between the two versions of the WAIS, separately conducted for the VIQ, PIQ, and FSIQ, were .91, .79, and .88, respectively (Sprandel, 1985).

However, some controversy has arisen in the literature regarding the degree to which the WAIS and WAIS-R produce equivalent scores. Several studies have suggested that at least for certain age groups, VIQ, PIQ, and FSIQ scores on the WAIS may average from 5 to 8 points higher than those for the WAIS-R (Mishra & Brown, 1983; Prifitera & Ryan, 1983; Smith, 1983; Wechsler, 1981). In response to this concern, Wagner and Gianakos (1985) examined the stability of WAIS and WAIS-R scores among a heterogeneous group of psychiatric outpatients over an 8-year period (a considerably longer period of time than was used in most studies). The results indicated that whereas WAIS scaled scores were consistently higher than the WAIS-R scores, the discrepancies were not as great as previously reported. The authors concluded that, overall, WAIS scores are good estimates of performance on the WAIS-R.

Consistent with the views of Wagner and Gianakos, we recommend that clinicians apply the same *general* principles of interpretation to the WAIS-R that are applied to the WAIS (e.g., Matarazzo, 1972; Maloney & Ward, 1976). We believe that the WAIS-R results can be considered to be valid for assessing a person's strengths and weaknesses, and that the factors that have been identified and used for interpreting the WAIS are similarly captured by the WAIS-R. However, clinicians should assume neither that IQ levels obtained on the WAIS and WAIS-R are equivalent, nor that the subtest composition of each factor is identical for the two tests (Kaufman, 1990).

Wechsler's Definition of Intelligence

Wechsler's (1968, 1975, 1981) definition of intelligence is broad and pragmatic. Wechsler (1981) described intelligence as "multifaceted as well as multidetermined" (p. 8). Specifically, he stated:

> Intelligence, operationally defined, is the aggregate or global capacity of the individual to act purposefully, to think rationally and to deal effectively with his [or her] environment. It is aggregate or global because

it is composed of elements or abilities which, though not entirely independent, are qualitatively differentiable. By measurement of these abilities, we ultimately evaluate intelligence. But intelligence is not identical
with the mere sum of these abilities, however inclusive. . . . The only
way we can evaluate it quantitatively is by the measurement of various
aspects of these abilities. (Wechsler, 1958, p. 7)

Traditional views of intelligence have been of four general types (Groth-
Marnat, 1990): (1) psychometric, (2) developmental, (3) neurobiological,
and (4) information-processing approaches (see also Kail & Pellegrino, 1985;
Sternberg & Salter, 1982). The definition of intelligence that guided
Wechsler in developing the WAIS and that still underlies the WAIS-R contains elements of each of these views. Wechsler's definition resembles a
psychometric approach to the study of intelligence, in that he described
intelligence as an *aggregate* of abilities, similar to what Spearman (1927)
called a "*g* factor." Similarly, Wechsler's conceptualization of specific abilities
resembles Spearman's (1927) "*s* factors." However, according to Wechsler
(1968, 1981), abilities are differentiable, but not entirely independent of
one another. That is, the *s* and *g* factors share some commonality. Factor-
analytic studies (Beck, Horwitz, Seidenberg, Parker, & Frank, 1985; Waller
& Waldman, 1990) of the WAIS-R have generally supported Wechsler's view.
There has been only limited and contradictory evidence for the existence
of unique abilities that do not share any variance with the "*g* factor." At
least among patient groups, a general factor (rather than several specific
factors) seems to be the rule. Nonetheless, there are two relatively broad
and reliable specific factors that are helpful in defining one's general learning style, as subsets of general intellectual ability. These factors are verbal
and perceptual ability (Piedmont, Sokolove, & Fleming, 1992).

At the same time, Wechsler's (1981) approach to intelligence deviates
from a purely psychometric view, in that he argued that the *way* in which
intellectual abilities are combined is just as important as the number or
quality of these abilities. How abilities are integrated is not easily expressed
as a mathematical term. Moreover, by raising the consideration of "how,"
Wechsler (1968) inserted such "nonintellective" aspects of intelligence as
personality and motivation into his definition. Thereby, he introduced a
developmental component to understanding intelligent behavior. He argued
that the development of intelligence is motivated by a human being's drive
to comprehend the surrounding environment and to accommodate or adapt
to the challenges that it presents (Wechsler, 1981). This view was similar to
that espoused by Piaget (1950; Phillips, 1975) in formulating his developmental theory of intelligence. Piaget construed intelligence as the mechanism for the assimilation of new information into existing cognitive structures and for the alteration of those same structures in order to accommodate
extraordinarily novel experiences.

Wechsler's definition of intelligence less obviously incorporates an information-processing perspective. Only a close examination reveals the striking similarities between these two approaches. For example, Wechsler's (1968) argument that intelligence is more than a compilation of abilities implies the operation of an "executive system" (Borokowski, 1985; Campione & Brown, 1978) that organizes and directs intelligent behavior. In addition, despite information-processing proponents' reliance on sequential and hierarchical models, there is some recognition in this approach that the components of intelligent behavior are organized and operate in concert with one another (Kail & Pellegrino, 1985).

Yet Wechsler's view of intelligence and the view espoused by information-processing proponents are also distinctly different in some respects. For example, Wechsler described intelligence as a gestalt. In contrast, information-processing proponents are more explicit about the precise operation of specific hypothetical components of intelligent behavior (Kail & Pellegrino, 1985). Nonetheless, the results of WAIS-R administrations are easily amenable to interpretations within an information-processing framework. For example, Digit Span results can provide information about the patient's ability to encode, store, and recall chunks of information; the Arithmetic problems can inform the examiner as to the patient's ability to choose the most essential pieces of information from an array (the story problem) and then to perform the correct mental operations (an arithmetic function); and the overall level of the patient's performance reflects the efficiency of his/her executive functions.

Wechsler's (1968) definition, in addition to including aspects of the other three aforementioned perspectives, assumes that the expression of intelligent behavior depends on the successful operation of a neurobiological system (Groth-Marnat, 1990). Horn and Cattell (1966, 1967) made a distinction between "fluid" or biologically based intelligence and "crystallized" or environmentally based intelligence. Fluid intelligence was considered to be sensitive to brain injury and was thought to be reflected in a patient's inherent ability to solve novel problems (Kaufman, 1990). Evidence of crystallized intelligence was seen in the extent of the patient's knowledge base, especially in its resistance to the effects of brain damage. The Verbal scales in both the WAIS and WAIS-R correspond roughly to this view of crystallized intelligence, and the Performance scales correspond to the concept of fluid intelligence.

Psychometric Properties

To say that the psychometric characteristics of the WAIS-R are well documented is an understatement. This test has proven to be a reliable and valid measure of intelligence (Kaufman, 1990).

Reliability

Split-half reliabilities for the 11 subscales comprising the WAIS-R range from .68 for Object Assembly to .96 for Vocabulary, with most coefficients in the .80 to .89 range. Split-half reliabilities for the IQ scales are .97 for VIQ, .93 for PIQ, and .97 for FSIQ (Kaufman, 1990). Subtest test–retest reliabilities range from .70 for Object Assembly to .92 for Vocabulary; most coefficients are in the .80s. The test–retest reliabilities for the scales are .96 for VIQ, .90 for PIQ, and .96 for FSIQ. Reliability estimates are somewhat lower for elderly populations (over 75 years old), but the figures are still in the acceptable range (Ryan, Paolo, & Brungardt, 1990, 1992). For a psychiatric population, Boone (1992a) reported that the most reliable subtests (split-half) were Digit Symbol, Information, and Picture Completion. Boone concluded that Object Assembly was unreliable for a psychiatric population ($r_{tt} = .38$). In contrast, Cyr and Atkinson (1991) estimated the split-half reliabilities of nine of the WAIS-R subscales and determined that Vocabulary, Similarities, and Arithmetic were the most reliable. Object Assembly was still the least reliable subtest, however, with a split-half coefficient of .64.

There is some evidence that subtest scores may be affected by the mood of the patient during administration. Wolff and Gregory (1991) found that subjects with experimentally induced dysphoria scored significantly lower than subjects in a control group on Block Design and Object Assembly. There were no differences between the groups on their scores for Arithmetic and Similarities. These results suggest that dysphoric mood may not have an overall depressive effect on scores, but affects various subtests differentially. Wolff and Gregory hypothesized that depression deflates perceptual–motor scores because it produces motor deficits or disrupts perceptual organization (Tucker, Stenslie, Roth, & Shearer, 1981).

Validity

The construct validity of the WAIS-R as a measure of adult intelligence is supported by its conformity with expected developmental changes in IQ. For example, the FSIQ increases with years of education (Sattler, 1988) and is curvilinearly related to age; the FSIQ steadily increases and then slowly decreases with age (Kaufman, 1990). The construct validity of the WAIS-R is further supported by an examination of correlations between the WAIS-R and other measures of intellectual ability, such as the Stanford–Binet ($r = .85$) and the Wide Range Achievement Test (reading, .62; spelling, .60, and arithmetic, .76) (Groth-Marnat, 1990).

Furthermore, factor-analytic studies have confirmed the construct validity of the WAIS-R by yielding results that match the organization of Wechsler's (1981) scales. A majority of factor-analytic studies of the structure of the WAIS-R have produced two factors (Silverstein, 1982b) or three factors, similar to those originally appearing on the WAIS (Waller & Wald-man, 1990). The two primary factors that combine to produce intelligent behavior are Verbal Comprehension and Perceptual Organization. The less consistently observed third factor is most commonly referred to as Freedom from Distractibility. The Verbal subtests of the WAIS-R load well on the Verbal Comprehension factor (factor loadings range from .47 to .84). The same holds true for the Performance scales, which load well on the Perceptual Organization factor (loadings range from .45 to .72) (Kaufman, 1990). Arithmetic and Digit Span usually comprise the Freedom from Distractibility factor (.55 and .64, respectively) (Kaufman, 1990).

As noted earlier, WAIS-R and WAIS scores are not precisely equivalent among all age groups. The 5- to 8-point discrepancies observed between tests pose a significant challenge to the validity of the WAIS-R, especially among 18- to 19-year-olds. Kaufman (1990) observed that members of this age group performed significantly less well on the WAIS-R than their cohorts from both the WAIS and the W-B standardization samples. In addition, members of this group failed to perform better than 16- to 17-year-olds, even though they were more mature and had more education than the younger group. Kaufman (1990) has interpreted these findings as indicating that the differences reflect a systemic bias in the selection of the standardization sample for this age group. Accordingly, Kaufman advises examiners to use caution when interpreting scaled scores for this age group.

WAIS-R Short Forms

Numerous WAIS-R short forms have been developed and tested (Boone, 1991b, 1992b, Cella, 1984; Kaufman, 1990; Kaufman & Ishikuma, 1989). These short forms differ in several ways, including the time required for administration and scoring. Clinicians who are searching for abbreviated forms of the WAIS-R are well advised to review those that are available (e.g., Kaufman, 1990) and to base their selection on the validity of the short forms being considered relative to the time constraints imposed, the specific subscales used, and any special needs of the population being tested.

Two approaches have been employed to shorten the time required for WAIS-R administration (Boone, 1991a). The first method limits the number of items administered on all or most subtests. For example, the Satz–Mogel technique (Adams, Smigielski, & Jenkins, 1984; Satz & Mogel, 1962) employs (with some variation) an every-other-item format for most subtests and an empirically derived correction. Another method (Cella, 1984) uses the patient's Information subtest score to establish a starting point for other subtests (except for Digit Span, Object Assembly, and Digit Symbol), thus reducing the length of each subtest. Cella reported that correlations of this procedure with the complete WAIS-R VIQ, PIQ, and FSIQ were .995, .996, and .998, respectively.

The advantage of Cella's (1984) Modified version of the WAIS-R (WAIS-RM) over the Satz–Mogel version is that subtest variability can be retained and the examiner can perform a profile analysis. However, Boone (1991a) investigated the ability of the WAIS-RM to predict intersubtest scatter, and found that the overall accuracy rate was only 49%. In addition, the time saved in administering the WAIS-RM to a low-functioning psychiatric population was only 15 minutes.

An alternative to item reduction formats is the subtest reduction format. Boone (1992b) compared five popular short forms of this type: Silverstein's (1982a) procedure, which combines the Vocabulary, Block Design, Picture Arrangement, and Arithmetic subscales; Reynolds, Willson, and Clark's (1983) procedure, which combines the Information, Picture Completion, Arithmetic, and Block Design subscales; and Kaufman and Ishikuma's (1989) dyadic (Information, Picture Completion), triadic (Information, Picture Completion, Digit Span), and tetradic (Similarities, Arithmetic, Picture Completion, Digit Symbol) forms. The triadic combination proved to be the most accurate and efficient short form tested (Boone, 1992b). The triad takes approximately 16 minutes to administer. The Kaufman tetrad is just as accurate as the triad and takes only 19 minutes to do, but is reportedly more difficult to administer and score (Boone, 1992b). The Silverstein (1982a) and Reynolds et al. (1983) tetrads are also just as accurate and reliable as the Kaufman triad, but these formats took longer to administer to the psychiatric inpatients tested (36 and 28 minutes, respectively).

The efficacy of item reduction (the Satz–Mogel technique) and subtest reduction (the Silverstein combination) techniques has been compared. Boone (1991b) found that the item reduction technique failed to produce subscale test scores accurately; the author concluded that the full battery of subtests should be administered if an examiner wants to assess the patient's strengths and weaknesses. To obtain a quick estimate of the patient's FSIQ, both approaches work, but the subtest reduction technique is more reliable and leaves the examiner with the opportunity to complete the administration of the remaining subtests later (Kaufman, 1977).

Administering and Scoring the WAIS-R

Administration

The WAIS-R was designed for use among adults aged 16 to 74. As noted earlier, it generates scores in the form of deviation IQs with a mean of 100 and a standard deviation of 15. FSIQ scores below 50 and above 150 are insensitive and imprecise (Sattler, 1992; Wechsler, 1981). Alternative measures of intelligence should be used if one's task is to differentiate among individuals within these extremes. Low-scoring adults may be evaluated with the Wechsler Intelligence Scale for Children—Revised (WISC-R) (see Feingold, 1985), but it is also apparent that in these groups, scores should be supplemented by a functional analysis of adaptive behaviors (Greenspan, 1979, 1981; H. J. Grossman, 1983; Kaufman, 1990; Sattler, 1988). The Vineland Adaptive Behavior Scales (Sparrow, Balla, & Cicchetti, 1984a, 1984b), the Scales of Independent Behavior (Bruininks, Woodcock, Hill, & Weatherman, 1984, 1985), the Functional Intelligence scale of the Kaufman Adolescent and Adult Intelligence Test (Kaufman & Kaufman, 1992), and the American Association of Mental Deficiency's Adaptive Behavior Scale (Lambert, 1981; Lambert & Windmiller, 1981; Nihira, Foster, Shellhaas, & Leland, 1975) are all suitable instruments that focus on adaptive behaviors among low-functioning individuals.

In a similar way, Kaufman recommends that the intellectual assessment of gifted adults should consist of the WAIS-R combined with supplementary tests of achievement, cognitive abilities, and thought processes. For example, an examiner might evaluate a gifted person's creativity with the Torrance Tests of Creative Thinking (Torrance, 1984).

IQ equivalents based on the normative group of 70- to 74-year-olds may also be used to estimate IQs for examinees whose ages are over 74 years (Wechsler, 1981). When applied in this way, the WAIS-R is a reliable measure of intelligence for examinees 75 years of age and older (Ryan et al., 1990, 1992).

Order of Administration

On the original WAIS (Wechsler, 1955), the administration of the six Verbal subtests preceded that of the five Performance subtests. Wechsler (1981) instituted a change with the introduction of the WAIS-R and chose to alternate presentation of the Verbal and Performance subtests. Alternating the type of subtest is thought to enhance the patient's motivation and to maintain interest better. The established order of administration may also be revised in order to accommodate the special needs of the examinee (Wechsler, 1981). For example, all the Verbal subtests may be administered first to examinees who are easily frustrated by perceptual–motor problems (Sattler, 1992).

Moreover, examinees who fatigue easily may benefit from multiple testing sessions with periodic breaks (Wechsler, 1981). Generally, it is best to cease administration in such cases at the end of a subtest, but if the subtest is unavoidably interrupted, administration can be resumed at a later time at the point where the patient terminated the administration without negative consequences. This is true except for the Picture Arrangement, Block

Design, and Similarities subtests, where resumption should be preceded by the administration of several items to compensate for interitem practice effects (Sattler, 1992). If an examinee refuses to start or complete a subtest, it may be omitted from the profile, and the examiner can estimate the appropriate IQ by using Appendix E in the WAIS-R manual (Wechsler, 1981).

Preparation

A clinician who administers the WAIS-R should be able to perform three essential tasks: (1) to follow the manual, (2) to observe the patient's behavior, and (3) to record the patient's responses verbatim (Wechsler, 1981). This is no small feat. The examiner should be sufficiently comfortable with the physical management of the materials so as to avoid looking clumsy or suspicious, and should be sufficiently familiar with scoring procedures to recognize incorrect responses during administration (Sprandel, 1985; Wechsler, 1981). These levels of proficiency are only achieved by experience. For example, overall accuracy in administration for preinternship students is about 59% (Moon, Fantuzzo, & Gorsuch, 1986). Postinternship students are 67% accurate in their administrations (Moon et al., 1986). The most frequent administration error committed by beginning and advanced WAIS-R trainees is a failure to record the subject's responses (Slate, Jones, & Murray, 1991). Slate et al.'s (1991) finding is remarkable, in that transcription is the simplest of the three essential tasks. Incomplete transcription diminishes the accuracy of IQ scores and results in the loss of a significant amount of anecdotal information. Clinicians can improve their accuracy by increasing their familiarity with the testing materials and by participating in training programs that provide active feedback from experienced supervisors (Slate et al., 1991).

Establishing Rapport and Introducing the Procedure

As pointed out in Chapters 2 and 4, the clinician must consider the physical arrangements in which the test is administered (see also Sprandel, 1985). The setting must be comfortable for both the clinician and patient, with no distractions and a minimal amount of outside noise. In administering the WAIS-R, the clinician may be seated either across from or next to the patient. The table should be at a comfortable height with a smooth writing surface. The lighting and temperature of the room should be adequate (Sprandel, 1985). Testing materials should be kept out of sight until needed (Wechsler, 1981). The clinician should allow time for brief, informal conversation at the beginning of the session, and should allot a few minutes at the end of test (the test takes 60–90 minutes to administer) for debriefing.

Some adults are concerned about "failing" the test; an examiner can reduce a patient's anxiety by assuring him/her that "no one fails, but that some parts go better than others" (Sprandel, 1985, p. 23). An examiner may also help contain a patient's anxiety by describing the testing process; stating that each task begins with easy questions and then gets progressively more difficult; and telling the examinee that not everyone is expected to succeed on all the problems (Wechsler, 1981).

While the examiner is introducing the test, he/she can provide the patient with a rationale or explanation of the various subtests. The clinician should point out that some tasks require answering questions and other tasks do not require words (Wechsler, 1981); the length of time required for each subtest should be estimated, and the respondent should be told that responses will be recorded throughout the administration (Sprandel, 1985). It is wise to offer the patient a description of his/her strengths and weaknesses *at a later time*. It is also wise, when asked, to provide some reasons for not offering a specific IQ score (i.e., the complexity of intelligence and the nonspecificity of a single score's meaning).

Although it is unacceptable to tell examinees whether a response is correct, the examiner can provide encouragement (Wechsler, 1981). Rapport may be enhanced or maintained by periodically asking the examinee how the test is going and responding to visibly difficult subtests with comments such as "That was rather difficult, wasn't it?" or "The next part has different kinds of questions in it; you'll probably like it better" (Sprandel, 1985, p. 24; Wechsler, 1981).

Other Considerations

"Dos and Don'ts."   Sattler (1992, p. 232) offers the conscientious examiner a list of "dos and don'ts" that may serve as useful last-minute reminders about proper administration. Briefly, it is best if the examiner (1) follows the test protocol exactly; (2) memorizes the discontinuance rules; (3) queries all ambiguous responses and indicates this on the record form (i.e., writes "Q"); (4) records the responses completely; (5) after scoring, checks his/her work; (6) identifies spoiled and skipped items; (7) transforms scores carefully and accurately; and (8) starts preparation for the interpretation immediately by looking up percentiles, confidence intervals, and classifications after scoring is complete.

Probing and Recording Responses.   Probing patients in order to determine whether their responses are accurate does not come naturally to most clinicians, whose training as therapists directs them to be nonjudgmental regarding the truth or accuracy of patient reports. It is difficult to judge when responses are ambiguous enough to warrant additional inquiry (Wechsler, 1981). Wechsler recommends that examiners use nonthreatening statements such as "Tell me more about it," and "How do you mean?" (1981, p. 54) when querying examinees. An examiner must avoid communicating any information about the accuracy of a response to an examinee. Clinicians will find the task of evaluating the accuracy of patient responses easier if they (1) memorize samples of correct answers to the Vocabulary, Comprehension, and Similarities subtests, so that judgments about whether to query can be made quickly (Wechsler, 1981); (2) practice querying respondents in a neutral, pleasant manner; and (3) remember to write "Q" on the record form to identify those questions for which an inquiry was made (Wechsler, 1981).

Testing the Limits. "Testing the limits" refers to a process by which a clinician can estimate the extent of a patient's cognitive ability by stepping outside of the normal administrative procedures. This process often involves asking direct questions and providing alternative responses from which to choose. Asking questions of this type in order to test the limits of the patient's knowledge can provide cues that stimulate memories and enhance abstracting processes. Hence, it is best to test the limits after the entire administration has been completed, in order to minimize the degree to which the clinician's comments might assist the patient inordinately, and thereby invalidate subsequent responses. Nonetheless, it is often valuable to test the limits when a clinician suspects neurological deficiencies or learning disabilities, in order to get the best estimate of the patient's abilities under the most advantageous conditions.

For example, R. D.[1] was a 53-year-old, third-generation Mexican-American, monolingual (English-only) male who had first begun to experience a progressive loss of his auditory, vocal, and psychomotor abilities about 5 years earlier. Preliminary neurological testing failed to reveal an organic cause for his condition. R. D. was referred for a WAIS-R administration by his therapist. R. D.'s WAIS-R results are provided in Table 5.1.

To test the limits, R. D.'s examiner administered the Arithmetic subtest to him untimed, and permitted him to use paper and pencil to answer the questions. In addition, the examiner read the test items very slowly, about one word a second. R. D.'s performance improved markedly with these provisions. The patient originally scored only a 3 on Arithmetic, but under unrestricted conditions he computed the answers to items 1 through 12 correctly. His initial low score was apparently the result of his inability to remember each part of a question when it was read at a normal pace. In addition, his speech problem prohibited him from communicating his response. He could *write* his response, but he could not *say* it.

---

[1]Cases in this chapter are based on a compilation of clinical material from several different cases. Some of the assessment data were fabricated for educational purposes. All identifying information has been altered to protect the anonymity of the patients.

TABLE 5.1. WAIS-R Results for R. D.

Subtest	Raw score	Scaled score	Age-corrected scaled score
	Verbal Tests		
Information	22	11	12
Digit Span	8	5	5
Vocabulary	7	2	2
Arithmetic	3	3	1
Comprehension	3	2	2
Similarities	0	1	2
	Performance tests		
Picture Completion	12	6	8
Picture Arrangement	10	7	9
Block Design	27	9	10
Object Assembly	29	8	10
Digit Symbol	19	3	5

Note. Verbal score (sum of scaled scores) = 24; Performance score (sum of scaled scores) = 33; VIQ = 69; PIQ = 87; FSIQ = 77; Verbal Comprehension = 69.2; Perceptual Organization = 96; Freedom from Distractibility = 60.8.

Scoring: An Overview

The signal rule for scoring is to follow the scoring procedures outlined in the WAIS-R manual (Wechsler, 1981). Once each item has been scored, the examiner should convert the raw scores to scaled scores using the table of scaled score equivalents located on the front of the record form, or Table 19 in the WAIS-R manual. The subtest scaled scores should be entered in the appropriate column on the record form. To obtain the VIQ, PIQ, and FSIQ, the examiner should sum the scaled scores for the six Verbal tests, the five Performance tests, and then all 11 subtests, and use Table 20 to locate the IQ equivalents. The correct age grouping in Table 20 must be used. For purposes of scoring and interpretation, the patient's age is the number of years accumulated by his/her last birthday (Wechsler, 1981).

It is frequently valuable to use a patient's raw scores to compute age-corrected scaled scores. These scores can be recorded in the extra column on the front of the record form. Table 21 can be used to determine the age-related scaled scores, which have a mean of 10 and a standard deviation of 3. Age-corrected scaled scores can be used to compare a patient with his/her peers and examine changes in IQ that are not related to age. For example, notice in Table 5.1 that R. D.'s age-corrected scaled scores were somewhat higher than the scaled scores based on the reference group. In the normal course of things, one would expect the difference between these two types of scaled scores to continue to increase as the patient ages (Kaufman, 1990). The age-corrected scale scores themselves should change very little with maturation (because both the individual and the age-related reference group are maturing). For R. D. and his therapist, it was more informative to watch the progress of R. D.'s symptoms by comparing his performance on the subscales with the performance of his age-related peers. It was likely that, compared to those of his peers, R. D.'s age-corrected scaled scores would decline more rapidly as his symptoms worsened.

VIQs, PIQs, and FSIQs can be converted to percentile rank scores by using either Table 8 in the WAIS-R manual or Appendix 5.1 of this chapter. A patient's IQ scores can be further described by categorizing them according to Wechsler's (1981, p. 28) intelligence classification scheme, or, if needed, according to the DSM-III-R (American Psychiatric Association, 1987).[2]

Spoiled Responses

A response is considered "spoiled" if the patient, in response to the examiner's request to elaborate an apparently correct response, provides a worse response and thereby reveals a failure to understand (Wechsler, 1981). For example, to item 7 on the Vocabulary test, R. D. described fabric as "cloth," which would be scored 2, but he then elaborated on the response and added "pants, skirt, shorts, socks." This demonstrated R. D.'s confusion about the test question, "What does cloth mean?", and spoiled the response. R. D. repeated the latter statement after he was queried with "Which is it?" Wechsler (1981, pp. 56–57) provides the following guidelines to scoring multiple responses:

1. If a response is intended to replace an earlier response, the earlier response should be ignored and the later one scored.
2. Any spoiled response is scored 0.
3. If two independent answers are given to a question, the examiner must ask which answer is intended. For example, in response to the Information question, "What is the capital of Italy?" a subject may say, "Rome—but maybe it's Naples." The examiner should then ask, "Which one is it?"
4. If a subject gives two or more answers to a question, none of which spoil the response, the best answer of the group should be scored.

Scoring Errors

Student examiners need to approach scoring cautiously. There is a tendency for novice clinicians to assign too many points to responses in the Vocabulary, Comprehension, and Similarities subtests (Slate et al., 1991). Incorrect point assignments appear to reflect a lack of understanding of the scor-

[2]Statements made about the DSM-III-R also apply to the DSM-IV, which was released just prior to the publication of this chapter.

ing criteria. An examiner should pay close attention to the criteria listed in Appendices A, B, and C of the WAIS-R manual, and remember to follow Wechsler's (1981) guidelines for scoring multiple responses. It is essential that the examiner record *every* response that is provided by the patient. Subsequent responses may spoil the patient's first answer and reveal the full extent of the patient's poverty of knowledge or lack of comprehension. Failure to record the patient's responses fully and accurately is one of the three most common errors made by examiners (Moon, Blakey, Gorsuch, & Fantuzzo, 1991; Slate et al., 1991). Faulty recording naturally leads to error-ridden scoring and inaccurate estimates of IQ.

Demand Characteristics of the WAIS-R

The WAIS-R can provide an astute examiner with a wealth of information about the patient's intellect, perceptions, thought content, coping style, and interpersonal manner *as these characteristics are expressed in the testing situation*. The degree to which the examiner's observations of the patient's behavior will become manifest in treatment depends on the degree to which the demands of treatment and the demands of the testing environment approximate each other.

Degree of Environmental Structure

The administration procedures of the WAIS-R present the patient with a highly structured environment. The patient's responses are limited by the implied expectation for accuracy. In addition, responses are limited by the presence of rules for discontinuing further inquiry (Sattler, 1992). The number of responses, the time taken to respond, and the number of consecutively incorrect responses are used by the examiner to cut off further explanation or response. Moreover, there is little ambiguity in the role of the patient and examiner. The examiner directs the proceedings, and the patient responds in turn.

The patient's response to this level of structure and clinician control may reveal how well he/she functions in a highly controlled interpersonal situation and how able he/she is to assert an opinion. The content of the patient's responses and the manner in which the answers are communicated may unveil the breadth of the patient's knowledge base, the efficiency of his/her cognitive processes, his/her thought content, and the extent of his/her perceptual and observational skills, as well as other personal characteristics.

Response to structure is exemplified in the performance of B. W., a 21-year-old Caucasian female who had an evening job as a factory worker and attended classes at community college full-time. She was raised in a working-class family and, during her childhood, lived in a large rural county in the Midwest. She and her family moved to an urban area when she was 10 years old. She sought treatment at the college's counseling center for depression and suicidal feelings. B. W. reported that she felt "different" from everyone around her, and she attributed this feeling to her superior intelligence. B. W. sought an intelligence test to validate her perceptions of her own "giftedness" and "superior intellect."

B. W.'s WAIS-R results are reported in Table 5.2. Ordinarily, when a patient is self-referred like B. W., the actual scores of each subtest and the patient's VIQ, PIQ, and FSIQ are not reported to the examinee. Generally, the written description of the patient's intellectual strengths and weaknesses includes examples and *useful* percentile scores. If any IQ values are reported at all, they are usually presented in the form of confidence intervals. The raw and scaled scores have been reported here for explanatory purposes.

B. W. obtained relatively high scores on subtests that posed direct unambiguous questions—namely, Information, Vocabulary, and Arithmetic —but performed relatively poorly on Picture Completion and Picture Arrangement. Collectively, these latter tests present novel stimuli, an ambiguous set of demands, unclear expectations, and open-ended (unstructured) questions (e.g., "What is missing? Tell a story").

Likewise, the VIQ–PIQ discrepancy (+20 points) in her scores suggested that B. W. had no trouble responding to Verbal items that relied primarily

TABLE 5.2. WAIS-R Results for B. W.

Subtest	Raw score	Scaled score	Age-corrected scaled score
Verbal tests			
Information	27	15	15
Digit Span	13	8	9
Vocabulary	55	12	12
Arithmetic	15	12	12
Comprehension	15	7	7
Similarities	22	6	11
Performance tests			
Picture Completion	10	5	5
Picture Arrangement	8	7	6
Block Design	39	12	12
Object Assembly	32	10	9
Digit Symbol	46	7	7

Note. Verbal score (sum of scaled scores) = 64; Performance score (sum of scaled scores) = 41; VIQ = 105; PIQ = 85; FSIQ = 96; Verbal Comprehension = 107; Perceptual Organization = 92; Freedom from Distractibility = 102.8.

on prior schooling and previous cognitive rehearsal. She seemed confused by the unfamiliar test demands of some of the Performance subtests. The content of her test responses—"The man has no friends" (to card 17 of Picture Completion, the man) and "The violin does not have enough strings" (to card 13, the violin)—suggested that she had a difficult time controlling and organizing extraneous thoughts. She was later able to provide correct responses to these items after being permitted to express all of her "creative musings" first. In correspondent fashion, the client's interpersonal behavior also mirrored her discomfort with a lack of structure. She seemed acutely uncomfortable at the beginning of the testing session and during a short period of chitchat, but she relaxed visibly once the administration was underway.

Type of Experience Assessed (Internal vs. External)

The testing demands of the WAIS-R require respondents to reflect on and reveal internal experience to formulate their responses. Individual differences in patients' cognitive processing abilities can only be *inferred* from the VIQ, PIQ, and FSIQ scores, PIQ–VIQ differences, inter- and intrasubtest scatter, the patient's verbatim responses, and anecdotal observations made by the examiner. If a patient is queried, an examiner may learn about the patient's mood and problem-solving strategies (internal experiences), as well as his/her social competencies (external behavior).

For example, B. W. perceived the "escape" scene from the Picture Arrangement task as an aborted rape attempt. Similarly, she saw other Picture Arrangement tasks as inherently violent and threatening. In response to the "robber" scene, she said, "If I had a gun, I would have shot that guy." B. W.'s responses gave evidence of a negatively toned bias in her perceptions that led her to be excessively quick to perceive danger and unhappy consequences to social interactions. She reportedly saw most social situations as adversarial, depressing, and negative. Her proclivity to foresee maleficence in others' intentions and her tendency to resolve social conflicts with imagined forms of violence would almost certainly hamper the development of a strong working alliance. Clearly, confrontational and intensive forms of individual therapy were contraindicated.

R. D.'s examiner observed that he had a difficult time following the verbal administration of the Arithmetic word problems (scaled score = 3). He appeared to comprehend the first few phrases and then forgot them as he tried to remember the remaining phrases. Consequently, he could not even begin to solve the problem, and demonstrated this by saying "Don't know" immediately after the problem was read. As noted above, he was later able to answer several of these items correctly when the questions were asked very slowly and he was not timed. R. D.'s scores on Digit Symbol (scaled score = 3) supported the existence of problems with encoding, memory, and/or recall (internal behaviors).

The manner in which the patient responds to perceived successes and failures on the WAIS-R can indicate what type of coping style he/she prefers. Externalizing patients (Welsh, 1952) may be inclined to blame and judge the examiner harshly when they fail, and to express their anger and frustration by complaining about the testing constraints and ridiculing the test itself (Sprandel, 1985). Internalizing patients (see Beutler & Clarkin, 1990) may respond to perceived failures with self-deprecation and increased self-scrutiny, which may in turn increase the latency of their responses, and seriously diminish their performance on the timed subtests.

Level and Type of Stress

The WAIS-R is perceived by most patients as interpersonally stressful (Kaufman, 1990). The presence and role of the WAIS-R examiner, whose attention is fully on the patient, adds an unfamiliar type of interpersonal stress that is typically absent from the familiar group setting of scholastic achievement tests. Hence, test anxiety is unavoidable (Sprandel, 1985) and is further exaggerated by several factors: (1) the imposition of directives from the test examiner (e.g., compliance is expected, and deviations from protocol are discouraged); (2) the limitation of response alternatives (e.g., patients are asked to give the right or "best" answer); (3) the limitation of the patient's perceived freedom by the authority of the examiner, who serves as a "judge" of performance, and thus determines the patient's IQ; (4) the demands for precision and speed; and (5) the need to override distracting thoughts or impulses in order to concentrate on the tasks.

Patients may respond to these stresses with either excessive or insufficient control of what they reveal in their responses, or by decompensating under the pressure. Response styles can become apparent to the examiner through observation or actual test scores. Overcontrolled responding will depress scores on the timed subtests (e.g., Block Design), and may enhance scores on the untimed tests (e.g., Information) by reduced levels of production and speed. Undercontrolled responding will depress the scores of average to below-average examinees by increasing the role of errors and the introduction of irrelevant ideas. This latter style may work to a bright patient's advantage on the timed tests. Bonus points are awarded on Block Design and Object Assembly for short latencies, and rapid response time is essential in scoring well on Digit Symbol. Undercontrolled responding also helps relatively bright impulsive patients score well on Information, Vocabulary, and Similarities, because they may provide many responses. In the case of multiple responses, as noted earlier, only the best response is scored or the examinee is asked, "Which one [response] is it?" (Wechsler, 1981, pp. 56–57). Thus, the respondent is given an opportunity to reflect on his/ her utterances and choose the best answer. Overcontrolled examinees, who offer only one response to items on these subtests, are penalized (e.g., some questions on Comprehension *require* two responses) and are denied the second chance to inspect their answers by choosing among several alternatives. On the other hand, impulsive or undercontrolled responding can impair performance on Performance tests and may inhibit the discovery of a useful problem-solving strategy. For example, examinees who persist in using a trial-and-error strategy on Block Design may tend to take longer to complete the task, and consequently score lower than those who mentally break the template down into component pieces and reconstruct the image for the examiner. The latter is a more reflective and controlled approach to the task.

Relating Test Demands to Treatment Demands

Meaningful interpretations of the WAIS-R test scores and profile patterns will help an astute clinician make recommendations for treatment. Treatment settings, contexts, and modalities vary on many different dimensions; the many different forms of psychotherapy pose different demands as well. In both cases, the situational demands posed to the patient vary in such parameters as intellectual, physical, perceived, and interpersonal demands. There is not sufficient room within the bounds of this chapter to provide a careful scrutiny of these four types of demands in various settings and formats of treatment, let alone all of the 400-plus forms of psychotherapy that are currently available (London, 1986; Parloff, 1980). However, there are distinctive differences in demand characteristics even among the most dominant and recognized therapies, and these parallel certain of those that are also present in the analogue environment of WAIS-R administration.

For example, in traditional psychoanalytic therapies, the therapist assumes the stance of a benign expert in a quest for understanding some truth that is hidden within the patient or analysand. This stance implies that the therapist holds the key to discovering "truth." When the analyst directs questions to the patient, it is the patient's job to look inwardly and to recall this truthful information. The information obtained is subjective and not externally observable, paralleling the implicit assumptions and subtle demand characteristics of the Verbal subscales of the WAIS-R. On the other hand, behavioral therapies value external or objective behaviors in a fashion that parallels the demand characteristics of the WAIS-R Performance subtests, where achievement is measured by speed and overt skill rather than inferred knowledge.

Therapies also differ in the degree to which they impose structure on the patient's responses. Psychodynamic and experiential therapies tend to be relatively unstructured, whereas behavioral and cognitive–behavioral therapies tend to be quite structured. By and large, the WAIS-R imposes a structured environment on the patient or respondent. Thus, observing how the patient reacts to the structure of the WAIS-R may provide a general indication of the degree to which he/she can manage structure. Comparisons of WAIS-R responses with those evoked by other tests may provide some indication of relative responsiveness to different therapy characteristics. For example, observing that a patient responds better to the WAIS-R than to the Rorschach may be an indication that he/she will be responsive to a structured therapy.

As one can see, the individual administration and structure of the WAIS-R testing environment imposes relatively high levels of interpersonal stress on the patient through the authoritative clinician role and demands for speed. The processes that are used to induce interpersonal stress are paralleled in various forms of psychotherapy. For example, the stress induced by the implicit assumption that there is an internal "truth" is magnified by the psychoanalytic therapist's role of authority and is expressed in interpretations of transference and resistance. Therapists who adhere to active approaches—especially experiential, behavioral, and cognitive-behavioral models—further impose sources of interpersonal stress on their patients by offering direct instructions and homework assignments, all of which are evaluated by the therapists' criteria. In time-limited forms of these models, time demands add an additional element of stress to the situation. The patient's response to the time demands of the Digit Symbol, Block Design, Object Assembly, and Arithmetic subscales provide an opportunity for the clinician to observe, in the analogue test environment, how the patient responds to the imposition of combined time, role, and structure pressures that may characterize different forms of therapy.

Analysis and Interpretation: Response Characteristics

One of the goals of this chapter is to help aspiring clinicians develop the deductive skills they need to form diagnostic impressions and make treatment recommendations. These cognitive operations follow a thorough analysis of the WAIS-R results. We assume that student clinicians are already familiar with one or more of the fundamental approaches to profile analysis and interpretation (see Kaufman, 1990, for several approaches; see also Sattler, 1992). Examiners should either choose among the systematic approaches that are available, or study these models and then formulate their own.

Hypotheses about a patient's intellectual strengths and weaknesses should be based on psychometrically reliable data and not clinical lore (Kaufman, 1990). Anecdotal clinical observation can be used to *supplement*, not to supplant, empirically based observations. An empirical analysis of the WAIS-R results should be at the heart of the profile analysis. Clinical observations are a useful source of information about the content of the patient's clinical issues and the manner in which the patient confronts or denies these issues. Clinical observation is *not* a useful source of information about clients' cognitive operations per se.

Given the emphasis that we are placing on a systematic and empirical approach to profile analysis and hypothesis formulation, we would like to present (1) a simple analytical scheme for constructing a WAIS-R interpretation (Groth-Marnat, 1990), and (2) summary information about the WAIS-R subtests and their common factors (Kaufman, 1990). In a later section, we provide case examples of profile analysis and interpretation, using the basic information presented here and the guidelines for hypothesis building presented in Figure 2.3 (Chapter 2). Sound hypothesis building is the result of creatively combining a solid scientific analysis of the WAIS-R results with knowledge of the patient's predisposing variables.

Levels of Analysis

Groth-Marnat (1990) presents a simple, straightforward approach to profile analysis that we believe warrants clinical use. This approach was first described by Sattler (1988). The material that we present is a summary of Groth-Marnat's method.[3]

Level I: The Full Scale IQ

The FSIQ is the most reliable score produced by a WAIS-R administration (.96 for ages 16–19, and .97–.98 for adults) (Kaufman, 1990). It is also the score that tends to generate the most public interest. In written reports, one may choose to describe the patient's skills and overall intellectual performance in terms of relative strengths and weaknesses. When reporting to the patient, however, special care is required. Unfortunately, many people assume that their cognitive strengths, weaknesses, and even their whole intellectual potential can be represented by an IQ number. When debriefing the patient, the examiner/consultant can avoid supporting this belief by explaining that the FSIQ is an "estimate" of a person's abilities. In addition, the examiner may describe the patient's FSIQ as (1) a percentile rank score (see Appendix 5.1), (2) a verbal descriptor (see Table 9 in the WAIS-R manual), and (3) a value existing somewhere within a selected confidence

---

[3]This summary is adapted from Groth-Marnat, G. (1990). *Handbook of psychological assessment* (2nd ed.), pp. 130–134. New York: Wiley. Copyright 1990 by John Wiley and Sons, Inc. Adapted by permission of the publisher.

interval (see Appendix 5.2). For example, there was a 95% probability that B. W.'s "true" FSIQ score lay somewhere between 91 and 101. Her percentile rank was 39 (Appendix 5.1), and her intellectual classification description was "average" (Wechsler, 1981, Table 9, p. 28). B. W.'s examiner made the following comments:

EXAMINER: Well, B. W., how well do you think you did on the WAIS-R?

B. W.: I think that I have a really high IQ. What did the test say?

EXAMINER: The test results do not match your self-evaluation completely. Let's start with a general description of your intellectual abilities and then look more closely at your strengths and weaknesses. According to the WAIS-R results, your intellectual abilities are considered to be "average," and your Full Scale score is higher than 39 out of 100 people in your age group.

B. W.: Oh, I thought that I would be better than "average."

EXAMINER: Frankly, "average" is not a very useful term. It doesn't tell us anything about what you do well. It does suggest that you have the same intellectual resources as a typical member of your age group. We will be able to identify your *unique* abilities when we look at your performance on the subtests.

B. W.: Okay, but what's my IQ?

EXAMINER: Unfortunately, intellectual assessment is not a perfect science. There is no way for me or any other consultant to obtain an exact measure of your intellectual abilities. There is a certain amount of measurement error in every IQ estimate. Therefore, I cannot give you a single score that represents your pure intellectual ability. A single score would not be accurate, because we don't know how much error has been included. I can say that there is a 95% probability that your true score is somewhere between 91 and 101.

B. W.: I think that my IQ is higher than that. That test is way off.

EXAMINER: Let's look at your scores on the Verbal and Performance subtests, and you'll see that *some* of the test results match your perceptions of *some* of your abilities better than others. Remember that everyone has both strengths *and* weaknesses. It is very unusual to have all strengths and *no* weaknesses.

Level IIa: Verbal and Performance IQs

Groth-Marnat (1990, p. 130) describes the VIQ as "an index of the person's verbal comprehensive abilities." The Verbal scales assess an individual's proficiency in the following areas (Groth-Marnat, 1990, p. 135):

1. The ability to work with abstract symbols
2. The amount and degree of benefit a person has received from his or her educational background
3. Verbal memory abilities
4. Verbal fluency

PIQ is "an estimate of one's perceptual organizational abilities" (Groth-Marnat, 1990, p. 130). The Performance scales reflect the following (Groth-Marnat, 1990, p. 139):

1. The individual's degree and quality of nonverbal contact with the environment
2. The ability to integrate perceptual stimuli with relevant motor responses
3. The capacity to work in concrete situations
4. The ability to work quickly

When documenting WAIS-R results, the examiner can discourage the reification of scores by converting the VIQ and PIQ to percentile ranks (Appendix 5.1) and verbal descriptors (Wechsler, 1981, Table 9), and by presenting any reported numerical scores as ranges (see Appendix 5.2).

The VIQ–PIQ difference is the first investigative step of a WAIS-R interpretation. Across all nine age groups, an average VIQ–PIQ discrepancy of 10 to 12 points is required for statistical significance at $p = .05$. A difference of 13 or more points is required to reach a $p = .01$ level of significance (Sattler, 1992, Table C-26, p. 841; see also Kaufman, 1990, Table 9.1, p. 264, for differences required per age group). Differences of 15 or more points warrant further cognitive, personality, or neuropsychological testing (Groth-Marnat, 1990), but a clinician should be aware that differences of this magnitude are not unusual. Twenty percent of the WAIS-R and 25% of the WISC-R standardization samples reported differences of this size (F. M. Grossman, 1983; Kaufman, 1976, 1979). Differences of 25 or more points are highly suggestive of the operation of some kind of pathology (Groth-Marnat, 1990).

Nonintellective factors, such as attentional ability and motivation, may contribute to VIQ–PIQ discrepancies. It is important to consider these factors when interpreting WAIS-R results. The incidence of VIQ–PIQ discrepancies does not seem to be related to age (Matarazzo & Herman, 1985) or gender (Matarazzo, Bornstein, McDermott, & Noonan, 1986), but does relate to FSIQ (Matarazzo & Herman, 1985). Individuals with IQs below 90 are less likely to produce VIQ–PIQ discrepancies of 9 or more points than individuals with IQs over 110 (Matarazzo & Herman, 1985). Large discrepancies are also more likely to occur for individuals from higher as opposed to lower socioeconomic groups (Kaufman, 1990). It is essential that the test interpreter examine the base rate for the patient's intellectual and socioeconomic group (Kaufman, 1990) before interpreting a discrepancy between VIQ and PIQ.

The direction of the discrepancy (VIQ > PIQ vs. PIQ > VIQ) has different meanings for individuals with varying personal and situational characteristics. Significantly higher VIQ than PIQ scores are associated with higher levels of education (Bornstein, Suga, & Prifitera, 1987; Kaufman, 1990); psychomotor retardation because of depression; a conscientious, deliberate approach to problem solving that hinders quick responding; or an overly eager response style that produces errors on timed Performance tests (Groth-Marnat, 1990), but does not affect Verbal tests, where multiple impulsive responses may eventually produce the correct answer. Higher PIQ than VIQ scores are frequently observed among those with poor educational backgrounds (Bornstein et al., 1987), keen perceptual and organizational abilities, an ability to cope with the stress induced by timed tests, low socioeconomic background (Matarazzo & Herman, 1985), language deficiency, problems with auditory conceptualization, and an ability to solve novel problems without the benefit of an extensive amount of accumulated knowledge (Groth-Marnat, 1990).

Level IIb: Factor Scores

WAIS (Wechsler, 1955) and WAIS-R (Wechsler, 1981) factor structures have been investigated thoroughly (see Atkinson et al., 1990, and Hill, Reddon, & Jackson, 1985, for reviews) and are considered stable across samples (Waller & Waldman, 1990), test administrations, statistical procedures, and time (Atkinson, 1991).

The number of factors and the composition of the factor structure are topics of tremendous debate. Factorial studies have produced single-factor structures (O'Grady, 1983; Silverstein, 1982b), two-factor structures (Ryan, Rosenberg, & DeWolfe, 1984; Siegert, Patten, Taylor, & McCormick, 1988), and three-factor solutions (Atkinson & Cyr, 1984; Beck et al., 1985; Parker, 1983; Tellegen & Briggs, 1967). A widely accepted version of the WAIS-R structure, as noted earlier, is represented by a three-factor solution: Verbal Comprehension, Perceptual Organization, and Freedom from Distractibility (Groth-Marnat, 1990; Kaufman, 1990; Leckliter, Matarazzo, & Silverstein, 1986; Sattler, 1992). Some evidence suggests that a two-factor solution (Verbal Comprehension and Perceptual Organization only) might best describe the factor-analytic structure of responses made both by examinees aged 70 to 74 years (Waller & Waldman, 1990) and by mental health patients (Piedmont et al., 1992). Waller and Waldman (1990) have hypothesized that the Freedom from Distractibility factor plays a nonsignificant role in response formation for the oldest standardization group because of age-related deterioration in memory and attention—factors that may also account for the findings among distressed mental health patients. In these groups, the variance of scores that measure concentration and distress may be very narrow, which complicates interpretation.

The Verbal Comprehension factor provides an estimate of the patient's overall verbal ability (Groth-Marnat, 1990). This factor is derived from four subtests—Information, Vocabulary, Comprehension, and Similarities (Groth-Marnat, 1990; Kaufman, 1990). Similarities is occasionally excluded from factor-analytic results, because it periodically fails to make a significant unique contribution to the explanation of variance (Leckliter et al., 1986).

The Perceptual Organization factor is used to estimate the patient's perceptual abilities (Groth-Marnat, 1990). This factor is comprised of the Picture Completion, Block Design, and Object Assembly subtests. Picture Arrangement is excluded from this triad because it is only weakly related to the construct of perceptual organization.

The Freedom from Distractibility factor is the most difficult to interpret among most examinees, except for relatively young and nondistressed persons. It is related to an individual's ability to attend, concentrate, engage in sequential cognitive processing, remember information, and avoid internal distractions produced by anxiety (Groth-Marnat, 1990). The Freedom from Distractibility factor is derived from the Arithmetic and Digit Span subtests. Digit Symbol is only weakly related to the latent variable of Freedom from Distractibility and is therefore excluded from interpretation as part of this construct.

The two "maverick" subtests, Picture Arrangement and Digit Symbol, can be considered to measure unique abilities (Kaufman, 1990). Picture Arrangement loads equally well on both the Verbal Comprehension and Perceptual Organization dimensions. Digit Symbol is not strongly related to any one construct (Kaufman, 1990). Picture Arrangement is thought to measure "anticipation of consequences, planning ability, temporal sequencing, and time concepts" (Kaufman, 1990, p. 405). Digit Symbol is thought to measure "ability to follow directions, clerical speed and accuracy, paper-and-pencil skill, psychomotor speed, and visual short-term memory" (Kaufman, 1990, p. 411).

Standardized factor scores for each of the three factors can be computed by following the procedures outlined in Atkinson (1991), Kaufman (1990, Table 13.6, p. 435), or Sattler (1992, Table C-28, p. 842). Factor scores are useful in the development of hypotheses about the patient's cognitive strengths and weaknesses. Appendix 5.3 contains a list of such hypotheses.

Level III: Variability within Subscales

The patient's verbal strengths and weaknesses can be further assessed by comparing the age-corrected scaled score of each Verbal subtest with the Verbal age-corrected scaled score mean (Groth-Marnat, 1990; Sattler, 1992). Likewise, the patient's nonverbal assets and deficits can be appraised by comparing the age-corrected scaled score of each Performance subtest with the Performance age-corrected scaled score mean (Groth-Marnat, 1990; Sattler, 1992).

Appendix 5.4 provides critical values for the differences required for significance when each age-corrected scaled score is compared to the age-corrected means of the Verbal, Performance, and Full Scale scores. The absolute values of these differences vary according to the reliability of the subtest. For example, Object Assembly is a notoriously unreliable measure of nonverbal ability ($r = .68$) and requires a deviation of 4.10 to reach a $p = .01$ level of significance, whereas Vocabulary is solidly reliable ($r = .96$) and requires a deviation of only 2.11 to reach a $p = .01$ level of significance (Groth-Marnat, 1990; Sattler, 1992, p. 842). For those clinicians who are unaccustomed to the use to sophisticated tables, Kaufman (1979, 1990) recommends that a difference of 3 points above or below the age-corrected scaled score mean be considered significant.

An assessment of patients' *strengths* can be derived from an inspection of those age-corrected subtest scores that are significantly greater than the age-corrected Verbal, Performance, or Full Scale age-corrected means. Conversely, patients' *weaknesses* are reflected in those subtests that are significantly below those same means. An examiner must keep in mind that these analyses of strengths and weaknesses only provide hypotheses about a patient's abilities; the examiner must seek out evidence from other sources to test the veracity and generalizability of these hypotheses. Other sources of information may include scholastic records, occupational performance evaluations, background information, medical history, presenting complaints, the clinical interview, and other kinds of psychological testing (neuropsychological, personality, career, achievement, etc.). The process of profile analysis resembles detective work (Kaufman, 1990). Each piece of information is used by the clinician to substantiate or falsify hypotheses about the patient's characteristics and conditions.

It is essential that the clinician consider the patient's testing behavior, background, and a variety of test-taking influences as he/she formulates hypotheses about the patient's relative strengths and weaknesses (Kaufman, 1990). Influences that might affect a patient's performance on a variety of subtests are catalogued in Appendix 5.5. For example, a foreign language background *may* impair performance on Information and Vocabulary subtests. The clinician must evaluate the patient's level of acculturation or familiarity with concepts, people, and events that are part of the two subtests and of the majority culture in the United States.

Profile analysis should be conducted with caution. A clinician should not form a hypothesis based on the results of only one subtest (Kaufman, 1990), because it is likely that any single result contains a considerable amount of measurement error. Kaufman advises the clinician to refer to Tables 14.1, 14.2, and 14.3 of his 1990 book to identify abilities that are reflected in two or more subtests. Kaufman (1990) then suggests that the examiner compare *groupings* of subtests in order to identify the person's relative strengths and weaknesses.

Level IV: Intersubtest Variability

Intersubtest scatter can be assessed by comparing each subtest age-corrected scale score with the mean of all 11 age-corrected scaled scores (Groth-Marnat, 1990; Sattler, 1992) (see Appendix 5.4 for differences required for significance). The caveats that we have reviewed above for interpreting within-scale scatter also apply to the interpretation of intersubtest scatter (Groth-Marnat, 1990).

Level V: Intrasubtest Variability

An additional source of hypotheses regarding the patient's strengths and weaknesses can be found through an examination of intrasubtest variability. The items within each subtest are designed to become more difficult as the examinee progresses through them (Wechsler, 1981). Typically, an examinee responds to questions until a designated number of consecutive failures is achieved. Examinees who fail items in an inconsistent pattern may be highly distractible, overly anxious, or purposely malingering. Sporadic responding should be explored further (Groth-Marnat, 1990). Testing the limits (as described earlier) is recommended.

Level VI: Qualitative Analyses

Used alone, the Wechsler scales are poor tools for psychiatric diagnosis (Matarazzo, 1972). Intensive research on the diagnostic power of the original WAIS led to the conclusion that none of the WAIS IQ scores, scale scores, profile patterns, scale deviations, or other statistical indices could consistently differentiate schizophrenic from other psychiatric and normal populations (Matarazzo, 1972). The WAIS-R seems to offer greater validity and reliability than did the WAIS for differential psychiatric diagnosis when broad categories (i.e., affective vs. psychotic disorders) are considered (Kaufman, 1990; Piedmont, Sokolove, & Fleming, 1989). The WAIS-R can help clinicians understand some of the perceptual and cognitive dysfunctions (Zillmer, Ball, Fowler, Newman, & Stutts, 1991) that accompany certain psychiatric disorders (e.g., cognitive "integrity" and schizophrenia) (Feinberg & McIlvried, 1991).

More research is needed to understand the relationship between the WAIS-R and particular psychiatric diagnoses, because of the complex variability of performance that characterizes patients within any psychiatric grouping. The patient's VIQ, PIQ, intra- and intersubtest scatter, item content, and background all need to be integrated in order for an accurate assessment to be made (Piedmont et al., 1989).

Without corroboration of test results from other sources, the WAIS and WAIS-R are inappropriate methods for diagnosing mental and emotional states associated with functional psychiatric problems (Russell, 1987), but they are a fertile source of information about the content of the patient's mentation, the patient's interpersonal style, and his/her coping strategies. The content and manner in which the patient responds can reveal characteristics of the patient's diagnostic condition, such as psychotic features (e.g., "clang" associations, evidence of delusions), aggressive tendencies (e.g., oppositional testing behavior, violent content in responses), and paranoia (e.g., suspiciousness, cautious responding) (Blatt & Allison, 1981; Groth-Marnat, 1990; Matarazzo, 1972).

Types of responses that are suggestive of various psychiatric conditions are included in our presentation of the Wechsler subscales (see Table 5.3, below). Much of this information is based on "clinical lore" rather than empirical evidence. Indeed, empirical efforts to verify an association between test scores and broad diagnostic categories (e.g., "schizophrenic," "anxious," and "neurotic") have produced inconsistent results (Matarazzo, 1972; Kaufman, 1990). We recommend that examiners pursue hypotheses that have a foundation in multiple data bases.

Matarazzo (1972) has described psychological assessment as an "art" (p. 507). As an "artisan," the examiner is not completely objective and unbiased in his/her view of the patient. The examiner's values, cultural history, theoretical stance, educational experiences, and personal and professional views will influence even the most structured interactions with the patient. As a psychological "detective" and hypothesis builder, a clinician must strive to be conscious of his/her intrapersonal influences as he/she begins to form a picture of the patient's problem and devises steps to ameliorate those problems.

Subtests

Comprehensive descriptions of the WAIS-R (Wechsler, 1981) subtests are available in Groth-Marnat (1990), Kaufman (1990), Sattler (1992), and Sprandel (1985). Table 5.3 is a catalog of subtest interpretations adapted from these four sources, plus, where relevant, information from Matarazzo (1972) and Blatt and Allison (1981) has been added. Table 5.3 can be used as a starting point for test interpretation and hypothesis building. We recommend that the original sources serve as a foundation for more extensive profile analysis.

TABLE 5.3. Descriptions of the WAIS-R Subtests

Subtest	Empirical analysis	High and low scores[a]	Clinical analysis	Neuropsychological analysis[b]	Extratest influences
Information (I) Measures general knowledge base; facts and dates, over-learned material; crystallized intelligence and retrieval. Correlated with FSIQ and educational level. Requires attention, long-term memory (LTM), and verbal responding.	g loading: $r = .81$. Highest r is with V, $r = .81$. Lowest r is with OA, $r = .39$. *Reliability:* split-half $= .89$, test-retest $(r_{tt}) = .91$. *Percent of variance:* VC = 56%, PO = 7%, FD = 9%, Other = 17%, Specificity = 20%*, g = 67%, Error = 11%.[c]	High scores suggest high level of verbal comprehension, ability to learn and recall facts, adequate schooling. Low scores suggest lack of educational/cultural opportunities, difficulty retaining or recalling learned material, anxiety, narrow range of interests.	Bizarre responses suggest schizophrenia, psychopathology, or manic–depressive diagnoses. Explore patterns of pass–fail and content of responses. Observe speed of responding; may suggest impulsive or overcontrolled coping style. Note subject's (S's) reaction to failure and need for reinforcement from examiner (E).	Resistant to brain damage. Test the limits to identify source of errors, if cerebral dysfunction suspected. Low scores for highly educated, acculturated, or U.S.-born Ss suggest left-hemisphere damage. Rule out (R/O) temporal lobe epilepsy.	Quality and extent of education, cultural background, specific interests, foreign language, learning disabilities, literary interest, early environment.
Digit Span (DSp) An auditory short-term memory (STM) task. Measures fluid intelligence and retrieval. Requires attention, concentration, encoding, STM, recall, sequencing, and vocalization.	g loading: $r = .62, .71$ for African-Americans. Highest r is with A, $r = .56$. Lowest r is with OA, $r = .33$. *Reliability:* $r_{tt} = .83$. *Percent of variance:* VC = 9%, PO = 5%, FD = 41%, Other = 28%, Specificity = 45%*, g = 38%, Error = 17%.	High scores suggest good attention, retention, and recall; use of auditory mnemonics or visual imagery; freedom from distractibility; comfort with numbers and sequencing tasks. Low scores suggest problems with attention, concentration,	Test limits and identify source of errors. For normal adults, digits forward (DF) exceeds digits backward (DB) by 1 point. Aberrations from this are meaningful. How well did S focus and attend? Ask Ss to describe their mnemonic strategies. Note S's	DF resistant to dementia, DB more sensitive to diffuse cerebral damage. Suspect brain dysfunction if DF more than 5 points greater than DB or if DB score is 3 or less. DF/DB *span* is more predictive of brain damage than the *scores*. DF and DB	Not a valid indicator of IQ if S is hearing-impaired. State anxiety, attention span, numerical sequencing ability, auditory discrimination, improper testing conditions, distractibility, learning disabilities, and negativism affect performance.

150

Subtest	g loading; Reliability; Percent of variance	Score interpretation	Interpretive suggestions	Clinical/neuropsychological notes	Influences on scores
		memory, verbal production, cognitive manipulations; anxiety.	anecdotal comments. Intrusive thoughts and preoccupations affect scores.	sensitive to left-brain damage; DF sensitive to right-brain defects and visual impairment.	
Vocabulary (V) Measures acquired knowledge, verbal comprehension, and expressive language skills; crystallized intelligence. Requires attention, auditory and visual perception, LTM, abstraction, and verbal expression. Best measure of g.	g loading: $r = .86$ (best subtest). Highest r is with I, $r = .81$. Lowest r is with OA, $r = .42$. *Reliability:* split-half $= .96$, $r_{tt} = .92$. *Percent of variance:* VC $= 66\%$, PO $= 7\%$, FD $= 12\%$, Other $= 11\%$, Specificity $= 19\%*$, $g = 64\%$, Error $= 4\%$.	High scores suggest good vocabulary, early environment, education, LTM, verbal expression, and intellectual interest. Low scores suggest heavy use of colloquialisms; lack of educational and cultural experiences; and psychological problems, if responses laden with personal and/or bizarre references. Repressive coping style hinders acquisition and recall of words.	Length and quality of response can reveal cognitive style. Note precision or verbosity. Attend to S's language skills. Are responses concrete or abstract? Study progression of 0-, 1-, and 2-point responses. Any patterns? Examine errors for apparent source. Examine content of responses for personal issues. Beware of overelaboration, overinclusion, ellipsis,[d] self-reference,[c] and perseveration.	Resistant to psychopathology and neurological deficits. Good estimate of premorbid IQ. Slightly sensitive to left-hemisphere lesions. Ss with cerebral damage may tire due to length of administration. Good subtest for differentiating brain damage from thought disorders. Latter indicated by bizarre responses, "clang" associations, idiosyncratic or confabulatory responses.	Cultural and educational experiences, foreign language, outside reading, S's occupation, willingness to risk, reading ability, early environment. Speech deficits may hinder productivity of response, which affects scores.
Arithmetic (A) Measures numerical reasoning; the ability to analyze a problem, select the correct method for computation, mentally per-	g loading: $r = .75$. Highest r is with V, $r = .63$, and I, $r = .61$. Lowest r is with OA, $r = .42$. *Reliability:* split-half $= .84$, $r_{tt} = .85$.	High scores suggest comfort and skill with numbers, good numerical STM, ability to solve problems, math skills, ability to concentrate,	Attend to how S responds to being timed. Assess S's distress level. Are errors due to perceptual, attentional, cognitive, communication, or	Administer item 1 to Ss with suspected brain dysfunction to evaluate their response to visual stimuli. Ss with memory deficits will	Attention span, distractibility, anxiety, concentration, learning disabilities, vocational history, math anxiety, schooling, and response to timing.

(continued)

151

TABLE 5.3. (Continued)

Subtest	Empirical analysis	High and low scores[a]	Clinical analysis	Neuropsychological analysis[b]	Extratest influences
form the arithmetic operation, and express the correct response; retrieval. Requires knowledge of addition, subtraction, multiplication, and division, as well as STM for problem solving. Also requires attention and concentration; ability to extract pertinent information from what is provided.	*Percent of variance:* VC = 19%, PO = 12%, FD = 30%, Other = 23%, Specificity = 30%*, *g* = 58%, Error = 16%.	freedom from distractibility. Low scores suggest possible lack of math education, state or math-related anxiety, poor STM and recall, difficulty in problem solving, attentional deficits, distractibility.	mathematical deficits? Test the limits by providing ample time and paper and pencil. Note S's remarks. Missing early items suggests inadequate living skills. If DSp is high and A is low, problem may be lack of concentration, not attention.	have depressed scores that are not indicative of their math ability. Oral format prevents discovery of figure or number alexia. Low scores associated with left- and right-hemisphere damage.	
Comprehension (C) Measures social judgment and concept formation, social intelligence, verbal comprehension and conceptualization; fluid and crystallized intelligence. Requires knowledge and acceptance of social mores, high-level reasoning, understanding of	*g* loading; *r* = .78. Highest *r* is with V, *r* = .74. Lowest *r* is with OA, *r* = .40. *Reliability:* split-half = .84, r_{tt} = .80. *Percent of variance:* VC = 50%, PO = 9%, FD = 7%, Other = 18%, Specificity = 23%*, *g* = 61%, Error = 16%.	High scores suggest high levels of verbal comprehension and general intelligence, good common sense, abstract thinking; S has and can apply knowledge of social conventions. Good problem-solving abilities, especially in a novel context. Social conventionality, conformity.	Responses reveal S's world view, coping style, personality, attitude toward society. Also assesses S's ability to think and respond coherently to ambiguous cultural situations. Maladjustment depresses scores. Responses may indicate areas of conflict or emotionality.	Very sensitive to left-hemisphere lesions. Good measure of premorbid intelligence for right-hemisphere, bilateral, and diffuse brain lesions. Right-hemisphere-damaged Ss may score well, but act impetuously.	Limited social experience and cultural or educational opportunities, rejection of social customs, and negativism can depress scores. Ability to understand and express abstract concepts moderates scores. Social knowledge may have been gained through vicari-

152

cause-and-effect relationships, audition, attention, LTM, and STM.		Low scores suggest low levels of verbal ability; lack of knowledge of or rejection of social convention; possible confusion in ambiguous situations; inhibition by trait anxiety; impaired judgment.	Convergent problem-solving style rewarded. Test limits to determine true levels of understanding. For low scores or unusual responses, R/O schizophrenia and antisocial personality.		ous means. S's personal experiences may be part of response.
Similarities (S) Measures verbal comprehension, concept formation and fluency, ability to see relationships, ability to classify auditory stimuli, crystallized and fluid intelligence. Requires audition, LTM, abstraction, categorization, verbal expression. Related to general intelligence. Typically, four levels of concept formation exhibited by Ss: (1) no recognition of similarity, (2) concrete descriptive similarity, (3) functional similarity, and (4) abstraction.	g loading: r = .79, r = .86 for African-Americans. Highest r is with V, r = .72. Lowest r is with DSp, r = .45. *Reliability:* Split-half = .84, r_{tt} = .84. *Percent of variance:* VC = 45%, PO = 13%, FD = 7%, Other = 19%, Specificity = 24%*, g = 62%, Error = 16%.	High scores suggest ability to classify, generalize, comprehend, and discriminate essential from trivial attributes. Low scores suggest lack of cultural and educational experiences; low intelligence; problems with LTM, classification; concrete thinking.	Note content of responses and comments. Observe progression of responses—from concrete to abstract, or mixed? Mixed responding suggests disordered thinking or guessing. Observe reactions to failure. Early items can be answered by rote. Look at later responses to discern level of abstraction used. Note bizarre, overinclusive, or overelaborate responding. Watch for self-referents; content may reveal clinical issues. Scores depressed by psychopathology.	Poverty of 2-point responses associated with brain dysfunction. Scores sensitive to left-hemisphere lesions. Low scores not associated with right frontal lobe damage.	General intelligence, cultural and educational opportunities, range of interests, outside reading, and occupation. Negativism, inflexible concrete thinking can depress scores.

(continued)

153

TABLE 5.3. (Continued)

Subtest	Empirical analysis	High and low scores[a]	Clinical analysis	Neuropsychological analysis[b]	Extratest influences
Picture Completion (PC) Measures visual acuity, discrimination, and judgment. Ss must distinguish essential from nonessential components and observe inconsistencies, nonverbal and fluid intelligence. Requires attention, perception, concentration, LTM, visual closure, decision making, and verbal or nonverbal communication.	g loading: $r = .70$. Highest r is with V, $r = .55$; S, $r = .54$; BD, $r = .54$. Lowest r is with DSp, $r = .37$. *Reliability:* Split-half $= .81$, $r_{tt} = .88$. *Percent of variance:* VC = 19%, PO = 31%, FD = 3%, Other = 28% Specificity = 34%*, $g = 37$%, Error = 19%.	High scores suggest good visual imagery, perception, and memory; ability to concentrate and use LTM to recall and select correct response. Low scores suggest poor concentration and poor visual acuity and organization; intrusive thoughts; lack of experience with test stimuli; impulsivity.	Bizarre, confabulatory responses or more than two responses that have no obvious relevance to the stimulus are pathognomonic (e.g., "hand is missing" for pitcher item). If Ss say "nothing is missing" this suggests negativity, hostility. First timed subtest. Note response, response rate. Subtest reveals S's contact with reality.	Very resilient to effects of brain damage; may measure premorbid intelligence; good subtest for Ss with verbal production problems. If visual agnosia suspected, test is unrepresentative of S's abilities.	Attention, visual acuity, anxiety, concentration, cognitive style (field dependence or independence), negativism, and willingness to risk when uncertain about correct response influence scores.
Picture Arrangement (PA) A nonverbal reasoning test that measures S's ability to comprehend and evaluate a whole situation. Measures social intelligence and logical sequencing abilities,	g loading: $r = .63$. Highest r is with PC, $r = .51$; V, $r = .51$; I, $r = .50$; S, $r = .50$. Lowest r is with DSp, $r = .37$, and DSym, $r = .39$. *Reliability:* split-half $= .74$, $r_{tt} = .72$. *Percent of variance:*	High scores suggest ability to recognize elements in a social interaction, anticipate consequences of acts, and arrange elements logically; high level of social intelligence; ability to perceive and understand the mean-	Note S's strategy—random or orderly manipulation of cards? Invite Ss to verbalize stories after completing all subtests. Note content and construction of sequences. Responses to items 2, 8, and 10	Sensitive to brain damage, especially to right anterior temporal lobe. Frontal lobe damage obfuscates the response. Place cards vertically for some visually impaired Ss. Low PA, BD, and OA scores	Scores can be depressed by unfamiliarity with majority culture in United States, depression, distractibility, poor visual acuity, or poor motor coordination. Exposure to comic strips, ability to work when

fluid intelligence. Requires visual and auditory processing, visual organization, logical and sequential thought, motor activity, and humor. Ability to anticipate consequences of social interactions.	VC = 18%, PO = 18%, FD = 5%, Other = 33%, Specificity = 35%*, g = 26%.	ing of a series of social exchanges; knowledge of social customs in majority culture of the United States. Low scores suggest lack of experience in majority culture of United States, lack of social skills, low IQ, poor organizational abilities, depression.	good stimuli for content. Note S's response to being timed. Conduct error analysis—any patterns? With low scores, R/O poor visual acuity. Scores seriously depressed by psychopathology.	associated with right-hemisphere lesions.	timed, and broad social knowledge may enhance scores.
Block Design (BD) Measures ability to analyze and synthesize two- and three-dimensional information, fluid intelligence, nonverbal abstract concept formation, recognition of part-whole relationships, visual-motor coordination. Relatively culture-free measure of intelligence. Highly correlated with g. Requires visual perception, analysis, and integration, a solution-focused strategy, concentration, and motor response.	g loading; r = .72 (best Performance scale), r = .67 for African-Americans. Highest r is with OA, r = .63. Lowest r is with DSp, r = .43. *Reliability:* Split-half = .87, r_{tt} = .86. *Percent of variance:* VC = 7%, PO = 48%, FD = 11%, Other = 21%, Specificity = 32%*, g = 53%, Error = 13%.	High scores suggest good visual–spatial–motor processing, nonverbal reasoning, and perceptual organization; high IQ; ability to synthesize and understand relationships among parts. Low scores suggest limited IQ, perceptual or visual problems, perceptual-organizational deficiencies, and poor concentration.	Note strategy used to duplicate pattern—random, organized, deliberate, compulsive, flexible? Trial and error or mental visualization before solving? How do Ss respond to novelty of the task? Note S's response to failure—persist or quit? What is response when 9 blocks introduced, when last (rotated) template is given? Analyze errors. Note bizarre solutions (stacking, lack of closure).	Testing the limits can reveal visual perception problems. Test limits with brain-damaged Ss. Test is sensitive to any kind of cerebral dysfunction, especially right parietal lesions. Errors associated with left-hemisphere damage include missing small details, confusion, simplification; for right-hemisphere damage: design distortions, misperceptions.	Perceptual problems, cognitive style, response to timing, anxiety, distractibility, compulsiveness, and occupational/educational background affect scores.

(continued)

155

TABLE 5.3. (Continued)

Subtest	Empirical analysis	High and low scores[a]	Clinical analysis	Neuropsychological analysis[b]	Extratest influences
Object Assembly (OA) Measures ability to analyze and synthesize parts into a whole, fluid intelligence. Requires visual–motor coordination, perceptual organization, identification of the object being formed, and perseverance.	g loading: $r = .61$. Highest r is with BD, $r = .63$. Lowest r is with DSp, $r = .33$. *Reliability:* Split-half = .68, $r_{tt} = .70$. *Percent of variance:* VC = 4%, PO = 53%, FD = 3%, Other = 8%, Specificity = 23%[+], g = 38%, Error = 32%.	High scores suggest superior analytic and synthetic abilities; good perceptual–motor coordination and visual organization; flexible approach to problems. Low scores suggest inhibitory anxiety, visual–motor disorganization, lack of analytic and synthetic abilities. *Note:* All scores should be interpreted with caution because of relatively low levels of reliability and specificity.	Note S's strategy–trial and error, mental imaging, random rotation? Observe S's reaction to failure or difficulty. Is S careful, logical, impulsive, deliberate? Watch for affect. How does S react to E's use of screen to set up task? Compulsivity, rigidity, anxiety, distractibility can depress scores. Observe S's response to the Hand (no clues drawn in).	Scores severely depressed in brain-damaged patients, such as those with posterior lesions in right-hemisphere, frontal lobe damage. Right posterior damage associated with disorganized assembly and lack of recognition until object is complete. Left-hemisphere damage associated with errors of detail. Conduct an error analysis—any patterns?	Trait anxiety and stress from being timed, physical disabilities, motor problems, carelessness, and distractibility can lower scores. Willingness to risk, cognitive style and flexibility, and experience with puzzles also moderate scores.
Digit Symbol (DSym) Measures visual–motor speed and coordination, ability to learn a novel task quickly, associative learning. Requires attention, concentra-	g loading: $r = .59$ (worst subtest), $r = .70$ for African-Americans. Highest r is with BD, $r = .47$; V, $r = .47$; S, $r = .46$; A, $r = .45$. Lowest r is with OA, $r = .38$, and PA, $r = .39$.	High scores suggest good reading and writing skills, adaptability when faced with novel task, visual–motor dexterity, perceptual organization, quick learning, persistence.	*Hypotheses:* Low DSym compared to V: depression. Low DSp and high DSym: anxiety expressed in activity. High DSp and low DSym: depression. Psychomo-	Best indicator of cerebral impairment; insensitive to site of lesion. Symbol orientation errors suggest right-hemisphere damage.	Performance relatively nondependent on previous learning. Content of task is neutral. Anxiety, clerical ability, occupational history, STM, and eye-hand coordi-

tion, coordination, visual acuity, STM, and ability to work when timed. Aided by facility with numbers.

Reliability: r_{tt} = .82.
Percent of variance: VC = 10%, PO = 14%, FD = 13%, Other = 45%, Specificity = 48%*, g = 36%, Error = 18%.

Low scores suggest visual problems, debilitating anxiety, diminished associative learning ability, inattention.

tor slowing suggests depression and schizophrenia. R/O visual problems. Assess S's learning facility; after exam, see how many pairs memorized. Scores depressed by illiteracy; left-handers may block key. Watch for compulsive coding, changes in response rate (fatigue, boredom).

nation can moderate scores.

---

[a]Meaning of high and low scores from Groth-Marnat (1990, pp. 134–143) and Sprandel (1985, pp. 63–116).
[b]Neuropsychological analysis from Kaufman (1990, pp. 393–412) and Groth-Marnat (1990, pp. 134–143).
[c]VC, Verbal Comprehension factor; PO, Perceptual Organization factor; FD, Freedom from Distractibility factor; Other, other abilities; Specificity, subtest specificity (*, adequate; †, inadequate).
[d]Ellipsis is "the omission of words, such as defining breakfast as 'eggs and toast'" (Kaufman, 1990, p. 397).
[e]Matarazzo (1972, pp. 487–489) lists examples of aberrant responses.
[f]See Sprandel (1985, pp. 104–105) for interpretations of a sample of Ss' responses.

The following tables from Kaufman (1990) will be particularly useful to clinicians as they develop interpretive hypotheses: Tables 14.1 (abilities shared by two or more WAIS-R Verbal subtests), 14.2 (abilities shared by two or more Performance subtests), and 14.3 (abilities shared by two or more Performance or Verbal subtests). Kaufman's Table 14.4 (influences likely to affect scores on two or more Verbal or Performance subtests) is reprinted here as Appendix 5.5.

Hypothesis Building

The principal goals of a WAIS-R administration are threefold: (1) to assess current and/or premorbid levels of intelligence, (2) to test or generate hypotheses about the presence of organic brain dysfunction and psycho-pathological conditions, and (3) to make predictions as to how these conditions will affect the patient's response to treatment.

The clinician's decision-making process of diagnosis and treatment selection should follow the patient's progress through treatment. Highlen and Hill (1984) have described a patient's phenomenological experience of therapy as a spiral movement forward and upward, then backward and upward. As a patient make gains in therapy, he/she has the perception of forward movement. With this perception of improvement comes an even greater awareness of all the "work" that needs to be done, and the patient often experiences the emergence of this unexpected work as backsliding.

The process of clinical assessment, diagnosis, and treatment formulation is just as cyclical. The therapist must continually adapt treatment to accommodate the patient's newly discovered strengths and needs. The assessment process does not end with an initial diagnosis. Assessment also guides treatment selection and aids in the development of mediating treatment goals. Repeated assessments stimulate treatment reformulations and serve as measures of therapeutic progress.

Diagnostic Hypotheses

Some of the most expedient assessment procedures available to clinicians today lead to the nominal categorization of a patient's symptom composition or personality (e.g., the Structured Clinical Interview for DSM-III-R [SCID], the Minnesota Multiphasic Personality Inventory [MMPI]). These approaches are attractive because they can appear to provide a baffled assessor with the "answers" to fundamental questions about a patient's condition. Unfortunately, taken out of context, these instruments are a hazard because they can lead to faulty conclusions about the patient's psychological state. The handiest assessment tools are best used as part of a testing package that includes a keen clinical interview and an open-ended approach to hypothesis building.

A diagnostic tool like the DSM-III-R is a useful method for organizing one's perceptions of a patient's psychological condition. However, over-reliance on a nonprescriptive categorical system, such as the DSM-III-R, can lead to a fractionated and incomplete view of the patient and his/her treatment needs (Beutler & Clarkin, 1990). The DSM-III-R emphasizes patient weakness and ignores the context in which the patient's problems emerged. An integrative model of assessment (Beutler & Clarkin, 1990) goes beyond the nosological categorization of patient symptoms and includes a thorough evaluation of patient predisposing variables. These variables include the patient's complaints, personal characteristics (e.g., expectations, coping ability, and personality), and his/her environment and circumstances (e.g., environmental stressors and resources).

The WAIS-R can provide information on many of these dimensions, if the clinician is thorough, attentive, and thoughtful in his/her administration. Specifically, the WAIS-R can be used to make differential diagnoses of the patient's symptoms. For example, deficits in visual organization can be differentiated from problems with visual–motor coordination by comparing the patient's performance on Picture Completion and Picture Arrangement with that on the visual–motor triad of Block Design, Object Assembly, and Digit Symbol (Kaufman, 1990).

Likewise, estimates of premorbid intelligence are generally not accurate when they are based solely on patient demographic variables (Silverstein, 1987). Premorbid intelligence may be estimated by evaluating the strength of the patient's performance on the Information and Vocabulary subtests. Scores on these subtests are based on overlearned material that is resistant to the effects of brain injury or severe psychopathology (Blatt & Allison, 1968; Kaufman, 1990; Maloney & Ward, 1976).

Finally, the patient's expectations, coping strategies, and environmental stressors can be detected by inviting a patient to verbalize his/her responses to the Performance subtests (Kaufman, 1990). For example, the patient's responses to Picture Arrangement can reveal how the patient interprets interpersonal experiences and copes with interpersonal conflict (Sipps, Berry, & Lynch, 1987; Zimmerman & Woo-Sam, 1973). In addition, the patient's exchanges with the examiner and attitude toward testing can reveal how he/she responds to authority, evaluative circumstances, and failure (Maloney & Ward, 1976).

Treatment Hypotheses

A patient's ability to encode, recall, and process information will affect how well he/she responds to the selected treatment context, approach, and techniques. For example, visual–motor deficiencies and significant deficits in fluid intelligence (Horn & Cattell, 1966, 1967), as measured by performance on Digit Span, Similarities, Picture Completion, Picture Arrangement, Block Design, and Object Assembly, have been noted to occur with conditions and events that are expected to impair conceptual fluency, such as chronic alcohol use and cirrhosis of the liver (Smith & Smith, 1977).

Fluid intelligence is thought to indicate one's ability to adapt to new situations, problems, and circumstances (Sattler, 1992). Deficiencies in an alcoholic's ability to accommodate to new patterns of living, for example, suggests that rapid and lasting abstinence from alcohol is not a realistic goal for treatment unless the alcoholic is provided with a structured treatment context (e.g., a hospital) and a concrete directive therapeutic approach (e.g., cognitive–behavioral therapy; Wakefield, Yost, Williams, & Patterson, in press).

A patient's cognitive, emotional, and interpersonal strengths and weaknesses need to be considered when selecting treatments (Beutler & Clarkin, 1990). Likewise, the cognitive, affective, and interpersonal demands of treatment need to be considered.

Hypotheses about Perceptual, Cognitive, and Ideational Processes

The WAIS-R can be used to develop hypotheses about the quality and character of the patient's perceptual, cognitive, and ideational processes. Examiners may want to explore the following areas:

Organicity
1. Premorbid intelligence
2. Degree of impairment and probable cause
3. Prognosis

Perceptual Processes
1. Information processing (encoding, memory, and recall)
2. Attention and concentration (distractibility)
3. Perceptual–motor functioning

Cognitive Processes
1. Problem-solving skills (concrete and abstract operations, integration, conceptualization, generalization)
2. Intelligence
3. Intellectual strengths and weaknesses (using ipsative and normative standards)
4. Psychopathology (thought disorders)

Hypotheses about Emotional Functioning, Motivation, and Investment

Likewise, the WAIS-R can be used to generate hypotheses about the patient's affective states, motivation, and investment in treatment and recovery. The following areas may be assessed:

Mood
1. Dominant trait and state moods (euphoria, euthymia, or dysphoria)
2. Pre- and postmorbid affect
3. Emotional responsiveness (range, lability, modulation)
4. Degree of affective disturbance
5. Chronicity versus acuteness

Motivation and Investment
1. Attitude toward testing
2. Response to frustration
3. Patient involvement and commitment to change

Hypotheses about Interpersonal–Intrapersonal Functioning and Coping Strategies

Finally, hypotheses about a patient's interpersonal–intrapersonal functioning and coping strategies can be formed by examining the content of the patient's responses and the way in which the patient interacts with the examiner. The following areas may be assessed:

Interpersonal–Intrapersonal Functioning
1. Personality
2. Attitude toward examiner
3. Interpersonal conflict
4. Social intelligence

Coping Strategies
1. Response style
2. Testing behavior

Diagnosis and Treatment Plans

As indicated in Chapter 3, diagnosis and treatment plans in an integrative approach to assessment must be based on multiple sources of information. The WAIS-R is one such source. The complexity and the severity of the patient's symptoms, coupled with his/her distress levels, coping style, and level of reactance, serve as the foundation for treatment planning. Treatment planning should include an assessment of the patient's risk for deterioration, need for confinement, and medication. Decisions about the duration, frequency, and modality of treatment should also be made.

Case Studies

The Case of R. D.

R. D.'s WAIS-R results are recorded in Table 5.1.

More Background

In addition to a progressive deterioration of his auditory, vocal, and psychomotor abilities, R. D.'s verbal disabilities led to his early retirement from teaching high school and exacerbated problems in his marital relationship. The patient and his wife were seeking couples counseling for long-standing marital problems at a Department of Veterans Affairs outpatient clinic.

R. D. reported that his stuttering had increased over the last year. He could apparently understand what was being said to him, but struggled to formulate his responses. He frequently reversed syllables when speaking, and failed to answer when faced with questions requiring more than a one-word reply. The patient reported that he was having difficulty reading and periodically felt depressed. He had had two "panic attacks" in the last year; he described these attacks as a sudden loss of breath, heart palpitations, and sweaty palms.

The WAIS-R was requested by the patient's therapist. The therapist wanted more information on the patient's cognitive functioning in order to clarify the diagnosis, and, more importantly, to evaluate the patient's request for marital therapy and determine an appropriate course of treatment.

R. D.'s presenting concerns—namely, visual, auditory, vocal, and psychomotor difficulties—confounded the assessment of his IQ. R. D.'s FSIQ, VIQ, and PIQ were not very useful when studied in isolation. For R. D., the best use of the WAIS-R was to provide the patient and therapist with an assessment of the patient's relative strengths and weaknesses in each of the following domains.

R. D.'s Perceptual, Cognitive, and Ideational Processes

Organicity. An outstanding feature of R. D.'s profile was the large VIQ–PIQ discrepancy. The therapist speculated that the patient suffered from primary degenerative dementia of the Alzheimer type or from presenile dementia "not otherwise specified." The patient's Performance score was significantly higher than his Verbal score (VIQ–PIQ = –18, p = .01). The magnitude of this discrepancy ($\geq$ 15 points) suggested that the odds were about 2 to 1 that this difference was not attributable to chance. That is, it probably represented an actual inconsistency in cognitive processing. Interestingly, R. D.'s PIQ > VIQ profile did not match the profile that most frequently characterizes Alzheimer-type dementia. Alzheimer patients typically produce VIQ > PIQ profiles of 15 or more points (Brinkman & Braun, 1984; Fuld, 1984)—a pattern that often indicates greater impairment in the areas of spatial relations and pattern perception. A PIQ > VIQ difference, as found in R. D.'s profile, is often taken to signify left-hemisphere brain damage (Kaufman, 1990).

Although PIQ and VIQ results are useful, the resulting lateralization of brain damage is often inaccurate, because the sensitivity of the WAIS-R to such damage is questionable (Kaufman, 1990). Specific patterns that can be related to discrete organic conditions are, in reality, less likely to occur than commonly thought. For example, lesions of the left hemisphere are often associated with PIQ > VIQ profiles, but the magnitude rarely exceeds 6 points (Kaufman, 1990), and they are thus often linked with normal profiles as well. Actually, patients with damage to the left hemisphere are almost equally likely to produce VIQ > PIQ profiles or no discrepancy at all (Kaufman, 1990; Todd, Coolidge, & Satz, 1977; Smith, 1966). PIQ > VIQ differences are therefore not very useful diagnostically. Nonetheless, the large VIQ–PIQ difference in R. D.'s profile, and the large difference in his Verbal Comprehension and Perceptual Organization factor scores, supported the hypothesis that the source of his cognitive deficits was an organic disorder.

Another significant aspect of R. D.'s profile was his relatively high Information score. This score was significantly greater than his age-corrected verbal and Full Scale means (p < .01). This subtest is resistant to the effects of brain damage; the score thus suggested that R. D.'s premorbid intellectual level was at least average for his age and that his long-term memory was intact. Vocabulary is also a good estimate of premorbid IQ, but R. D. did not score well on it. R. D. experienced a great deal of frustration during administration of this subtest. He often responded to the items by listing related terms. To item 1 (bed), he responded, "Sheets and pillowcases, blankets, and spread." Likewise, for item 5 (breakfast), he said, "Eggs, bacon, orange juice, coffee." He seemed to know that these responses were not accurate. He shook his head and finally started saying "Don't know" right away, after each word was read.

Perceptual and Cognitive Processes. Nearly all the remaining Verbal subtest scores were significantly lower than the Full Scale age-corrected mean, suggesting severe deficits in verbal comprehension. R. D.'s score on Digit Span was the second highest in the Verbal subtests (though it was still rather low), but Digit Span is not strongly related to Verbal Comprehension and is more directly related to Freedom from Distractibility.

R. D. performed least well on Arithmetic, which requires verbal encoding, memory, mental arithmetic operations, verbal report, attention, and concentration. Interestingly, R. D. was able to answer many of these items correctly when the examiner tested the limits with him, as described earlier. Therefore, R. D.'s low Arithmetic score was probably attributable not to a lack of mathematical skills, but to deficits in either attentional or cognitive processes.

R. D.'s strengths lay in his perceptual abilities. His Perceptual Organization factor score was near the mean for his age group, and he scored near or at the mean on four out of five of the Performance subtests. R. D.'s age-corrected score on Block Design, which is highly correlated with g, was significantly higher than his Full Scale age-corrected mean ($p < .01$). High scores on Block Design suggest good visual–spatial abilities, nonverbal reasoning, and perceptual organization.

Digit Symbol is particularly sensitive to cerebral impairment, and R. D.'s poor performance on this subtest was further evidence for brain damage and psychomotor deficits.

It was possible that R. D.'s problem-solving skills were limited by his reduced capacity to encode, manipulate, and communicate information. Abstract operations involving complicated mental manipulations were difficult for him to perform without the benefit of concrete representations. His premorbid intellectual abilities were probably compromised by the progressive deterioration of varied cognitive, perceptual, and motor processes. There was no evidence of psychopathology; all of R. D.'s responses were rational and meaningful.

R. D.'s Emotional Functioning, Motivation, and Investment

Mood.   R. D.'s mood was typically pleasant at the beginning of the assessment sessions (the WAIS-R was administered over three sessions because of patient fatigue). The range of his affect was appropriate to the assessment situation. He did express frustration with himself when he could not communicate his responses smoothly or quickly. He did not respond well to encouragement from the examiner. For example, he would not take time to think before responding "Don't know" during the latter portion of the Vocabulary subtest.

Motivation and Investment.   Despite his frustration, the patient endured three long assessment sessions. In addition, he readily followed through on suggested referrals to a neurologist, neuropsychologist, and speech therapist. He repeatedly expressed interest in working on improving his speech, the quality of his life, and his marital relationship.

R. D.'s Interpersonal–Intrapersonal Functioning and Coping Strategies

Interpersonal–Intrapersonal Functioning. The patient evidenced no explicit signs of interpersonal dysfunction as it might be expressed in the analogue environment of assessment. The attitude toward the examiner was one of appropriate respect with requests for professional assistance. R. D.'s social behaviors were appropriate.

Coping Strategies. R. D. did appear to tense up when feeling frustrated by his performance on the WAIS-R. His breathing became shallow and he tightened his fists periodically. He seemed to internalize his negative affect. In addition, it appeared that R. D. did not have a ready coping strategy for his condition. He was experiencing a serious and significant deterioration of his cognitive abilities, and he was probably at a loss as to how to prevent or deter any further decay.

Diagnosis and Treatment Plans

The external validity of the WAIS-R results seemed strong. It was likely that the patient's method of responding and cognitive deficits were not restricted to performance on highly structured assessment tools, but were legitimate concerns for the patient as he tried to function in his daily life. Neuropsychological assessment supported the hypothesis that an organic disorder was the basis for his symptoms. The additional assessment revealed signs indicating a significant deficit in receptive language skills, bilateral motor impairment, and slowed mental processing. The neuropsychologist concluded that the bilateral nature of the patient's ailments suggested the possibility of a progressive demyelination syndrome, and he recommended that the patient work to enhance the quality of his life by increasing his involvement in social activities. The neuropsychologist did not support the patient's pursuit of couples therapy, because of the treatment's reliance on verbal comprehension and production.

R. D.'s therapist used the neuropsychologist's report and WAIS-R results to formulate a diagnosis and make a decision about the patient's treatment request. The following diagnosis was made:

DSM-III-R
  I. 294.10, Dementia associated with Axis III physical disorder or condition
     Severity: mild
     V61.10, Marital Problem
 II. V71.09, no diagnosis
III. Progressive demyelination syndrome

IV. Psychosocial stressors: Speech problem, early retirement, marital problems
Severity: 5—extreme (predominantly enduring circumstances)
V. Global Assessment of Functioning (GAF):
Current GAF: 60, moderate symptoms
Highest GAF past year: 70, some mild symptoms

The patient did not seem to be at risk for rapid increases in his rate of deterioration. He also did not seem to require hospitalization or medication.

The therapist concluded that strictly verbal forms of therapy were contraindicated. The therapist accepted the couple as patients and met with them weekly. He sought to draw upon the patient's nonverbal strengths and applied an experiential approach to treatment. Together, they engaged in stress reduction and breathing exercises to help R. D. relax and slow the pace of his speech production. The therapist used role playing and experiential homework assignments to help the spouses alter the ways in which they communicated their wants and needs to each other. He also supported the wife as she tried to adjust to her husband's increasing debilitation. Therapy was terminated by the couple after 4 months when they had achieved their goals of greater acceptance of R. D.'s condition and improved communication.

The Case of B. W.

B. W.'s WAIS-R results are listed in Table 5.2.

More Background

B. W. reported that she could remember feeling depressed as early as age 12, with only one short respite from her negative feelings. This period was when she was 18 and she was having an affair with her 40-year-old marksmanship teacher. The sexual relationship ended after B. W.'s father threatened to harm the instructor if the affair continued. She remained friends with her instructor and continued to shoot with him regularly.

In addition to her subjective experience of depression, B. W. suffered from migraine headaches and a host of other physical complaints (i.e., backaches, frequent colds, and vertigo). She was the youngest of four biological siblings, all girls. When B. W.'s father realized that his last child was another girl, he swore that he would raise her as the son he was never given. She learned how to hunt, shoot, handle knives, and fix cars in her youth.

B. W.'s family was unsupportive of her academic pursuits and devalued her efforts at achievement. She requested an "intelligence test" to verify her explanation about why she felt so different from her classmates. She also reported that she was leery of psychologists, who, in her opinion, had special mind-reading abilities. Later, she explained that her reference to mind reading simply meant that she expected psychologists to be ultra-intuitive.

B. W. described her classmates as "stupid and immature" because they failed to extract important concepts from course material. She saw her classmates as flirtatious and frivolous. She reported that she had had few childhood friends and that she could not think of anyone with whom she might like to form a friendship at college.

B. W.'s academic record suggested that she was an exceptional student. She received A's in courses requiring either the acquisition of knowledge (e.g., introductory psychology) or divergent creative thought (e.g., creative writing). She performed least well in classes requiring group discussion or cooperative effort (e.g., laboratory science with group projects).

B. W.'s therapist chose to fulfill the patient's request for an "intelligence test," and viewed the WAIS-R administration as the first step toward gaining the patient's cooperation in completing a battery of assessment instruments that would include measures of personality, mood, and affect. The results of the WAIS-R would be used in conjunction with an intensive clinical interview as a starting point for diagnosis. The results would also be used to strengthen the fledgling therapeutic relationship and begin the process of treatment planning.

B. W.'s Perceptual, Cognitive, and Ideational Processes

Organicity.   B. W.'s depression was chronic and apparently unrelated to any specific event. The origins of her depression might have been biochemical, and a psychiatric consultation was recommended.

Perceptual and Cognitive Processes.   B. W.'s FSIQ was 96, which placed her in the 39th percentile. Her VIQ was in the "average" range, and her PIQ was "low average." B. W.'s Verbal Comprehension and Perceptual Organization factor scores were also in the "average" range. These findings suggested that she had an adequate knowledge base and average verbal comprehension abilities, concept formation, achievement orientation, and understanding of the majority culture (Groth-Marnat, 1990). In addition, B. W. had average perceptual organization abilities, alertness to detail, nonverbal reasoning ability, persistence, work speed and efficiency, and spatial ability. B. W.'s Freedom from Distractibility factor score was also average, suggesting that she had a general ability to sustain attention and average numerical ability, encoding ability, use of rehearsal strategies, short-term memory, ability to self-monitor, and ability to perform symbolic cognitive operations (Groth-Marnat, 1990).

B. W.'s intellectual abilities were classified as "average," but several aspects of the test administration made this examinee unusual. Many of B. W.'s responses were atypical, and her response style varied from steady, deliberate, and focused to distracted, obtuse, and unsure. A closer look at the patient's intellectual strengths and weaknesses was needed to understand how someone who saw herself as gifted scored in the average range so consistently.

The first noticeable aberration in this profile was the difference in B. W.'s VIQ and PIQ, which was quite significant (20 points, VIQ > PIQ; $p < .001$). The size and direction of this discrepancy were unexpected, given her low socioeconomic status and masculine upbringing. Higher VIQs are associated with psychomotor slowing, a deliberate response style, or impulsive responding. It was possible that any of these conditions could have been in operation during assessment.

B. W.'s response latencies in the timed procedures were not extraordinarily long. She performed above or just below the age-corrected Performance mean for both Block Design and Object Assembly, which rely on psychomotor coordination (Kaufman, 1990, Table 14.2, pp. 473–474). She did appear to have some trouble completing the Digit Symbol subtest, which also requires psychomotor skills. She used a very deliberate approach to this task by looking at the key each time she transformed a number to a symbol. Responses to the five Performance subtests are all expressed through a visual–motor channel (Kaufman, 1990, Table 14.2). Interestingly, B. W.'s worst subtest was Picture Completion; her score on this was significantly ($p < .01$) below the age-corrected mean for all the subtests. She also obtained relatively low scores on Picture Arrangement and Digit Symbol, so it remained possible that some kind of psychomotor disruption or delay was occurring. This delay might have been produced by lethargy associated with her depression, resistance to the task presented, or cogitation that was interfering with her responses. The deviant content of her responses supported the third explanation.

B. W.'s score on Information was significantly greater than her age-corrected Verbal mean ($p < .01$) and the age-corrected mean for all the subscales ($p < .01$), which suggested that her knowledge base was broad and well developed compared to her other abilities. Her scores on Vocabulary and Arithmetic were very near the age-corrected Verbal mean, and that on Vocabulary also appeared to be significantly greater than the age-corrected Full Scale mean ($p < .01$). Block Design was the only Performance scale that emerged as a strength; that score was significantly greater than the age-corrected Performance scale mean ($p < .01$). Block Design is also highly correlated with g.

To summarize, B. W.'s verbal strengths were (1) long-term semantic memory, (2) expansive knowledge base, and (3) verbal concept formation. Her perceptual and performance strengths were (1) visual–motor coordination, (2) visual–spatial perception, (3) nonverbal reasoning, and (4) perceptual organization. Abilities that she might possess, which are shared by Block Design, Information, and Vocabulary, were generalizability and abstract thought (Kaufman, 1990).

B. W.'s weakest subtests were Comprehension, which was significantly below the age-corrected Verbal mean ($p < .01$) and Picture Completion, which was significantly below the age-corrected mean of all 11 subtests ($p < .01$). Her low score on Comprehension suggested a lack of social judgment and knowledge of social mores. This hypothesis seemed likely because B. W. had grown up in a rural community, read avidly, and acquired her knowledge of the world through the impersonal conduit of library books. Her social experiences were very limited; even relationships within her family were constricted and atypical. The content of her responses to the Comprehension questions revealed some of her confusion about the world around her. To item 5 (deaf), she replied, "Because she can't hear and their parents probably don't talk to them." To item 6 (borrow), she said, "Friends will stab you in the back." To item 12 (iron), she said, "That sounds weird; hit someone at the right time."

The Picture Completion subtest requires the examinee to respond when uncertain, pay attention to the stimulus card, concentrate, and act under time pressure. Bizarre responses to this subtest are pathognomonic. The accuracy of B. W.'s responses was very mixed. She got items 1 through 5 correct; then to item 6 (pitcher) she offered, "No one is holding it," and to item 7 (glasses), she replied, "He misses his wife." To item 17 (man), she said, "The man has no friends." Low scores on Picture Completion suggest the operation of intrusive thoughts and impulsivity. This subtest can also be influenced by negativity. After the exam, the administrator asked B. W. to describe her experience in taking the test. B. W. reported that she often did not know which answer to provide. She described herself as a quick and smart thinker, and she said that she often had many answers in her head and tried hard to choose the one that she thought the examiner wanted.

When combined, B. W.'s cognitive processes appeared to be suitable for her academic activities as a community college student. Her perceptions of herself as bright and gifted were not supported by the WAIS-R results. She had some outstanding strengths, but her verbal comprehension skills and psychomotor function seemed to be constrained by her limited developmental experiences, depression, and intrusive thoughts. She was accurate in her perception of herself as "different," and her attribution that she was extremely intelligent appeared to be her way of explaining her isolation.

B. W.'s Emotional Functioning, Motivation, and Investment

Mood. According to her self-report, B. W.'s predominant mood was dysphoria. During intellectual assessment, her affect varied. She seemed to be happy when answering questions that allowed her to demonstrate her intelligence (e.g., Information and Block Design), but appeared confused and anxious when responding to the Picture Arrangement and Picture Completion subtests. Her emotions were well modulated, but not congruent with some of her statements. For example, for Picture Arrangement item 9 (robber), she arranged the cards correctly and saw humor in the series, but then laughed and said, "If I had a gun, I would have shot that guy." She was confused and agitated while she arranged the cards for item 6 (escape), which she saw as an attempted rape.

It seemed likely that B. W.'s affective disturbance was chronic and at times extreme. During the clinical interview she reported experiencing intense migraines, which usually led her to consider suicide, though she had never made any attempts.

Motivation and Investment. B. W.'s attitude toward assessment was generally positive. She reported little frustration with the demands of the evaluation. Her involvement in treatment and commitment to change were questionable because of her inherent lack of trust in others. She was very judgmental and expressed hostility toward her classmates, who seemed to be more interested in socializing than learning during class. It was surmised that this patient might present challenges to the therapist as she attempted to cultivate the therapeutic relationship.

B. W.'s Interpersonal–Intrapersonal Functioning and Coping Strategies

Interpersonal–Intrapersonal Functioning. B. W.'s intratest behavior suggested that she might have some interpersonal deficits. She was anxious and suspicious at that start of the assessment, then warmed up after structure was imposed. Ambiguous social situations seemed to be intolerable for her. B. W. looked and acted differently from other college students, and though she reported that she had never had a close friend, she did not seem to want one. It was possible that she lacked social intelligence, which Sipps et al. (1987) defined as an ability to be insightful, flexible, and adaptable in new social situations. Scores on both Picture Arrangement and Comprehension are related to these abilities (Sipps et al., 1987), and B. W. performed poorly on both.

Coping Strategies. According to B. W., she often screened her responses in an effort to please the examiner. It seemed possible that she used her cognitive resources to edit intrusive deviant thoughts. These thoughts were contained and released sporadically throughout the administration. It was determined that it would be useful for the therapist to learn more about her personality and coping style by asking her to complete a Rorschach and inviting her to reveal her thought processes as she responded to the assessment stimuli. An MMPI was also administered in an effort to get a better summary of her physical and psychological symptomatology.

Diagnosis and Treatment Plans

B. W.'s therapist chose to administer the WAIS-R as a means for engaging the patient in the therapeutic process. The results of the assessment challenged B. W.'s self-perceptions and allowed the therapist to observe her reaction to contradictory feedback. B. W. responded to the unexpected results with surprise followed by silence. Later, B. W. disclosed suicidal feelings and thoughts—an apparent reaction to the incongruities between her self-concept and the results of the cognitive assessment.

At the time of the WAIS-R administration, the patient did not seem to be at risk for rapid deterioration, though this impression changed after she reported the suicidal thoughts. As therapy progressed, however, the significance of these suicidal feelings diminished. Indeed, she later reported that the depressive and suicidal feelings did not seem to be extraordinary to her. Although she acknowledged feeling worthless and depressed for much of her life, the patient's tenacity and cognitive strength were sufficient that she did not need hospitalization. B. W. was referred to a psychiatrist to be evaluated for antidepressive medication. The therapist made the following diagnosis:

> *DSM-III-R*
> I. 296.32, Major Depression, recurrent, moderate severity
> II. 301.22, Schizotypal Personality Disorder
> III. Migraine headaches
> IV. Psychosocial stressors: Social isolation, parental problems
> Severity: 3—moderate (predominantly enduring circumstances)
> V. GAF:
> Current GAF: 45, serious symptoms, some impairment in reality testing
> Highest GAF past year: 50, serious symptoms

The therapist initially concluded that she had erred by administering and interpreting the intellectual test so quickly, because it seemed to precipitate the expression of suicidal feelings. With time, however, it became apparent that the patient's acknowledgment of suicidal feelings was an important step in the therapeutic process. It facilitated the establishment of a relationship and a focus for therapeutic work.

Because of B. W.'s fragile control, the therapist surmised that intensive interpersonal forms of therapy were contraindicated. Thus, she presented herself as an advisor or consultant rather than as an authority. The therapist focused on reinforcing the patient's cognitive assets and engaged her in social skills training. Together, they pursued two goals: (1) to help B. W. become confident in social situations while gaining self-monitoring skills, and (2) to manage her depressive symptoms. The patient stayed in treatment for a year and terminated when she graduated from community college.

Limitations of the WAIS-R

The WAIS-R is best suited for the intellectual assessment of persons who are within two standard deviations of average intelligence, highly accultur-ated, and comfortable with the English language. The WAIS-R has more limited applicability to the intellectual assessment of mentally retarded, learning-disabled, and intellectually gifted individuals (Groth-Marnat, 1990). In addition, the validity of the WAIS-R results must be called into question and thoroughly evaluated when the test is administered to ethnic minority persons (Groth-Marnat, 1990), particularly monolingual and minimally bilingual Spanish-speaking adults (Gomez, Piedmont, & Fleming, 1992; Lopez & Romero, 1988; Lopez & Taussig, 1991). Examiners must consider patients' ethnic, cultural, and socioeconomic background when selecting and interpreting the WAIS-R. Extraneous factors such as socioeconomic status, educational level, and familiarity with the majority culture in the United States can elevate or depress IQ scores (Kaufman, 1990).

Other limitations of the WAIS-R include (1) inconsistencies in the adolescent norms (Kaufman, 1990), which reduce the validity of IQ scores obtained for persons under 20 years of age (Groth-Marnat, 1990); (2) the use of the 20- to 34-year-old subsample as the reference group for the deri-vation of scaled scores, which creates the appearance of a non-normative decline in intelligence over time (Kaufman, 1990); (3) the subjectivity of some of the scoring criteria and the preponderance of examiner error (Moon et al., 1991); and (4) a lack of research that ties WAIS-R scores to an individual's ability to function on a daily basis (Groth-Marnat, 1990).

Gender and Ethnic Differences

There are consistent gender and ethnic differences in FSIQ, VIQ–PIQ dis-crepancies, and subtest scores for the WAIS-R (Kaufman, 1990; Kaufman, McLean, & Reynolds, 1988; Reynolds & Brown, 1984), though some ethnic differences have narrowed in the last decade (Vincent, 1991). Generally, men tend to outperform women on the FSIQ, PIQ, and VIQ scales and on the Information, Arithmetic, and Block Design subscales; women out-perform men on the Digit Symbol subscale (Kaufman, 1990). Ethnic differences are much more complicated and are confounded by systematic differences in education, socioeconomic status, and cultural experience (Saccuzzo, Johnson, & Russell, 1992). The bulk of research on ethnic differences has compared the performance of African-Americans and European-Americans. Compared to African-Americans, European-Americans have received consistently higher scores on the FSIQ, VIQ, and PIQ (Kaufman, 1990) within each age, education, and occupational grouping assessed (Reynolds, Chastain, Kaufman, & McLean, 1987). Reynolds et al. (1987) reported point differences ranging from a low 8.4 for persons with 0 to 8 years of education on the FSIQ to 16.3 for persons with 13 or more years of education on the VIQ. The origins of ethnic differences in IQ are hotly debated and frequently boil down to familiar arguments about heredity versus environmental influences (Scarr & Barker, 1981; Scarr & Carter-Saltzman, 1982).

Using Group Differences

In addition to other characteristics, a patient's gender, ethnicity, and cultural history can serve as a basis for developing hypotheses about the patient's strengths and weaknesses. For example, a male patient who scores particularly well on Digit Symbol is demonstrating atypical strengths in visual–motor processing (Snow & Weinstock, 1990). An examiner who is acting as a good detective can use this observation to develop hypotheses about the patient's occupational history or avocational interests.

The patient's gender and ethnicity may also provide clues as to the patient's predominant mode of information processing. In a comparative investigation of the factor-analytic structure of the WAIS-R for men, women, African-Americans, and European-Americans, Kaufman, McLean, and Reynolds (1991) found that the typical two- and three-factor solutions were generally valid across all four groups, but that in some instances subtests loaded heavily on *both* the Verbal Comprehension and the Perceptual Organization factors. Specifically, Digit Span, Arithmetic, and Similarities had substantial secondary loadings on the Perceptual Organization factor, and Picture Completion and Picture Arrangement loaded well on the Verbal Comprehension factor for females and for African-Americans. Similarities had a substantial secondary loading on the Perceptual Organization factor for males and for European-Americans. These results suggest that both verbal and nonverbal abilities were used to respond to questions on these subtests.

In an even closer examination of factor loadings by race × gender, Digit Span, Arithmetic, and Similarities loaded about equally well on Verbal Comprehension and Perceptual Organization for African-American males, which suggests that they may have used nonverbal processing strategies on some of the Verbal subtests. Alternatively, the Picture Completion and Picture Arrangement subtests loaded most heavily on the Verbal Comprehension dimension for African-American women, which suggests that they may have used verbal strategies to solve what previous studies have identified as predominantly perceptual problems. Digit Span, Arithmetic, and Similarities loaded on both factors for European-American women, which suggests that they used both verbal and nonverbal strategies to answer questions on those subtests. Finally, the factor-analytic structure of the responses of European-American males conformed to the expected two-factor structure best (Similarities had only a slight secondary loading on Perceptual Organization). The WAIS-R scores themselves tell the examiner and patient little about *what* strategies examinees use to solve the problems presented to them. Information about a demographic group's typical factor-analytic structure may be useful to an examiner who is trying to develop hypotheses about *how* individual patients achieve their scores.

Conclusion

The WAIS-R is a strong addition to a complete and integrated approach to psychological assessment. It is a reliable source of information about the patient's intellectual strengths and weaknesses, and an unexpectedly rich resource for clinically relevant content.

In this chapter we have reviewed the development, administration, scoring, and interpretation of the WAIS-R. Within the context of our integrative model of assessment, we have emphasized that the WAIS-R provides a structured and moderately stressful environment that draws on the patient's internal experience. When analyzed by levels, it provides important information on cognitive functioning and secondary information on emotional and mood factors, as well as allowing the development of some tentative hypotheses regarding the nature of conflicts and interpersonal relationships. A careful, empirically based interpretation of WAIS-R results can guide the clinician in the formulation of tenable hypotheses about the patient's perceptual and cognitive processes, emotional functioning and motivation, and interpersonal functioning and coping strategies.

The WAIS-R complements the use of other instruments that vary in the degree of interpersonal stress imposed on the situation, that focus on external or objective behavior and diagnostic symptoms, and that provide a less structured environment. When used in this way, this instrument can provide data to assist the clinician in formulating a diagnosis and in selecting the types of treatment environments to which the patient is most likely to respond.

APPENDIX 5.1. Percentile Rankings for Wechsler Deviation IQs

IQ	Percentile rank	IQ	Percentile rank	IQ	Percentile rank	IQ	Percentile rank
155	99.99	127	96	99	47	71	3
154	99.98	126	96	98	45	70	2
153	99.98	125	95	97	42	69	2
152	99.97	124	95	96	39	68	2
151	99.97	123	94	95	37	67	1
150	99.96	122	93	94	34	66	1
149	99.95	121	92	93	32	65	1
148	99.93	120	91	92	30	64	1
147	99.91	119	90	91	27	63	1
146	99.89	118	88	90	25	62	1
145	99.87	117	87	89	23	61	0.47
144	99.83	116	86	88	21	60	0.38
143	99.79	115	84	87	19	59	0.31
142	99.74	114	82	86	18	58	0.26
141	99.69	113	81	85	16	57	0.21
140	99.62	112	79	84	14	56	0.17
139	99.53	111	77	83	13	55	0.13
138	99	110	75	82	12	54	0.11
137	99	109	73	81	10	53	0.09
136	99	108	70	80	9	52	0.07
135	99	107	68	79	8	51	0.05
134	99	106	66	78	7	50	0.04
133	99	105	63	77	6	49	0.03
132	98	104	61	76	5	48	0.03
131	98	103	58	75	5	47	0.02
130	98	102	55	74	4	46	0.02
129	97	101	53	73	4	45	0.01
128	97	100	50	72	3		

Note. From Groth-Marnat, G. (1990). *Handbook of psychological assessment* (2nd ed.), p. 447. New York: Wiley. Copyright 1990 by John Wiley and Sons, Inc. Reprinted by permission of the publisher.

APPENDIX 5.2. Confidence Intervals for the WAIS-R Scales

Age level	Scale	Confidence level				
		68%	85%	90%	95%	99%
16–17	VIQ	±3	±5	±5	± 7	± 9
	PIQ	±5	±8	±9	±10	±13
	FSIQ	±3	±4	±5	± 6	± 8
18–19	VIQ	±3	±4	±5	± 6	± 7
	PIQ	±5	±7	±8	± 9	±12
	FSIQ	±3	±4	±5	± 6	± 8
20–24	VIQ	±3	±4	±5	± 6	± 8
	PIQ	±4	±6	±7	± 8	±11
	FSIQ	±3	±4	±4	± 5	± 7
25–34	VIQ	±3	±4	±4	± 5	± 7
	PIQ	±4	±6	±6	± 8	±10
	FSIQ	±2	±3	±4	± 4	± 6
35–44	VIQ	±3	±4	±4	± 5	± 7
	PIQ	±4	±5	±6	± 7	±10
	FSIQ	±2	±3	±4	± 4	± 6
45–54	VIQ	±3	±4	±4	± 5	± 7
	PIQ	±4	±5	±6	± 7	±10
	FSIQ	±3	±4	±4	± 5	± 7
55–64	VIQ	±3	±4	±4	± 5	± 7
	PIQ	±4	±6	±6	± 8	±10
	FSIQ	±3	±4	±4	± 5	± 7
65–69	VIQ	±3	±4	±4	± 5	± 7
	PIQ	±4	±5	±6	± 7	±10
	FSIQ	±2	±3	±4	± 4	± 6
70–74	VIQ	±3	±4	±4	± 5	± 6
	PIQ	±4	±6	±7	± 8	±10
	FSIQ	±2	±4	±4	± 5	± 6
Average	VIQ	±3	±4	±4	± 5	± 7
	PIQ	±4	±6	±7	± 8	±10
	FSIQ	±3	±4	±4	± 5	± 7

Note. From Sattler, J. M. (1992). *Assessment of children* (rev. 3rd ed.), p. 840. San Diego: Author. Copyright 1992 by Jerome M. Sattler, Publisher, Inc. Reprinted by permission of the author/publisher.

Ability	Background factors	Possible implications of high scores	Possible implications of low scores	Instructional implications
		Full Scale		
General intelligence Scholastic aptitude Academic aptitude Readiness to master a school curriculum	Natural endowment Richness of early environment Extent of schooling Cultural opportunities Interests Rate of motor activity Persistence Visual–motor organization Alertness	Good general intelligence Good scholastic aptitude Readiness to master a school curriculum	Poor general intelligence Poor scholastic aptitude Not ready to master school curriculum	Focus on language development activities Focus on visual learning activities Develop concept formation skills Reinforce persistence
		Verbal scale or Verbal Comprehension factor		
Verbal comprehension Application of verbal skills and information to the solution of new problems Verbal ability Ability to process verbal information Ability to think with words	Natural endowment Richness of early environment Extent of schooling Cultural opportunities Interests	Good verbal comprehension Good scholastic aptitude Possession of knowledge of the cultural milieu Good concept formation Readiness to master school curriculum Achievement orientation	Poor verbal comprehension Poor scholastic aptitude Inadequate understanding of the cultural milieu Poor concept formation Bilingual background Foreign background Not ready to master school curriculum Poor achievement orientation	Stress language development activities Use verbal enrichment activities Focus on current events Use exercises involving concept formation

(continued)

Ability	Background factors	Possible implications of high scores	Possible implications of low scores	Instructional implications
Performance scale or Perceptual Organization factor				
Perceptual organization Ability to think in terms of visual images and manipulate them with fluency, flexibility, and relative speed Ability to interpret or organize visually perceived material against a time limit Nonverbal ability Ability to form relatively abstract concepts and relationships without the use of words	Natural endowment Rate of motor activity Persistence Visual–motor organization Alertness Cultural opportunities Interests	Good perceptual organization Good alertness to detail Good nonverbal reasoning ability Good persistence Good ability to work quickly and efficiently Good spatial ability	Poor perceptual organization Poor alertness to detail Poor nonverbal reasoning ability Limited persistence Poor ability to work quickly and efficiently Poor spatial ability	Focus on visual learning activities Focus on part–whole relationships Use spatial–visual tasks Encourage trial-and-error activities Reinforce persistence Focus on visual planning activities Improve scanning techniques
Freedom from Distractibility factor				
Ability to sustain attention Short-term memory Numerical ability Encoding ability Ability to use rehearsal strategies Ability to shift mental operations on symbolic material Ability to self-monitor	Natural endowment Ability to passively receive stimuli	Good ability to sustain attention Good short-term memory Good numerical ability Good encoding ability Good use of rehearsal strategies Good ability to shift mental operations on symbolic material Good ability to self-monitor	Difficulty in sustaining attention Distractibility Anxiety Short-term retention deficits Encoding difficulties Poor rehearsal strategies Difficulty in rapidly shifting mental operations on symbolic material Inadequate self-monitoring skills	Develop attention skills Develop concentration skills Focus on small, meaningful units of instruction

Note. From Sattler, J. M. (1992). *Assessment of children* (rev. 3rd ed.), pp. 856–857. San Diego: Author. Copyright 1992 by Jerome M. Sattler, Publisher, Inc. Reprinted by permission of the author/publisher.

APPENDIX 5.4. Differences Required for Significance When Each WAIS-R Age-Corrected Subtest Scaled Score Is Compared to the Mean Age-Corrected Scaled Score for Any Individual Examinee

Subtest	Mean of 6 Verbal scale subtests		Mean of 5 Performance scale subtests		Mean of 11 Full Scale subtests	
	.05	.01	.05	.01	.05	.01
Information	2.33	2.78	—	—	2.59	3.07
Digit Span	2.91	3.47	—	—	3.31	3.92
Vocabulary	1.77	2.11	—	—	1.87	2.21
Arithmetic	2.73	3.26	—	—	3.09	3.66
Comprehension	2.85	3.40	—	—	3.24	3.84
Similarities	2.93	3.49	—	—	3.34	3.95
Picture Completion	—	—	2.92	3.49	3.36	3.98
Picture Arrangement	—	—	3.19	3.83	3.75	4.44
Block Design	—	—	2.47	2.96	2.71	3.21
Object Assembly	—	—	3.43	4.10	4.08	4.83
Digit Symbol	—	—	2.94	3.53	3.41	4.04

APPENDIX 5.5. Influences Likely to Affect Scores on Two or More WAIS-R Verbal or Performance Subtests

Influence	Verbal subtest						Performance subtest					Reliability[a]	
	I	DSp	V	A	C	S	PC	PA	BD	OA	DSym	Teens (16–19)	Adults (20–74)
Ability to respond when uncertain	I						PC			OA		.76	.85
Alertness to environment	I						PC				DSym	.86	.89
Anxiety		DSp		A							DSym	.87	.92
Attention span		DSp		A								.82	.90
Cognitive style (field dependence/independence)							PC		BD	OA		.87	.91
Concentration	I			A			PC				DSym	.86	.92
Cultural opportunities			V		C			PA				.94	.95
Distractibility		DSp		A							DSym	.87	.92
Flexibility						S				OA		.83	.89
Foreign language background	I		V									.96	.96
Intellectual curiosity and striving	I		V									.96	.96
Interests	I		V			S						.96	.96
Learning disabilities	I	DSp		A							DSym	.91	.94
Negativism		DSp			C	S	PC					.89	.94
Outside reading	I		V			S						.96	.96
Overly concrete thinking					C	S						.88	.91
Persistence	I									OA	DSym	.74	.83
Richness of early environment	I		V	A								.96	.96
School learning	I		V	A								.95	.96
Working under time pressure							PC	PA	BD	OA	DSym	.91	.94

Note. Abbreviations: I, Information; DSp, Digit Span; V, Vocabulary; A, Arithmetic; C, Comprehension; S, Similarities; PC, Picture Completion; PA, Picture Arrangement; BD, Block Design; OA, Object Assembly; DSym, Digit Symbol. Examiners should never infer a person's background or behaviors from the pattern of subtest scores. Background information must be verified by reliable sources, and behaviors must be observed or inferred by the examiner during the testing session. The subtests listed in this table are the ones most likely to be affected by each influence (background or behavioral variable). However, it is likely that *all* subtests listed for a given influence will be affected, and it is conceivable that tasks not listed may be affected. For example, a person with a poor attention span is likely to perform poorly on whatever subtests failed to attract his/her interest (not just Arithmetic and Digit Span). Thanks are due to Toshinori Ishikuma and Harue Ishikuma for computing the reliability coefficients shown in the table. From Kaufman, A. S. (1990). *Assessing adolescent and adult intelligence*, pp. 477–478. Boston: Allyn & Bacon. Copyright 1990 by Allyn & Bacon, Inc. Reprinted by permission of the publisher.

[a]Reliability is test–retest.

References

Adams, R. L., Smigielski, J., & Jenkins, R. L. (1984). Development of the Satz–Mogel short form of the WAIS-R. *Journal of Consulting and Clinical Psychology, 52,* 908.

American Psychiatric Association. (1987). *Diagnostic and statistical manual of mental disorders* (3rd ed., rev.). Washington, DC: Author.

Atkinson, L. (1991). Some tables for statistically based interpretation of WAIS-R factor scores. *Psychological Assessment, 3,* 288–291.

Atkinson, L., Bowman, T. G., Dickens, S., Blackwell, J., Vasarhelyi, J., Szep, P., Dunleavy, B., MacIntyre, R., & Bury, A. (1990). Stability of Wechsler Adult Intelligence Scale—Revised factor scores across time. *Psychological Assessment, 2,* 447–450.

Atkinson, L., & Cyr, J. J. (1984). Factor analysis of the WAIS-R: Psychiatric and standardization samples. *Journal of Consulting and Clinical Psychology, 52,* 714–716.

Beck, N. C., Horwitz, E., Seidenberg, M., Parker, J., & Frank, R. (1985). WAIS-R factor structure in psychiatric and general patients. *Journal of Consulting and Clinical Psychology, 53,* 402–405.

Beutler, L. E., & Clarkin, J. F. (1990). *Systematic treatment selection: Toward targeted therapeutic interventions.* New York: Brunner/Mazel.

Blatt, S. J., & Allison, J. (1968). The intelligence test in personality assessment. In A. I. Rabin (Ed.), *Projective techniques in personality assessment.* New York: Springer.

Blatt, S. J., & Allison, J. (1981). The intelligence test in personality assessment. In A. I. Rabin (Ed.), *Projective techniques in personality assessment* (2nd ed.). New York: Springer.

Boone, D. E. (1991a). Use of the modified WAIS-R with psychiatric inpatients: A caution. *Perceptual and Motor Skills, 73,* 315–322.

Boone, D. E. (1991b). Item-reduction vs. subtest-reduction short forms on the WAIS-R with psychiatric patients. *Journal of Clinical Psychology, 47,* 271–276.

Boone, D. E. (1992a). Reliability of the WAIS-R with psychiatric inpatients. *Journal of Clinical Psychology, 48,* 72–76.

Boone, D. E. (1992b). Evaluation of Kaufman's short forms of the WAIS-R with psychiatric inpatients. *Journal of Clinical Psychology, 48,* 239–245.

Bornstein, R. A., Suga, L., & Prifitera, A. (1987). Incidence of Verbal IQ–Performance IQ discrepancies at various levels of education. *Journal of Clinical Psychology, 43,* 387–389.

Borokowski, J. G. (1985). Signs of intelligence: Strategy, generalization, and metacognition. In S. R. Yussen (Ed.), *The growth of reflection in children.* Orlando, FL: Academic Press.

Brinkman, S. D., & Braun, P. (1984). Classification of dementia patients by a WAIS profile related to central cholinergic deficiencies. *Journal of Clinical Neuropsychology, 6,* 393–400.

Bruininks, R. H., Woodcock, R. W., Hill, B. K., & Weatherman, R. F. (1984). *Scales of Independent Behavior examiner's manual.* Allen, TX: DLM/Teaching Resources.

Bruininks, R. H., Woodcock, R. W., Hill, B. K., & Weatherman, R. F. (1985). *Devel-*

opment and standardization of the Scales of Independent Behavior. Allen, TX: DLM/Teaching Resources.

Campione, J. C., & Brown, A. L. (1978). Toward a theory of intelligence: Contributions from research with retarded children. *Intelligence, 2,* 279–304.

Cella, D. F. (1984). The Modified WAIS-R: An extension and revision. *Journal of Clinical Psychology, 40,* 801–804.

Cyr, J. J., & Atkinson, L. (1991). Use of population specific parameters in generating WAIS-R short forms. *Psychological Reports, 69,* 151–167.

Feinberg, J. R., & McIlvried, E. J. (1991). WAIS-R intrasubtest scatter in a chronic schizophrenic population: Is it an attentional problem? *Journal of Clinical Psychology, 47,* 327–335.

Feingold, A. (1985). Wechsler Adult Intelligence Scale—Revised IQ equivalents of Wechsler Intelligence Scale for Children—Revised scores for adults. *Perceptual and Motor Skills, 61,* 189–190.

Fuld, P. A. (1984). Test profile of cholinergic dysfunction of Alzheimer-type dementia. *Journal of Clinical Neuropsychology, 6,* 380–392.

Gomez, F. C., Piedmont, R. L., & Fleming, M. Z. (1992). Factor analysis of the Spanish version of the WAIS: The Escala de Inteligencia Wechsler para Adultos (EIWA). *Psychological Assessment, 4,* 317–321.

Greenspan, S. (1979). Social intelligence in the retarded. In N. R. Ellis (Ed.), *Handbook of mental deficiency: Psychological theory and research* (2nd ed., pp. 483–531). Hillsdale, NJ: Erlbaum.

Greenspan, S. (1981). Social competence and handicapped individuals: Practical implications and a proposed model. *Advances in Special Education, 3,* 41–82.

Grossman, F. M. (1983). Percentage of WAIS-R standardization sample obtaining Verbal–Performance discrepancies. *Journal of Consulting and Clinical Psychology, 51,* 641–642.

Grossman, H. J. (1983). *Classification in mental retardation.* Washington, DC: American Association on Mental Deficiency.

Groth-Marnat, G. (1990). *Handbook of psychological assessment* (2nd ed.). New York: Wiley.

Highlen, P. S., & Hill, C. E. (1984). Factors affecting client change. In S. D. Brown & R. W. Lent (Eds.), *Handbook of counseling psychology* (pp. 334–396). New York: Wiley.

Hill, T. D., Reddon, J. R., & Jackson, D. N. (1985). The factor structure of the Wechsler scales: A brief review. *Clinical Psychology Review, 5* 287–306.

Horn, J. L., & Cattell, R. B. (1966). Refinement and test of the theory of fluid and crystallized intelligence. *Journal of Educational Psychology, 57,* 253–270.

Horn, J. L., & Cattell, R. B. (1967). Age differences in fluid and crystallized intelligence. *Acta Psychologica, 26,* 107–129.

Kail, R., & Pellegrino, J. W. (1985). *Human intelligence: Perspectives and prospects.* New York: W. H. Freeman.

Kaufman, A. S. (1976). Verbal–Performance I.Q. discrepancies on the WISC-R. *Journal of Consulting and Clinical Psychology, 44,* 739–744.

Kaufman, A. S. (1977). Should short form validity coefficients be corrected? *Journal of Consulting and Clinical Psychology, 45,* 1159–1161.

Kaufman, A. S. (1979). *Intelligence testing with the WISC-R.* New York: Wiley.

Kaufman, A. S. (1990). *Assessing adolescent and adult intelligence.* Boston: Allyn & Bacon.

Kaufman, A. S., & Ishikuma, T. (1989). *Amazingly short forms of the WAIS-R*. Unpublished manuscript, University of Alabama.

Kaufman, A. S., & Kaufman, N. L. (1992). *Kaufman Adolescent and Adult Intelligence Test (KAIT)*. Circle Pines, MN: American Guidance Service.

Kaufman, A. S., McLean, J. E., & Reynolds, C. R. (1988). Sex, race, residence, region, and education differences on the 11 WAIS-R subtests. *Journal of Clinical Psychology, 44*, 231–248.

Kaufman, A. S., McLean, J. E., & Reynolds, C. R. (1991). Analysis of WAIS-R factor patterns by sex and race. *Journal of Clinical Psychology, 47*, 548–557.

Lambert, N. M. (1981). *AAMD Adaptive Behavior Scale, school edition: Diagnostic and technical manual*. Monterey, CA: Publishers Test Service.

Lambert, N. M., & Windmiller, M. (1981). *AAMD Adaptive Behavior Scale, school edition*. Monterey, CA: Publishers Test Service.

Leckliter, I. N., Matarazzo, J. D., & Silverstein, A. B. (1986). A literature review of factor analytic studies of the WAIS-R. *Journal of Clinical Psychology, 42*, 332–342.

Lezak, M. (1983). *Neuropsychological assessment*. New York: Oxford University Press.

London, P. (1986). *The modes and morals of psychotherapy* (2nd ed.). Washington, DC: Hemisphere.

Lopez, S. R., & Romero, A. (1988). Assessing the intellectual functioning of Spanish-speaking adults: Comparison of the EIWA and the WAIS. *Professional Psychology: Research and Practice, 19*, 263–270.

Lopez, S. R., & Taussig, I. M. (1991). Cognitive–intellectual functioning of Spanish speaking impaired and nonimpaired elderly: Implications for culturally sensitive assessment. *Psychological Assessment, 3*, 448–454.

Lubi, B., Larsen, R. M., Matarazzo, T. D., & Seever, M. (1985). Psychological test image patterns in five professional settings. *American Psychologist, 7*, 857–861.

Maloney, M. P., & Ward, M. P. (1976). *Psychological assessment: A conceptual approach*. New York: Oxford University Press.

Matarazzo, J. D. (1972). *Wechsler's measurement and appraisal of adult intelligence* (5th ed.). Baltimore: Williams & Wilkins.

Matarazzo, J. D., Bornstein, R. A., McDermott, P. A., & Noonan, J. V. (1986). Verbal IQ versus Performance IQ difference scores in male and females from the WAIS-R standardization sample. *Journal of Clinical Psychology, 42*, 965–974.

Matarazzo, J. D., & Herman, D. O. (1985). Clinical uses of the WAIS-R: Base rates of differences between VIQ and PIQ in the WAIS-R standardization sample. In B. B. Wolman (Ed.), *Handbook of intelligence* (pp. 899–932). New York: Wiley.

Mishra, S. P., & Brown, K. H. (1983). The comparability of WAIS and WAIS-R IQs and subtest scores. *Journal of Clinical Psychology, 39*, 754–757.

Moon, G. W., Blakey, W. A., Gorsuch, R. L., & Fantuzzo, J. W. (1991). Frequent WAIS-R administration errors: An ignored source of inaccurate measurement. *Professional Psychology: Research and Practice, 22*, 256–258.

Moon, G. W., Fantuzzo, J. W., & Gorsuch, R. L. (1986). Teaching WAIS-R administration skills: Comparison of the MASTERY model to other existing clinical training modalities. *Professional Psychology: Research and Practice, 17*, 31–35.

Nihira, K., Foster, R., Shellhaas, M., & Leland, H. (1975). *AAMD Adaptive Behavior Scale*. Monterey, CA: Publishers Test Service.

O'Grady, K. E. (1983). A confirmatory maximum likelihood factor analysis of the WAIS-R. *Journal of Consulting and Clinical Psychology, 51*, 826–831.

Parker, K. (1983). Factor analysis of the WAIS-R at nine age levels between 16 and 74 years. *Journal of Consulting and Clinical Psychology, 51*, 302–308.

Parloff, M. B. (1980). Psychotherapy and research: An anaclitic depression (The twenty-third annual Frieda Fromm-Reichman Memorial Lecture). *Psychiatry, 43*, 279–293.

Phillips, J. L., Jr. (1975). *The origins of intellect: Piaget's theory* (2nd ed.). San Francisco: W. H. Freeman.

Piaget, J. (1950). *The psychology of intelligence.* New York: Harcourt, Brace & World.

Piedmont, R. L., Sokolove, R. L., & Fleming, M. Z. (1989). Discriminating psychotic and affective disorders using the WAIS-R. *Journal of Personality Assessment, 53*, 739–748.

Piedmont, R. L., Sokolove, R. L., & Fleming, M. Z. (1992). An evaluation of various WAIS-R factor structures in a psychiatric sample. *Journal of Clinical Psychology, 48*, 658–666.

Piotrowski, C., & Keller, J. (1989). Psychological testing in outpatient mental health facilities: A national study. *Professional Psychology: Research and Practice, 20*, 423–425.

Prifitera, A., & Ryan, J. J. (1983). WAIS-R/WAIS comparisons in a clinical sample. *Clinical Neuropsychology, 5*, 97–99.

Rapaport, D., Gill, M., & Schafer, R. (1968). *Diagnostic psychological testing* (rev. ed. by R. R. Holt). New York: International Universities Press.

Reynolds, C. R., & Brown, R. T. (Eds.). (1984). *Perspectives on bias in mental testing.* New York: Plenum.

Reynolds, C. R., Chastain, R. L., Kaufman, A. S., & McLean, J. E. (1987). Demographic characteristics and IQ among adults: Analysis of the WAIS-R standardization sample as a function of stratification variables. *Journal of School Psychology, 25*, 323–342.

Reynolds, C. R., Willson, V. L., & Clark, P. L. (1983). A four-subtest short form of the WAIS-R for clinical screening. *Clinical Neuropsychology, 5*, 111–116.

Russell, E. W. (1987). Neuropsychological interpretation of the WAIS. *Neuropsychology, 1*, 1–6.

Ryan, J. J., Paolo, A. M., & Brungardt, T. M. (1990). WAIS-R reliability and standard errors for persons 75 to 79, 80 to 84, and 85 and older. *Journal of Psychoeducational Assessment, 8*, 9–14.

Ryan, J. J., Paolo, A. M., & Brungardt, T. M. (1992). WAIS-R test–retest stability in normal persons 75 years and older. *Clinical Neuropsychologist, 6*, 3–8.

Ryan, J. J., Rosenberg, S. J., & DeWolfe, A. S. (1984). Generalization of the WAIS-R factor structure with a vocational rehabilitation sample. *Journal of Consulting and Clinical Psychology, 52*, 311–312.

Saccuzzo, D. P., Johnson, N. E., & Russell, G. (1992). Verbal versus performance IQs for gifted African-American, Caucasian, Filipino, and Hispanic children. *Psychological Assessment, 4*, 239–244.

Sattler, J. M. (1988). *Assessment of children* (3rd ed.). San Diego: Author.

Sattler, J. M. (1992). *Assessment of children* (rev. 3rd ed.). San Diego: Author.

Satz, P., & Mogel, S. (1962). An abbreviation of the WAIS for clinical use. *Journal of Clinical Psychology, 18*, 77–79.

Scarr, S., & Barker, W. (1981). The effects of family background: A study of cognitive differences among black and white twins. In S. Scarr (Ed.), *IQ: Social class and individual differences* (pp. 261–315). Hillsdale, NJ: Erlbaum.

Scarr, S., & Carter-Saltzman, L. (1982). Genetics and intelligence. In R. J. Sternberg (Ed.), *Handbook of human intelligence* (pp. 792–896). Cambridge, England: Cambridge University Press.

Siegert, R. J., Patten, M. D., Taylor, A. J. W., & McCormick, I. A. (1988). Factor analysis of the WAIS-R using the factor replication procedure, FACTOREP. *Multivariate Behavioral Research, 23*, 481–489.

Silverstein, A. B. (1982a). Two- and four-subtest short forms of the WAIS-R. *Journal of Consulting and Clinical Psychology, 50*, 415–418.

Silverstein, A. B. (1982b). Factor structure of the Wechsler Adult Intelligence Scale—Revised. *Journal of Consulting and Clinical Psychology, 50*, 661–664.

Silverstein, A. B. (1987). Accuracy estimates of premorbid intelligence based on demographic variables. *Journal of Clinical Psychology, 43*, 493–495.

Sipps, G. J., Berry, W., & Lynch, E. M. (1987). WAIS-R and social intelligence: A test of established assumptions that uses the CPI. *Journal of Clinical Psychology, 43*, 499–504.

Slate, J. R., Jones, C. H., & Murray, R. A. (1991). Teaching administration and scoring of the Wechsler Adult Intelligence Scale—Revised: An empirical evaluation of practice administrations. *Professional Psychology: Research and Practice, 22*, 375–379.

Smith, A. (1966). Certain hypothesized hemispheric differences in language and visual functions in human adults. *Cortex, 2*, 109–126.

Smith, H. H., & Smith, L. S. (1977). WAIS functioning of cirrhotic and non-cirrhotic alcoholics. *Journal of Clinical Psychology, 33*, 309–313.

Smith, R. S. (1983). A comparison of the Wechsler Adult Intelligence Scale and Wechsler Intelligence Scale—Revised in a college population. *Journal of Consulting and Clinical Psychology, 51*, 414–419.

Snow, W. G., & Weinstock, J. (1990). Sex differences among non-brain-damaged adults on the Wechsler Adult Intelligence Scales: A review of the literature. *Journal of Clinical and Experimental Neuropsychology, 12*, 873–886.

Sparrow, S. S., Balla, D. A., & Cicchetti, D. V. (1984a). *Vineland Adaptive Behavior Scales, Expanded Form manual*. Circle Pines, MN: American Guidance Service.

Sparrow, S. S., Balla, D. A., & Cicchetti, D. V. (1984b). *Vineland Adaptive Behavior Scales, Survey Form manual*. Circle Pines, MN: American Guidance Service.

Spearman, C. E. (1927). *The abilities of man*. New York: Macmillan.

Sprandel, H. Z. (1985). *The psychoeducational use and interpretation of the Wechsler Adult Intelligence Scale—Revised*. Springfield, IL: Charles C Thomas.

Sternberg, R. J., & Salter, W. (1982). Conceptions of intelligence. In R. J. Sternberg (Ed.), *Handbook of human intelligence* (pp. 3–28). Cambridge, England: Cambridge University Press.

Tellegen, A., & Briggs, P. F. (1967). Old wine in new skins: Grouping Wechsler subtests into new scales. *Journal of Consulting and Clinical Psychology, 31*, 499–506.

Terman, L. M. (1916). *The measurement of intelligence*. Boston: Houghton Mifflin.

Terman, L. M., & Merrill, M. A. (1937). *Measuring intelligence*. Boston: Houghton-Mifflin.

Todd, J., Coolidge, F., & Satz, P. (1977). The Wechsler Adult Intelligence Scale Discrepancy Index: A neuropsychological evaluation. *Journal of Consulting and Clinical Psychology, 45,* 450–454.

Torrance, E. P. (1984). *Torrance Tests of Creative Thinking.* Bensenville, IL: Scholastic Testing Service.

Tucker, D. M., Stenslie, C., Roth, R., & Shearer, S. (1981). Right frontal lobe activation and right hemisphere performance: Decrement during a depressed mood. *Archives of General Psychiatry, 38,* 169–174.

Vincent, K. R. (1991). Black/white IQ differences: Does age make the difference? *Journal of Clinical Psychology, 47,* 266–270.

Wagner, E. E., & Gianakos, I. (1985). Comparison of WAIS and WAIS-R scaled scores for an outpatient clinic sample retested over extended intervals. *Perceptual and Motor Skills, 61,* 87–90.

Wakefield, P. J., Yost, E., Williams, R. E., & Patterson, K. P. (in press). *Thoughts, actions, and alcohol: Cognitive–behavioral treatment manual for alcoholic couples.* New York: Guilford Press.

Waller, N. G., & Waldman, I. D. (1990). A reexamination of the WAIS-R factor structure. *Psychological Assessment, 2,* 139–144.

Wechsler, D. (1939). *Measurement of adult intelligence.* Baltimore: Williams & Wilkins.

Wechsler, D. (1955). *Manual for the Wechsler Adult Intelligence Scale.* New York: Psychological Corporation.

Wechsler, D. (1958). *The measurement and appraisal of adult intelligence* (4th ed.). Baltimore: Williams & Wilkins.

Wechsler, D. (1968). *The measurement and appraisal of adult intelligence* (5th ed.). Baltimore: Williams & Wilkins.

Wechsler, D. (1975). Intelligence defined and undefined. *American Psychologist, 30,* 135–139.

Wechsler, D. (1981). *Manual for the Wechsler Adult Intelligence Scale—Revised.* New York: Psychological Corporation.

Welsh, G. S. (1952). An anxiety index and an internalization ratio for the MMPI. *Journal of Consulting Psychology, 16,* 65–72.

Wolff, K. C., & Gregory, R. J. (1991). The effects of a temporary dysphoric mood upon selected WAIS-R subtests. *Journal of Psychoeducational Assessment, 9,* 340–344.

Zillmer, E. A., & Ball, J. D. (1987). Psychological and neuropsychological testing in the medical setting. *Staff and Resident Physician, 6,* 602–609.

Zillmer, E. A., Ball, J. D., Fowler, P. C., Newman, A. C., & Stutts, M. L. (1991). Wechsler Verbal–Performance IQ discrepancies among psychiatric inpatients: Implications for subtle neuropsychological dysfunction. *Archives of Clinical Neuropsychology, 6,* 61–71.

Zimmerman, I. L., & Woo-Sam, J. M. (1973). *Clinical interpretations of the Wechsler Adult Intelligence Scale.* New York: Grune & Stratton.

6

The Rorschach

Stephen W. Hurt
Marvin Reznikoff
John F. Clarkin

Background

Historical Development

The Rorschach is perhaps the most extensively researched projective instrument, and it is among the most frequently used tests in a variety of clinical settings (Lubin, Larsen, Matarazzo, & Seever, 1984). The concept of projection has a lengthy history and relies on the idea that individuals exposed to comparatively unstructured or ambiguous materials organize and interpret them in a manner characteristic of their own personalities and perceptions of the world, and in doing so, "project" aspects of their inner lives and modes of thinking. Historical examples that rely on this concept include Leonardo da Vinci's 15th-century description of the artistic inspiration Botticelli received from a sponge full of color thrown against a wall, thereby producing a blot in which various shapes of animals and people could be seen (cited in Zubin, Eron, & Schumer, 1965). In *Hamlet*, Act III, Scene 2, Shakespeare depicts an interesting exchange between Hamlet and Polonius with respect to the ever-changing animal forms that can be perceived in clouds.

To Kerner, however, goes the distinction for first recognizing the potential for studying personality through inkblots as such. In his book *Kleksographien*, published in 1857, Kerner observed that inkblots seem to impose their own meaning upon the viewer (Klopfer & Kelley, 1942). He failed to recognize the wide sweep of individual differences in inkblot interpretations, but did find the blots a major source of stimulation for writing poetry.

Hermann Rorschach was born in 1884 in Zurich, Switzerland, the son of a minor artist and art teacher (Rorschach, 1944). Apparently influenced by Kerner while in school, he became fascinated with inkblots, to the extent that he was nicknamed "Kleks" (meaning "inkblot") by his classmates. Instead of pursuing a career in the arts, Rorschach decided to become a psychiatrist; for a 10-year period he investigated the diagnostic potential of inkblots, administering them to diverse groups of psychiatric patients, as well as to nonpsychiatric populations for comparative purposes. His fundamental goals were to choose a set of blots and devise a scoring system that could be useful in the differential diagnosis of various forms of psychopathology.

Highly encouraged by his findings, Rorschach decided to write a monograph describing his work. However, before the monograph could be completed, a report by Hens appeared in 1917 addressing the usefulness of inkblots with normal children and adults as well as the mentally ill. Rorschach criticized Hens's, approach largely because of his efforts to link inkblot responses to such variables as vocational interests and current events.

Rorschach's own monograph *Psychodiagnostik*, containing his scoring system and reproduction of his inkblots still currently in use, was subsequently published in 1921. Although Rorschach had done a great deal of his experimentation with 15 blots, the printer agreed to include only 10, 5 of which were achromatic and the remainder chromatic. Furthermore, he reduced the blots in size, eliminated parts of them, altered their colors to some degree, and (as a result of a very imperfect printing process) varied the shading. This last printer's error was serendipitous, in that shading ultimately became a very important Rorschach interpretive feature.

Rorschach presented his work to various professional groups; it was not particularly well received, nor did it create much interest. After Rorschach's untimely death of a burst appendix in 1922, Oberholzer, a close coworker, continued his work and introduced the procedure to David Levy, an American psychiatrist studying under him at the time. Upon returning to America, Levy introduced the method to Samuel Beck, then a doctoral student at Columbia. Beck managed to obtain a fellowship permitting him to study the test with Oberholzer in Zurich, which resulted in the first American dissertation on the Rorschach procedure (Beck, 1944). An English translation of Rorschach's *Psychodiagnostik* was not published until 1942.

Klopfer, Piotrowski, and Rapaport were among the many psychologists in the United States who shortly thereafter made major contributions to Rorschach methodology. Although the Rorschach gained enormous popularity among clinicians in the United States and in other parts of the world, it was subject to a variety of criticisms even during its early period of use. In a survey of book reviews dealing with the Rorschach (Aronow & Reznikoff, 1973), the Rorschach was described as enmeshed in overly complex terminology, essentially undecipherable to outsiders. The absence of comprehensive norms was also noted. At the same time, it was compared most positively with the Stanford–Binet in terms of significance and application.

With World War II, a need for psychodiagnostic evaluations in the armed forces helped promote the Rorschach as a major assessment tool. Following the war, graduate training in the Rorschach experienced enormous growth. However, during this postwar period, failure to validate many of the Rorschach hypotheses and an intense and often rancorous rivalry among major Rorschach schools of scoring and interpretation, among other factors, led to a significant shift from optimism to a more pessimistic attitude about the test's inherent value. Thus, after an impressive growth spurt of psychodiagnostic evaluation in the 1940s, interest in the Rorschach and other projective instruments began declining somewhat in the 1950s. This stemmed from overselling the usefulness of very time-consuming, demanding procedures that often produced highly speculative conclusions, which served to raise serious questions about the reliability and validity of the instruments. Equally significant to the declining interest in testing was the fact that psychologists were slowly but successfully expanding their professional roles to include such previously restricted activities as psychotherapy and community consultation—activities that were proving more gratifying than psychodiagnostic activities.

Recently, there has been renewed vigor in the testing sphere. The publication of the various versions of the American Psychiatric Association's *Diagnostic and Statistical Manual* and their progressively more reliable and clinically meaningful psychiatric taxonomy, as well as the emergence of neuropsychological testing and computer-based test interpretation, have been the major contributors to this resurgence (Clarkin, Hurt, & Mattis, 1994). Specifically, in regard to the Rorschach, there have been impressive accomplishments in making it psychometrically more robust and utilizing it in a more creative and probing manner—developments discussed below.

Comparative or Alternative Procedures Available

Of the older scoring–interpretive systems, the one by Klopfer, Ainsworth, Klopfer, and Holt (1954) is still widespread and has its advocates at universities and clinical facilities throughout the United States. Whereas Klopfer et al. stressed perceptual scoring rather than content aspects of Rorschach percepts (as indeed did Rorschach himself), by comparison Exner's Comprehensive System (Exner, 1985) is much more emphatically structural and psychometrically driven in its approach, and clearly predominates in the United States today. The Comprehensive System reflects Exner's review of previously existing systems and an integration and extension of components distilled from these other scoring approaches. It is fundamentally atheoretical and provides extensive norms for scoring and interpretation, based on a substantial body of psychometric data collected by Exner, his students, and his colleagues. It has been an evolving and changing system, rather complex in nature, with over 300 structural components. Although it is hardly free of criticisms, by and large the favorable reliability and validity data emerging from research with the Comprehensive System have invigorated the Rorschach as a potentially dependable psychometric instrument (Anastasi, 1988).

Exner's statistically oriented Rorschach scoring system lends itself to computer interpretation. A Rorschach Interpretation Assistance Program (RIAP) has been developed that employs coded responses and generates approximately a five-page-long set of interpretative hypotheses, which can be integrated into a report (Exner, 1985). Piotrowski (1964) made an initial attempt to computerize Rorschach interpretation utilizing both structural and content scoring. The system, however, is not now commercially available.

Mention should be made here of the Holtzman Inkblot Technique (Holtzman, 1968), which is an effort to deal with the psychometric insufficiencies of the Rorschach by providing two parallel series of 45 cards each, with scores obtained on 22 response variables. The changes in the inkblot stimuli in combination with the procedure that restricts the number of responses to one per card, however, are sufficiently sweeping that the Holtzman Inkblot Technique should be considered quite a different instrument from the Rorschach.

Another approach to Rorschach interpretation, which may best reflect the manner in which many practicing clinicians actually use the instrument, is the content approach (Aronow & Reznikoff, 1976, 1983; Aronow, Reznikoff, & Moreland, 1994). A key concept in this approach is that the Rorschach can be treated as a semistructured interview; within this context, an emphasis on content rather than structural aspects permits a better understanding of the unique parameters of the individual's personality. Contrasted with the nomothetic approach of the Comprehensive System, content interpretation taps an individual's idiographic view of his/her world.

Focusing largely on content aspects in Rorschach interpretation is not new. In fact, in their classic work *Diagnostic Psychological Testing*, Rapaport, Gill, and Schafer (1946) presented an analysis of pathological verbalizations on the Rorschach that has held up well in the research literature (Aronow & Reznikoff, 1976). In 1949 two separate major content approaches were published—namely, the Anxiety and Hostility Scales of Elizur and the Wheeler Signs of Homosexuality. Among other very important interpretive frameworks of Rorschach content were Schafer's psychoanalytic perspective, emphasizing defenses, which appeared in 1954. Four years later Fisher and Cleveland produced their Barrier and Penetration Scales, which provided a conceptual framework for assessing permeability of body boundaries on the Rorschach. Most recently, several scales have been developed to assess various aspects of object relations, incorporating a significant content component (Blatt, 1990; Lerner & Lerner, 1990).

Nature of the Test Demands

The Rorschach is considered to be an unstructured test. That is, subjects are given a relatively open-ended set of instructions prior to beginning the test, and these instructions provide few clues as to how the subjects are to approach the test materials. Questions about these instructions are usually handled by stressing the fact that there are no right or wrong answers and that subjects' approach to responding to the test is left up to them. During the inquiry phase of the examination, questions are generally open-ended and directed at encouraging subjects to elaborate on their responses, rather than to answer specific questions regarding determinants.

Subjects' responses to the Rorschach inkblots depend on their history of experience, style of perception, preferences for information processing, and modes of self-expression; all these factors influence the way in which they provide meaning and structure to the test situation. This approach is in keeping with the projective hypothesis discussed above. Occasionally, subjects will attempt to justify their percepts on the basis of external events, but such instances are usually interpreted as reflecting some anxiety with the testing situation, rather than providing direct, observable information pertinent to the interpretation of test data.

Most examiners assume that the Rorschach places a mild or moderate degree of stress on the subject. This results in part from the ambiguous nature of the test stimuli themselves, and in part from the open-ended nature of the instructions and form of the examination. The examiner's efforts to be interested in and engaged with the subject, but at the same time to remain relatively unobtrusive and nondirectional, help to maintain the anxiety most subjects experience within tolerable bounds. There are no demands, explicit or implicit, for either speedy response or prolonged deliberation. Neither are there any indications given as to how many responses should be provided or what their nature should be, other than to encourage subjects who attempt to unduly restrict the number of their responses to provide additional associations if they can.

Administration and Scoring

Administration

The Rorschach should be administered in standardized but not mechanical fashion. The examiner should interact with the subject, establishing if possible a "testing alliance" in which the examiner is perceived by the subject as trustworthy and helpful. At the same time, the examiner should scrupulously avoid a directive stance when the subject raises questions about such matters as whether the cards can be turned or the number of responses to give. There is some disagreement as to the proper seating arrangement for Rorschach testing. We recommend that the subject sit at the corner of a desk or table closest to the examiner. The desk or table then does not become a potential "barrier" between the examiner and subject. Examiner influence in terms of unintentional reinforcement of selected Rorschach responses is an important variable to consider in the administration procedure. Apart from verbal comments, the examiner should be mindful of nonverbal cues derived from facial expressions and postural movement.

The usual Rorschach administration procedure involves two distinct phases: the "association phase" and the "inquiry phase." In the association phase, the subject is asked to look at each of the 10 symmetrical inkblot cards and to state what each inkblot might be or represent. Reassurance can be offered that there are no right or wrong answers and that different people see different things. The examiner keeps a verbatim record of all responses, as well as noting reaction times, the position in which the cards are held, other behaviors, spontaneous comments, and emotional expression of any type.

Immediately after the association phase is completed, the inquiry phase of testing begins. This phase consists of a systematic effort to explore further and clarify the subject's associations. The subject's responses are read back, and he/she is asked where on the blot the percept was seen and what it was about the blot that might have helped to develop the association. A location sheet, on which the blots are reproduced in miniature, assists the examiner in delineating the inkblot areas utilized by the subject. The inquiry may occur after the entire series of 10 blots is presented, or it may occur after each blot. Some methods, such as that proposed by Exner (1985), prefer the former approach. However, in systems such as that of Rapaport et al. (1946), the inquiry phase is completed after each card—in order to provide an opportunity to explore the subject's associations more closely while they are still fresh, and particularly to enhance the opportunity to capture the associations behind peculiar or deviant responses and verbalizations.

In addition to the two major phases of the Rorschach administration process, a "testing-the-limits" procedure is occasionally used. This allows the examiner to assess the subject's ability to perceive responses that were not reported initially. For example, if the record is an impoverished one and there are no popularly seen percepts, the examiner may suggest such a percept for one of the cards and ask if the subject can, in fact, point it out.

If a content Rorschach is being administered (Aronow & Reznikoff, 1983; Aronow et al., 1994), the inquiry is rather different. Rather than merely locating specific percepts and investigating what specific inkblot properties determine them, the examiner may ask a series of questions that endeavor to stimulate further associations to the responses, even as they may relate to the subject's own life.

Scoring

Although the major Rorschach scoring systems differ from one another in the definition of certain of the scoring features, all of the systems rely on several general characteristics. These include (1) location of the response; (2) perceptual features that contribute to the response (e.g., form, color, or shading); (3) content of the response; (4) conventionality of the response; and (5) form level of the response. In addition, some systems consider the kind and structure of the patient's verbalizations an important scoring category (see Table 6.1).

Scoring of location depends on determining where the percept was seen and how much of the blot was utilized. The subject may elect to incorporate the whole blot, large details of the blot, or small unusual areas and white space. When all or nearly all of the blot is used, location is scored as W. Examples include "a butterfly" to card I, "a monster" to card IV, or "a bat" to card V. If a large, well-defined detail is used as the basis of the response, the location scoring is D. Large details include the side (excluding the central) figures on card I; the central figure alone on card I; the two black areas, the upper or lower red areas, and the central white space on card II; the side human figures, the central red, the upper red, and the lower central figures on card III; the central projection at the bottom of card IV; the top of card VI; the three separate areas of card VII; the side details on card VIII; the upper orange on card IX; and several of the areas of card X. Each scoring system defines large and small details somewhat differently; however, since there is a great deal of overlap, tables from any manual are likely to be quite consistent with those of another.

Second, perceptual features or "determinants" are scored. These include whether the percept is influenced by form, movement, color, and/or shading qualities of the blot. Since there is obviously no movement in the inkblot per se, including movement in a response reflects a subject's ability to project some form of action or life, and movement can be especially revealing of the individual's imaginative activity. Most responses are exclusively or nearly exclusively determined by the form or shape of the blot. As clinicians become more familiar with the Rorschach, popular or conventional responses that require little inquiry are generally form-based. On inquiry, a general question such as "What made it look like . . . ?" usually provokes an answer such as "Because of its shape," and indicates that form is probably the primary determinant.

Depending on the scoring system being used, movement responses may be confined to human percepts or may also be scored for animals or inanimate objects. Movement responses are often apparent from the initial response of the subject. Responses such as "two women dancing" (card I), "two men bowing" (card III), or "a rocket taking off" (card II) are clear examples of responses in which movement is a determinant. Less clear, and

TABLE 6.1. Rorschach Scoring Features

Feature	Scoring types	Examples
Location	Whole blot (W)	Card I, "A butterfly"
	Large detail (D)	Card X, "A crab" (upper right and left blue figures)
	Small detail (d, Dd)	Card I, "Two hands" (small details at top, center)
	White space (S)	Card II, "A plane" (central white space)
Perceptual features	Form (F)	Card VIII, "Two wolves" (pink details on side)
	Movement (M, m)	Card II, "Two people bowing"
	Color (C)	Card III, "A butterfly" (central red detail)
	Black–white (C')	Card IV, "A lump of black coal"
	Shading (K, Ch, C, c)	Card II, "Two elephants with baggy skin" (large black areas, mottled grey/black used to define "baggy")
	Texture (T, c, Y)	Card VI, "An animal skin" (mottled grey/black used to define fur)
Content	Animal, whole (A)	Card II, "Two elephants"
	Animal, part (Ad)	Card IV, "A dragon's head" (lower, central detail)
	Human, whole (H)	Card VII, "Two girls dancing"
	Human, part (Hd)	Card I, "Torso of a woman" (central figure)
	Object (Obj)	Card III, "Two guitars" (upper red details)
	Landscape (Ldsc)	Card X, "A coral reef" (whole blot)
	Art	Card IX, "A child's watercolor" (whole blot)
	Sex	Card II, "A vagina" (lower red detail)
	Anatomy (At, An)	Card VIII, "A ribcage" (small, upper, central detail)
	Clothing (Cg)	Card V, "A Halloween cape" (whole blot)
	Clouds (Cl)	Card VII, "Clouds" (whole blot)
	X-ray	Card IV, "X-ray of a spine" (center detail)
	Blood (Bl)	Card III, "Dripping blood" (top red details)
	Plants (Pl)	Card X, "Some type of seaweed" (lower green detail)
Conventionality	Popular (P)	Card V, "A bat"
	Original (O)	Card IX, "Women drinking tea" (green areas)

(continued)

TABLE 6.1. (Continued)

Feature	Scoring types	Examples
Form level	Good (+)	Card V, "A bat"
	Poor (−)	Card II, "An exploding volcano"
Verbalizations	Peculiar (Pec)	Card II, "An upside-down top" (central white space)
	Fabulized (Fab)	Card VIII, "Two squirrels having a race to the top of the tree"
	Fabulized combination (FabComb)	Card X, "Two bugs attacking the Eiffel Tower" (top, center detail)
	Confabulation (Confab)	Card IX, "Twins inside a woman's pelvis" (bottom pink [twins] and middle green)
	Autistic logic (Aut)	Card I, "Genesis, because it's the first card"
	Contamination (Contam)	Card III, "Two men beating their brains out" (usual human figures; lower details are drums; upper red details "look like brains")

handled somewhat differently by the various scoring systems in widespread use, are examples of "frozen" movement or lifelike posture or movement not based on gross motor involvement. Examples of these types of movement include "a woman with her hands up" (center detail, card I), "two monkeys falling" (upper red, card III), or "two animals halfway up a tree" (side details, card VIII). Instances such as these are not as obviously based on movement and may reflect a tendency to view oneself and others as largely "acted on" rather than as "acting."

Color as a determinant can be used alone, but is most often used in conjunction with form. In scoring the response, it becomes necessary to determine whether color is the sole determinant or is used in combination with form to some degree. If color is the sole determinant, it is scored C. For example, "Art" as a response to card IX is almost always based solely on the colors of the card. If color predominates or is the primary determinant, the response is scored CF. If, instead, form is primary and the color is a secondary feature, the response is scored FC. Generally, differentiating between CF and FC is a task for inquiry. Beginning with a general question often prompts a spontaneous mention of color or form as the primary determinant (e.g., association: card III, central red as "a butterfly"; inquiry: "What made it look like . . . ?" "It was shaped like a butterfly and it was a bright red color"; scoring: FC). Since the scoring depends on the subject's perceptual approach and not on the actual inkblot, careful inquiry is important. The central red detail mentioned above is often seen as a butterfly. For some, the red color is of primary importance in seeing it as a butterfly; for others, the form predominates but the color is helpful; for still others, no mention of the color is made. "Blood spots" on cards II and III, in particular, are examples of the use of color with indefinite form and are scored CF. Mention of achromatic color—that is, the blackness or whiteness of something—is scored as C'. Like the C score for chromatic color, the C' score is often combined with F for scores of FC' or C'F. Clear examples involving C' include the following: card II, "Large black bears standing on their hind legs and pressing their paws together"; card V, "A black bat"; or card I, "Ghosts" (seen as the four interior white spaces). When scoring achromatic color, the examiner must be careful not to confuse it with the W, D, and S location scorings. For example, "A Halloween mask," seen as the whole of card I with the upper interior white forming the eyeholes and the lower interior white forming a mouth opening, is probably better scored to reflect the use of white space in the whole response (WS) rather than the white space as part of the response's determinants (FC').

Shading is a less frequently encountered determinant. It is represented in the scoring summary by either K, Ch, c, or (C). Shading responses are based on the use of the lighter and darker grey areas in the achromatic parts of the blot as part of the determinant of the response. This can include responses such as "mottled," "furry," or "hairy," all of which suggest that this contrast may be influencing the response. In other cases, the actual response given during the association phase of the examination will contain no explicit clue to the use of shading as a determinant, but with increasing experience, responses likely to involve shading become more apparent. Cards IV and VI, especially, fall into this latter group. A response of "monster" on card IV or "an animal skin" on card VI often involves shading as a determinant, as do other furry mammal responses (e.g., "bears" to card II or "rabbits" to card VII). In those systems that score shading as texture differently from shading used to denote perspective or surface reflection such as marble (e.g., Beck or Klopfer), careful inquiry is required to choose the appropriate determinant.

The third category of scoring deals with content—namely, the subject matter of the response. Key content categories encompass human and animal figures and details, clouds, anatomy, X-rays, blood, plants, and sexual objects. The breadth and variety of content categories give some indication of the educational and cultural background of subjects.

A fourth component of scoring involves the degree of conventionality or creativity of a particular response, based on its frequency of occurrence in the population in general. Most percepts are scored as neither popular nor original. However, a record should contain at least a few popular responses. Overreliance on popular responses indicates a cautiousness or blandness in subjects, and an avoidance of popular responses may be cause for clinical concern. Other aspects of content interpretation are discussed in more detail below.

Lastly, a form level score is assigned to each response in which form is the chief determinant. The form level conveys the degree of congruence between the outline and structural features of the blot area chosen and the shape and characteristics of the concept seen. When poor form level is scored because a reasonable fit has not been achieved, it may be indicative of poor reality appreciation. Several sources (Exner, 1985; Hertz, 1970) are available for assigning form level scores to responses, and their use is recommended for inexperienced examiners. Most examples of good form responses are perceptually obvious, but some of indeterminate nature are typically assigned a good form level score, based on the frequency with which they are given by otherwise normal individuals.

In addition to the major scoring categories of the Rorschach, the clinician also examines various more qualitative aspects of a subject's performance. These include an analysis of the sequence of responses, pathological verbalizations (i.e., examples of peculiar, highly personalized thinking; see Table 6.1 for examples), and behavioral accompaniments of various percepts.

After the Rorschach responses are scored or coded and the numbers of responses falling into various categories are tabulated, the examiner computes a series of ratios and percentages representing various combinations of different Rorschach variables and their interrelationships. Confronted by this wide array of indices derived from a Rorschach record, the clinician's daunting task is then to integrate the results to present a meaningful description or picture of the individual. As mentioned earlier, if the clinician elects to use the RIAP, a computerized set of hypotheses based on Exner's Comprehensive System is produced; this highlights features of the record, which the clinician can then integrate into the final report.

In contrast to the nomothetic approach to perceptual scoring discussed above, scoring of a content Rorschach provides a more idiographic approach. Although no formal content scoring approach is recommended, some interpretive guidelines have been suggested (Aronow & Reznikoff, 1983). Aronow and Reznikoff caution that overly speculative interpretation of content that is restricted and/or unclear should be avoided. They also suggest eschewing interpretations that rely on fixed symbolic meaning for various content categories, or depending primarily upon content associations that certain blots are assumed invariably to evoke. It is asserted that the more original, emotionally charged, and imaginative the content of a percept is, the more likely it is to be symbolically significant and dynamically revealing of the individual.

Advantages and Limitations

The Rorschach is a very useful test on many counts. It is helpful in making a differential diagnosis, particularly when there are issues of reality appreciation and mood disturbance. It can also add information about the influence of organically based difficulties, and can reveal characteristic defense mechanisms and modes of coping with anxiety.

The Rorschach provides data on the nature of an individual's self-concept, as well as on his/her object relations and manner of dealing with emotions (both expression and control). The Rorschach can address various aspects of a person's intellectual functioning, assess insight, and afford a basis for some educated guesses on resilience. In sum, it can present an overall picture of a person's assets and liabilities that may be particularly useful in a therapeutic planning context.

With regard to the Rorschach's major limitations, the primary ones may very well be (1) the length of time it takes to do a Rorschach, score it, and write a report; and (2) the amount of training and experience necessary to develop the skills to use it effectively. Although the status of the Rorschach has improved notably in recent years with regard to reliability and validity of both its perceptual and content components, there are still some questions to be resolved in these areas. It would also appear that despite the great enhancement of its psychometric status, there is more than a modicum of subjectivity in Rorschach interpretation and report writing. Fortunately, examiners' proclivities for being both overly speculative and rigid in their Rorschach evaluations diminish considerably with experiential factors.

The Rorschach can be integrated extremely well with other projective instruments, such as the more psychodynamically oriented Thematic Apperception Test (TAT) and the self-concept-focused Draw-a-Person. As a measure of less conscious aspects of personality, it nicely complements self-report inventories such as the Minnesota Multiphasic Personality Inventory (MMPI), the Millon Clinical Multiaxial Inventory (MCMI), and the Personality Assessment Inventory (PAI).

Interpretation

Validity of the Record

As in all examination procedures, an understanding of the motivation and investment of the subject in the testing process is crucial to subsequent interpretation of the test data, and bears directly on issues of the validity of the record. Since the testing procedure is interactional, motivation and investment are generally easy to gauge, and are in part reflected in the number of responses offered during the association phase. Depending on the goal of the evaluation, protocols with 20 to 30 responses demonstrate sufficient interest and motivation in the examination procedure to provide an adequate basis for interpretation. Shorter protocols are typical of individuals during hospitalization for psychological or psychiatric problems. With such cases, the chief referral question is often diagnostic in nature; given the impact of the psychological disorders that bring people to treatment in such settings, protocols with 10 to 15 responses are often sufficiently informative to provide an adequate basis for interpretation. A protocol that includes rejections of several of the cards or includes only a few terse popular responses will probably provide few data for interpretation and are of questionable validity. Selective and repeated rejection of certain cards or parts of cards, however—for example, those having a pull for sexual associations—may be of some interpretive value.

Cognition/Ideation

In keeping with the projective hypothesis upon which Rorschach interpretation is based, cognitive and ideational processes are tapped quite extensively by the Rorschach. Since the task of constructing a response to an amorphous blot requires imagination and explication on the part of the subject, a good verbatim record of the subject's responses can be quite revealing of his/her typical modes of thinking in ambiguous situations. Typical features of cognition examined in a Rorschach protocol include the subject's appreciation of consensual reality; capacity to make use of multiple determinants in creative or novel ways; range and breadth of content categories; ability to integrate disparate parts of the blot into a single, well-integrated whole; use of symbolism; attention to detail; and integration of affective and ideational aspects of the response.

The subject's appreciation of conventional reality is reflected in the overall form level of the Rorschach protocol and the percentage of popular responses in the protocol, taking into consideration the total number of responses offered during the association phase. An appropriate balance between more complex responses with multiple determinants and simpler responses tending toward the more conventional also gives indication of an ability to appreciate subtlety or nuance while still maintaining an adequate grasp of consensual meaning. The record should also contain a balance between whole responses and detail responses; the absence of such a balance suggests a certain rigidity in cognitive style.

Cognitive abilities and general ideational style are also evident in an individual's preferences for using small areas of the blot as opposed to the entire blot, as well as his/her willingness to engage in more fanciful efforts versus hewing to the clearly seen and more mundane. Range and breadth of categories involving content are often used as other indicators of cognitive abilities, although these are generally conceded to be heavily influenced by education and experience. During the inquiry phase, the examiner has the opportunity to explore the subject's responses. How these questions are managed, and whether the explanations are helpful in understanding the perceptions of the subject or whether they introduce new material, are all useful indicators of cognitive and ideational processes.

As a general rule, the more disorganized an individual's thinking on the Rorschach—particularly if this is apparent in more minor ways in other tests in the battery—the greater the need for more intense treatment. Very disorganized protocols with many peculiar verbalizations, confabulations, contaminations, or other evidence of poor reality testing may form the basis for a recommendation for formal psychiatric evaluation, and perhaps in-patient treatment.

Mood/Affect

The subject's current affective state undoubtedly colors both the quantitative and qualitative aspects of the Rorschach protocol. Because the typical instructions offered to subjects just prior to taking the test provide few clues to guide their behavior during the test, most subjects, as previously indicated, experience some mild to moderate degree of anxiety on confronting the test materials. This is to be expected, and unless their anxiety fails to abate during the testing or escalates throughout the examination, no particular meaning should be attached to their initial apprehensiveness.

Clinically significant depression or other, milder forms of dysphoria also leave their imprint on test protocols. Depressed subjects may provide rather direct indications of their affective state by describing stooped, prone, or fatigued human percepts, withered or decaying leaves, or other damaged or incomplete responses. Other indicators of a possible dysphoric state include an emphasis on skeletal remains or other anatomical preoccupations, a diminished reactivity to the chromatic cards, or a failure to integrate color successfully into responses.

Elevated mood states, such as those found in the manic phase of a bipolar or schizoaffective episode or in certain cyclothymic or self-absorbed subjects, can also influence the test protocol. As in the case of depressed subjects, human figures and the descriptions of their character, posture, or engagement with one another often lend themselves to opportunities for descriptions of expansive, elevated, or irritable affective states.

An absence of human percepts, or a pronounced tendency to avoid ascribing movement, feelings, or motivations to them, may suggest a more generalized discomfort with emotions or interpersonal situations. At its most extreme, this tendency is often evident in protocols with a large number of abstract, geometric, or geographic responses at the expense of the easily perceived human forms on cards I, II, III, and VII.

Coping Styles and Personality

As noted above, certain of the Rorschach inkblots easily lend themselves to being perceived as human or human-like figures, and the Rorschach literature has most typically viewed these responses as reflecting characteristic ways of interpreting and dealing with interpersonal interactions. Figures seen fighting, arguing, or otherwise engaged in conflictual relationships connote a mental attitude that seems tuned to the perception and expectation of hostility and threat from others. Alternatively, figures dancing, carrying, talking, or celebrating connote an emphasis on cooperation and mutually satisfactory engagement with others. Issues involving dependence, autonomy, and mutuality are all judged from the qualities of movement imparted to human figures and, in some systems, to animals and inanimate objects as well. The nature of the relationship between the figures may vary, depending on the gender of the perceived figures or their assigned roles in relationship to one another—a feature of the analysis that may provide additional insight into the subject's repertoire of interpersonal behavior and areas of conflict.

For example, a young man who had recently been asked to take a leave of absence from his postgraduate training program because of his declining academic performance saw the two human figures on card III as "boxers with gloves on, exhausted after a long match." In contrast, a middle-aged woman cautiously beginning a relationship with a man she had recently met after completing a bitter divorce saw these same figures as "two people sitting down to dinner." Whereas the first response suggested struggle and depletion of resources, the second offered a more guardedly optimistic view of interpersonal situations, with some potential for a gratifying outcome.

Diagnosis

Insofar as diagnostic clarification remains among the chief reasons for referring individuals for psychological assessment, the potential of the Rorschach to contribute to this task should be carefully evaluated. The Rorschach's value in this regard derives in part from its status as a projective test instrument and in part from its style of administration, during which examiners are provided with multiple opportunities to engage subjects in exploring their modes of perceiving and thinking, their affective states and styles, and the significance of their perceptions to their own experiential worlds.

Early attempts to use the Rorschach as a diagnostic instrument focused on efforts to develop catalogs of "signs" of organic, psychological, or psychiatric disorders. These efforts were largely unsuccessful. Such signs can be sensitive to the presence of a disorder, but may also be very nonspecific indicators. That is, members of a certain diagnostic group may often have a particular sign somewhere in their protocols, but many individuals who do not belong to the diagnostic group also have these same signs, making the sign approach of limited value. The hope that pathognomonic signs might be found in the Rorschach (i.e., *everyone* with the diagnosis displays the sign, and *only* those individuals with the diagnosis display the sign) appears to have disappeared. What value remains in scrutinizing the record for various indicators is no different from that derived from careful scoring and calculation of various indices and ratios—the value of using the test data to generate diagnostic hypotheses, which can be checked against other features of the test protocol and other test materials in the battery. Taken together, the signs approach and the requirements of a complete verbatim record and careful scoring form the basis for refining diagnostic hypotheses, making some more likely than others.

Behind the assertion that tests such as the Rorschach can play a role in the diagnostic process is an assumption that the impact of the various organic, psychological, and psychiatric disorders being considered exert identifiable influences on the Rorschach percepts. However, since modern diagnostic nomenclature depends on the identification of clear behavioral manifestations of the diagnosis as well as on a history that supports it, psychological test results can never be the sole basis for a diagnostic conclusion. At best, psychological tests can make a contribution to the differential diagnostic process by offering a source of behavioral data that can be reviewed for evidence of psychopathological functioning. In accepting the fact that Rorschach data, when applied to the problem of differential diagnosis, do not make unequivocal statements, it is helpful to have at hand some information about the individual being examined. These include age, gender, ethnicity, recent life circumstances, range of diagnostic possibilities under consideration, and relevant background information (including previous experience with psychological testing, command of the language in which the examination is being carried out, and recent substance use). Examples of the use of the Rorschach, as well as a number of other tests in wide use in clinical diagnostic settings, can be found in Hurt, Reznikoff, and Clarkin (1991).

Treatment Recommendations

Although much has been written about the value of the Rorschach in exploring more enduring and unconscious attitudes in individuals, clinicians familiar with the use of the test are generally aware of the influence of more situational variables on a person's responses. This is particularly true when individuals are being seen in situational distress or in the midst of an episode of a psychiatric disorder. For this reason, it is best to have some information concerning a person's immediate life circumstances and the reason for the testing referral when evaluating the results. Such information is helpful in sorting out and understanding the test data and in using the data for treatment planning. Under the impact of moderate situational distress, there may be fewer responses with a conventional flavor. The responses may be of poor form quality, or may have unusual or idiosyncratic elements that can be understood in the context of situational factors. Preoccupation with certain types of responses—for example, body parts in someone recently diagnosed with a life-threatening illness—may say more about the person's preoccupation with current circumstances than about his/her more general tendencies to somatize difficulties.

On the basis of the notion that it is not just a test but a clinical technique, the Rorschach can be seen as lending itself to becoming an important part of the therapeutic process. Historically, the posture that assessment has the potential to combine with and add to psychotherapy goes back at least to Jung (1910), who, in the early 1900s, described giving feedback about the results of an association test to a schizophrenic woman he was treating; the woman consequently quickly improved. Jung asserted that it is not easy to differentiate where assessment ends and psychotherapy commences.

Harrower, Vorhaus, Roman, and Bauman (1960) coined the term "projective counseling" to describe sharing projective test responses with the patient. A number of other authors have also written about sharing projective data. From Craddick's (1975) perspective, the examiner and the subject should jointly interpret a Rorschach record. Richman (1967) and Mosak and Gushurst (1972) have similarly stressed the efficacy of sharing test-based information with patients in the context of a psychotherapy relationship.

Schlesinger (1973) emphasizes the continuity between the diagnostic and treatment processes, and feels that a patient should be encouraged to participate as much as possible in the assessment endeavor, because invaluable information is gained from the patient's spontaneous reactions to his/her own test responses. In a comprehensive discussion of the specific use of the TAT in psychotherapy, Bellak (1993) asserts that as a therapeutic tool it may be especially useful in conducting short-term therapy. Bellak permits patients to interpret their own TAT stories, feeling that in the process the patients may actually learn to search for common denominators in their own behavior.

Aronow et al. (1994) summarize four general uses of the Rorschach in connection with psychotherapy:

1. Prior to the onset of therapy, to provide a "road map" (of psychodynamics, ego strengths and weaknesses, etc.).
2. Either during the course of therapy or at the very end, to serve as a means of evaluating progress; this is particularly useful if there is, in fact, a "before" measure with which to provide comparisons.
3. To serve as a tool to gain a better understanding of blockages that may occur in the psychotherapy process and that may otherwise be impenetrable.
4. To serve as a means for insight and change in psychotherapy through the actual process of sharing the interpretation of responses with the subjects.

Thus, discussing the results of a psychological evaluation with a patient can be legitimately viewed as a therapeutic intervention; as observed by Finn and Tonsager (1992), this represents a "major paradigm shift" in how assessment is ordinarily regarded.

References

Anastasi, A. (1988). *Psychological testing* (6th ed.). New York: Macmillan.

Aronow, E., & Reznikoff, M. (1973). Attitudes toward the Rorschach expressed in book reviews: A historical perspective. *Journal of Personality Assessment, 37*, 309–315.

Aronow, E., & Reznikoff, M. (1976). *Rorschach content interpretation*. New York: Grune & Stratton.

Aronow, E., & Reznikoff, M. (1983). *A Rorschach introduction: Content and perceptual approach*. New York: Grune & Stratton.

Aronow, E., Reznikoff, M., & Moreland, K. L. (1994). *The Rorschach technique: Perceptual basics and content analysis*. Needham Heights, MA: Allyn & Bacon.

Beck, S. J. (1944). *Rorschach's test: I. Basic processes*. New York: Grune & Stratton.

Bellak, L. (1993). *The Thematic Apperception Test, the Children's Apperception Test and the Senior Apperception Test in clinical use* (5th ed.). Needham Heights, MA: Allyn & Bacon.

Blatt, S. J. (1990). The Rorschach: A test of perception or an evaluation of representation. *Journal of Personality Assessment, 55*, 394–416.

Clarkin, J. F., Hurt, S. W., & Mattis, S. (1994). Psychological and neuropsychological assessment. In J. A. Talbott, R. E. Hales, & S. C. Yudofsky (Eds.), *Textbook of psychiatry* (2nd ed., pp. 247–276). Washington, DC: American Psychiatric Press.

Craddick, R. A. (1975). Sharing oneself in the assessment procedure. *Professional Psychology, 6*, 279–282.

Elizur, A. (1949). Content analysis of the Rorschach with regard to anxiety and hostility. *Rorschach Research Exchange, 13*, 247–284.

Exner, J. E., Jr. (1985). *A Rorschach workbook for the comprehensive system* (2nd ed.). Bayville, NY: Rorschach Workshops.

Finn, S. E., & Tonsager, M. E. (1992). Therapeutic effects of providing MMPI-2 test feedback to college students awaiting therapy. *Psychological Assessment, 4*, 278–287.

Fisher, S., & Cleveland, S. L. (1958). *Body image and personality*. New York: Dover.

Harrower, M., Vorhaus, P., Roman, M., & Bauman, G. (1960). *Creative variations in projective techniques*. Springfield, IL: Charles C Thomas.

Hens, S. (1917). *Phantasieprufung mit formlosen Klecksen bei Schulkindern mormalen Erwachsenen und Geisteskranken*. Dissertation, Zurich, Switzerland.

Hertz, M. R. (1970). *Frequency tables for scoring Rorschach responses* (5th ed.). Cleveland, OH: Press of Case Western Reserve University.

Holtzman, W. H. (1968). Holtzman Inkblot Technique. In A. I. Ragin (Ed.), *Projective techniques in personality assessment* (pp. 136–170). New York: Springer.

Hurt, S. W., Reznikoff, M., & Clarkin, J. F. (1991). *Psychological assessment, psychiatric diagnosis and treatment planning*. New York: Brunner/Mazel.

Jung, C. G. (1910). The association method. *American Journal of Psychology, 21*, 219–269.

Klopfer, B., Ainsworth, M. D., Klopfer, W. G., & Holt, R. R. (Eds.). (1954). *Developments in the Rorschach techniques: Vol. 1. Technique and theory.* Yonkers-on-Hudson, NY: World Book.

Klopfer, B., & Kelley, D. M. (1942). *The Rorschach technique.* New York: World Book.

Lerner, P., & Lerner, H. (1990). Rorschach measures of psychoanalytic theories of defense. In J. R. Butcher & C. D. Spielberger (Eds.), *Advances in personality assessment* (Vol. 8, pp. 121–160). Hillsdale, NJ: Erlbaum.

Lubin, B., Larsen, R. M., Matarazzo, J. D., & Seever, M. (1984). Patterns of psychological test usage in the United States 1935–1982. *American Psychologist, 39*, 451–453.

Mosak, H. H., & Gushurst, R. S. (1972). Some therapeutic uses of psychological testing. *American Journal of Psychotherapy, 26*, 539–546.

Piotrowski, Z. A. (1964). A digital computer administration of inkblot test data. *Psychiatric Quarterly, 38*, 1–26.

Rapaport, D., Gill, M., & Schafer, R. (1946). *Diagnostic psychological testing* (2 vols.). Chicago: Year Book Medical.

Richman, J. (1967). Reporting diagnostic test results to patients and their families. *Journal of Projective Techniques and Personality Assessment, 31*, 62–70.

Rorschach, H. (1942). *Psychodiagnostics.* Bern: Verlag Hans Huber.

Rorschach, O. (1944). Ueber das Leben und die Wesenart von Hermann Rorschach. *Schweizer Archiv fuer Neurologie und Psychiatrie, 53*, 1–11.

Schafer, R. (1954). *Psychoanalytic interpretation in Rorschach testing.* New York: Grune & Stratton.

Schlesinger, H. J. (1973). Interaction of dynamic and reality factors in the diagnostic testing interview. *Bulletin of the Menninger Clinic, 37*, 495–517.

Wheeler, W. M. (1949). An analysis of Rorschach indices of male homosexuality. *Journal of Projective Techniques, 13*, 97–126.

Zubin, J., Eron, L. D. & Schumer, F. (1965). *An experimental approach to projective techniques.* New York: Wiley.

7

Interpretation of the MMPI-2

James N. Butcher

Clinical assessment of mental health patients in the 1930s was a difficult and somewhat flawed activity. The difficulties resulted, for the most part, from the lack of a valid, objective means of obtaining information about patients' problems and symptoms. Although there were personality questionnaires available, they were not considered to be effective in clinical assessment of psychiatric patients: They were too closely tied to psychological theories to be useful, were developed with college students, or simply attempted to measure variables that were unrelated to psychopathology. A developer of the Minnesota Multiphasic Personality Inventory (MMPI), Starke Hathaway (1965), pointed out that sheer frustration in understanding clinical patients was what led him and psychiatrist J. C. McKinley to begin the research in 1939 that resulted in the publication of the original MMPI. Initially, the MMPI was developed at the University of Minnesota Hospitals to aid clinicians in the routine tasks of assessing and diagnosing patients with mental disorders; however, it came to be immediately successful at filling the void in clinical assessment by providing a useful and practical assessment technique for individuals reporting mental health symptoms and problems in a variety of settings.

The MMPI provides information that is useful in predicting individual clients' problems and behaviors in a cost-effective manner. More than 50 years after its publication, the MMPI (now the MMPI-2 and MMPI-A) is still the first and most frequent choice for practitioners when it comes to understanding patients' problems. What gave the MMPI approach to assessment the utility and tenacity it has enjoyed? Hathaway (1965) pointed out several features of the MMPI, in addition to its validity, that he considered important in accounting for the MMPI's popularity as a clinical assessment device: "the provisions for some control over undesirable response patterns, detection of invalid records such as those from nonreaders, the use of simple language, the simplicity of administration and scoring, and, finally, the general clinical familiarity of the profile variables" (p. 463). He further noted that other qualities of the MMPI enhanced its reputation as an objective psychological assessment procedure. It furnished reliable evaluations across administrations, and provided a ready means of comparing a person's score on a scale in a normative framework. That is, a patient's scores on the test could be compared with others to determine whether his/her scores were low or high compared with those of normals.

Development of the Original MMPI

In developing the MMPI, Hathaway and McKinley (1940) chose as their response format the use of statements to which the client could respond either "True" or "False." This relatively straightforward self-administration task enabled individuals with a relatively low reading level to complete the inventory in a short time, usually about 1½ hours. Hathaway and McKinley did not select items for the scales according to their content; they considered the selection of scale items based on face validity to be too subjective. Instead, they compiled a large pool of potential items (about 1,000), which were, for the most part, indicative of symptoms of mental disorders. Before the initial norm development, they reduced the item pool to 504 items. (Later, the MMPI item pool was expanded to 550 items by the inclusion of two additional scales, Masculinity–Femininity and Social Introversion.) In constructing scales, Hathaway and McKinley had no preconceived idea as to how items were to be grouped. Instead, they used empirical contrasts between a sample of normal subjects and groups of well-defined patients to determine the items comprising a particular scale. Their concept of "scale" for the MMPI was relatively uncomplicated. Hathaway and McKinley believed that patients who endorsed similar symptoms or items in the MMPI pool were diagnostically more alike than they were different. If an item empirically discriminated a criterion group (say, depressives) from a normal group, it was considered to have validity and was included on the Depression scale. For example, they believed that individuals endorsing many symptoms related to having a depressed mood were likely to be more similar to other depressed patients than they would be to other clinical diagnostic groups. In order to quantify the relationship between reported psychological symptoms and diagnostic similarity, Hathaway and McKinley developed scales (groups of items) with norms by which individuals could be compared on particular variables. The MMPI scales were viewed as dimensions reflecting particular problems, such as depression or psychopathic deviation.

In developing norms for the original MMPI, Hathaway and McKinley collected responses from a large group of "normals," defined as men and women who were not presently under a doctor's care. Most of the subjects in the original normative sample were visitors to the University of Minnesota Hospital. These individuals were usually people waiting at the hospital who had time on their hands and were willing to participate in the study. The means of the scale distributions were assigned a value of 50, and the standard deviations of each distribution were assigned a value of 10. The *T*-score distributions allow for comparison of scale scores across scales. A score of 70, two standard deviations above the mean, was considered clinically significant.

Almost as soon as the inventory was published (Hathaway & McKinley, 1943), it began to gain acceptance in clinical assessment settings. The scale construction method produced clinical scales that proved to have high generalizability across diverse settings, and the MMPI became the most widely used and researched objective personality inventory in the United States (Lubin, Larsen, & Matarazzo, 1984; Lubin, Larsen, Matarazzo, & Seever, 1985; Piotrowski & Lubin, 1990) for patients in general medical settings, adolescents in schools, inmates in correctional facilities, individuals in alcohol and drug problem treatment units, military personnel, and eventually applicants for highly responsible or sensitive positions in industrial settings (e.g., airline pilots, police officers, or nuclear power plant operators). The MMPI also became the most widely used measure of psychopathology in psychological, psychiatric, and medical research studies.

International adaptation of the MMPI followed shortly after its publication. During the 1940s translations were completed in Cuba, Germany, Italy, Japan, and Puerto Rico, and by 1976 there were over 130 foreign language translations available in over 40 countries (Butcher & Pancheri, 1976; Butcher, 1985). The MMPI has been seen by mental health professionals in other countries as a more efficient way of providing effective assessment instruments than constructing entirely new indigenous instruments. Various reviews of cross-national MMPI research (Butcher & Pancheri, 1976; Butcher, 1985; Cheung, 1985) have suggested that the MMPI has demonstrated the same level of acceptance in mental health settings in many other countries as in the United States.

Revision of the MMPI: The MMPI-2 and MMPI-A

Over time, several problems with the original MMPI became apparent. Many of the items in the inventory were found to be out-of-date or objectionable (Butcher, 1972; Butcher & Owen, 1978), and it was recommended that the instrument be revised by deleting obsolete items and broadening the item pool to include more contemporary topics. In addition, the use of the original MMPI norms became problematic, because the normative sample on which the original MMPI scales were based was not appropriate for many present-day comparisons (Butcher, 1972). The original MMPI normative sample was comprised of white, rural subjects from Minnesota, yet it was being used across the United States with broadly diverse clients. Colligan, Osborne, Swenson, and Offord (1983) and Parkison and Fishburne (1984) conducted studies showing that the original MMPI norms were inappropriate for use with today's subjects.

In the early 1980s, the University of Minnesota Press, the copyright holder, decided to sponsor a revision of the MMPI. The revision program was initiated in 1982 by a committee comprised of Grant Dahlstrom, John Graham, Auke Tellegen, and myself; it was aimed at maintaining the integrity of many scales of the original MMPI, because of their demonstrated advantages, as well as at expanding the range of clinically relevant measures in the inventory (Butcher, Graham, Williams, & Ben-Porath, 1990). Of primary concern to the committee was the need to maintain the acceptability of the original instrument in its restandardized versions, the MMPI-2 and the MMPI-A.[1] Initially, the MMPI revision committee decided to develop two separate experimental booklets, one for adults and one for adolescents, for use in data collection. Each experimental booklet included all the original MMPI items, some with minor wording improvements (Butcher, Dahlstrom, Graham, Tellegen, & Kaemmer, 1989; Butcher et al., 1992). Items measuring new content (e.g., suicidal behavior, treatment readiness, Type A behaviors, problematic substance drug use) were added to both experimental booklets. In addition, developmentally relevant items were added to the appropriate booklets (e.g., work adjustment items were added to the adult form, and school adjustment items to the adolescent form).

Items comprising the validity and standard scales, except for the objectionable items, were retained in the MMPI-2. However, new items measuring additional clinical problems and applications were added to the inventory, replacing the out-of-date, nonfunctional items from the original booklet. Thus, broader content coverage, allowing for new scale development, was accomplished without altering the standard scales. In order to modernize the MMPI, new normative and clinical data were collected on adults (Butcher et al., 1989) and adolescents (Butcher et al., 1992). In the development of the MMPI-2 and MMPI-A, the following goals were pursued: (1) to revise and modernize the MMPI item domain by deleting objectionable, nonworking, or otherwise obsolete items and replacing them with items addressing contemporary clinical problems and applications; (2) to assure the continuity of the original validity, standard, and several supplementary scales by keeping these measures relatively intact; (3) to develop new scales to address problems that were not covered in the original MMPI; (4) to collect

[1]This chapter focuses upon assessment of adults and does not present detailed information about the MMPI-A. Readers interested in the assessment of adolescents should consult the manual for the MMPI-A (Butcher et al., 1992) or the interpretive guide by Butcher and Williams (1992).

new, representative, randomly solicited, and nationally based nonpatient samples of adults and adolescents, in order to develop age-appropriate norms; (5) to develop new normative distributions for the MMPI-2 and MMPI-A scales that would better reflect clinical problems; and (6) to collect a broad range of clinical data for evaluating changes in the original scales and for validating the new scales.

Development of New Norms

The MMPI-2 normative sample consisted of 2,600 subjects (1,462 women and 1,138 men, ages 18 through the adult years), sampled from seven states in different geographic regions (California, Minnesota, North Carolina, Ohio, Pennsylvania, Virginia, and Washington). The normative sample was balanced for gender and important demographic characteristics such as ethnic group membership. Normative subjects were randomly selected, initially contacted by letter, and asked to come to a prearranged testing site for completion of the test battery. All subjects were administered the 704-item experimental form of the MMPI, a biographical questionnaire, and a questionnaire assessing significant life events in the past 6 months. In addition to the normative study described in the manual for the MMPI-2, a number of other normative and clinical studies provided additional validation for the MMPI-2 standard scales and new content scales.

The norms for the MMPI-2 were constructed to eliminate two problems with the original MMPI norms. First, as noted above, the norms were based upon a large contemporary sample of individuals drawn from across the United States. Second, the norms were derived by procedures that assured that the T scores for each scale would be uniform for a given level of T scores. That is, for a given T score, the percentile value of the clinical and content scale scores would be equivalent. As a result of the new normative procedures, there are small differences between T scores generated by the original and new procedures. However, it is important to realize that the relationship between the *uniform* T-score distribution and the original MMPI distribution is very strong, and that both are based on a linear T-score transformation for the raw scores (Tellegen & Ben-Porath, 1992).

As a result of the maintenance of continuity between the original MMPI and the MMPI-2, the validity research on the original scales has been shown to apply equally well to the MMPI-2 (Graham, 1988, 1990). In addition, a number of studies were conducted to provide new validation information for the scales, to ensure that they maintained their validity during the revision process. Several recent studies have provided evidence of the validity of the traditional clinical scales on the MMPI-2 (Ben-Porath & Butcher, 1989a, 1989b; Ben-Porath, Butcher, & Graham, 1991; Butcher et al., 1991; Butcher, Jeffrey, Cayton, Colligan, DeVore, & Minnegawa, 1990; Butcher,

Graham, Dahlstrom, & Bowman, 1990; Egeland, Erickson, Butcher, & Ben-Porath, 1991; Hjemboe & Butcher, 1991; Keller & Butcher, 1991). Several additional scales, often referred to as "supplemental scales," were maintained on the MMPI-2 (the Anxiety, Repression, Ego Strength, MacAndrew Alcoholism, and Overcontrolled Hostility scales). In addition, several new supplementary scales were published in the MMPI-2 to assess specific problems such as drug and alcohol abuse (the Addiction Potential scale and Addiction Acknowledgment scale), as well as marital problems (the Marital Distress scale) (Weed, Butcher, Ben-Porath, & McKenna, 1992). A brief description of the MMPI-2 validity scales is provided in Table 7.1, and the clinical and supplemental scales are described in Table 7.2.

Development of the MMPI-2 Content Scales

Interpretation of item content is based on the view that responses to items are communications about an individual's feelings, personality style, and past or current problems. It is assumed that the individual wishes to reveal his/her ideas, attitudes, beliefs, and problems, and then cooperates with the testing by truthfully acknowledging them. Most people taking the inventory provide accurate information about themselves.

The content scales for the MMPI-2, described more fully in Table 7.3, were developed (Butcher, Graham, Williams, & Ben-Porath, 1990) to assess the main content dimensions in the revised inventory. The new MMPI-2 content scales were developed by a multimethod, multistage scale construction strategy, in which both rational and statistical procedures were employed to ensure content homogeneity and strong statistical properties. The new MMPI-2 content scales assess several important areas of symptomatic behavior with several scales (Anxiety, Fears, Obsessiveness, Depression, Health Concerns, and Bizarre Mentation). They also include two personality factor scales (Type A Behavior, Cynicism), two externalizing scales (Anger, Antisocial Practices), a negative self-views scale (Low Self-Esteem), and important clinical problem area scales (Family Problems, Work Interference, Negative Treatment Indicators).

The MMPI-2 content scales have been shown to have strong internal psychometric properties, along with external validity. For example, comparisons between the MMPI-2 content scales and the original MMPI clinical scales using the same behavioral descriptors showed the content scales to possess external validity equal to or greater than that of the clinical scales (Ben-Porath et al., 1991; Butcher, Graham, Williams, & Ben-Porath, 1990). Two recent studies provided empirical verification for MMPI-2 content scales. In a recent study, Faull and Meyer (1993) found that the Depression content scale on MMPI-2 outperformed the MMPI-2 Depression clinical scale in assessment of subjective depression in a group of primary medical pa-

TABLE 7.1. Description of the MMPI-2 Validity Scales

Cannot Say (?) score. The total number of unanswered items. A defensive proto-col with possible attenuation of scale scores is suggested if the ? raw score is more than 30. The actual item omissions are listed in the report. In addition, the actual impact of item omissions on each scale is provided by showing the percentage of items endorsed on each scale.

Lie (L) scale. A measure of rather unsophisticated or self-consciously "virtuous" test-taking attitude. Elevated scores (*T* above 65) suggest that the individual is presenting himself/herself in an overly positive light—attempting to create an unrealistically favorable view of his/her adjustment.

Infrequency (F) scale. The items on this scale are answered in the nonkeyed direction by most people. A high score (*T* above 80) suggests an exaggerated pattern of symptom checking that is inconsistent with accurate self-appraisal and suggests confusion, disorganization, or actual faking of mental illness. Scores above 110 invalidate the profile.

Defensiveness (K) scale. Measures an individual's willingness to disclose personal information and discuss his/her problems. High scores (*T* above 65) reflect an uncooperative attitude and an unwillingness or reluctance to disclose personal information. Low scores (*T* below 45) suggest openness and frankness. This scale is positively correlated with intelligence and educational level, which should be taken into account when interpreting the scores.

Back F (F_B) scale. This scale was incorporated into the MMPI-2 to detect possible deviant responding to items located toward the end of the item pool. Some sub-jects, tiring of taking the test, may modify their approach to the items part way through the item pool and answer in a random or unselective manner. Since all of the items on the F scale occur before item 370, the F scale or F − K may not detect such changes in response pattern. This 40-item scale was developed in a manner analogous to the development of the original F scale—that is, by including items that had low endorsement percentages in the normal population. Within the Min-nesota Report, no interpretation of the F_B scale is provided if the *T* score is above 90 or if the profile is invalid by F-scale criteria. If the F_B *T* score is elevated above 90 and the original F scale is valid, then interpretations of F_B are provided depending upon the level of the original F score.

Variable Response Inconsistency (VRIN) scale. The VRIN scale consists of 49 pairs of specially selected items. The members of each VRIN item pair have either similar or opposite content; each pair is scored for the occurrence of an incon-sistency in responses to the two items. The scale score is the total number of item pairs answered inconsistently. A high VRIN score is a warning that a test subject may have been answering the items in the inventory in an indiscriminate manner, and raises the possibility that the protocol may be invalid and that the profile is essentially uninterpretable.

True Response Inconsistency (TRIN) scale. The TRIN scale is made up of 20 pairs of items that are opposite in content. If a subject responds inconsistently by an-swering "True" to both items of certain pairs, 1 point is added to the TRIN score; if the subject responds inconsistently by answering "False" to certain item

(continued)

TABLE 7.1. (Continued)

pairs, 1 point is subtracted. A very high TRIN score indicates a tendency to give "True" answers to the items indiscriminately ("acquiescence"); a very low TRIN score indicates a tendency to answer "False" indiscriminately ("nonacquiescence"). (Negative TRIN scores are avoided by adding a constant to the raw score.) A very low or very high TRIN score is a warning that the test subject may have been answering the inventory indiscriminately, so that the profile may be invalid and uninterpretable.

Note. Adapted from J. N. Butcher, MMPI-2 workshops and symposia, University of Minnesota.

tients. In another study, Clark (1993) reported that high-scoring patients in a Department of Veterans Affairs chronic pain program who had high scores on the MMPI-2 Anger content scale showed frequent and intense anger, felt unfairly treated by others, felt frustrated, were oversensitive to criticism, were quick-tempered, tended to externalize anger, had tenuous anger control, were impulsive, and had anger control problems.

Nature of the Test Demands

The MMPI-2 provides a highly structured environment for subjects. Respondents are asked to consider their own problem situations and the symptoms they are experiencing at this time, and to share that information by endorsing structured items in the inventory. In most respects, the MMPI-2 does not require a great deal of interpersonal involvement or produce a great deal of interpersonal stress. Once rapport has been established with a client, the reason for administering the test is explained, and specific test instructions are provided, the test items are usually answered in private (either by paper and pencil or by computer).

Traditionally, there were several variables that needed to be considered in evaluating MMPI profiles. The original normative sample was quite restricted in the types of people that were included in the norms; therefore, the test was considered by some to be influenced by such factors as ethnicity. However, because the revised forms of the MMPI were normed on highly diverse, nationally based samples, the contemporary norms are more appropriate for the diverse patient populations to whom the tests are administered today. Recent research has shown that the MMPI-2 norms are appropriate for minority clients (Shondrick, Ben-Porath, & Stafford, 1992).

If an individual is appropriately instructed as to how to respond to the test items, any deviation from those procedures—for example, being defensive or exaggerating symptoms—should be considered "subject variables" that require careful evaluation (Pope, Butcher, & Seelen, 1993). The MMPI-2

TABLE 7.2. Description of the MMPI-2 Clinical and Supplemental Scales

Clinical scales

Scale 1: Hypochondriasis (Hs)
    High scores: Excessive bodily concern; somatic symptoms that tend to be
vague and undefined; epigastric complaints; fatigue, pain, weakness; lacks manifest anxiety; selfish, self-centered, and narcissistic; pessimistic, defeatist, cynical
outlook on life; dissatisfied and unhappy; makes others miserable; whines, complains; demanding and critical of others; expresses hostility indirectly; rarely
acts out; dull, unenthusiastic, unambitious; ineffective in oral expression; long-
standing health concerns; functions at a reduced level of efficiency without
major incapacity; not very responsive to therapy; tends to terminate therapy
when therapist is seen as not giving enough attention and support; seeks medical solutions to problems.

Scale 2: Depression (D)
    High scores: Depressed, unhappy, and dysphoric; pessimistic; self-deprecat-
ing; guilty; sluggish; somatic complaints; weakness, fatigue, and loss of energy;
agitated, tense, high-strung, and irritable; prone to worry; lacks self-confidence;
feels useless and unable to function; feels like a failure at school or on the job;
introverted, shy, retiring, timid, and seclusive; aloof; maintains psychological
distance; avoids interpersonal involvement; cautious and conventional; has difficulty making decisions; nonaggressive; overcontrolled, denies impulses; makes
concessions to avoid conflict; motivated for therapy.

Scale 3: Hysteria (Hy)
    High scores: Reacts to stress and avoids responsibility through development
of physical symptoms; has headaches, chest pains, weakness, and tachycardia;
anxiety attacks; symptoms appear and disappear suddenly; lacks insight about
causes of symptoms; lacks insight about own motives and feelings; lacks anxiety,
tension, and depression; rarely reports delusions, hallucinations, or suspiciousness; psychologically immature, childish, and infantile; self-centered, narcissistic,
and egocentric; expects attention and affection from others; uses indirect and
devious means to get attention and affection; does not express hostility and resentment openly; socially involved; friendly, talkative, and enthusiastic; superficial and immature in interpersonal relationships; shows interest in others for
selfish reasons; occasionally acts out in sexual or aggressive manner with little
apparent insight; initially enthusiastic about treatment; responds well to direct
advice or suggestion; slow to gain insight into causes of own behavior; resistant
to psychological interpretations.

Scale 4: Psychopathic Deviate (Pd)
    High scores: Antisocial behavior; rebellious toward authority figures; stormy
family relationships; blames parents for problems; history of underachievement
in school; poor work history; marital problems; impulsive; strives for immediate
gratification of impulses; does not plan well; acts without considering consequences of actions; impatient; limited frustration tolerance; poor judgment;
takes risks; doesn't profit from experience; immature, childish, narcissistic, self-
centered, and selfish; ostentatious, exhibitionistic; insensitive; interested in

(continued)

TABLE 7.2. (Continued)

Clinical scales

others in terms of *how* they can be used; likable and usually creates a good first impression; shallow, superficial relationships, unable to form warm attachments; extraverted, outgoing; talkative, active, energetic, and spontaneous; intelligent; asserts self-confidence; has a wide range of interests; lacks definite goals; hostile, aggressive; sarcastic, cynical; resentful, rebellious; acts out; antagonistic; aggressive outbursts, assaultive behavior; little guilt over negative behavior; may feign guilt and remorse when in trouble; is free from disabling anxiety, depression, and psychotic symptoms; likely to have personality disorder diagnosis (antisocial or passive–aggressive); prone to worry; is dissatisfied; shows absence of deep emotional response; feels bored and empty; poor prognosis for change in therapy; blames others for problems; intellectualizes; may agree to treatment to avoid jail or some other unpleasant experience, but is likely to terminate before change is effected.

Scale 5: Masculinity–Femininity (Mf)
Males
   High scores (T > 80): Shows conflicts about sexual identity; insecure in masculine role; effeminate; aesthetic and artistic interests; intelligent and capable; values cognitive pursuits; ambitious, competitive, and persevering; clever, clear-thinking, organized, logical; shows good judgment and common sense; curious; creative, imaginative, and individualistic in approach to problems; sociable; sensitive to others; tolerant; capable of expressing warm feelings toward others; passive, dependent, and submissive; peace-loving; makes concessions to avoid confrontations; good self-control; rarely acts out. (The interpretation of high scores should be tempered for males with advanced academic degrees.)
   High scores (T between 70 and 79): May be viewed as sensitive; insightful; tolerant; effeminate; showing broad cultural interests; submissive, passive. (In clinical settings, the patient may show sex role confusion or heterosexual adjustment problems.)
   Low scores (T < 35): "Macho" self-image, presents self as extremely masculine; overemphasizes strength and physical prowess; aggressive, thrill-seeking, adventurous, and reckless; coarse, crude, and vulgar; harbors doubts about own masculinity; has limited intellectual ability; narrow range of interests; inflexible and unoriginal approach to problems; prefers action to thought; is practical and nontheoretical; easy-going, leisurely, and relaxed; cheerful, jolly, humorous; contented; willing to settle down; unaware of social stimulus value; lacks insight into own motives; unsophisticated.

Females
   High scores (T > 70): Rejects traditional female roles and activities; masculine interests in work, sports, hobbies; active, vigorous, and assertive; competitive, aggressive, and dominating; coarse, rough, and tough; outgoing, uninhibited, and self-confident; easy-going, relaxed, balanced; logical, calculated; unemotional, and unfriendly.
   Low scores (T < 35): Describes self in terms of stereotyped female role; doubts about own femininity; passive, submissive, and yielding; defers to males

(continued)

TABLE 7.2. (Continued)

Clinical scales

in decision making; self-pitying; complaining, fault finding; constricted; sensitive; modest; idealistic. (This interpretation for low scores does *not* apply for
females with postgraduate degrees.)

Scale 6: Paranoia (Pa)

Extremely high scores (T > 80): Frankly psychotic behavior; disturbed thinking; delusions of persecution and/or grandeur; ideas of reference; feels mis-
treated and picked on; angry and resentful; harbors grudges; uses projection as
defense; most frequently diagnosed as schizophrenic or paranoid.

Moderately high scores (T = 65 to 79 for males, 71 to 79 for females): Paranoid
predisposition; sensitive; overly responsive to reactions of others; feels he/she is
getting a raw deal from life; rationalizes and blames others; suspicious and
guarded; hostile, resentful, and argumentative; moralistic and rigid; overemphasizes rationality; poor prognosis for therapy; does not like to talk about emotional problems; difficulty in establishing rapport with therapist.

Extremely low scores (T < 35): Should be interpreted with caution. In a clinical setting, low scores, in the context of a defensive response set, may suggest
frankly psychotic disorder; delusions, suspiciousness, ideas of reference; symptoms less obvious than for high scorers; evasive, defensive, guarded; shy, secretive, withdrawn.

Scale 7: Psychasthenia (Pt)

High scores: Anxious, tense, and agitated; high discomfort; worried and ap-
prehensive; high-strung and jumpy; difficulties in concentrating; introspective,
ruminative; obsessive and compulsive; feels insecure and inferior; lacks self-confidence; self-doubting, self-critical, self-conscious, and self-derogatory; rigid and
moralistic; maintains high standards for self and others; overly perfectionistic
and conscientious; guilty and depressed; neat, orderly, organized, and meticu-
lous; persistent; reliable; lacks ingenuity and originality in problem solving; dull
and formal; vacillates; is indecisive; distorts importance of problems, overreacts;
shy; does not interact well socially; hard to get to know; worries about popularity and acceptance; sensitive, physical complaints; shows some insight into problems; intellectualizes and rationalizes; resistant to interpretations in therapy;
expresses hostility toward therapist; remains in therapy longer than most patients; makes slow but steady progress in therapy.

Scale 8: Schizophrenia (Sc)

Very high scores (T = over 80 to 90): Blatantly psychotic behavior; confused,
disorganized, and disoriented; unusual thoughts or attitudes; delusions; hallucinations; poor judgment.

High scores (T = 65 to 79): Schizoid lifestyle; does not feel a part of social
environment; feels isolated, alienated, and misunderstood; feels unaccepted by
peers; withdrawn, seclusive, secretive, and inaccessible; avoids dealing with
people and new situations; shy, aloof, and uninvolved; experiences generalized
anxiety; resentful, hostile, and aggressive; unable to express feelings; reacts to
stress by withdrawing into fantasy and daydreaming; difficulty in separating reality and fantasy; self-doubts; feels inferior, incompetent, and dissatisfied; sexual

(continued)

TABLE 7.2. (Continued)

Clinical scales

preoccupation and sex role confusion; nonconforming, unusual, unconventional, and eccentric; vague, long-standing physical complaints; stubborn, moody, and opinionated; immature and impulsive; high-strung; imaginative; abstract, vague goals; lacks basic information for problem solving; poor prognosis for therapy; reluctant to relate in meaningful way to therapist; stays in therapy longer than most patients; may eventually come to trust therapist.

Scale 9: Hypomania (Ma)

High scores (T > 80): Overactivity; accelerated speech; may have hallucinations or delusions of grandeur; energetic and talkative; prefers action to thought; wide range of interest; does not utilize energy wisely; does not see projects through to completion; creative, enterprising, and ingenious; little interest in routine or detail; easily bored and restless; low frustration tolerance; difficulty in inhibiting expression of impulses; episodes of irritability, hostility, and aggressive outbursts; unrealistic, unqualified optimism; grandiose aspirations; exaggerates self-worth and self-importance; unable to see own limitations; outgoing, sociable, and gregarious; likes to be around other people; creates good first impression; friendly, pleasant, and enthusiastic; poised, self-confident; superficial relationships; manipulative, deceptive, unreliable; feelings of dissatisfaction; agitated; may have periodic episodes of depression; difficulties at school or work; resistant to interpretations in therapy; attends therapy irregularly; may terminate therapy prematurely; repeats problems in stereotyped manner; not likely to become dependent on therapist; becomes hostile and aggressive toward therapist.

Moderately elevated scores (T > 65, ≤ 79): Overactivity; exaggerated sense of self-worth; energetic and talkative; prefers action to thought; wide range of interest; does not utilize energy wisely; does not see projects through to completion; enterprising and ingenious; lacks interest in routine matters; becomes bored and restless easily; low frustration tolerance; impulsive; episodes of irritability, hostility, and aggressive outbursts; unrealistic, overly optimistic at times; shows some grandiose aspirations; unable to see own limitations; outgoing, sociable, and gregarious; likes to be around other people; creates good first impression; friendly, pleasant, and enthusiastic; poised, self-confident; superficial relationships; manipulative, deceptive, unreliable; feelings of dissatisfaction; agitated; views therapy as unnecessary; resistant to interpretations in therapy; attends therapy irregularly; may terminate therapy prematurely; repeats problems in stereotyped manner; not likely to become dependent on therapist; becomes hostile and aggressive toward therapist.

Low scores (T < 40): Low energy level; low activity level; lethargic, listless, apathetic, and phlegmatic; difficult to motivate; reports chronic fatigue, physical exhaustion; depressed, anxious, and tense; reliable, responsible, and dependable; approaches problems in conventional, practical, and reasonable way; lacks self-confidence; sincere, quiet, modest, withdrawn, seclusive; unpopular; overcontrolled; unlikely to express feelings openly.

Scale 0: Social Introversion (Si)

High scores (T > 65): Socially introverted; is more comfortable alone or with a few close friends; reserved, shy, and retiring; uncomfortable around members

(continued)

TABLE 7.2. (Continued)

Clinical scales

of opposite sex; hard to get to know; sensitive to what others think; troubled by lack of involvement with other people; overcontrolled; not likely to display feelings openly; submissive and compliant; overly accepting of authority; serious, slow personal tempo; reliable, dependable; cautious, conventional, unoriginal in approach to problems; rigid, inflexible in attitudes and opinions; difficulty making even minor decisions; enjoys work; gains pleasure from productive personal achievement; tends to worry; is irritable and anxious; moody, experiences guilt feelings; has episodes of depression or low mood.

Low scores (T < 45): Sociable and extraverted; outgoing, gregarious, friendly, and talkative; strong need to be around other people; mixes well; intelligent, expressive, verbally fluent; active, energetic, vigorous; interested in status, power, and recognition; seeks out competitive situations; has problem with impulse control; acts without considering the consequences of actions; immature, self-indulgent; superficial, insincere relationships; manipulative, opportunistic; arouses resentment and hostility in others.

Supplementary scales

Anxiety (A) scale. This scale defines the first, and largest, factor dimension in the MMPI-2. It measures general maladjustment or emotional upset.

Repression (R) scale. This scale assesses emotional overcontrol and reliance on denial and repression. It defines the second main factor in the MMPI-2.

Ego Strength (Es) scale. This scale was developed as a means of predicting successful response to psychotherapy. To develop the scale, "successful" therapy patients were contrasted with another group of patients who failed to benefit from treatment.

MacAndrew Alcoholism (MAC-R) scale. The MAC-R scale is the revised version of the MAC scale on the original MMPI. It is an empirically derived scale that assesses the potential for developing substance abuse problems.

Dominance (Do) scale. This scale was developed to identify dominant individuals by asking their peers to identify them as one or the other. The Do scale measures comfort in social relationships, self-confidence, strong opinions, persevering at tasks, and ability to concentrate.

Social Responsibility (Re) scale. This scale was developed as a means of predicting an individual's feelings of responsibility to others.

Overcontrolled Hostility (O-H) scale. This scale was developed to identify individuals who have difficulty expressing anger and usually overcontrol their hostile impulses, yet have actually engaged in assaultive behavior.

Post-Traumatic Stress Disorder (PTSD-PK/PS) scales. The PK scale was developed using an empirical scale construction strategy to discriminate individuals who are experiencing symptoms of PTSD. The PS scale was developed to assess PTSD in veterans.

Marital Distress scale (MDS). This scale was newly developed for the MMPI-2 and was designed to identify distress or discord in close relationships.

(continued)

TABLE 7.2. (Continued)

Supplementary scales

Addiction Potential scale (APS). This scale was constructed as a measure of personality characteristics and life situations associated with substance abuse.

Addiction Acknowledgment scale (AAS). The development of this scale began with a rational search through the pool for items with content indicating substance abuse problems, and was refined by statistical methods. The scale assesses the degree to which the individual acknowledges alcohol or drug problems.

Note. Adapted from J. N. Butcher, MMPI-2 workshops and symposia, University of Minnesota.

---

contains a number of measures that provide estimates of the individual's cooperativeness in taking the test. These validity indices, to be discussed below, need to be carefully evaluated to determine whether the profiles can be interpreted.

Administration and Scoring

The MMPI-2 provides a relatively easy administration format compared with many other clinical assessment methods. Most people are accustomed to completing paper-and-pencil surveys, and can, with brief instructions, become readily engaged in the task. Since the MMPI-2 is a structured task, it is important that the person administering the test follow the test instructions closely. It is also important to determine, in advance, whether clients can understand the items and mark their responses in the appropriate place. It takes a fifth- or sixth-grade reading level to understand the MMPI-2 items. The inventory can be administered in several ways: by the traditional paper-and-pencil form, by audiocassette, or by electronic computer. Individuals are instructed to read the items and determine whether each item is true or false as applied to them. They are asked to mark a T or F in the appropriate place on the answer sheet, or to respond by pressing the appropriate key on the computer keyboard.

The scoring of the MMPI-2 scales is easy and objective. In the case of manual scoring of the test, the practitioner simply places a scoring template over the answer sheet and counts the number of items endorsed in the scored direction on each scale. The raw scores are then placed in the appropriate place on the profile sheet. Once all of the scales are scored, the profile is drawn by connecting the dots that mark the appropriate raw score level on the profile. In the case of five of the clinical scales, a correction factor for test defensiveness (the Defensiveness or K factor) is added to the raw score before plotting the profile.

TABLE 7.3. Description of the MMPI-2 Content Scales

1. Anxiety (ANX; 23 items)—High scorers on ANX report general symptoms of anxiety, including tension, somatic problems (i.e., heart pounding and shortness of breath), sleep difficulties, worries, and poor concentration. They fear losing their minds, find life a strain, and have difficulties making decisions. They appear to be readily aware of these symptoms and problems, and are willing to admit to them.

2. Fears (FRS; 23 items)—A high score on FRS indicates an individual with many specific fears. These specific fears can include blood; high places; money; animals such as snakes, mice, or spiders; leaving home; fire; storms and natural disasters; water; the dark; being indoors; and dirt.

3. Obsessiveness (OBS; 16 items)—High scorers on OBS have tremendous difficulties making decisions and are likely to ruminate excessively about issues and problems, causing others to become impatient. Having to make changes distresses them, and they may report some compulsive behaviors, like counting or saving unimportant things. They are excessive worriers who frequently become overwhelmed by their own thoughts.

4. Depression (DEP; 33 items)—High scores on this scale characterize individuals with significant depressive thoughts. They report feeling blue, uncertain about their future, and uninterested in their lives. They are likely to brood, be unhappy, cry easily, and feel hopeless and empty. They may report thoughts of suicide or wishes that they were dead. They may believe that they are condemned or have committed unpardonable sins. Other people may not be viewed as a source of support.

5. Health Concerns (HEA; 36 items)—Individuals with high scores on HEA report many physical symptoms across several body systems. Included are gastrointestinal symptoms (e.g., constipation, nausea and vomiting, stomach trouble), neurological problems (e.g., convulsions, dizzy and fainting spells, paralysis), sensory problems (e.g., poor hearing or eyesight), cardiovascular symptoms (e.g., heart or chest pains), skin problems, pain (e.g., headaches, neck pains), and respiratory troubles (e.g., coughs, hay fever or asthma). These individuals worry about their health and feel sicker than the average person.

6. Bizarre Mentation (BIZ; 24 items)—Psychotic thought processes characterize individuals high on the BIZ scale. They may report auditory, visual, or olfactory hallucinations, and may recognize that their thoughts are strange and peculiar. Paranoid ideation (e.g., the belief that they are being plotted against or that someone is trying to poison them) may be reported as well. These individuals may feel that they have a special mission or powers.

7. Anger (ANG; 16 items)—High scores on the ANG scale suggest anger control problems. These individuals report being irritable, grouchy, impatient, hotheaded, annoyed, and stubborn. They sometimes feel like swearing or smashing things. They may lose self-control and report having been physically abusive toward people and objects.

8. Cynicism (CYN; 23 items)—Misanthropic beliefs characterize high scorers on CYN. They expect hidden, negative motives behind the acts of others—for example, believing that most people are honest simply for fear of being caught. Other people are to be distrusted, for people use each other and

(continued)

TABLE 7.3. (Continued)

are only friendly for selfish reasons. They likely hold negative attitudes about those close to them, including fellow workers, family, and friends.

9. Antisocial Practices (ASP; 22 items)—In addition to holding similar misan-thropic attitudes as high scorers on the CYN scale, high scorers on the ASP scale report problem behaviors during their school years and other antiso-cial practices, like being in trouble with the law, stealing, or shoplifting. They report sometimes enjoying the antics of criminals and believe that it is all right to get around the law, as long as it is not broken.

10. Type A Behavior (TPA; 19 items)—High scorers on TPA are hard-driving, fast-moving, and work-oriented individuals, who frequently become impa-tient, irritable, and annoyed. They do not like to wait or be interrupted. There is never enough time in a day for them to complete their tasks. They are direct and may be overbearing in their relationships with others.

11. Low Self-Esteem (LSE; 24 items)—High scores on LSE characterize individu-als with low opinions of themselves. They do not believe that they are liked by others or that they are important. They hold many negative attitudes about themselves, including beliefs that they are unattractive, awkward and clumsy, useless, and a burden to others. They certainly lack self-confidence, and find it hard to accept compliments from others. They may be over-whelmed by all the faults they see in themselves.

12. Social Discomfort (SOD; 24 items)—SOD high scorers are very uneasy around others, preferring to be by themselves. When in social situations, they are likely to sit alone, rather than joining in the group. They see them-selves as shy and dislike parties and other group events.

13. Family Problems (FAM; 25 items)—Considerable family discord is reported by high scorers on FAM. Their families are described as lacking in love, quarrelsome, and unpleasant. They even may report hating members of their families. Their childhood may be portrayed as abusive, and marriages may be seen as unhappy and lacking in affection.

14. Work Interference (WRK; 33 items)—A high score on WRK is indicative of behaviors or attitudes likely to contribute to poor work performance. Some of the problems relate to low self-confidence, concentration difficulties, ob-sessiveness, tension and pressure, and decision-making problems. Others suggest lack of family support for the career choice, personal questioning of career choice, and negative attitudes toward coworkers.

15. Negative Treatment Indicators (TRT; 26 items)—High scores on TRT indi-cate individuals with negative attitudes toward doctors and mental health treatment. High scorers do not believe that anyone can understand or help them. They have issues or problems that they are not comfortable discuss-ing with anyone. They may not want to change anything in their lives, nor do they feel that change is possible. They prefer giving up, rather than fac-ing a crisis or difficulty.

The objective administration, scoring, and interpretation procedures for the MMPI-2 make it particularly well suited to computer processing. Many practitioners today employ a computer interpretation program to provide the "raw material" or test-based hypotheses for interpreting the MMPI-2. Later in this chapter, a computer-interpreted MMPI-2 protocol is presented to provide the reader with an illustration of an objective test interpretation.

Developing Hypotheses about Clients with the MMPI-2

Useful hypotheses about client functioning can be obtained from various sources of information within the MMPI-2. One valuable interpretive strategy involves examining the MMPI-2-based test indices with certain questions in mind, in order to generate interpretive hypotheses about the individual's personality functioning and current behavior:

What is the motivation of the client to participate in the assessment process?
What are the client's cognitive and ideational processes like?
How is the individual functioning in interpersonal contexts?
Is he/she likely to remain stable over time, or is change possible?
What are the likely clinical diagnostic issues?
Is this individual amenable to psychological treatment?

In the discussion that follows, I first examine a general strategy for interpreting MMPI-2 profiles and explore the variables in the MMPI-2 that address the questions of interest. Then I present a case illustration, analyzed by a computer-based MMPI-2 system, to show how an objective appraisal of the MMPI-2 indices can provide the practitioner with a substantial amount of information that can be incorporated into a diagnostic evaluation.

The interpretation of MMPI-2 scales and profiles involves a sequential analysis based on several types of information in the test. First, and often considered to be the most important to interpretation, is an assessment of the individual's approach to the test items through an appraisal of the MMPI-2 validity scales. The next step in the interpretation process involves the determination of the likely empirical behavioral correlates that have been established for the clinical and supplementary scales. In the third step, the MMPI-2 item content, as noted above, can be viewed as a direct source of important client information and incorporated into the interpretive process.

Assessment of Profile Validity

Understanding the client's motivation and investment in the assessment process is a key factor in the interpretation of self-report instruments (Ben-

Porath & Tellegen, 1993). Individuals taking the MMPI-2 under some conditions may have clear motivations to present themselves in particular ways. For example, litigants in personal injury cases may tend to exaggerate their complaints; men and women being evaluated in family custody cases tend to present themselves in a highly virtuous and unrealistic manner. It is extremely important for a practitioner to assure that a test protocol was produced in a cooperative and open manner, without test-taking response patterns that prevent the practitioner from obtaining valid information.

The MMPI-2 contains a number of measures that address test-taking attitudes and provide the clinician with a means of knowing whether the client has cooperated sufficiently with the evaluation to provide an accurate portrayal of his/her personality characteristics and problems (see Table 7.1). For example, the motivation to present oneself in a favorable light or to be defensive in the assessment is usually detected by the Lie scale or the Defensiveness scale (Baer, Wetter, & Berry, 1992). On the other hand, individuals who present themselves in a way as to be viewed by others as having extreme psychological problems tend to exaggerate their symptoms. This exaggerated symptom-checking approach usually produces extreme elevations on the two scales that assess Faking, the Infrequency scale and the Back F scale (Berry, Baer, & Harris, 1991; Rogers, Bagby, & Chakraborty, 1993; Wetter, Baer, Berry, Smith, & Larsen, 1992; Wetter, Baer, Berry, Robison, & Sumpter, 1993; Schretlen, 1988; Graham, Watts, & Timbrook, 1991). In addition to these invalidating conditions, there may be unusual, non-content-oriented response sets operating in the test performance. These conditions are detected by other measures in the MMPI-2: For example, random responding is detected by the Variable Response Inconsistency scale, and mostly true or mostly false response patterns are detected by the True Response Inconsistency scale (Berry et al., 1992; Tellegen & Ben-Porath, 1992).

Assessment of Personality Functioning and Symptomatic Behavior

This section demonstrates how the MMPI-2 clinical, supplemental, and content measures can be employed to provide information about the client's functioning in several areas: (1) cognitive/ideational functions, (2) mood and affect (including emotional stability), (3) specific conflict areas, (4) intra- and interpersonal coping styles, (5) diagnostic considerations, and (6) treatment recommendations.

1. *Cognitive/ideational functions.* The MMPI-2 clinical scales provide a valid picture of the behavioral problems or symptoms the individual is experiencing. The correlates that have been empirically established for the clinical scales provide a description of the individual's cognitive functioning. For example, elevations on the Paranoia and Schizophrenia clinical

scales are associated with extreme cognitive impairment and thought disorder. High elevations on the Psychasthenia clinical scale or the Obsessiveness content scale suggest extreme preoccupation with disordered thinking, such as pathological rumination and obsessive–compulsive behavior.

2. *Mood and affect.* The individual's symptomatic behavior and mood are reflected in the MMPI-2 clinical and content scales. Examination of the correlates for high scores on the Depression clinical scale (see Table 7.2) suggests that the high-scoring individual is likely to be depressed, unhappy, and dysphoric at the present time. The individual is likely to be feeling somewhat sluggish, has many somatic complaints, feels weak and tired much of the time, and reports having low energy. In addition to these symptoms of depressed mood, the individual is likely to be prone to worry and lacking in self-confidence. Individuals with the Depression scale score elevated show personality characteristics such as a pessimistic attitude about life, a self-deprecating self concept, tendencies toward feeling guilty, and concern over failure on the job. They are usually introverted, shy, and timid, and they tend to avoid interpersonal involvement. Substantial information on the empirical correlates of the MMPI-2 clinical scales has accumulated over the past 50 years (see Marks, Seeman, & Haller, 1974; Gilberstadt & Duker, 1965; Lewandowski & Graham, 1972).

3. *Specific conflict areas.* In addition to the extensive information available on symptomatic status of individuals from the MMPI-2 clinical scales, several of the supplemental scales provide information about specific problems (see Table 7.2). For example, several scales address possible problems with alcohol or drug abuse; one scale, the Marital Distress scale, focuses upon marital problems; and the Post-Traumatic Stress Disorder scales address symptomatic behavior related to this disorder.

4. *Intra- and interpersonal coping styles.* The MMPI-2 provides several types of information related to interpersonal–intrapersonal functioning. First, many of the MMPI-2 clinical scales have established empirical correlates that reflect the manner in which the individual deals with others. For example, the Psychopathic Deviate scale on the MMPI-2 is associated with interpersonal difficulty, aggressiveness, and the tendency to manipulate others for the subject's own gain. However, there are also several specific indicators that address social skills—for example, the Social Introversion scale. High scores on this scale are characteristic of introverted, reclusive persons who have great difficulty in interpersonal contexts. Finally, specific interpersonal problem scales such as the Family Problems content scale can provide information as to specific interpersonal difficulties the individual may be encountering.

5. *Diagnostic considerations.* Information is also available on the relationship between diagnostic classification and MMPI-2 scores. Although it is usually not a good practice to attempt to use MMPI-2 scores to signify a particular *Diagnostic and Statistical Manual* (DSM) code, some MMPI-2 pro-

file types have been found to correspond fairly well with some DSM patterns (for examples, see Manos, 1985; Savasir & Erol, 1990). The value of the MMPI-2 in the diagnostic process is to provide likely behavioral correlates and symptom patterns for particular profile types.

6. *Treatment planning.* The MMPI and MMPI-2 have been extensively used in treatment planning, and a substantial base of information is available on the use of the scales in predicting response to treatment. Several studies detailing the utility of the MMPI and MMPI-2 in treatment planning have been published (e.g., Aronoff & Evans, 1982; Apostal, 1971; Barron, 1953; Brandwin & Kewman, 1982; Butcher, 1990; Distler, May, & Tuma, 1964; Elliott, Anderson, & Adams, 1967; Haase & Ivey, 1970; Hollon & Mandell, 1979; Kuperman, Golden, & Blume, 1979; Moore, Armentraut, Parker, & Kivlahan, 1986; Reich, Steward, Tupin, & Rosenblatt, 1985; Pustell, 1958; Raab, Rickels, & Moore, 1964; Schofield, 1950, 1953; Shealy, Lowe, & Ritzler, 1980; and Wagner & Dobbins, 1967). In treatment planning with the MMPI-2, the following types of information can be used to provide a client with an important perspective on his/her problems:

a. The MMPI-2 scores can provide objective, "outside" information about the client's problems that the therapist can employ in treatment sessions to bring into focus particular problems or personality characteristics relevant to the therapy.

b. The scale scores can provide important problem summaries. When MMPI-2 content scales are used, the summaries are considered to be "highly relevant" content themes highlighting the patient's problems and concerns (Butcher, Graham, Williams, & Ben-Porath, 1990).

c. The validity scales provide an appraisal of possible treatment resistance or negative factors that could bear on the treatment process.

d. The validity and clinical scales can provide an appraisal of the individual's treatment motivation.

e. The clinical, content, and supplemental scales provide information as the client's need for therapy.

f. The MMPI-2 variables provide an excellent mechanism for providing test feedback to clients in therapy—an important process that is described below.

Content-Based Hypotheses

Patients being assessed in a mental health setting usually expect that the mental health professional they are seeing will pay careful attention to the content of their communications about their symptoms. With respect to the MMPI-2, in which patients are asked to share personal information about their symptoms and adjustment, clients expect that the information they share will be incorporated in their evaluation. The content of test item responses, at least when a person being assessed is motivated to participate with the evaluation, can be viewed as direct communications between the patient and the clinician. Patients, of course, will not be able to provide information they do not have; however, they are able to provide such information about themselves as whether they feel sad at times, whether they have been in trouble with the law, or whether they enjoy going to parties.

If clients are motivated to share personal information and have access to the information being requested, they are usually excellent witnesses as to the presence or absence of mental health problems. In fact, patients generally hold the key to understanding their problems and, under appropriate conditions, can provide accurate, useful information about themselves. As described earlier, the MMPI-2 content scales provide a means of summarizing an individual's problems and attitudes in terms of important themes. The content scales provide an objective framework for appraising the major content dimensions represented in the MMPI-2 (see Table 7.3 for a discussion of the MMPI-2 content themes).

Case Description

Let us now turn to an examination of how the information available in the MMPI-2 can be searched and organized to bear on a particular case. The patient, who was seen in an outpatient mental health evaluation, was administered the MMPI-2 following an intake interview conducted by the psychologist. Following completion of the test, the client was scheduled for follow-up appointment to discuss the results of the testing and the recommendations of the psychologist.

Background

David C., a 43-year-old businessman, had become quite despondent over several family and business problems in recent months. He reportedly was having great difficulty sleeping, felt tense much of the time, worried a great deal over situations he felt were overwhelming him, and had recently begun to believe that his problems were hopeless and unsolvable. On a few recent occasions, he wondered whether the only solution for him might be to end his own life.

In addition to his low mood state, Mr. C. was quite concerned over his constant "fatigue" and other physical symptoms. Mr. C. went to see his family physician for a physical examination. After completing the physical examination and finding no physical problems, the doctor suggested that Mr. C. obtain help for his mental health symptoms and referred him for further psychological evaluation.

Mr. C. considered his current psychological problems to stem from two main sources: his increased family difficulties and work stress. One of his three children, a 14-year-old girl, was beginning to stay out all night and drink with a "crowd of mostly school dropouts." He was very troubled by her behavior, but felt that he was unable to provide the support and structure that his daughter needed at this time because of his own lack of energy. He also reported that his wife, a "cold, distant, and unloving" person, seemed unable to provide emotional support for him or his daughter at this time. Mr. C. and his wife, Evelyn, were experiencing marital difficulties and were considering a separation and a possible termination of their 20-year marriage. Their relationship was marked by great tension and lack of communication over the problems. Mr. C. reported that he had not enjoyed his marriage for several years, and that lately he felt that his marriage had "reached a dead end."

Mr. C. was also experiencing major stresses at work. The company at which he had been employed for about 20 years was undergoing a major labor dispute, the result of which was a deteriorating financial situation. There had been a great deal of talk in recent weeks about a possible company shut-down, and he was very concerned that his position was being threatened.

Mr. C. came to see the psychologist by himself. He indicated that he did not believe that his wife and family would want to be involved in his present problems. During the initial interview, Mr. C. appeared to be quite depressed, sighed frequently, and was tearful throughout the interview.

Mr. C. 's MMPI-2 answer sheet was submitted for computer interpretation. The MMPI-2 profiles are shown in Figures 7.1 and 7.2, and the computer-generated narrative summary from the Minnesota Report (Butcher, 1993) is given in Figure 7.3.

Recommendations Based on the MMPI-2 Results

The MMPI-2 narrative report provided a comprehensive picture of Mr. C.'s depressed mood, suicidal ideation, and generally confused cognitive emotional state. The narrative report suggested that Mr. C.'s symptomatic picture was more extreme than that of most people, and that a treatment intervention for this severe disorder would be recommended to alleviate his psychological adjustment problems. It was possible that his mood disorder would respond to treatment, such as psychotropic medications for his depression and cognitive restructuring therapy for his negative self-attitudes and pessimistic orientation toward others. Given his motivation to discuss his problems (as reflected through the validity scale analysis) and his intense feelings of despair, it was quite likely that he would follow up on treatment suggestions.

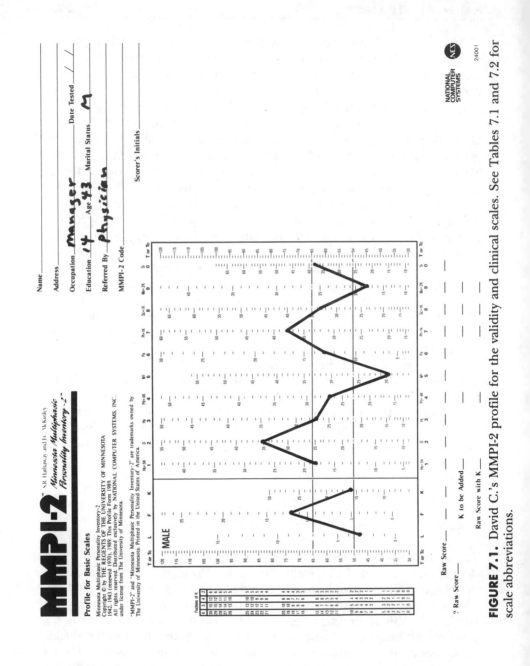

FIGURE 7.1. David C.'s MMPI-2 profile for the validity and clinical scales. See Tables 7.1 and 7.2 for scale abbreviations.

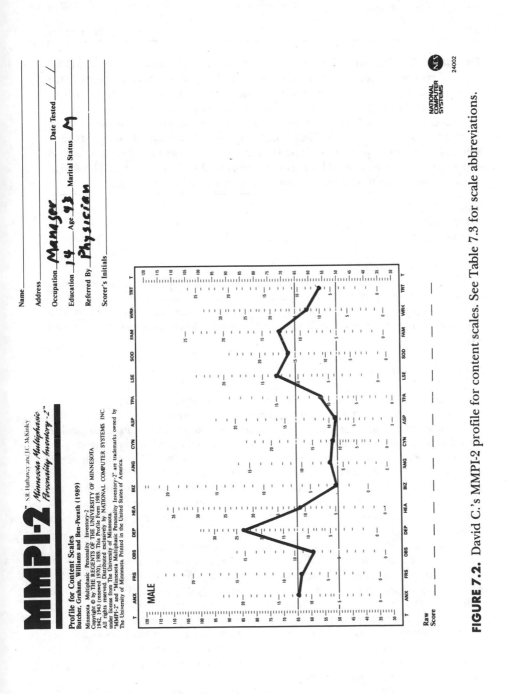

FIGURE 7.2. David C.'s MMPI-2 profile for content scales. See Table 7.3 for scale abbreviations.

FIGURE 7.3. Minnesota Report for David C. (*Note*: This type of MMPI-2 interpretation can serve as a useful source of hypotheses about clients. This report is based on objectively derived scale indices and scale interpretations that have been developed in diverse groups of patients. The personality descriptions, inferences, and recommendations contained herein need to be verified by other sources of clinical information, since individual clients may not fully match the prototype. The information in this type of report should most appropriately be used by a trained, qualified test interpreter. The information contained in the report should be considered confidential.)

Patient Age: 43
Status: Married
Setting: Outpatient

Validity Considerations
This is a valid MMPI-2 profile. The client was quite cooperative in describing his symptoms and problems. His frank and open response to the items can be viewed as a positive indication of his involvement with the evaluation. The MMPI-2 profile is probably a good indication of his present personality functioning and symptoms.

Symptomatic Behavior
The MMPI-2 clinical profile type (2-7/7-2—Depression [D] and Psychasthenia [Pt]) employed as the prototype to develop this report showed very high profile definition. The behavioral descriptions provided in the following narrative are likely to be an accurate portrayal of his personality and symptoms, because his profile closely matches the profile characteristics on which the correlates are based. The client's MMPI-2 profile reflects much psychological distress at this time. He is experiencing intense feelings of self-doubt and low morale in the context of a mixed pattern of psychological problems. He has major problems with anxiety and depression. He tends to be high-strung and insecure, and may also be having somatic problems. He is probably experiencing loss of sleep and appetite, and a slowness in personal tempo.

Individuals with this profile often have high standards and a strong need to achieve, but they feel that they fall short of their expectations and then blame themselves harshly. This client feels quite insecure and pessimistic about the future. He also feels quite inferior, has little self-confidence, and does not feel capable of solving his problems.

The client has a low Masculinity–Femininity (Mf) score, suggesting that he has a rather limited range of interests and tends to prefer stereotyped masculine activities over literary and artistic pursuits or introspective experiences. He tends to be somewhat competitive and needs to see himself as masculine. He probably prefers to view women in subservient roles.

Interpersonally, he is likely to be intolerant and insensitive, and others may find him rather crude, coarse, or narrow-minded. He seems to require an excessive amount of emotional support from his spouse.

He has endorsed a number of items suggesting that he is experiencing low morale and a depressed mood. He is preoccupied with feeling guilty and unwor-
(continued)

FIGURE 7.3. (Continued)

thy. He feels that he deserves to be punished for wrongs he has committed. He feels regretful and unhappy about life, and seems plagued by anxiety and worry about the future. He feels hopeless at times and feels that he is a condemned person. He has endorsed a number of attitudes that reflect feelings of low self-esteem and long-standing beliefs about his inadequacy. He has difficulty managing routine affairs, and the item content he has endorsed suggests a poor memory, concentration problems, and an inability to make decisions. He appears to be immobilized and withdrawn, and has no energy for life. He has acknowledged having suicidal thoughts recently. Although he denies suicidal attempts in the past, an assessment of suicidal potential appears indicated, given his current mood.

Profile interpretation can be greatly facilitated by examining the relative frequency of patterns in various settings. His high-point clinical scale score (D) occurs in 7.2% of the normative sample of men. However, only 2.4% of the normative sample have the D scale at or over a T score of 65, and only 1.1% have well-defined D spikes. This elevated MMPI-2 profile configuration (2-7/7-2) is very rare in samples of normals, occurring in less than 1% of the normative sample of men.

This high point MMPI-2 score on the D scale is relatively frequent in various outpatient settings. The NCS Archival Outpatient Sample (1993) showed that the high-point clinical scale score on D occurred in 12.7% of men in outpatient settings. Moreover, 9.0% of the outpatients have the D-scale spike at or over a T score of 65. His elevated MMPI-2 profile configuration (2-7/7-2) occurs in 4.8% of the NCS Outpatient Archival Sample.

Interpersonal Relations

He appears to be quite passive and dependent in interpersonal relationships, and does not speak up for himself even when others take advantage. He avoids confrontation and seeks nurturance from others, often at the price of his own independence. He forms deep emotional attachments and tends to be quite vulnerable to being hurt. He also tends to blame himself for interpersonal problems.

He is somewhat shy, with some social concerns and inhibitions. He is a bit hypersensitive about what others think of him, and is occasionally concerned over his relationships with others. He appears to be somewhat inhibited in personal relationships and social situations, and may have some difficulty expressing his feelings toward others.

Behavioral Stability

The relative elevation of the highest scales in his clinical profile shows very high profile definition. His peak scores on this testing are likely to be very prominent in his profile pattern if he is retested at a later date.

Individuals with this profile are often experiencing psychological distress in response to stressful events. The intense affect may diminish over time or with treatment.

Diagnostic Considerations

Individuals with this profile tend to be considered neurotic, and receive DSM Axis I diagnoses such as Dysthymic Disorder or Anxiety Disorder. They may also

(continued)

FIGURE 7.3. (Continued)

---

receive an Axis II diagnosis of Dependent or Obsessive Compulsive Personality Disorder.

Treatment Considerations

Individuals with this MMPI-2 pattern are feeling a great deal of discomfort and are in need of symptomatic relief for their depression. Some symptomatic relief may be provided by antidepressant medication. Psychotherapy, particularly a supportive approach, may be beneficial. He may also respond to cognitive–behavioral treatment.

His self-esteem is low, and he tends to blame himself too much for his difficulties. Although he worries a great deal about his problems, he seems to have little energy left over for action to resolve them.

The passive, unassertive personality style that seems to underlie this disorder may be a focus of behavior change. Individuals with these problems may learn to deal with others more effectively through assertiveness training.

His item content suggests some family conflicts that are giving him considerable concern at this time. He feels unhappy about his life and resents having an unpleasant home life. Psychological intervention with him could profitably focus, in part, upon clarifying his feelings about his family.

The MMPI-2 report also suggested that Mr. C.'s low self-esteem and generally negative mood state would need to be taken into consideration in any treatment program. Perhaps his negative appraisal of his current problem situation (and his negative views about family and work) might be somewhat discolored by his mood state. It would be important to obtain verification of his appraisal by other family members; moreover, including his family members in the treatment plan would be a very important consideration. The Minnesota Report noted that Mr. C. considered his family problems to be quite severe, and concluded that this should be an important area of focus for any psychological intervention with him. It would be important to assist him in clarifying his feelings about his family.

Importance of Providing Test Feedback to Patients

It is important for the psychologist to conduct a test feedback session with the client before therapy begins or as an integral part of the therapy. Elsewhere (Butcher, 1990), I have described a process for providing MMPI-2 feedback to therapy patients and have suggested guidelines for conducting feedback sessions with clients in treatment. Most practitioners who share MMPI-2 feedback with their patients early in the therapy are often very pleasantly surprised over the great therapeutic impact such information can have on the clients' progress in therapy.

What effect does test feedback have on the patient's behavior and adjustment? Finn and Tonsager (1992) recently showed that the test feedback process itself can be a powerful clinical intervention. They conducted a clinical study in which one group of patients from a therapy waiting list ($n = 32$) was provided with MMPI-2 test feedback according to a model developed by Finn (1990). The second group of patients ($n = 29$) from the waiting list was administered the MMPI-2 but not given test feedback. The results of the study were very informative: The authors found that individuals who were provided feedback on their MMPI-2 results showed a significant decline in reported symptoms and an increase in measured self-esteem, compared with the control group. Finn and Tonsager (1992) reported:

> This study provides support for the therapeutic impact of sharing MMPI-2 test results verbally with college age clients. Clients who completed an MMPI-2 and later heard their MMPI-2 test results reported a significant increase in their self-esteem immediately following the feedback session, an increase that continued to grow over the 2-week follow-up period. In addition, after hearing their MMPI-2 test results, clients showed a significant decrease in their symptomatic distress, and distress continued to decline during the subsequent 2-week period. Last, compared with clients receiving attention only from the examiner, clients who completed the MMPI-2 and received a feedback session showed more hopefulness about their problems immediately following the feedback session, and this persisted at the final follow-up. (p. 284)

The results of this study suggest that psychological test results can be effectively used more directly as a therapeutic intervention.

Limitations of the MMPI-2

The MMPI-2 can be used in a wide range of clinical situations for assessing clients. There are, however, some limitations or restrictions that should be considered in its use with clients. In some respects, the major strengths of the MMPI-2 can also be seen as possible limiting considerations.

The MMPI-2 is an empirically based instrument developed in a "blindly empirical" fashion, without regard to any theoretical orientation or guiding viewpoint. It provides observations that are not bound to any particular theoretical perspective. Some authorities have considered the lack of an underlying theory to be a major drawback of the MMPI. In the past, the MMPI has actually been criticized by some therapy theorists from quite divergent camps— for example, behaviorists, psychoanalysts, humanistic psychologists, and nondirective theorists. Therefore, psychologists who follow a strict therapeutic discipline or school may find that the patient information provided by the MMPI-2 cannot be readily integrated into their particular doctrine.

The MMPI-2 is a verbal instrument and requires certain reading and comprehension skills to complete. Individuals with a very low reading level or severe intellectual impairment may not be able to complete an MMPI-2. Similarly, since the MMPI-2 items usually require some motor responding, such as marking an answer sheet or punching a computer keyboard, some accommodation may be necessary if an individual is unable to engage in such responding. For example, in the case of blind or deaf clients, it may be necessary to use special forms for item presentation and response recording.

As noted at several points in this chapter, the quality of the information presented through the MMPI-2 items is limited by the motivation of the client. If a client is motivated to provide a distorted picture on the test, he/she can readily do so. The answer to the question "Can the MMPI-2 be faked?" is "Yes!" If individuals want to appear psychologically disturbed, they can certainly endorse the items in an extreme manner to present many symptoms. If they do not wish to cooperate with the evaluation, they may simply deny any and all symptoms. There are certainly times and situations when the only information gained through an MMPI-2 is that a person has faked the test. We do not then know much about the person except that he/she was uncooperative. In some situations, such as a forensic case, this may be important (though limited) information.

Although some patients and therapists alike may consider the MMPI-2 to be too long for a particular use, the opposite argument (that it does not contain enough range) can be made as well. The 567 items on the inventory address a broad range of problems and symptoms; however, there are areas in contemporary clinical practice that are not addressed. For example, the inventory is problem-oriented and does not contain much content with respect to assessing resources or strengths. Thus, the MMPI-2 does not provide much information with respect to this important aspect of personality functioning.

The question as to how much of the information needed by clinicians for assessment is provided by the MMPI-2 must also be addressed. Can the MMPI-2 be used as the only instrument in the assessment, or should the inventory always be employed as part of a more extensive battery of tests? Answers to this question obviously differ. Some clinicians, for some applications, use only the MMPI-2 in their clinical work because of its objectivity, validity, and easy-to-use format. Others employ the MMPI-2 as part of a test battery. Practitioners who employ a number of tests in their assessment study need then to integrate the results from differing tests into a integrated report. Practitioners interested in the issues of integrating psychological test results are referred to Tallent (1993) and Weiner (1992).

Summary

The MMPI, originally developed by Hathaway and McKinley to aid in diagnostic screening, soon became the most widely used personality instrument in psychological assessment. Moreover, the MMPI has been adapted in numerous other countries, indicating strong generalization of validity across cultural settings. Though enormously successful, the MMPI's use became problematic as time went by and as the applications expanded beyond the original purpose of the instrument. In 1982 the test's publisher, the University of Minnesota Press, initiated a program of revision that resulted in the publication of two separate but overlapping and parallel forms of the MMPI, the MMPI-2 for adults and the MMPI-A for adolescents.

The MMPI-2 is a revised version of the original instrument in which the clinical and validity scales have been kept relatively intact. In addition, a number of new scales for expanded clinical applications have been developed. New norms, based on a large, representative sample of normals, provide a more relevant comparison sample for today's test uses. A number of validity studies have documented the MMPI-2's effectiveness as a replacement for the original MMPI in the assessment of adults.

In interpreting the MMPI-2 in clinical practice, three major strategies are usually involved. First, careful consideration of the validity scale pattern is important, in order to ensure appropriate motivation for the assessment and cooperation with the assessment. Next, the empirically derived behavioral correlates are surveyed if the test is considered valid and interpretable. Finally, the MMPI-2 content scales are employed as direct communications between the patient and the clinician. Objective clinical interpretation by electronic computer has been illustrated with a case, and personality description and treatment recommendations have been provided.

References

Aronoff, G. M., & Evans, W. O. (1982). The prediction of treatment outcome at a multidisciplinary pain center. *Pain, 14,* 67–73.

Apostal, R. A. (1971). Personality descriptions of mental health center patients for use as pre-therapy information. *Mental Hygiene, 55,* 119–120.

Barron, F. (1953). Some test correlates of response to psychotherapy. *Journal of Consulting Psychology, 17*(4), 235–241.

Baer, R. A., Wetter, M. W., & Berry, D. T. (1992). Detection of under reporting of psychopathology on the MMPI: A meta-analysis. *Clinical Psychology Review, 12,* 509–525.

Ben-Porath, Y. S., & Butcher, J. N. (1989a). Psychometric stability of rewritten MMPI items. *Journal of Personality Assessment, 53,* 645–653.

Ben-Porath, Y. S., & Butcher, J. N. (1989b). The comparability of MMPI and MMPI-2 scales and profiles. *Psychological Assessment: A Journal of Consulting and Clinical Psychology, 1,* 345–347.

Ben-Porath, Y. S., Butcher, J. N., & Graham, J. R. (1991). Contribution of the MMPI-2 content scales to the differential diagnosis of psychopathology. *Psychological Assessment, 3,* 634–640.

Ben-Porath, Y. S., & Tellegen, A. (1993). Continuity and changes in MMPI-2 validity indicators: Points of clarification. *MMPI-2 News and Profiles, 3,* 6–8.

Berry, D. T., Baer, R. A., & Harris, M. J. (1991). Detection of malingering on the MMPI: A meta-analysis. *Clinical Psychology Review, 11*, 585–591.

Berry, D. T., Wetter, M. W., Baer, R. A., Larsen, L., Clark, C., & Monroe, K. (1992). MMPI-2 random responding indices: Validation using a self-report methodology. *Psychological Assessment, 4*, 340–345.

Brandwin, M. A., & Kewman, D. G. (1982). MMPI indicators of treatment response to spinal epidural stimulation in patients with chronic pain and patients with movement disorders. *Psychological Reports, 51*, 1059–1064.

Butcher, J. N. (Ed.). (1972). *Objective personality assessment: Changing perspectives.* New York: Academic Press.

Butcher, J. N. (1985). Current developments in MMPI use: An international perspective. In J. N. Butcher & C. D. Spielberger (Eds.), *Advances in personality assessment* (Vol. 4, pp. 83–92). Hillsdale, NJ: Erlbaum.

Butcher, J. N. (1990). *Use of the MMPI-2 in treatment planning.* New York: Oxford University Press.

Butcher, J. N. (1993). *User's guide for the MMPI-2 Minnesota Report: Adult clinical system* (rev. ed.). Minneapolis: National Computer Systems.

Butcher, J. N., Aldwin, C., Levenson, M., Ben-Porath, Y. S., Spiro, A., & Bosse, R. (1991). Personality and aging: A study of the MMPI-2 among elderly men. *Psychology of Aging, 6*, 361–370.

Butcher, J. N., Dahlstrom, W. G., Graham, J. R., & Tellegen, A. (1990, May). The MMPI-2 and Classic Coke. *APA Monitor*, p. 1.

Butcher, J. N., Dahlstrom, W. G., Graham, J. R., Tellegen, A. M., & Kaemmer, B. (1989). *Minnesota Multiphasic Personality Inventory–2 (MMPI-2): Manual for administration and scoring.* Minneapolis: University of Minnesota Press.

Butcher, J. N., Graham, J. R., Dahlstrom, W. G., & Bowman, E. (1990). The MMPI-2 with college students. *Journal of Personality Assessment, 54*, 1–15.

Butcher, J. N., Graham, J. R., Williams, C. L., & Ben-Porath, Y. S. (1990). *Development and use of the MMPI-2 content scales.* Minneapolis: University of Minnesota Press.

Butcher, J. N., Jeffrey, T., Cayton, T., Colligan, S., DeVore, J., & Minnegawa, R. (1990). A study of active duty military personnel with the MMPI-2. *Military Psychology, 2*, 47–61.

Butcher, J. N., & Owen, P. (1978). Survey of personality inventories: Recent research developments and contemporary issues. In B. Wolman (Ed.), *Handbook of clinical diagnosis.* New York: Plenum Press.

Butcher, J. N., & Pancheri, P. (1976). *Handbook of cross-national MMPI research.* Minneapolis: University of Minnesota Press.

Butcher, J. N., & Williams, C. L. (1992). *Essentials of MMPI-2 and MMPI-A interpretation.* Minneapolis: University of Minnesota Press.

Butcher, J. N., Williams, C. L., Graham, J. R., Archer, R., Tellegen, A., Ben-Porath, Y. S., & Kaemmer, B. (1992). *MMPI-A: Manual for administration, scoring, and interpretation.* Minneapolis: University of Minnesota Press.

Clark, M. E. (1993, March). *MMPI-2 Anger and Cynicism scales: Interpretive cautions.* Paper presented at the 28th Annual Symposium on Recent Developments in the Use of the MMPI/MMPI-2, St. Petersburg, FL.

Cheung, F. M. (1985). Cross-cultural considerations for the translation and adaptation of the Chinese MMPI in Hong Kong. In J. N. Butcher & C. D.

Spielberger (Eds.), *Advances in personality assessment* (Vol. 4, pp. 131–158). Hillsdale, N.J.: Erlbaum.

Colligan, R. C., Osborne, D., Swenson, W. M., & Offord, K. (1983). *The MMPI: A contemporary normative study*. New York: Praeger.

Distler, L. S., May, P. R., & Tuma, A. H. (1964). Anxiety and ego strength as predictors of response to treatment in schizophrenic patients. *Journal of Consulting Psychology, 28*, 1970–1977.

Egeland, B., Erickson, M., Butcher, J. N., & Ben-Porath, Y. S. (1991). MMPI-2 profiles of women at risk for child abuse. *Journal of Personality Assessment, 57*, 254–263.

Elliott, T. R., Anderson, W. P., & Adams, N. A. (1987). MMPI indicators of long-term therapy in a college counseling center. *Psychological Reports, 60*, 79–84.

Faull, R., & Meyer, G. J. (1993, March). *Assessment of depression with the MMPI-2: Distinctions between Scale 2 and the DEP*. Paper presented at the midwinter meeting of the Society for Personality Assessment, San Francisco.

Finn, S. (1990). *A model for providing test feedback with the MMPI-2*. Paper presented at the 25th Annual Symposium on Recent Developments in the Use of the MMPI/MMPI-2, Minneapolis.

Finn, S., & Tonsager, M. (1992). Therapeutic effects of providing MMPI-2 test feedback to college students awaiting therapy. *Psychological Assessment, 4*, 278–287.

Gilberstadt, H., & Duker, J. (1965). *A handbook for clinical and actuarial MMPI interpretation*. Philadelphia: W. B. Saunders.

Graham, J. R. (Chair). (1988, August). *Establishing validity of the revised form of the MMPI*. Symposium presented at the 96th Annual Convention of the American Psychological Association, Atlanta.

Graham, J. R. (1990). *MMPI-2: Assessing personality and psychopathology*. New York: Oxford University Press.

Graham, J. R., Watts, D., & Timbrook, R. (1991). Detecting fake-good and fake-bad MMPI-2 profiles. *Journal of Personality Assessment, 57*, 264–277.

Haase, R. F., and Ivey, A. E. (1970). Influence of client pretesting on counseling outcome. *Journal of Consulting and Clinical Psychology, 34*, 128.

Hathaway, S. R. (1965). Personality inventories. In B. Wolman (Ed.), *Handbook of clinical psychology* (pp. 451–476). New York: McGraw-Hill.

Hathaway, S. R., & McKinley, J. C. (1940). A multiphasic personality schedule (Minnesota): I. Construction of the schedule. *Journal of Psychology, 10*, 249– 254.

Hathaway, S. R., & McKinley, J. C. (1943). *The Minnesota Multiphasic Personality Inventory*. New York: Psychological Corporation.

Hjemboe, S., & Butcher, J. N. (1991). Couples in marital distress: A study of demographic and personality factors as measured by the MMPI-2. *Journal of Personality Assessment, 57*, 216–237.

Hollon, S., & Mandell, M. (1979). Use of the MMPI to measure treatment effects. In J. N. Butcher (Ed.), *New directions in MMPI research* (pp. 241–302). Minneapolis: University of Minnesota Press.

Keller, L. S. & Butcher, J. N. (1991). *Use of the MMPI-2 with chronic pain patients*. Minneapolis: University of Minnesota Press.

Kuperman, S. K., Golden, C. J., & Blume, H. G. (1979). Predicting pain treatment results by personality variables in organic and functional patients. *Journal of Clinical Psychology, 35*, 832–837.

Lewandowski, D., & Graham, J. R. (1972). Empirical correlates of frequently oc-curring two-point MMPI code types: A replicated study. *Journal of Consulting and Clinical Psychology, 39*, 467–472.

Lubin, B., Larsen, R. M., & Matarazzo, J. (1984). Patterns of psychological test usage in the United States 1935–1982. *American Psychologist, 39*, 451–454.

Lubin, B., Larsen, R. M., Matarazzo, J., & Seever, M. (1985). Psychological assessment services and psychological test usage in private practice and military settings. *Psychotherapy in Private Practice, 4*, 19–29.

Manos, N. (1985). Adaptation of the MMPI in Greece: Translation, standardization, and cross-cultural comparison. In J. N. Butcher & C. D. Spielberger (Eds.), *Advances in personality assessment* (Vol. 4, pp. 159–208). Hillsdale, NJ: Erlbaum.

Marks, P. A., Seeman, W., & Haller, D. L. (1974). *The actuarial use of the MMPI with adolescents and adults.* Baltimore: Williams & Wilkins.

Moore, J. E., Armentraut, D. P., Parker, J. C., & Kivlahan, D. R. (1986). Empiri-cally derived pain-patient MMPI subgroups: Prediction of treatment out-comes. *Journal of Behavioral Medicine, 9*, 51–63.

Parkison, S., & Fishburne, J. (1984). MMPI normative data for a male active duty Army population. In *Proceedings of the Psychology in the Department of Defense, Ninth Symposium* (USAFA No. TR-84-2). Colorado Springs, CO: U.S. Air Force Academy.

Piotrowski, C., & Lubin, B. (1990). Assessment practices of health psychologists: Survey of APA Division 38 clinicians. *Professional Psychology: Research and Practice, 21*, 99–106.

Pope, K. S., Butcher, J. N., & Seelen, J. (1993). *The MMPI/MMPI-2/MMPI-A in court: Assessment, testimony, and cross-examination.* Washington, DC: American Psy-chological Association.

Pustell, H. B. (1958). A note on use of the MMPI in college counseling. *Journal of Counseling Psychology, 5*, 69–70.

Raab, E., Rickels, K., & Moore, E. (1964). A double blind evaluation of tybamate in anxious neurotic medical clinic patients. *American Journal of Psychiatry, 120*, 1005–1007.

Reich, J., Steward, M. S., Tupin, J. P., & Rosenblatt, R. M. (1985). Prediction of response to treatment in chronic pain patients. *Journal of Clinical Psychol-ogy, 46*, 425–427.

Rogers, R., Bagby, R. M., & Chakraborty, D. (1993). Feigning schizophrenic disor-ders on the MMPI-2: Detection of coached simulators. *Journal of Personality Assessment, 60*, 215–226.

Savasir, I., & Erol, N. (1990). The Turkish MMPI: Translation, standardization and validation. In J. N. Butcher & C. D. Spielberger (Eds.), *Advances in personal-ity assessment* (Vol. 8, pp. 49–62). Hillsdale, NJ: Erlbaum.

Schofield, W. (1950). Changes in responses to the MMPI following certain thera-pies. *Psychological Monographs, 64*(5, Whole No. 311).

Schofield, W. (1953). A further study of the effects of therapies on MMPI responses. *Journal of Abnormal and Social Psychology, 48*, 67–77.

Schretlen, D. J. (1988). The use of psychological tests to identify malingered symp-toms of mental disorder. *Clinical Psychology Review, 8*, 451–476.

Shealy, R. C., Lowe, J. D., & Ritzler, B. A. (1980). Sleep onset insomnia: Personality characteristics and treatment outcomes. *Journal of Consulting and Clinical Psychology, 48,* 659–661.

Shondrick, D. D., Ben-Porath, Y. S., & Stafford, K. (1992, May). *Forensic assessment with the MMPI-2: Characteristics of individuals undergoing court-ordered evaluations.* Paper presented at the 27th Annual Symposium on Recent Developments in the Use of the MMPI/MMPI-2, Minneapolis.

Tallent, N. (1993). *Psychological report writing* (4th ed.). Englewood Cliffs, NJ: Prentice-Hall.

Tellegen, A., & Ben-Porath, Y. S. (1992). The new uniform *T* scores for the MMPI-2: Rationale, derivation, and appraisal. *Psychological Assessment, 4,* 145–155.

Wagner, E. E., & Dobbins, R. D. (1967). MMPI profiles of parishioners seeking pastoral counseling. *Journal of Consulting Psychology, 31,* 83–84.

Weed, N. C., Butcher, J. N., Ben-Porath, Y. S., & McKenna, T. (1992). New measures for assessing alcohol and drug abuse: The APS and AAS. *Journal of Personality Assessment, 58,* 389–404.

Weiner, I. B. (1992). Clinical considerations in the conjoint use of the Rorschach and MMPI. *Journal of Personality Assessment, 60,* 148–152.

Wetter, M. W., Baer, R. A., Berry, D. T., Robison, L. H., & Sumpter, J. (1993). MMPI-2 profiles of motivated fakers given specific symptom information. *Psychological Assessment, 5,* 317–323.

Wetter, M. W., Baer, R. A., Berry, D. T., Smith, G. T., & Larsen, L. (1992). Sensitivity of the MMPI-2 validity scales to random responding and malingering. *Psychological Assessment, 4,* 369–374.

8

Putting Humpty Dumpty Together Again: Using the MCMI in Psychological Assessment

Theodore Millon
Roger Davis

Paradoxically, the methodology through which assessment instruments are created is in spirit opposed to the goal that directs their use. In tapping dimensions of individual differences, we abstract from persons only those dimensions we take as being common to all. Yet in using our instruments, we seek to build up again as a reconstructive process the very individuality we have previously distilled, so that the circle completes itself: from rich idiographic individuality, to nomothetic commonalities, and finally to "nomothetic individuality." Apparently, we must first give up the person if we are ultimately to understand him/her.

Integrative assessment is concerned with the last two links of this process. The fractionated person, the person who has been dispersed across scales and instruments, must be put together again as the organic whole he/she once was. How is such a venture to be achieved? First and foremost, we argue that assessment is an eminently theoretical process. Indeed, it is an evolutionary process, which requires a weighing of this and a disqualifying of that across the idiosyncrasies and commonalities of methods and data sources, through multiple rounds of hypothesis generation and testing. The end goal, of course, is *the* theory of the client, wherein every loose end has been tied up in a theory that follows the logic of the client's own psyche—a theory so compelling that it seems things could be not be otherwise than they have been supposed to be. Only such an eminently integrative theory allows the referral question to be addressed with confident words and concrete suggestions.

Although we are undoubtedly biased in our appraisal, we believe that no other inventory offers as potentially complete an integrative assessment of problematic personality styles and classical psychiatric disorders as the Millon Clinical Multiaxial Inventory (MCMI). Moreover, perhaps no other instrument is as coordinated with the official DSM taxonomy of personality disorders as the MCMI, or as conceptually consonant with the multiaxial logic that underlies the DSM. In fact, the MCMI is but one (essential) link in what has emerged as an integrative schema by which to conceptualize both personality and abnormal behavior (Millon, 1969, 1981, 1990).

Let us explain. Integrative consonance is a worthy ideal not only in the individual assessment case, but within a science as well. Rather than being developed independently as free-standing and uncoordinated structures, a mature clinical science of psychopathology should embody explicit (1) theories (explanatory and heuristic conceptual schemas that are consistent with established knowledge), and (2) nosology (a taxonomic classification of disorders that has been logically derived from a theory, arranged to provide a cohesive organization within which major categories can be grouped and differentiated). The development of a theory and a nosology permits the development of (3) instrumentation—that is, tools that are empirically grounded and sufficiently sensitive quantitatively to enable the theory's propositions and hypotheses to be adequately investigated and evaluated, and to permit the categories comprising its nosology to be readily identified (diagnosed) and measured (dimensionalized). The instrumentation enables clinicians to specify target areas for (4) interventions—that is, strategies and techniques of therapy, designed in accord with the theory and oriented to modify problematic clinical characteristics (Millon, 1990).

The goals of this chapter are largely derived from the framework identified in the paragraph above. Operating on the assumption that clinicians want to know not only what they should do, but also why they should do it, we try to embed the "how" of the MCMI in its "why." Perhaps test users will then feel that they are doing something more than merely following a flowchart or a chain of stimulus–response bonds to its termination in the clinical report: They must understand the test to understand their clients. Since the test is embedded in a theoretical matrix, users must understand the theory to understand the test. This requires a justification, not merely a dispensation.

Before we begin, we must express a few reservations. In a chapter such as this, which features a particular instrument but nevertheless seeks to illuminate integrative links among the four domains of clinical science, some highly relevant issues must be greatly abbreviated or completely omitted. As a result, what otherwise might appear as a well-worn, incremental theoretical pathway now contains more abrupt transitions. Most of the more theoretical material presented may be found in *Toward a New Personology: An Evolutionary Model* (Millon, 1990). Other concerns have been treated at a level of abstraction more gross than their gravity requires. These include the descriptions, developmental pathways (all but omitted), and specific intervention opportunities for each of the personality disorders and their more common two-point variants. Much of this information is available in *Disorders of Personality* (Millon, 1981). In an ideal world, we should adopt ideal goals, but in a less than ideal world, we must often adopt pragmatic ones.

Integrative Logic and the Process of Assessment

The word "integrative" is now used so widely as to be a cliché: Obviously, given an equivalence of purpose, that which is more integrated is better than that which is less integrated. However, integration neither springs into being fully formed, nor is it unveiled or discovered in a single conceptual leap. Instead, integration is perhaps better understood as a dynamic process. Such a conception sees knowledge building as an ongoing activity in which internal inconsistencies are generated and resolved or transcended at higher and higher levels of conceptualization: While reality is undoubtedly integrated, our ideas about reality must be more or less so. An inquiry into the nature of this process will be worthwhile, because (as we intend to show) essentially the same logic underlies profile interpretation, thus creating another link between theory and instrumentation.

Pepper (1942) formalized the integrative means of knowledge building as a world view that he called "organicism," one of his four relatively adequate "world hypotheses" or metaphysical world views. Pepper described seven categories of organicism. These work in a kind of dialectical interplay between appearance and reality—one that always proceeds in the direction of increasing integration:

> These [categories] are (1) *fragments* of experience which appear with (2) *nexuses* or connections or implications, which spontaneously lead as a result of the aggravation of (3) *contradictions*, gaps, oppositions, or counteractions to resolution in (4) an *organic whole*, which is found to have been (5) *implicit* in the fragments, and to (6) *transcend* the previous contradictions by means of a coherent totality, which (7) *economizes*, saves, preserves all the original fragments of experience without any loss. (p. 283, emphasis Pepper's)

To translate this into terms more easily recognized, (1) observations (fragments) lead one to (2) form inchoate theoretical propositions (nexuses), which, unfortunately, do not all mesh harmoniously. This automatically produces (3) aggravating and ostensibly irreconcilable inconsistencies (contradictions) that are resolved through (4) a unified theory (organic whole), which, upon reflection, is found to have been (5) implicit in the observations (fragments) all along. Thus, it (6) transcends the initial, naive inconsistencies among observations by reconceptualizing these observations in terms of a new, coherent theoretical model—one that (7) integrates or accounts for all the evidence (economizes) according to its new terms and relationships.

Undoubtedly, even this is a lot to digest in a single paragraph. Extrapolating from the logic presented above, we might say that as a body of implicit theories is formalized, hiatuses are discovered, and the theories inevitably become enmeshed in inconsistencies and contradictions. Eventually, a new theory is formulated that unifies disparate observations and inconsistencies. What was believed to have been contradictory is discovered not to have been so at all, but only to have appeared contradictory, much as special cases are transcended by more general formulations.

By this account, science cannot exist merely as a descriptive venture that consists of observing, categorizing, and cross-correlating various phenomena at face value; instead, it proceeds by establishing higher-level (superordinate) theoretical principles that unify the manifestations of a subject domain by explaining why these particular observations or formulations obtain rather than others. The "limit of this series" (Pepper, 1942) is truth itself—what physicists have called "the theory of everything," and what philosophers (notably Hegel) have called "the absolute." In this ultimate integration, "logical necessity would become identified with ultimate fact" (Pepper, 1942, p. 301). Nothing would remain unassimilated; everything would be harmonized with everything else.

More than anything else, the question "Why this rather than that?" is what underlies the force toward integration in this world view. Only by answering this question can we escape what is arbitrary and capricious, and move in the direction of necessity. In its most radical form, this argument holds that even if reliable observations of great or even perfect positive predictive power could be made through some infallible methodology, these indicators would stand simply as isolated facts unassimilated as scientific knowledge until they were unified through some theoretical basis. Predictive power alone does not make a science. Scientific explanations appeal to theoretical principles that operate above the level of superficialities—principles that are sufficient because they predict, necessary because they explain.

The process of clinical assessment follows essentially the same logic. Modeling the following after Pepper, but substituting the appropriate terminology, we can say: The individual scales, instruments, and other data are the (1) fragments. These possess (2) nexuses—implications, or (statistically) intercorrelations both with one another and with other clinical phenomena—leading to inchoate theories about the individual and his/her psychopathology. Inevitably, these theories do not mesh, cannot be assimilated to one another exactly; this leads to (3) contradictions, gaps, or inconsistencies in the assessment thus far. The assessor then steps back, seeking (4) a more integrative theory or organic whole that makes sense of the gaps or inconsistencies. This integrative theory is then found to have been (5) implicit in the scales, observations, and other data (otherwise, an integrative assessment would not be possible at all), and to (6) transcend the foregoing inconsistencies, gaps, or contradictions by means of a coherent totality, which (7) makes sense of all the observations by tying up all loose ends.

In an integrative assessment, the assessor is required to step outside the theoretical fecundity and inevitable contradictions of a morass of scales and data domains, in order to develop a theory of the client in which all the data somehow make sense. This superordinate theory lies literally at a higher level of formulation than do the individual measures that constitute the "raw data" of the assessment. Thus the "loop" from idiographic individuality to nomothetic commonality to nomothetic individuality is brought to closure: Nomothetic individuality explicitly requires the reintegration of the individual who currently lies fractionated among various scales and dimensions. An integrative assessment, then, does not come into being of its own accord, but is constructed, and its validity is linked to the mode of its construction.

The underlying assumption here is that things do not fit together equally well in all possible combinations. What exists in one personological domain constrains what can exist in another; otherwise, there would be no nexuses or implications across domains. An individual born with an active temperament, for example, is unlikely to possess a phlegmatic phenomenology as an adult. In other words, biophysical construction constrains the quality of subjective realities that can evolve in the individual life. The same is true of all the domains of personality: They do not fit together equally well in all combinations. Functional and structural attributes for each of the personality prototypes have been delineated in several prior publications (Millon, 1986, 1990) and are explored below.

Interestingly, the logic presented above finds a point of contrast with that of inventories derived through factor analysis. Orthogonal factors, by definition, are independent: Scores on one factor do *not* constrain what can exist on any other. The extracted traits do not influence one another in any way. Thus, although factor analysis represents a parsimonious way of looking at a particular area, it implicitly holds that the structure of reality is distinctly unintegrated—that a few essential underlying dimensions determine a great variety of appearances, but these dimensions do not constrain one another. It is interesting, then, to speculate whether the methodology of factor-analytic test construction may be inherently inconsistent with the epistemology of test interpretation (indeed, of clinical psychology as a field). The position that fundamental dimensions exist independently runs counter to the clinician's desire to put the client together again.

On the Importance of Theory to a Taxonomy of Personality Disorders

Philosophers of science are agreed that theory provides the conceptual glue that binds a nosology together. Moreover, a good theory not only summarizes and incorporates extant knowledge; it possesses systematic import, in that it originates and develops new observations and new methods. In setting out a theory of personality prototypes, what is desired is not merely a *descriptive* list of disorders and their correlated attributes, but an *explanatory* derivation based on theoretical principles. Again, the question of interest is this: Why these particular personality disorders rather than others?

To address this question, a taxonomy must seek a theoretical schema that "carves nature at its joints," so to speak. The philosopher of science Carl Hempel (1965) clearly distinguished between natural and artificial classification systems. The difference, according to Hempel, is that natural classifications possess "systematic import." Hempel wrote:

> Distinctions between "natural" and "artificial" classifications may well be explicated as referring to the difference between classifications that are scientifically fruitful and those that are not: in a classification of the former kind, those characteristics of the elements which serve as criteria of membership in a given class are associated, universally or with high-probability, with more or less extensive clusters of other characteristics. . . . [A] classification of this sort should be viewed as somehow having objective existence in nature, as "carving nature at the joints" . . . (pp. 146–147)

The biological sexes, male and female, and the periodic table of elements are both examples of classification schemes that can be viewed as possessing "objective" existence in nature. The items we seek to classify are not genders or chemical elements, however, but persons. In so doing, we seek the ideal of a classification scheme or taxonomy that is "natural"—one that "inheres" in the subject domain, rather than being "imposed" on it. Such a scheme asserts its "the-ness" rather than its "a-ness": Not only is it sufficient with respect to the phenomena of a subject domain, it is necessary.

Again, to achieve such an end, the system of kinds that undergirds any domain of inquiry must itself be answerable to the question that forms the very point of departure for the scientific enterprise: Why does nature take this particular form rather than some other? The goal of science is to explain the objects and events we find in the world, and among the objects we find in the world are classification systems for objects themselves. Applied to a taxonomy, the question is thus rephrased: Why this particular system of kinds rather than some other? Accordingly, a taxonomic scheme must be justified, and to be justified scientifically, it must be justified theoretically. Consonant with integrative principles, then, theory and taxonomy are intimately intertwined. Rather than remaining an uncoordinated and free-floating fragment, each taxon finds its true nexus with others in transcending theoretical principles through which the entire taxonomy can be deduced as an organic whole: The validity of a taxonomy is linked to its theoretical construction. Quine (1977) makes a parallel case:

> . . . one's sense of similarity or one's system of kinds develops and changes . . . as one matures. . . . And at length standards of similarity set in which are geared to theoretical science. The development is away from the immediate, subjective, animal sense of similarity to the remoter objectivity of a similarity determined by scientific hypotheses . . . and constructs. Things are similar in the later or theoretical sense to the degree that they are . . . revealed by science. (p. 171)

This "remoter sense of objectivity" is essentially what is sought in the assessment process—most obviously in terms of the referral question, but also in terms of the intermediate constructs required to address the referral question, such as personality style. The purpose of an integrative assessment is to develop a theory of the person. That anyone would want to develop an integrative theory of the person without a proportionally integrative theory of the constructs used to explain the person is somewhat puzzling, if not amazing. But when theory is ignored in favor of exclusively empirical inductions or factor-analytically derived orthogonal dimensions, this is essentially what is being done.

Does this mean that an assessor has to buy into the theory that underlies the MCMI to buy into the test? Not at all. Although no other instrument is as coordinated with the official DSM taxonomy of personality disorders as the MCMI, the official position of the DSM with regard to all taxonomic categories, including personality prototypes, is atheoretical. Moreover, the MCMI was designed from the beginning to function as an explicitly clinical inventory. It is not set in stone. As substantive advances in knowledge take place, whether as the result of compelling empirical research or of well-justified theoretical deduction, the MCMI will be upgraded and refined as well. Minor elaborations and modifications have been introduced since the original formal publication of the MCMI-I in 1977, these fine-tunings will continue regularly as our understanding of the MCMI's strengths, limits, and potentials develops further.

We must add, however, that to jettison the theory would be to sell the

MCMI short. In the absence of a theoretical foundation, the outline of this chapter could be effectively abbreviated to read something like the following: "These are the disorders, and this is the test, and this is how to give the test, and this is what to watch out for, and this is what to expect when such and such shows up." No "why," just "that." In contrast, a theoretical perspective embodies well-ordered and codified links between constructs, providing a *generative* basis for making clinical inferences founded on a small number of fundamental principles. We now turn to these principles.

The Polarity Model of Personality Disorders

The theoretical model that follows is grounded in evolutionary theory. In essence, it seeks to explicate the structure and styles of personality with reference to deficient, imbalanced, or conflicted modes of ecological adaptation and reproductive strategy. The proposition that the development and functions of personological traits may be usefully explored through the lens of evolutionary principles has a long, if as yet unfulfilled, tradition. Spencer (1870) and Huxley (1870) offered suggestions of this nature shortly after Darwin's seminal *Origin of Species* was published. In more recent times, we have seen the emergence of sociobiology, an interdisciplinary science that explores the interface between human social functioning and evolutionary biology (Wilson, 1975, 1978).

Four domains or spheres in which evolutionary principles are demonstrated are labeled as "existence," "adaptation," "replication," and "abstraction." The first relates the serendipitous transformation of random or less organized states into those possessing distinct structures of greater organization; the second refers to homeostatic processes employed to sustain survival in open ecosystems; the third pertains to reproductive styles that maximize the diversification and selection of ecologically effective attributes; and the fourth concerns the emergence of competencies that foster anticipatory planning and reasoned decision making. Polarities derived from the first three phases (pleasure–pain, passive–active, other–self) are used to construct a theoretically embedded classification system of personality disorders.

These polarities have forerunners in psychological theory that may be traced as far back as the early 1900s. A number of pre-World War I theorists, including Freud, proposed a set of three polarities that were used time and again as the raw materials for constructing psychological processes. Aspects of these polarities were "discovered" and employed by theorists in France, Germany, Russia, and other European nations, as well as the United States. In addition, there is a growing group of contemporary scholars whose work has begun to illuminate aspects of these polar dimensions, including Eysenck (1957, 1967), Gray (1964, 1973), Buss and

Plomin (1975, 1984), Russell (1980), Tellegen (1985), and Cloninger (1986, 1987).

A more formal summary of the concordance between evolutionary model polarities and modern psychological constructs across (1) principles of learning, (2) psychoanalytic concepts, (3) components of emotion/ motivation, and (4) neurobiological substrates is presented in Millon (1990). Some may object, particularly because of the brief presentation that space allows, that the concordance suggested is an imperfect one. From a certain perspective, it is: The theorists and researchers from traditional perspectives possess unique vocabularies. These vocabularies are differentiated in proportion to the highly specified nature of their explorations and horizontal refinements, by virtue of which each resists assimilation to overarching perspectives. Accordingly, from that particular perspective, the concordance is indeed less than perfect.

From a metatheoretical perspective, however, each exists as a fragment to be transcended—a partial truth that attempts to describe an intrinsically indivisible world, and is only partially successful. Much as Godel argued that the consistency of a system cannot be proven at the same level as that system, disputations between these "subdisciplines" cannot be resolved by means of imperial ambitions and internecine battles; they can only be transcended at a superordinate level of integration in metatheory. Interested readers should consult Millon (1990) for an explication of these relationships. Table 8.1 derives the DSM personality disorders from the polarity model.

The first phase, existence, concerns the maintenance of integrative phenomena—whether nuclear particles, viruses, or human beings—against

TABLE 8.1. Polarity Model and Its Personality Disorder Derivatives

	Existential aim		Replication strategy	
	Life enhancement	Life preservation	Reproductive propagation	Reproductive nurturance
Polarity	Pleasure–pain		Self–other	
Pathology: Deficiency, imbalance, or conflict	Pleasure – Pain – +	Pleasure ↶ Pain ↷	Self – Other +	Self + Other –	Self Other
Adaptation mode	DSM-III-R personality disorders			
Passive: Accommodation	Schizoid	Self-Defeating	Dependent	Narcissistic	Compulsive
Active: Modification	Avoidant	Sadistic	Histrionic	Antisocial	Passive–Aggressive
Dysfunctional	Schizotypal	Borderline/ Paranoid	Borderline	Paranoid	Borderline/ Paranoid

Note. Adatped from Millon (1987).

the background of entropic decompensation. Evolutionary mechanisms derived from this stage have to do with life enhancement and life preservation. The former are concerned with orienting individuals toward improvement in the quality of life; the latter are concerned with orienting individuals away from actions or environments that decrease the quality of life, or even jeopardize existence itself. These may be called "existential aims." At the highest level of abstraction, such mechanisms form (whether phenomenologically or metaphorically expressed) a pleasure–pain polarity. Some personality types are conflicted in regard to these existential aims (e.g., the sadistic), while others possess deficits in these crucial substrates (e.g., the schizoid). In terms of neuropsychological growth stages (Millon, 1969, 1981), the pleasure–pain polarity is recapitulated in a "sensory–attachment" phase, the purpose of which is the largely innate and rather mechanical discrimination of pain and pleasure signals.

Existence, however, is but an initial phase. Once an integrative structure exists, it must maintain its existence through exchanges of energy and information with its environment. The second evolutionary stage relates to what are termed the "modes of adaptation." It is also framed as a two-part polarity—a passive orientation (a tendency to accommodate to one's ecological niche) versus an active orientation (a tendency to modify or intervene in one's surrounds). These modes of adaptation differ from the first phase of evolution, in that they regard how that which is endures. Unlike pleasure–pain and self–other, the active–passive polarity is truly unidimensional; one cannot be both active and passive at the same time. In terms of neurophysiological growth stages, these modes are recapitulated in a "sensorimotor–autonomy" phase, during which the child either progresses to an active disposition toward his/her physical and social context, or perpetuates the dependent mode of prenatal and infantile existence.

Although organisms may be well adapted to their environments, the existence of any life form is time-limited. To circumvent this limitation, organisms have developed "replicatory strategies" by which to leave progeny. These strategies regard what biologists have referred to as a "self-propagating strategy" at one polar extreme, and an "other-nurturing strategy" at the second extreme. Psychologically, the former strategy is disposed toward actions that are egotistic, insensitive, inconsiderate, and uncaring; the latter is disposed toward actions that are affiliative, intimate, protective, and solicitous (Gilligan, 1982; Rushton, 1985; Wilson, 1978). Like pleasure–pain, the self–other polarity is not truly unidimensional. Some personalities are conflicted on this polarity, such as the compulsive and passive–aggressive. In terms of a neuropsychological growth stages, an individual's orientation toward self and others is recapitulated in the "intracortical–initiative" stage. A description of each of the derived personality patterns follows.

Applying the Polarity Model
to the DSM Personality Disorders

In this section, our goal is to apply the polarity model to the DSM personality disorders. Some personalities exhibit a reasonable balance on one or other of the polarity pairs. Not all individuals fall at the center, of course; individual differences in both personality features and overall style will reflect the relative positions and strengths of each polarity component. Personalities we have termed "deficient" lack the capacity to experience or to enact certain aspects of the three polarities (e.g., the schizoid has a faulty substrate for both pleasure and pain). Those spoken of as "imbalanced" lean strongly toward one or another extreme of a polarity (e.g., the dependent is oriented almost exclusively to receiving the support and nurturance of others). Finally, those we judge "conflicted" struggle with ambivalences toward opposing ends of a bipolarity (e.g., the passive-aggressive vacillates between adhering to the expectancies of others and enacting what is wished for the self). In the explications that follow, it is suggested that the reader attend not only to the trait content of the various patterns, but particularly to their embeddedness in the polarity model. Consistent with integrative logic, this theoretical foundation will prove important both in MCMI interpretation and in intervention. (The numbering and lettering of the personality types correspond to the MCMI scheme presented later in Table 8.2.)

1. *Schizoid personality*. Schizoid patients are those in whom both pleasure and pain polarity systems are deficient. That is, they lack the capacity, relatively speaking, to experience life's events as either painful or pleasurable. These clients are notable for their lack of desire and their incapacity to experience depth in either pleasure or pain. They tend to be apathetic, listless, distant, and asocial. Affectionate needs and emotional feelings are minimal; the individual functions as a passive observer, detached from the rewards and affections as well as from the demands of human relationships. Deficits such as these across the entire pleasure–pain polarity underlie what is termed the "passive–detached" style.

2A. *Avoidant personality*. The second clinically meaningful combination based on problems in the pleasure–pain polarity comprises patients with a diminished ability to experience pleasure, but with an unusual sensitivity and responsiveness to pain. This imbalance causes these patients to experience few positive reinforcers from either self or others; they are vigilant, perennially on guard, and ever ready to distance themselves from an anxious anticipation of life's painful or negatively reinforcing experiences. Their adaptive strategy reflects a fear and mistrust of others. They maintain a constant vigil lest their impulses and longing for affection result in a repetition of the pain and anguish they previously experienced with others. Only by active withdrawal can they protect themselves. Despite desires to relate, they have learned that it is best to deny these feelings and keep a good measure of interpersonal distance. Unable to experience pleasures either from self or others, both schizoid and avoidant personalities tend to drift into isolating circumstances. Consequently, both are referred to as "detached" types. Because the avoidant secretly desires interpersonal contact, however, this pattern is differentiated as the "active–detached" type.

2B. *Depressive personality*. The avoidant and depressive personalities have in common a diminished ability to experience pleasure and a comparable tendency to be overly sensitive to pain (i.e., events of a forbidding, disquieting, and anguishing character). However, avoidants have learned to anticipate these troublesome events—by taking proactive steps to distance themselves from them, by minimizing involvements with others, and by aspiring to want or possess little lest it be unattainable or quickly withdrawn. Depressives are notably more passive then the anxiously proactive avoidants. They permit themselves to be stuck in the mire of feeling helpless and hopeless, do little to eschew pain, and simply give in to what they feel is life's inevitable helplessness. With nothing that can be done to alter their circumstances, depressives either sit immobile, feeling incompetent, sorrowful, useless, and unworthy, or simply cry out in painful misery.

3. *Dependent personality*. Following the polarity model, we must ask whether particular clinical consequences occur among individuals who are markedly imbalanced by virtue of turning almost exclusively toward others or toward themselves as a means of experiencing pleasure and avoiding pain. Dependents have learned not only to turn to others as their source of nurturance and security, but to wait passively for the others' leadership in providing them. They are characterized by a search for relationships in which they can lean upon others for affection, security, and leadership. Dependents' lack of both initiative and autonomy is often a consequence of parental overprotection. As a function of these experiences, they have simply learned the comforts of assuming a "passive–dependent" role in interpersonal relations, accepting what kindness and support they may find, and willingly submitting to the wishes of others in order to maintain their affection.

4. *Histrionic personality*. Also turning to others as their primary strategy are a group of personalities who take an actively dependent stance. They achieve their goal of maximizing protection, nurturance, and reproductive success by engaging busily in a series of manipulative, seductive, gregarious, and attention-getting maneuvers. This "active–dependent" imbalance characterizes the histrionic personality, according to the theory. These patients often show an insatiable, if not indiscriminate, search for stimulation and affection. Their clever and often artful social behaviors give the appearance of an inner confidence and independent self-assurance; beneath this guise, however, lie a fear of genuine autonomy and a need for repeated signs of acceptance and approval. Tribute and affection must constantly

be replenished, and are sought from every interpersonal source and in every social context.

5. *Narcissistic personality*. Clients falling into the "independent" personality pattern also exhibit an imbalance in their replication strategy; in this case, however, there is a primary reliance on self rather than others. These individuals are notable for their egotistic self-involvement, experiencing primary pleasure simply by passively being or focusing on themselves. Early experience has taught them to overvalue their self-worth; this confidence and superiority may be founded on false premises (i.e., may be unsustainable by real or mature achievements). Nevertheless, they blithely assume that others will recognize their specialness. Hence, they maintain an air of arrogant self-assurance and, without much thought or even conscious intent, benignly exploit others for their own advantage. Although the tributes of others are both welcome and encouraged, their air of snobbish and pretentious superiority requires little confirmation through either genuine accomplishment or social approval. Their sublime confidence that things will work out well provides them with little incentive to engage in the reciprocal give and take of social life.

6A. *Antisocial personality*. Those whom we characterize as exhibiting the "active–independent" orientation resemble the DSM antisocial personality in outlook, temperament, and socially unacceptable behaviors. These individuals act to counter the expectation of pain and depredation at the hands of others; this is done by engaging in duplicitous and often illegal behaviors designed to exploit the environment for self-gain. Their orientation reflects their skepticism concerning the motives of others, a desire for autonomy, and a wish for revenge over what are felt as past injustices. They are irresponsible and impulsive—actions they see as justified, because others are judged unreliable and disloyal. In contrast to the narcissistic personality, this second pattern develops as a form of protection and counteraction. These types turn to themselves, first to avoid the depredation they anticipate, and then to compensate by furnishing self-generated rewards in their stead. Insensitivity and ruthlessness are the only means of heading off abuse and victimization.

6B. *Sadistic personality*. In some clients, the usual properties associated with pain and pleasure are conflicted or reversed: These patients not only seek or create objectively "painful" events, but experience them as "pleasurable." Both the sadistic and self-defeating patterns can be labeled as "discordant" patterns, to reflect, on the one hand, the dissonant structure of their pain pleasure systems, and, on the other, the conflicting character of their interpersonal relations. The sadistic pattern reflects the "active–discordant" variant, recognizing individuals who are not judged publicly to be antisocial, but whose actions signify personal pleasure and satisfaction in behaviors that humiliate others and violate their rights and feelings. These aggressive personalities are generally hostile, pervasively combative, and appear indifferent to or even pleased by the destructive consequences of their contentious, if not abusive and brutal, behaviors. Although they may cloak their more malicious and power-oriented tendencies in publicly approved roles and vocations, they give themselves away in their dominating, antagonistic, and frequent persecutory actions. As is all too well known, competitive ambition and social brutality may readily be reinforced as a means toward achieving security, status, and pleasure in our society, by demonstrably resulting in personal achievement, material rewards, and dominance over others.

7. *Compulsive personality.* The compulsive personality represents a pattern conflicted on the self–other polarity, but with a passive bent. Such individuals display a picture of distinct other-directedness, consistency in social compliance, and interpersonal respect. Their histories usually reveal subjection to constraint and discipline, but only when they transgressed parental strictures and expectations. Beneath the conforming and other-oriented veneer, they exhibit intense desires to rebel and assert their own self-oriented feelings and impulses. These individuals have been intimidated and coerced into accepting the reinforcements imposed on them by others. They resolve this ambivalence not only by suppressing resentment, but by overconforming and by placing high demands on themselves and others. Their disciplined self-restraint serves to control intense though hidden oppositional feelings, resulting in an overt passivity and seeming public compliance. However, their intense anger and oppositional feelings occasionally break through their controls.

8A. *Negativistic (passive–aggressive) personality.* The negativistic pattern is also conflicted on the self–other polarity, but instead assumes a more active orientation toward this reversal than does the compulsive. Although this struggle represents an inability to resolve conflicts similar to that of "passive–ambivalent" individuals (compulsives), the conflicts of these "active–ambivalent" personalities remain close to consciousness and intrude into everyday life. They behave obediently one time and defiantly the next. Feeling intensely, yet unable to resolve their ambivalence, they weave an erratic course from voicing their self-depreciation and guilt for failing to meet the expectations of others, to expressing stubborn negativism and resistance over having submitted to the wishes of others rather than their own. These clients get themselves into endless wrangles and disappointments as they vacillate between deference and obedience, defiance and aggressive negativism, explosive anger and stubbornness, and guilt and shame.

8B. *Self-defeating personality.* Like sadistic personalities, self-defeating personalities are conflicted on the pleasure–pain polarity. These individuals interpret events and engage in relationships in a manner that not only is at variance with this deeply rooted polarity, but is contradictory to the associations these life-promoting emotions usually acquire through learning. Relating to others in an obsequious and self-sacrificing manner, these persons allow or even encourage others to exploit or take advantage of them. Focusing on their very worst features, many assert that they deserve being shamed and humbled. To compound their pain and anguish—states that they experience as comforting and that they strive to achieve—they actively and repetitively recall their past misfortunes, as well as transform otherwise fortunate circumstances into their potentially most problematic outcomes. Typically acting in an unpresuming and self-effacing way, they will often intensify their deficits and place themselves in an inferior light or abject position.

S. *Schizotypal personality*. The schizotypal personality represents a cognitively dysfunctional and maladaptively detached orientation in the polarity theory. Schizotypal personalities experience minimal pleasure; they also have difficulty consistently differentiating between self and other strategies, as well as active and passive modes of adaptation. Most prefer social isolation with minimal personal attachments and obligations. Inclined to be either autistic or cognitively confused, they think tangentially and often appear self-absorbed and ruminative. Behavioral eccentricities are notable, and the individuals are often perceived by others as strange or different. Depending on whether the pattern is basically more active or more passive, there will be either an anxious wariness and hypersensitivity or an emotional flattening and deficiency of affect. Estranged from external support systems, these individuals are likely to have few subliminatory channels and still fewer sources for emotional nurturance and cognitive stability, the lack of which disposes them to social regressions and autistic preoccupations.

C. *Borderline personality*. The borderline personality corresponds to the theory's emotionally dysfunctional and maladaptively ambivalent polarity orientation. Conflicts exist across the board—between pleasure and pain, active and passive, and self and other. Borderline individuals seem unable to take a consistent, neutral, or balanced position among these polar extremes, tending to fluctuate from one end to the other. These persons experience intense endogenous moods, with recurring periods of dejection and apathy, often interspersed with spells of anger, anxiety, or euphoria. Among the features that distinguish borderline personalities from their less severe personality covariants is the dysregulation of their affects, seen most clearly in the instability and lability of their moods. In addition, many express or even enact recurring self-mutilating and suicidal thoughts. Some appear overly preoccupied with securing affection. Many have difficulty maintaining a consistent sense of identity. Interpersonally, most display a cognitive–affective ambivalence, evident in simultaneous feelings of rage, love, and guilt toward others. These features represent a low level of structural cohesion in their psychic organization. For many, there is a split within both their interpersonal and their intrapsychic orientations. Unable to build inner structural coherence, they are unable to maintain a nonconflictual direction in their personal relationships, or a consistency in their defensive operations. There are fundamental intrapsychic dissensions—core splits between taking an independent *or* taking a dependent stance, between acting out impulsively *or* withdrawing into passive disengagement, between following the wishes of others *or* damning them and doing the opposite of what they wish. They repeatedly undo or reverse the actions they previously took, thereby embedding further the reality of being internally divided.

P. *Paranoid personality.* The paranoid personality exhibits a vigilant mistrust of others and an edgy defensiveness against anticipated criticism and deception. Driven by a high sensitivity to pain (rejection–humiliation) and oriented strongly toward the self polarity, these patients exhibit a touchy irritability, a need to assert themselves—not necessarily in action, but in an inner world of self-determined beliefs and assumptions. They are "prepared" to provoke social conflicts and fractious circumstances as a means of gratifying their confused mix of pain sensitivity and self assertion. The interplay of these polarities perpetuates their pathology: Not only is it sustained, but it is increased, as in a vicious circle. There is an ever-present abrasive irritability, which tends to precipitate exasperation and anger in others. Expressed often is a fear of losing self-autonomy, leading the clients to vigorously resist external influence and control. Whereas borderlines are notable for the instability of their polarity positions, paranoids are distinctive by virtue of the immutability and inflexibility of their respective positions.

History of the MCMI

It may be of interest to record a few words regarding the origin and sequential development of the various forms of the MCMI. A year or two after the publication of *Modern Psychopathology* (Millon, 1969), Millon began, with some regularity, to receive letters and phone calls from graduate students who had read the book and thought it provided ideas that could aid them in formulating their dissertations. Most inquired about the availability of an "operational" measure they could use to assess or diagnose the pathologies of personality that were generated by the text's theoretical model. Regrettably, no such tool was available. Nevertheless, they were encouraged to pursue whatever lines of interest they had in the subject. Some were sufficiently motivated to state that they would attempt to develop their own "Millon" instrument as part of the dissertation enterprise.

As the number of these potential "Millon" instruments grew into the teens, however, concern grew proportionately regarding both the diversity and adequacy of these representations of the theory. To establish a measure of instrumental uniformity for future investigators, as well as to assure at least a modicum of psychometric quality among tools that ostensibly reflected the theory's constructs, Millon was prompted (perhaps "driven" is a more accurate word) to consider undertaking the construction of a test himself. At that time, in early 1971, Millon was directing a research supervision group composed of psychologists and psychiatrists in training during their internship and residency periods. All of them had read *Modern Psychopathology*, and found the proposal of working together to develop instruments to identify and quantify the text's personality constructs to be both worthy and challenging.

The initial task was that of exploring alternate methods for gathering relevant clinical data. About 11 or 12 persons were involved in that early phase. Some were asked to analyze the possibilities of identifying new indices from well-established projective tests, such as the Rorschach and the Thematic Apperception Test (TAT); others were to investigate whether relevant scales could be composed from existing objective inventories, such as the Sixteen Factor Personality Questionnaire and the Minnesota Multiphasic Personality Inventory (MMPI). Another group examined the potential inherent in developing a new and original structured interview. After 4 or 5 months of weekly discussions, the group concluded that an entirely new instrument would be required to represent the full scope of the theory, especially its diverse and then-novel pathological personality patterns (this work, it should be recalled, preceded by several years that undertaken by the DSM-III task force). It was judged further that the group would attempt to construct both a self-report inventory and a semistructured interview schedule.

Naively, it was assumed that both construction tasks could be completed in about 18 months—a time period that would allow several members of the research group to participate on a continuing basis. Despite the fact that the development of the interview schedule was "postponed" after a brief initial period, the "more limited" task of the inventory took almost 7 years to complete. The framework and preliminary item selections of the inventory were well underway, however, by the end of the first full year of work, and were described briefly in *Research Methods in Psychopathology* (Millon & Diesenhaus, 1972). The initial forms of the clinical instrument were entitled the Millon–Illinois Self-Report Inventory (MI-SRI).

Millon became involved thereafter in the development of the DSM-III, playing a major role in formulating both the constructs and criteria that were to characterize its Axis II personality disorders. Although the MI-SRI was regularly refined and strengthened on the basis of theoretical logic and research data, an effort was made during this period to coordinate both its items and scales with the forthcoming syndromes of DSM-III. Thus modified, its name was changed to the Millon Clinical Multiaxial Inventory (MCMI), published in 1977 by National Computer Systems, Inc. (NCS).

In the ensuing 10-year period, numerous refinements of the inventory (retrospectively labeled the MCMI-I) were introduced (e.g., corrections for response-distorting tendencies such as current emotional state), as were expansions made to incorporate theoretical extensions and the newly published DSM-III-R (e.g., the addition of the Self-Defeating and Sadistic scales). The MCMI-II, reflecting the preceding changes and additions, was published in 1987. Ongoing investigations, further refinements in its undergirding theory, and modifications in the DSM-IV (American Psychiatric Association, 1994) personality disorders criteria served as the primary impetus to refashion the inventory into its latest form, the MCMI-III (Millon, 1994). The MCMI-III has been designed to reflect its theory optimally, and to maximize its consonance with the most recent and empirically grounded official classification system.

Structural Features of the MCMI

A principal goal in constructing the MCMI was to keep the total number of items small enough to encourage use in diverse diagnostic and treatment settings, yet large enough to permit the assessment of a wide range of clinically relevant behaviors. At 175 items, the final form is much shorter than comparable instruments. Potentially objectionable items have been screened out, and terminology has been geared to an eighth-grade reading level. The majority of patients can complete the MCMI in 20 to 30 minutes; this facilitates relatively simple and rapid administration, as well as minimizing patient resistance and fatigue.

The inventory itself currently consists of 24 clinical scales, as well as three "modifier" scales available for interpretive analysis. Table 8.2 lists the MCMI-III scales; a sample MCMI-II profile is given later in this chapter. The first three scales, Disclosure, Desirability, and Debasement, represent modifier indices; their purpose is to identify distorting tendencies that characterize clients and their responses. The next two sections constitute the basic personality disorder scales, essentially reflecting Axis II of the DSM. The first section appraises what are viewed as the moderately severe personality pathologies, ranging from the Schizoid to the Self-Defeating scales; the second section represents more severe personality pathologies, encompassing the Schizotypal, Borderline, and Paranoid scales. The following two sections cover several of the more prevalent Axis I disorders, ranging from the more moderate clinical syndromes (the Anxiety Disorder to Post-Traumatic Stress Disorder scales) to those of greater severity (the Thought Disorder, Major Depression, and Delusional Disorder scales). The division between personality and clinical syndrome scales is congruent with multiaxial logic, and has important interpretive implications.

TABLE 8.2. MCMI-III Scales

Modifying indices
- X   Disclosure
- Y   Desirability
- Z   Debasement

Clinical personality patterns
- 1   Schizoid
- 2A   Avoidant
- 2B   Depressive
- 3   Dependent
- 4   Histrionic
- 5   Narcissistic
- 6A   Antisocial
- 6B   Aggressive/Sadistic
- 7   Compulsive
- 8A   Negativistic (Passive–Aggressive)
- 8B   Self-Defeating

Severe personality pathology
- S   Schizotypal
- C   Borderline
- P   Paranoid

Clinical syndrome
- A   Anxiety Disorder
- H   Somatoform Disorder
- N   Bipolar:Manic Disorder
- D   Dysthymic Disorder
- B   Alcohol Dependence
- T   Drug Dependence
- PT   Post-Traumatic Stress Disorder

Severe syndrome
- SS   Thought Disorder
- CC   Major Depression
- PP   Delusional Disorder

Administration and Scoring

The MCMI is administered much like other self-report inventories. No special instructions are necessary to administer the test beyond those printed on the front page of the answer sheet itself, and these are self-explanatory. The entire answer booklet forms a single-fold, four-page sheet, complete with test directions, client information chart, and a special coding section for clinicians on the front page. The 175 test items are printed with adjacent "true–false" bubbles on the remaining pages. Thus, although some clients may require supervision, the MCMI can be administered routinely by office or hospital personnel with a minimum of training. The examiner should scan the test booklet for double markings and excessive omissions when it is returned; examinees should be gently encouraged to resolve such ambiguities. A Spanish-language version is available.

Computer scoring is the fastest and most convenient method for obtaining MCMI profiles. The MCMI interpretive report, available from NCS, consists of a computer-plotted profile report and a theoretically and empirically based narrative that integrates clients' primary Axis II personality styles and Axis I symptom features. These reports can be obtained from NCS in several ways. Mail-in scoring provides 24-hour turnaround. Alternately, results can be keyed in item by item through teleprocessing technology. By far the popular, however, is computer administration through the MICROTEST™ assessment software. Here the traditional paper-and-pencil format is bypassed completely in favor of computer administration and scoring. Results can be printed on most popular printers. Although item weighting, modifying indices, and look-up tables greatly complicate hand scoring (research indicates that most scorers make one or more errors, sometimes severe enough to change the resulting profile), scoring templates have been made available primarily for students, researchers, and public agencies.

Case Interpretation

The MCMI offers several layers or levels of interpretation. Consistent with integrative logic, each level subsumes the previous one in an explanatory hierarchy, demanding a higher order of complexity and integration. At the first level, the assessor merely examines the personality and clinical syndrome scales for single-scale elevations. If any scales are sufficiently elevated, certain diagnoses may be warranted. At the second level, the interpretive process branches to follow one of two pathways, depending upon whether any of the severe personality pathology scales are elevated, or whether elevations are confined to the less severe personality pattern scales. Regardless of which branch the interpretive process follows, the goal at the second layer is to obtain an integrated picture of the patient's personality functioning and dynamics. The third layer seeks to integrate the patient's Axis II personality disorders and Axis I clinical syndromes according to multiaxial logic. Here the full promise of the MCMI is realized. The following sections address each of these levels in turn, and include illustrations from the featured case. We refrain from making statements about the strengths and weaknesses of particular scales, and instead concentrate on the general interpretive logic of the instrument. In the interest of anchoring these abstract interpretive principles to concrete clinical reality, a case is now presented in order to illustrate the interpretive process. The details are as follows:

Cathy, a 31-year-old female graduate student from Venezuela majoring in English literature, presented at the outpatient center of a large psychiatric hospital with tiredness and difficulty in falling asleep as her primary complaints. In her words, "my mind just doesn't want to shut down, so I only get about 5 or 6 hours [of sleep] each night." She had endured this pattern for the last 5 years, and was at a loss to explain it. Medical examination suggested no relevant physiological problems. She was referred for psychiatric impressions and treatment recommendations.

Cathy responded easily during the interview, readily offering psychologically salient information. She noted that her first graduate major was chemical engineering, from which she was forced to withdraw "when it was discovered that I wasn't intelligent." She stated difficulty in understanding some of the more abstract coursework, as well as an embarrassing incident in which an expensive apparatus in her charge was damaged. Cathy was the older of two girls; her sister was 4 years younger than she. She reported that her parents at one time feared she was autistic, and that she was examined by a child psychologist at her mother's request when she was 4. Her father, a physicist, passed away when she was 7 years old, and she regretted that they had not been able to spend more time together. She confided that she had never had a boyfriend. When asked if she ever felt lonely, she replied, "It's always been that way, you get used to it." Her mother and sister remained in Venezuela.

Diagnostic testing revealed a Wechsler Adult Intelligence Scale—Revised (WAIS-R) Verbal IQ of 128 and a Performance IQ of 115, with relative strengths in Vocabulary and Comprehension. The Spanish-language version of the MCMI-II revealed three basic personality scales in the disordered range—Schizoid (base rate [BR] = 90), Avoidant (BR = 78), and Dependent (BR = 77), with a subthreshold Axis I peak on the Dysthymic Disorder scale (BR = 74). On the MMPI-2, a three-point 7-8-0 profile (Psychasthenia, Schizophrenia, Social Introversion) was obtained. The Rorschach Inkblot Test, scored according to the Comprehensive System, revealed positive Schizophrenia and Depression indices, several Level 2 special scores, many Level 1 deviant verbalizations, and a high X-minus percent, indicating numerous violations of the contours of the blots. Her TAT responses emphasized facial expressions and motives, and featured quick and almost magical endings. Several of her responses to the Incomplete Sentences Blank (ISB) were notable: #1, "I like to lie in bed with my dog and my cat"; #2, "The happiest time I can remember was playing with my little sister when I was a child"; #10, "People are not nearly as enjoyable or comfortable to be around as animals"; #11, "A mother is someone who makes you a part of herself"; #16, "Sports are wonderful except for team sports"; #28, "Sometimes I long for someone to spend my life with"; and #29, "What pains me is not feeling cared for."

Isolating Scale Elevations and Making Diagnoses

When self-report instruments consist of multiple scales, the results are usually presented in the form of a profile. Cathy's full MCMI-II profile is presented in Figure 8.1. At the first layer of interpretation, we are only interested in determining which scales are elevated and their importance for making diagnostic decisions. For two reasons, this must be viewed as the most basic level of interpretation: First, this layer looks only at single scales rather than at the profile as a whole; and, second, it collapses continuous data down to a dichotomous level—information is first ignored, then actively discarded.

Base Rates

For MCMI neophytes, perhaps the first thing to notice is this: The elevation of each scale of Cathy's profile is given in terms of a BR score, rather than a more familiar T score or percentile rank. Each is a transformation of the raw scores, and each has the purpose of putting the raw scores on a common metric. Unlike T scores or percentile ranks, however, the BR scores are created such that the percentage of the clinical population deemed diagnosable with a particular disorder falls (1) either at or above a common threshold (clinical scales), or (2) at a particular rank order in the profile (personality scales). Thus, if 5% of the clinical population is deemed to possess a schizoid pattern as its primary personality style, and another 2% is thought to possess the schizoid pattern as a secondary feature, then the raw scores are transformed so that the normative sample reflects these *prevalence* or *base* rates.

Obviously, the BR score implies that we are not so much interested in the "absolute quantity" of a particular trait as in the implications of that quantity for psychological functioning. Although a certain level of narcissism is considered healthy in our society, the same level of antisocial behavior may not be; we may treat the second, but not the first. Thus, the BR concept recognizes that equal quantities of a trait or characteristic have differential pathological implications. Such scales have been equated in terms of the implications of a particular quantity for psychological functioning. The BR score simply represents the most direct way of getting at such considerations. BR scores are superior to T scores, which implicitly assume the converse—namely, that pathology varies directly with the absolute quantity of a trait or pattern.

Conceptualization and Diagnosis

The BR score is intended to suggest positive characteristics of psychopathology. In Pepper's (1942) terms, it represents something of a fragment,

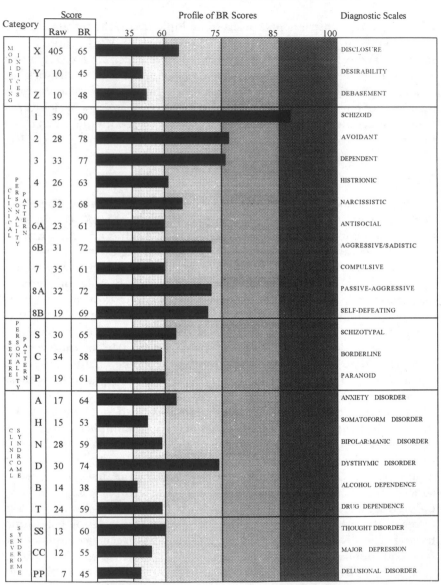

FIGURE 8.1. Cathy's MCMI-II profile.

in that it makes a prediction in and of itself without appealing to anything immediately outside itself (i.e., auxiliary evidence) for corroboration. Consequently, there is a possibility of interpretive error in always diagnosing a personality disorder—or, worse, multiple personality disorders—whenever BR scores equal or exceed 75 (85 for MCMI-III). Although it has become traditional to view a BR score of 75 as indicating the presence of either a significant personality trait or a personality disorder, there are always false positives and false negatives, as with every test. In a false-positive result, the test indicates the present of pathology where pathology does not exist. In a false-negative result, the test indicates the absence of pathology where pathology in fact exists. As with most tests, false positives and false negatives derive principally from the insensitivity of any rigorous procedure—whether a self-report, an interview, or a physiological measure—to contextual factors. Such factors must always be taken into consideration; this is a function of trained clinical judgment. In Cathy's case, three personality scales were diagnostic candidates, and there was no reason to believe that any other Axis II disorders might be applicable. Since we need not worry about false negatives, our attitude in the dichotomous world of diagnostic judgment is one of culling the true positives from the set of all positives.

To elaborate on this problem, let us consider some definitions of personality pathology. "Personality disorders" are defined as clinical syndromes composed of intrinsic, deeply embedded, and pervasive ways of functioning (Millon, 1981). The DSM-III-R (American Psychiatric Association, 1987) states that it is "only when *personality traits* are inflexible and maladaptive and cause either significant functional impairment or subjective distress that they constitute *Personality Disorders*" (p. 335, emphasis in the original). Thus, when constructing an inventory, the problem is to separate scale elevations that have become inflexible or pervasive from those that have not. However, the degree to which a trait is problematic is not a direct function of the quantity of the trait, but instead is a function of (1) its interaction with other characteristics of the organism in which the trait is embedded, and (2) the interaction between the organism and the context in which *it* is embedded. Thus, not one, but two interactions separate the quantity of a trait and its flexibility or pervasiveness. Obviously, then, scale elevations that are problematic for one individual may not be pathological for another. Schizoid individuals, for example, are notable for their lack of emotional reactivity. Such individuals not only function well in, but actively seek out, environments that make few interpersonal demands. An accountant whose job requires long hours of tedious work may be well served by such characteristics. If this individual were suddenly thrust into a management position, would difficulties ensue? Quite possibly. Nevertheless, what exists can only be said to represent a vulnerability to contextual change, not a disorder per se.

This prefigures a second way of falling into error—that of viewing personality disorders as medical illnesses for which some discrete pathogen can be found, or for which there exists some underlying unitary cause, either past or present. The use of the term "disorder" is indeed unfortunate, for personality disorders are not "disorders" at all in the medical sense. Instead, personality disorders are best conceptualized as disorders of the entire matrix of the person. Hence, we prefer the terms "pattern" or "style," rather than the intrinsically reifying "disorder." This misconception is more paradigmatic than diagnostic, but it leads to subsequent distortions in multiaxial logic: It encourages the view that classical clinical syndromes and personality disorders exist alongside each other in a horizontal relationship, rather than as clinical symptoms embedded in personality patterns. What threatens to undermine the interpretive process will surely undermine the intervention as well.

Configural Interpretation of MCMI Personality Scales

The quality of information that can be deduced from the profile analysis of a test is a function of several factors: the adequacy and generativity of the theory that provides the logic underlying its various scales; the overall empirical validity of the inventory; and its internal consistency and scale generalizability. An interpretation that in fact mirrors the patient's characteristic style of functioning as well as his/her current problems depends ultimately on the clinician's skill in weighing the degree to which a variety of client variables interact in order to corroborate, moderate, or even disqualify straightforward hypotheses, as well as suggest ones that are more subtle. As noted by Wetzler and Marlowe (1992), even the best inventory is only as good as the clinician interpreting it. Perfect construct validity and generalizability will not make up for inadequate knowledge of the theory undergirding an inventory, or for ignorance of fundamental principles of psychopathology.

Although examining the elevation of single scales may be useful for making diagnostic assignments, their interpretive value is greatly amplified when viewed in the context of the remaining profile of scales. Why? The explanation of this obvious and widely accepted tenet of test interpretation can be traced back to metatheoretical assumptions addressed in the section of this chapter that has dealt with what we call "integrative logic." The short answer is that the process of profile interpretation is similar to that of the knowledge building in the integrative world view. We are working our way toward an integrative conception of the client—what we have called "nomothetic individuality." In doing so, we take distance from the individual scales and diagnoses in order to reconstruct the personality as an organic whole: In the context of the entire profile, the meaning of each scale becomes something other than it would have been, had that scale alone been available for interpretation. Thus we want to know more than just "avoidant" or "schizoid." In Pepper's (1942) more metaphysical terminology, each scale or even each diagnosis becomes a mere fragment, to be transcended by increasingly integrative formulations; the limit of the series (Pepper, 1942) is reality itself (here, the client). From the superordinate vista of this final product, it is little wonder that diagnoses as such often seem pathetic, inadequate, and next to useless, just as Ptolemy's crystal spheres must seem to modern astronomers.

In Cathy's case, the test results suggested several diagnoses and other characteristics, each being a hypothesis about the nature of her pathology. True to Pepper's (1942) model, however, some of these diagnoses were already enmeshed in contradictions. According to the various theory-derived personality prototype descriptions given above, Cathy's score on the MCMI-II Schizoid scale (BR = 90) would argue for an apathetic attitude and an absence of emotionality—in other words, that Cathy functioned as a passive observer, detached from rewards and affections as well as the demands of human relationships. Her scores on the Avoidant (BR = 78) and Dependent (BR = 77) scales, and the ISB findings (e.g., # 34, "I wish I could find true love"), however, would argue against such procrustean first-order interpretive logic, as would the elevation of the MMPI-2 Psychasthenia and Schizophrenia scales. The schizoid hypothesis perhaps finds some corroboration in the elevation of the MMPI-2 Social Introversion scale. However, social introversion is a trait more narrow in scope than the schizoid personality; worse, both the schizoid and the avoidant personality styles often give "introverted" presentations, though for different reasons. In fact, the undergirding theory of the MCMI holds that both are detached types— one passively, the other actively so. How, then, would the assessor make sense of these ostensibly disparate findings? One means would be to conceptualize Cathy as a "mixed" type, with features of each of the schizoid, avoidant, and dependent prototypes.

Such integrative configural logic is inherently nonlinear or nonmechanistic. Although it asks for a level of sophistication, in return it breaks the pattern of labeling clients and fitting them to discrete diagnostic categories: It conceptualizes a diagnostic construct as a beginning of an assessment rather than its endpoint. A narcissistic–antisocial pattern, for example, is somewhat different from either the purely narcissistic pattern or the purely antisocial pattern. Although the "two-point" pattern in part resembles these focal constructs (nomothetic commonality), it is also more than either of these two patterns added together (nomothetic individuality), by virtue of the synergism of these elements. A narcissistic–antisocial pattern is something more than narcissism plus antisocial behavior.

In making configural personality interpretations, a separation should also be made between those scales pertaining to the *basic* clinical personality pattern and those pointing to the presence of more *severe* Axis II pathology—the Borderline, Schizotypal, and Paranoid scales. These structural pathologies differ from the other clinical personality patterns by several criteria, notably deficits in social competence and frequent (but readily reversible) psychotic episodes. Less integrated in terms of their personality organization and less effective in coping than their more mildly disordered counterparts, such individuals are especially vulnerable to decompensation when confronted with the strains of everyday life.

In terms of the theoretical model, these patterns are significantly less adaptable in the face of ecological vicissitudes. They are dysfunctional variants of the more moderately pathological patterns—a feature that leads to several predictions concerning these patterns and MCMI profiles. First, we have noted earlier that at least two interactions mediate the role of a single personality trait for psychological functioning, and that for this reason, the quantity of that trait constrains but does not determine the level of personality pathology. The elevation of the Schizotypal, Borderline, and Paranoid scales may be used as a rough index of the degree to which the client's basic personality pattern has become structurally compromised. If, for example, a client receives a BR score of 105 on the Narcissistic scale, but the scores on the three "severe" scales are low, then structurally the personality appears to be fundamentally intact, despite the elevated Narcissistic score. If, on the other hand, a client receives a BR score of 80 on the Narcissistic scale, but the BR score for the Paranoid scale is also at 75, this suggests a basic narcissistic pattern with paranoid tendencies, possibility an incipient structural pathology.

In Cathy's case, a somewhat elevated score (BR = 69) on the Schizotypal scale was achieved. This finding corroborated those obtained with the basic personality scales—that is, her schizoid–avoidant–dependent pattern. Significantly, the schizoid and avoidant personalities bracket the schizotypal personality on the circumplex model of DSM personality disorders designed by Millon (1987). This circumplex has as its axes impassive versus expressive and autonomous versus enmeshed. Cathy's pattern would be located in the impassive–enmeshed quadrant. Interestingly, this would appear to converge with her response to ISB #11: "A mother is someone who makes you a part of herself." Accordingly, it could be expected that in the face of severe stressors, Cathy might evidence the schizotypal's somewhat autistic ideations, mixed perhaps with personal irrelevancies and delusions of reference, depending on the nature and intensity of the stressors. The positive Schizophrenia index obtained on the Rorschach with the Comprehensive System would further support this interpretation. Some authors, in fact, conceptualize the avoidant personality, the schizotypal personality, and schizophrenia as a spectrum of psychopathology.

Generating Domain Hypotheses

Not all clients with the same personality diagnosis possess the same problem. A single diagnostic label rarely if ever provides information specific and comprehensive enough to serve as a sound basis for intervention efforts. Not only do patients differ with respect to the magnitude of their pathology within a diagnostic kind; they differ in the features with which they approximate the kind. Whether diagnostic taxons are derived through clinical observation, mathematical analyses, or theoretical deduction, clients differ in *how* they meet taxonic requirements—a fact institutionalized in DSM-III with the adoption of the polythetic model. In and of itself, then, a diagnosis alone *underspecifies* pathology, especially with regard to treatment considerations. Moreover, the vast majority of clients do represent so-called "mixed types." In moving toward nomothetic individuality, then, we must ask "what part of the mix" is relevant to interpreting the individual case.

One option is to systematically investigate characteristics associated with each MCMI suggested personality prototype in a domain-oriented fashion. Recall Hempel's (1965) remark that "those characteristics . . . which serve as criteria of membership in a given class [should be] associated, universally or with high probability, with more or less extensive clusters of other characteristics." These characteristics or clinical domains have been usefully organized in a manner similar to distinctions drawn in the biological realm—that is, by dividing them into "structural" and "functional" attributes. Functional characteristics represent dynamic processes that transpire within the intrapsychic world and between the individual's self and psychosocial environment. They represent "expressive" modes of regulatory action. Structural attributes represent a deeply embedded and relatively enduring template of imprinted memories, attitudes, needs, fears, conflicts, and so on, which guide experience and transform the nature of ongoing events in accord with these imprintings. Obviously, this distinction is rooted in integrative logic. Pepper (1942), in fact, regarded both "integration" and "organism" as first approximations to the root metaphor, or "organicism." No organism exists that is composed exclusively of functional or exclusively of structural domains. Both are required if the organism is to exist as a self-regulating whole: Function animates structure; structure undergirds or substratizes function.

These domains are further differentiated according to their respective data level—either biophysical, intrapsychic, phenomenological, or behavioral, reflecting the four historic approaches that characterize the study of psychopathology (namely, the biological, the psychoanalytic, the cognitive, and the behavioral). The grouping of functional–structural clinical domains within the four traditional data levels of psychopathology is schematized in Table 8.3.

TABLE 8.3. Functional (F) and
Structural (S) Clinical Domains

Behavioral level
   (F) Expressive acts
   (F) Interpersonal conduct

Phenomenological level
   (F) Cognitive style
   (S) Object representations
   (S) Self-image

Intrapsychic level
   (F) Regulatory mechanisms
   (S) Morphological organization

Biophysical level
   (S) Mood/temperament

Note. Adapted from Millon (1990).

Several criteria were used to select and develop the clinical domains comprising this assessment schema: (1) They should be varied in the features they embody—that is, not be limited just to behaviors or cognitions, but encompass a full range of clinically relevant characteristics. (2) They should parallel, if not correspond to, many of our profession's current therapeutic modalities, as evidenced by the four data levels. (3) They should not only be coordinated to the official DSM schema of personality disorder prototypes, as well as its guiding model of evolutionary polarities; each disorder should also be characterized by a distinctive feature within each clinical domain. Brief descriptions of these functional and structural domains have been given in several publications (Millon, 1986, 1987, 1990).

In the context of the individual case, the question then becomes: "Which functional processes and structural attributes are necessary for the client's personality pattern to exist as the organic whole represented by the code type?" Answering this question engages a synthesizing process of clinical inference for which the end point is the mutual corroboration of parts and whole, a picture of the organism as a totality. If the personality assessment is to be exhaustive, then, with the guidance of the code type, a description of the client in each clinical domain should be formulated. Each domain description may be said to represent a within-domain hypothesis about client functioning in that circumscribed clinical area, and this hypothesis should be evaluated and amended as needed until it fits with auxiliary data and represents what is indeed believed to be the case. Given a two- or three-point code and a particular domain of interest, the client's functioning may be prototypical of the domain description for the primary code, may be prototypical of the domain description for the secondary code, or may lie somewhere in between.

We are now in a position to advance a remarkably detailed assessment of the individual, and to illustrate this process with regard to the featured case of Cathy. Structural attributes and functional processes relevant to the schizoid–avoidant–dependent patterns are presented in Table 8.4. We can simply move down the chart from domain to domain, asking ourselves which description Cathy most resembled, and synthesizing these descriptions when needed. Behaviorally, Cathy's presentation during diagnostic testing strongly suggested a dependent–avoidant behavioral style, with its incumbent passivity, docility, immaturity, and heightened awareness of others' reactions to her; this was seen especially in her attentiveness to facial expressions on the TAT, and her willingness to self-disclose in the interview. Interpersonally, she seemed to alternate between the schizoid and the dependent–avoidant styles, perhaps as a defense against the feared rejection and helplessness that typify the latter: If what one desperately desires appears completely unobtainable, then one solution is to deny that such needs exist at all, remaining aloof from others as well as from oneself. Such an analysis conceptualizes this schizoid feature as a compromise that reflects conflictual dispositions, but has nevertheless taken on characterological pervasiveness. Cathy's ISB responses corroborated this interpretation: Animals were more enjoyable and comfortable than people, but wouldn't true love be nice! Here we see the avoidant's view that others are critical and humiliating, the dependent's desire to be rescued, and a blunting of affect typical of the schizoid. Cognitively, the intrusive and perplexing quality of Cathy's ideations appeared more like the avoidant, possibly even the schizotypal, than like the schizoid or the dependent. Cathy herself noted that her parents at one time believed she was autistic; moreover, the large number of poor form responses in her Rorschach protocol, as represented by the inflated X-minus percent, argued for poor reality testing and perceptual distortion. Defensively, Cathy appeared to combine the mechanisms of the avoidant with those of the dependent. While her TAT stories possessed nearly magical endings, she seemed incapable of separating her goals for herself from those of her introjected father image. Although her affective expression was blunted in an effort to avoid pain, lending her presentation a numb or flattened quality, Cathy's mood resembled more the avoidant's anguished desire for affection and constant fear of rebuff. As for her self-image, much like the dependent–avoidant, Cathy saw herself as weak and inadequate, belittled her own intelligence and achievements, and regarded herself as a failure in her chosen profession. Her internalizations and intrapsychic organization resembled those of the avoidant and dependent more closely than those of the schizoid (ISB #2, "The happiest time I can remember was playing with my little sister when I was a child").

Often the yield of domain hypotheses will be much richer than can be practically evaluated with data internal to the MCMI. As seen above, we have readily drawn on the TAT and Rorschach data, as well as the inter-

TABLE 8.4. Comparison of Suggested Functional Processes and Structural Attributes across Three High Codes

Schizoid personality	Avoidant personality	Dependent personality
	Functional processes	
Behaviorally Lethargic: Appears to be in a state of fatigue, low energy, and lack of vitality; is phlegmatic, sluggish, displaying deficits in activation, motoric expressiveness, and spontaneity.	*Behaviorally Guarded*: Warily scans environment for potential threats; overreacts to innocuous events and anxiously judges them to signify personal ridicule and threat.	*Behaviorally Incompetent*: Ill-equipped to assume mature and independent roles; is docile and passive, lacking functional competencies, avoiding self-assertion, and withdrawing from adult responsibilities.
Interpersonally Aloof: Seems indifferent and remote, rarely responsive to the actions and feelings of others, possessing minimal "human" interests; fades into the background, is unobtrusive, has few close relationships, and prefers a peripheral role in social, work and family settings.	*Interpersonally Aversive*: Extensive history of social pan-anxiety and distrust; seeks acceptance, but maintains distance and privacy to avoid humiliation and derogation.	*Interpersonally Submissive*: Subordinates need to stronger, nurturing figure, without whom feels anxiously helpless; is compliant, conciliatory, placating, and self-sacrificing.
Cognitively Impoverished: Seems deficient across broad spheres of knowledge and evidences vague and obscure thought processes that are below intellectual level; communication is easily derailed, loses its sequence of thought, or is conveyed via circuitous logic.	*Cognitively Distracted*: Is preoccupied and bothered by disruptive and often perplexing inner thoughts; the upsurge from within of irrelevant and digressive ideation upsets thought continuity and interferes with social communication.	*Cognitively Naive*: Is easily persuaded, unsuspicious, and gullible; reveals a Pollyanna attitude toward interpersonal difficulties, watering down objective problems, and smoothing over troubling events.
Intellectualization Mechanism: Describes interpersonal and affective experiences in a matter-of-fact, abstract, impersonal, or mechanical manner; pays primary attention to formal and objective aspects of social and emotional events.	*Fantasy Mechanism*: Depends excessively on imagination to achieve need gratification and conflict resolution; withdraws into reveries as a means of safely discharging affectionate, as well as aggressive impulses.	*Introjection Mechanism*: Is firmly devoted to another to strengthen the belief that an inseparable bond exists between them; jettisons any independent views in favor of those of another to preclude conflicts and threats to the relationship.
	Structural attributes	
Flat Mood: Is emotionally impassive, exhibiting an intrinsic unfeeling, cold and stark quality; reports weak affectionate or erotic needs, rarely displaying warm of intense feelings, and apparently unable to experience	*Anguished Mood*: Describes constant and confusing undercurrents of tension, sadness, and anger; vacillates between desire for affection, fear of rebuff, and numbness of feeling.	*Pacific Mood*: Is characteristically warm, tender, and noncompetitive; timidly avoids social tension and interpersonal conflicts.

(continued)

TABLE 8.4. (Continued)

Schizoid personality	Avoidant personality	Dependent personality
	Structural attributes	
pleasure, sadness, or anger in any depth.		
Complacent Self Image: Reveals minimal introspection and awareness of self; seems impervious to the emotional and personal implications of everyday social life.	*Alienated Self-Image*: Sees self as a person who is socially isolated and rejected by others; devalues self-achievements and reports feelings of aloneness and emptiness, if not depersonalization.	*Inept Self-Image*: Views self as weak, fragile, and inadequate; exhibits lack of self-confidence by belittling own aptitudes and competencies.
Meager Internalizations: Inner representations are few in number and minimally articulated, largely devoid of the manifold percepts and memories, or the dynamic interplay among drives and conflicts that typify even well-adjusted persons.	*Vexatious Internalizations*: Inner representations are composed of readily reactivated, intense, and conflict-ridden memories, limited avenues of gratification, and few mechanisms to channel needs, bind impulses, resolve conflicts, or deflect external stressors.	*Immature Internalizations*: Inner representations are composed of unsophisticated ideas and incomplete memories, rudimentary drives, and childlike impulses, as well as minimal competencies to manage and resolve stressors.
Undifferentiated Intrapsychic Organization: Given an inner barrenness, a feeble drive to fulfill needs, and minimal pressures to defend against or resolve internal conflicts or to cope with external demands, internal structures may best be characterized by their limited coordination and sterile order.	*Fragile Intrapsychic Organization*: A precarious complex of tortuous emotions depends almost exclusively on a single modality for its resolution and discharge, that of avoidance, escape, and fantasy; and hence, when faced with unanticipated stress, there are few resources available to deploy and few positions to revert to, short of regressive decompensation.	*Inchoate Intrapsychic Organization*: Entrusts others with the responsibility to fulfill needs and to cope with adult tasks; thus there is both a deficit and lack of diversity in internal mechanisms and regulatory controls, leaving a miscellany of relatively undeveloped and undifferentiated adaptive abilities, as well as an elementary system for functioning independently.

Note. Adapted from Millon (1990).

personal impressions of the examiner. Some domain hypotheses will be thoroughly corroborated (e.g., by a therapist's own clinical observations); others will be only partially so, perhaps because the evidence simply suggests something else, but more often because not enough data exist to permit an informed judgment. Evaluation of such hypotheses must await the accrual of extra-MCMI data, whether through additional testing or across therapy sessions. As with any form of clinical inference, the combination of various gauges from diverse settings provide the data aggregates (Epstein, 1979, 1983) necessary to increase the likelihood of drawing correct inferences, especially when coupled with multimethod approaches (Campbell & Fiske, 1959).

Putting Symptoms in Perspective

Since diagnoses exist as "fragments" to be transcended in increasingly integrative formulations, they are, in the final analysis, somewhat trivial. We
have already noted that diagnosis represents an underspecification of pathology with regard to treatment planning. In fact, as more integrative formulations are achieved—that is, as the limit of the series is reached in the
necessary theory of the client—this theory becomes eminently more suitable for treatment planning than simple Axis I and Axis II diagnoses. The
various diagnoses are only important for how they have been transformed,
not in themselves. Just as theoretical evolutions in a science transform the
meaning of pre-existing constructs, increasingly integrative syntheses transform the meaning of our clinical constructs for the individual case. In this
sense, there are no personality "givens"—that is, clinical constructs that
explain but are not themselves explained. In a pure scientific sense, clinical constructs seek their explanation in terms of an overarching theory; in
an applied clinical sense, these constructs are compounded in an effort to
understand the individual.

The proper question, then, in understanding the individual's pathology is not a "whether," but a "how"—how the interaction of individual characteristics and contextual factors (i.e., the interaction of Axis II and Axis
IV) produces Axis I, classical psychiatric symptomatology.[1] Answering this
"how" question requires that the symptoms be put in context of the Axis II–
Axis IV interaction. Consequently, determination of the level of personality pathology—that is, making a diagnosis—is secondary to a knowledge of
the client's basic personality pattern. For this reason, the profile of MCMI
BR scores is often more informative than their overall elevation, arguing
against the strict use of cutoff scores for the basic clinical personality pattern scales. Thus, although the scales of interest in Cathy's case were all
elevated above the traditional MCMI-II cutoff score, they need not have
been to be relevant to the interpretive process.

How do Axis II and Axis IV interact to produce the bedtime worries
observed in Cathy's case? Answering this question requires that the symptom complaint and psychosocial history and functioning be integrated with
the personality style as explicated above. Accordingly, Cathy would emerge
as a basically avoidant–dependent individual—someone who was far from

---

[1]Numerous researchers and theorists have noted the possibility of spectrum disorders—superordinate taxa that encompass a personality disorder as one end and classical psychiatric symptomatology at the other. Some have proposed that Axis I and Axis
II be collapsed together. However, the fact that Axis I disorders and Axis II disorders
often covary in no way undoes the logic of the multiaxial model: The separation of
clinical symptomatology into multiple axes is purely heuristic. Thus, the rise of an
emphasis on spectrum disorders is perhaps best seen as a reaction against the wrong-
ful reification of these axes.

home (Venezuela), felt herself to be a failure at her chosen career, was questioning her intellectual competency, and was desperately longing for companionship (ISB #34, "I wish I could find true love"). If what one desperately needs or desires is believed to be completely unattainable, too painful to pursue yet too painful to exist without, one solution is to deny that the need or desire exists at all. Thus it appeared that Cathy was socially inhibited and self-doubting, yet often secretive and intellectualizing.

In part because of the enmeshment of her family system, Cathy was probably less individuated and more developmentally immature than would be required for the professional life she was ostensibly seeking. Anchored in another culture, away from friends and family who could be relied upon to gratify affectionate needs, a failure at what she valued most, she longed to return to the security of an earlier developmental epoch—a security that, in all likelihood, would now sadly perpetuate the very immaturity and impoverishment of interpersonal abilities that it originally engendered. As noted on the ISB, "The happiest time I can remember was playing with my little sister when I was a child." Given the lack of reinforcers in her current setting, Cathy might turn inward, depending excessively on imagination to achieve need gratification and conflict resolution, withdrawing into reverie to discharge occasionally overwhelming affectionate needs (and perhaps aggressive impulses as well) when these could no longer be readily denied or intellectualized. In fact, this mechanism might have achieved pathological proportions, suggesting that she might be predisposed to temporary, but readily reversible, episodes of an almost psychotic nature. Depending on the intensity of stressors, her cognitive/ideational state might vary along a continuum of disruptive and irrelevant intrusions but generally good reality testing at one (the more normal) end, to more schizotypal and schizophrenic ideations at the other. During the near-psychotic episodes, reality testing would be poor. Given the client's high intellectual level, her position on this continuum at any one moment might be difficult to judge. She was intelligent enough to know what would constitute a good presentation.

No less problematic in sustaining Cathy's psychopathology was a generally inept, alienated, and devalued self-image. Her dependent style (specifically, her generally fragile and inchoate intrapsychic organization) probably inclined her toward globalized beliefs of inefficacy, rather than more realistic and differentiated appraisals of her performance in more narrow domains of competency. Her implicitly dichotomous conception of intellectual ability ("when I found out that I was not intelligent") would support this interpretation. In her eyes, her "failure" in chemical engineering probably validated her belief in her incompetency. Perhaps if she were not somewhat dependent, she could generate her own solutions and work toward realizing her possibilities. Perhaps if she were not somewhat avoidant, she could pursue whatever solutions and possibilities she envisioned. As a dependent–avoidant, however, she could do neither, creating and sustaining her dysthymic mood. At bedtime, when she was undistracted by the events of the day, a ruminative cycle began that focused on present unfulfilled needs and future impossibilities.

Intervention: Integrative Therapy for Personality Disorders

The polarity schema and clinical domains delineated above serve as useful points of focus for corresponding modalities of therapy. Ideally, of course, clients would be "pure" prototypes, and all polarities would be prototypical and invariably present. Were this so, each diagnosis would automatically match its polarity configuration. As we have stressed, "real" clients are rarely pure textbook prototypes; most, like Cathy, are complex mixtures.

The question of which domains and which polarities should be selected for therapeutic intervention is not, therefore, merely a matter of making "the diagnosis," but requires a comprehensive assessment of the kind explained above—one that not only appraises the overall configuration of polarities and domains, but differentiates their balance and degrees of salience. By careful homework, the clinician will arrive at what we have called a "nomothetically individuated" formulation, which is necessary in a theoretical sense, and therefore sufficient to serve as an intervention guide. In aiming for theoretical necessity in the individual case (a compelling theory of the client), we achieve a certain superordinate level of complexity and sophistication in the conceptualization of that case. Any discussion of integrative psychotherapy, then, must take place at a level of abstraction or integration commensurate with that of personality itself. Personality disorders cannot be remedied if the personality is tenaciously integrated while the therapy is not. Since the therapy must be as individuated as the case, those who week concrete pointers applicable across all situations are likely to be disappointed.

To the credit of those of an eclectic persuasion, they have recognized the arbitrary if not illogical character of contentions that cognitive, behavioral, biological, or intrapsychic formulations are "closer to the truth," as well as the need to bridge schisms that have been constructed less by philosophical considerations, theoretical logic, or pragmatic goals than by the accidents of history and professional rivalries. Interested readers should see Beutler, Consoli, and Williams (1994) and Beutler and Clarkin (1990) for notable contributions in this regard.

Integrative therapies, thought not inapplicable to more focal pathologies, are *specifically* required for the personality disorders (whereas depression may successfully be treated either cognitively or pharmacologically); the interwoven nature of the components of personality disorders is exactly what makes a multifaceted approach a necessity. The integration labeled "personological psychotherapy" (Millon, 1988) insists on the primacy of an overarching gestalt that gives coherence, provides an interactive framework, and creates an organic order among otherwise discrete polarities and attributes. We have created such an organic order for Cathy above. It is eclectic, in the sense that it borrows from here and there to address the client in his or her "nomothetic individuality," but it is more. It is synthesized from a substantive theory whose overall utility and orientation derives from that old chestnut, "The whole is greater than the sum of its parts." As we know well, the personality problems our clients bring to us are an inextricably linked nexus of interpersonal behaviors, cognitive styles, regulatory processes, and so on. They flow through a tangle of feedback loops and serially unfolding concatenations that emerge at different times in dynamic and changing configurations. Each component of these configurations has its role and significance altered by virtue of its place in these continually evolving constellations. In parallel form, so should personological psychotherapy be conceived as an integrated configuration of strategies and tactics in which each intervention technique is selected not only for its efficacy in resolving particular pathological attributes, but also for its contribution to the overall constellation of treatment procedures of which it is but one.

Why should we formulate an integrated therapeutic strategy for the personality disorders? The answer may perhaps be best grasped if we think of the polarities of personality as analogous to the sections of an orchestra, and the clinical attributes of a client as a clustering of discordant instruments that exhibit imbalances, deficiencies, or conflicts within these sections. To extend this analogy, a therapist may be seen as a conductor whose task is to bring forth a harmonious balance among all the sections as well as their specifically discordant instruments—muting some here, accentuating others there, all to the end of fulfilling the conductor's knowledge of how "the composition" can best be made consonant. The task is not that of altering one instrument, but of all, in concert. What is sought in music is a balanced score, one composed of harmonic counterpoints, rhythmic patterns, and melodic combinations. What is needed in therapy, then, is a similarly balanced program—a coordinated strategy of counterpoised techniques designed to optimize sequential and combinatorial treatment effects.

In personological therapy, then, there are psychologically designed composites and progressions among diverse techniques. In an attempt to formulate them in an early paper (Millon, 1988), terms such as "catalytic sequences" and "potentiating pairings" are employed to represent the nature and intent of these polarity-oriented and attribute-focused treatment plans. In essence, they comprise therapeutic arrangements and timing series, which promote polarity balances and effect attributed changes that would otherwise not occur by use of only one technique.

In a "catalytic sequence," for example, one might seek first to alter the socially aversive feelings of a client like Cathy by direct modification procedures, which, if successful, might facilitate the use of cognitive methods in producing self-image changes in confidence, which might, in their turn, foster the utility of interpersonal techniques in effecting improvements in relationships with others. In "poten tiated pairing," one may simultaneously combine behavioral and cognitive methods (as is commonly done these days), so as to overcome both problematic interactions with *others* and conceptions of *self* that might be refractory to either technique alone.

A defining feature of personality disorders is that they are themselves pathogenic. Millon (1969) has described this process as "self-perpetuation"; Horney (1937) characterized it earlier in her use of the concept of "vicious circles"; Wachtel (1977) has suggested the term "cyclical psychodynamics." These ceaseless and entangled sequences of repetitive cognitions, interpersonal behaviors, and unconscious mechanisms call for the use of simultaneous or alternately focused methods. The synergism and enhancement produced by such catalytic and potentiating processes are what comprise genuine personological strategies.

As a general philosophy, then, it seems that we should select our specific treatment techniques only as tactics to achieve polarity-oriented goals through the clinical domains. Depending on the pathological polarity and domains to be modified, and the overall treatment sequence we have in mind, the goals of therapy should be oriented toward the improvement of imbalanced or deficient polarities by the use of techniques that are optimally suited to modify their expression in those clinical domains that constrain clients' flexibility.

Table 8.5 provides a synopsis of what may be considered the primary goals of personological therapy according to the polarity model. Therapeutic efforts responsive to problems in the pain–pleasure polarity would, for example, have as their essential aim the enhancement of pleasure among schizoid and avoidant personalities ("+ pleasure"). Given the probability of intrinsic deficits in this area, schizoids might require the use of pharmacological agents designed to activate their "flat" mood/temperament. Increments in pleasure for avoidants, however, are likely to depend more on cognitive techniques designed to alter their "alienated" self-image, and behavioral methods oriented to counter their "aversive" interpersonal inclinations. Equally important for avoidants is reducing their hypersensitivities, especially to social rejection ("– pain"); this may be achieved by coordinating the use of medications for their characteristic "anguished" mood/temperament with cognitive methods geared to desensitization. In the passive–active polarity. increments in the capacity and skills to take a less reactive and more proactive role in dealing with the affairs of their lives ("– passive, + active") would be a major goal of treatment for schizoids, dependents, narcissists, self-defeatists, and compulsives. To turn to the other–self polarity, the imbalances found among narcissists and antisocials, for example, suggest that a major aim of their treatment would be a reduction in their predominant self-focus and a corresponding augmentation of their sensitivity to the needs of others ("+ other, – self").

TABLE 8.5. Polarity-Oriented Personological Therapy

Modifying the pain–pleasure polarity
  + Pleasure (Schizoid/Avoidant)
  – Pain (Avoidant)
  Pain ↔ pleasure (Self-Defeating/Sadistic)

Balancing the passive–active polarity
  + Passive, – active (Avoidant/Histrionic/Antisocial/Sadistic/Passive–Aggressive)
  – Passive, + active (Schizoid/Dependent/Narcissistic/Self-Defeating/Compulsive

Altering the other–self polarity
  – Other, + self (Dependent/Histrionic)
  + Other, – self (Narcissistic/Antisocial)
  Other ↔ self (Compulsive/Passive–Aggressive)

Rebuilding the personality structure
  + Cognitive–interpersonal cohesion (Schizotypal)
  + Affective–self cohesion (Borderline)
  – Cognitive–affective cohesion (Paranoid)

Note. Adapted from Millon (1990).

To make unbalanced or deficient polarities the primary aim of therapy is a new focus and a goal as yet untested. In contrast, the clinical domains in which problems are expressed lend themselves to a wide variety of therapeutic techniques. We can address dysfunctions in the realm of "interpersonal conduct" by employing any number of family (Gurman & Kniskern, 1981) or group (Yalom, 1986) therapeutic methods, as well as a series of recently evolved and explicitly formulated interpersonal techniques (Anchin & Kiesler, 1982). Methods of classical analysis or of more contemporary analytic schools may be especially suited to the realm of "object representations." The methods of Beck (1976), Ellis (1970), and Meichenbaum (1977) may be well chosen to modify difficulties of "cognitive style" and "self-image." The goals, as well as the strategies and modes of action, for when and how we might practice personological therapy have only begun to be specified.

References

American Psychiatric Association. (1987). *Diagnostic and statistical manual of mental disorders* (3rd ed., rev.). Washington, DC: Author.

American Psychiatric Association. (1994). *Diagnostic and statistical manual of mental disorders* (4th ed.). Washington, DC: Author.

Anchin, J. C., & Kiesler. D. J. (Eds.), (1982). *Handbook of interpersonal psychotherapy.* Elmsford, NY: Pergamon Press.

Beck, A. T. (1976). *Cognitive therapy and the emotional disorders.* New York: International Universities Press.

Beutler, L. E., & Clarkin, E. (1990). *Systematic treatment selection: Toward targeted therapeutic interventions.* New York: Brunner/Mazel.

Beutler, L. E., Consoli, A. J., & Williams, R. E. (1994). Integrative and eclectic thera-
   pies in practice. In B. Bonger & L. E. Beutler (Eds.), *Foundations of psycho-
   therapy: Theory, research, and practice*. New York: Oxford University Press.
Buss, A. H., & Plomin, R. (1975). *A temperament theory of personality development*.
   New York: Wiley.
Buss, A. J., & Plomin, R. (1984). *Temperament: Early developing personality traits*.
   Hillsdale, NJ: Erlbaum.
Campbell, D. T., & Fiske, D. W. (1959). Convergent and discriminant validation
   by the multitrait–multimethod matrix. *Psychological Bulletin, 56*, 81–105.
Cloninger, C. R. (1986). A unified biosocial theory of personality and its role in
   the development of anxiety states. *Psychiatric Developments, 3*, 167–226.
Cloninger, C. R. (1987). A systematic method for clinical description and classifi-
   cation of personality variants. *Archives of General Psychiatry, 44*, 573–588.
Ellis, A. (1970). *The essence of rational psychotherapy: A comprehensive approach to treat-
   ment*. New York: Institute for Rational Living.
Eysenck, H. J. (1957). *The dynamics of anxiety and hysteria*. London: Routledge &
   Kegan Paul.
Eysenck, H. J. (1967). *The biological basis of personality*. Springfield, IL: Charles C
   Thomas.
Epstein, S. (1979). The stability of behavior: I. On predicting most of the people
   much of the time. *Journal of Personality and Social Psychology, 37*, 1097–1126.
Epstein, S. (1983). Aggregation and beyond: Some basic issues on the prediction
   of behavior. *Journal of Personality, 51*, 360–392.
Gilligan, C. (1982). *In a different voice*. Cambridge, MA: Harvard University Press.
Gray, J. A. (Ed.). (1964). *Pavlov's typology*. Elmsford, NY: Pergamon Press.
Gray, J. A. (1973). Causal theories of personality and how to test them. In J. R. Royce
   (Ed.), *Multivariate analysis and psychological theory*. New York: Academic Press.
Gurman, A. S., & Kniskern, D. (Eds.). (1981). *The handbook of family therapy*. New
   York: Brunner/Mazel.
Hempel, C. G. (1965). *Aspects of scientific explanation*. New York: Free Press.
Horney, K. (1937). *The neurotic personality of our time*. New York: Norton.
Huxley, T. H. (1870). Mr. Darwin's critics. *Contemporary Review, 18*, 443–476.
Meichenbaum, D. (1977). Cognitive–behavioral genesis and prevalence of the
   borderline personality disorder: A social learning thesis. *Journal of Personal-
   ity Disorders, 1*, 354–372.
Millon, T. (1969). *Modern psychopathology*. Philadelphia: W. B. Saunders.
Millon, T. (1981). *Disorders of personality: DSM-III, Axis II*. New York: Wiley-
   Interscience.
Millon, T. (1986). Personality prototypes and their diagnostic criteria. In T. Millon
   & G. L. Klerman (Eds.), *Contemporary directions in psychopathology*. New York:
   Guilford Press.
Millon, T. (1987). *Millon Clinical Multiaxial Inventory—II (MCMI-II) manual*. Min-
   neapolis: National Computer Systems.
Millon, T. (1988) Personologic psychotherapy: Ten commandments for a post-
   eclectic approach to integrative treatment. *Psychotherapy, 25*, 209–219.
Millon, T. (1990). *Toward a new personology: An evolutionary model*. New York: Wiley.
Millon, T. (1994). *Millon Clinical Multiaxial Inventory—III (MCMI-III) manual*. Min-
   neapolis: National Computer Systems.

Millon, T., & Diesenhaus, H. (1972). *Research methods in psychopathology*. New York: Wiley.

Pepper, S. C. (1942). *World hypotheses: A study in evidence*. Berkeley: University of California Press.

Quine, W. V. O. (1977). Natural kinds. In S. P. Schwartz (Ed.), *Naming, necessity, and natural groups*. Ithaca, NY: Cornell University Press.

Rushton, J. P. (1985). Differential K theory: The sociobiology of individual and group differences. *Personality and Individual Differences, 6*, 441–452.

Russell, J. A. (1980). A circumplex model of affect. *Journal of Personality and Social Psychology, 39*, 1161–1178.

Spencer, H. (1870). *The principles of psychology*. London: Williams & Norgate.

Tellegen, A. (1985). Structures of mood and personality and relevance to assessing anxiety, with an emphasis on self-report. In A. H. Tuma & J. Maser (Eds.), *Anxiety and the anxiety disorders*. Hillsdale, NJ: Erlbaum.

Wachtel, P. (1977). *Psychoanalysis and behavior therapy: Toward an interpretation*. New York: Basic Books.

Wetzler, S., & Marlowe, D. (1992). What they don't tell you in test manuals: A response to Millon. *Journal of Counseling and Development, 70*, 327–428.

Wilson, E. O. (1975). *Sociobiology: The new synthesis*. Cambridge, MA: Harvard University Press.

Wilson, E. O. (1978). *On human nature*. Cambridge, MA: Harvard University Press.

Yalom, I. D. (1986). *The theory and practice of group psychotherapy* (3rd ed.). New York: Basic Books.

9

Integrating Treatment Recommendations

Kevin F. Gaw
Larry E. Beutler

The last section of the psychological report is devoted to answering the referral question and providing recommendations for treatment. This section is the point in which all other information in the report culminates. Descriptions of the patient's presenting problems, personal history, level of functioning, pattern of adjustment, and problems are useful only to the degree that they direct the clinician's attention to the implementation of effective treatment. Thus, it is imperative that this section of the report be informative, helpful, and specific. This chapter illustrates how formal assessment data and clinical indicators can be integrated into clear and systematic treatment plans.

The dimensions of treatment planning to be presented here are based upon the model of "systematic treatment selection" initially set forth by Beutler and Clarkin (1990) and outlined briefly in Chapter 2. Systematic treatment selection is a pragmatic approach to the complex and often confusing process of treatment planning. It offers the clinician a structured, planned, and purposeful approach to designing treatment plans—one that is independent of any specific theory of psychotherapy or psychopathology. Among the criticisms directed at the eclecticism, of which Beutler and Clarkin's prescriptive approach is one model, is that it is indefinite, is applied in a haphazard fashion, and means something different to each eclectic therapist (Beutler & Clarkin, 1990; Norcross, 1986). Although this may be true of nonsystematic efforts to bridge among the procedures of different theories, technical eclectic approaches to prescriptive treatment specify both the theories that guide the planning of treatment and the indicators that direct the selection of specific strategies and procedures.

To the degree that these approaches make these specifications in advance of initiating treatment, they represent "prescriptions" for treatment. It is the planned and purposeful aspect of systematic treatment selection that makes this prescriptive–eclectic approach to psychotherapy valuable and powerful.

This chapter is designed to present a pragmatic approach to the application of systematic treatment selection. Since it is not our intention to review at length the increasing empirical literature that supports the principles and practices of this approach, the interested reader is referred to the original volume by Beutler and Clarkin (1990). Our presentation here focuses on demonstrating the use of psychological tests and clinical judgments in the construction of treatment plans, including the provision of decision rules for applying the dimensions initially described in Chapter 2. Although the chapter addresses the broad scope of mental health treatment, attention is focused most closely upon planning psychotherapy strategies and selecting specific interventions. This presentation follows the logic outlined in Chapter 2 as well as elsewhere (Beutler, 1986, 1987; Beutler & Clarkin, 1990; Beutler & Consoli, 1992; Beutler, Consoli, & Williams, 1994).

For purposes of illustration, we use a limited number and type of formal assessment devices to illustrate the principles expressed in this chapter. The omission from our discussion of some tests should not be taken as an indication that these procedures are not useful for answering specific referral questions. However, the following procedures serve the purpose of illustrating the process of treatment planning within the systematic treatment selection model:

> The Beck Depression Inventory (BDI; Beck & Steer, 1987; Beck, Ward, Mendelson, Mock, & Erbaugh, 1961)
>
> The Beck Hopelessness Scale (BHS; Beck & Steer, 1988; Beck, Weissman, Lester, & Trexler, 1974)
>
> The Brief Symptom Inventory (BSI; Derogatis, 1992)
>
> The DSM-IV multiaxial evaluation (American Psychiatric Association, 1994)
>
> The Global Assessment of Functioning (GAF) scale (American Psychiatric Association, 1994)
>
> The Minnesota Multiphasic Personality Inventory (e.g., MMPI-2; Butcher, Dahlstrom, Graham, Tellegen, & Kaemmer, 1989)
>
> The Millon Clinical Multiaxial Inventory (e.g., MCMI-II; Millon, 1987)
>
> The Social Support Questionnaire (SSQ; Sarason, Levine, Basham, & Sarason, 1983)
>
> The State–Trait Anxiety Inventory (STAI; Spielberger, Gorsuch, Lushene, Vagg, & Jacobs, 1983)
>
> The Therapeutic Reactance Scale (TRS; Dowd, Milne, & Wise, 1991)

In addition, relevant clinical indicators generated from cognitive assessment and the clinical interview are presented for integration with formal assessment data, including the Mental Status Examination (MSE; Amchin, 1991), the Wechsler Adult Intelligence Scale–Revised (WAIS-R; Wechsler, 1981; see Chapter 5), and the Structured Clinical Interview for DSM-III-R (SCID; Spitzer, Williams, & Gibbon, 1986). Other procedures can replace or supplement the ones illustrated here to the degree that they possess adequate psychometric properties, they include standardized administration procedures, they tap the relevant dimensions of patient function and dysfunction, and the user is familiar with the strengths and limitations of the instrument for the purposes selected.

To organize assessment material around psychotherapy strategies and techniques, we introduce a set of treatment planning forms at the end of this chapter. The use of these forms for developing comprehensive proposals for psychological treatment is illustrated. A final form allows verification that the treatment plan is implemented as intended and with at least a modicum of therapist skill.

The Five Dimensions of Systematic Treatment Selection

Before we embark upon the task of linking formal assessment data and clinical indicators with mental health treatment plans, the basic dimensions of systematic treatment selection (Beutler & Clarkin, 1990) require some definition. This section briefly examines the five dimensions (i.e., predisposing patient variables) that we believe are the most firmly linked to contemporary clinical research and the most pragmatically useful of those initially proposed by Beutler and Clarkin in planning treatment programs for patients.[1] The dimensions to be illustrated here are (1) problem severity; (2) motivational distress; (3) problem complexity; (4) resistance potential or reactance level; and (5) coping style. These dimensions represent aspects of patient functioning that were initially introduced in Chapter 2.

Each of these five dimensions has unique characteristics that strongly influence the patient's experiences (positive and negative) in psychotherapy, and it is therefore important that the clinician attend carefully to the patient's expression of each dimension. It should be noted that these concepts are discussed at length elsewhere (Beutler, 1986; Beutler & Clarkin, 1990; Beutler & Consoli, 1992; Beutler, Consoli, & Williams, 1994; Beutler, Wakefield, & Williams, 1994), and the reader is referred to these resources if further study is necessary.

---

[1]There is some variation in the labels used to define these constructs in various renditions of systematic treatment selection. This variation reflects changes and refinements that have accrued as the approach has evolved and as research has accumulated.

"Problem severity" represents a continuum of functioning, ranging from no or little impairment to incapacitation. Estimates of problem severity are estimates of the degree to which a patient's problem interferes with his/her life and the intensity of the problem. From an assessment of problem severity, the clinician identifies which treatment setting, modality, and format will be appropriate for the patient. That is, the clinician must identify which treatment environment the patient requires (the "least restrictive environment" rule is always employed), what treatment modes (i.e., medical/somatic, psychosocial, or combinations) are appropriate, how long and intensive the treatment may be, and what the immediate goals of treatment are. Because of the diversity of decisions that depend in part on this assessment, an estimate of problem severity is an essential entry dimension into the systematic treatment selection model. Among the indices of severity are psychiatric diagnoses, availability of social support networks, and the degree to which life functions are interrupted because of the problem(s) presented.

"Motivational distress" is a concept that is related to problem severity, but one that is treated separately because of its implications for treatment selection. Motivational distress is indicated by the degree of subjective distress experienced by the patient in regard to his/her problems. Since distress is a subjective phenomenon, however, the patient's level of distress is not identical with the degree of problem severity as described above. Distress motivates change and movement in the service of reducing discomfort. Although this movement is not growth-enhancing itself, if channeled in therapeutic directions it can facilitate the attainment of treatment objectives. Other aspects of severity, in contrast, may be good indicators of the need for intervention, but imprecise indicators of the degree of effort that is available to be expended in achieving change. Thus, treatment planning benefits from considering subjective distress separately from external or "objective" indicators of impaired functioning.

It should not be assumed that the relationship between degree of distress and motivation or ability to change is linear. If a patient's subjective distress is too high, treatment efforts may be muted by the patient's efforts to avoid the challenges of therapy; the patient may become rigid and unable to benefit from treatment, following old patterns of coping with stress rather than learning and experimenting with new ones. Rigidification of coping patterns increases the patient's level of distress, symptoms, and emotional pain further as adjustment fails to accommodate new experience. Alternatively, if the motivational distress level is very low, the patient may fail to become invested in the treatment at all. Thus, level of subjective distress can be motivating if it is not so intense as to preclude focusing on the interpersonal sources of discomfort. At the same time, maintaining *some* discomfort about the problem is important as a mediating therapeutic goal, in order to ensure that the patient will engage in enough practice and learning to be protected from a recurrence of problems. The clinician should identify and attempt to maintain the particular arousal level at which the patient is open to and motivated for change.

"Problem complexity" is also related to severity, but represents a unique aspect of a patient's problem, in that it is associated both with historical patterns and with prognosis. Thus, problem complexity is more of a factor in setting the goals for treatment than in specifying the means of treatment.

For simplicity, problem complexity is considered to be a dichotomous variable, and patients are judged to present either thematic and "complex" problems or symptomatic and "noncomplex" problems. Complex presentations are characterized by enduring patterns of symptoms and behaviors across events and over time. Such presentations are often symbolized expressions of underlying intrapsychic conflict, and serve as indicators for interventions that are focused on changing themes and lifestyle patterns. It is important to note that the interventions used for complex and noncomplex problems may be quite diverse. For example, working toward resolution of thematic conflicts need not necessarily involve the use of procedures that facilitate insight. Complex problems can also be treated with interventions that alter patterns through a process of changing the system in which it occurs, such as is done in many strategic and systems approaches. These procedures do not rely on patient insight. Thus, it is our assertion that complexity is more accurately considered to be a means of defining the *goals* of treatment (i.e., symptom removal vs. pattern change) than of defining the procedures for doing so.

Restricting the goals of treatment to symptomatic change is appropriate for problems that arise from transient symptoms, those that arise in response to clearly defined environmental events, and those that are related to immediate or acute stressors. These symptomatic goals contrast with thematic ones that are indicated when problems bear only an indirect or symbolic relationship to contemporary events, when they persist and reoccur in unrelated situations, and when multiple areas of life functioning are impaired by them.

At a different level, some characteristics of patients predispose them to respond differently to interpersonal sources of threat. One of the most important of these characteristics is expressed as receptivity to therapeutic interventions. When a patient responds with resistance and/or opposition to interpersonal demands, such as the recommendations or suggestions of a therapist, the patient is manifesting a pattern that has been called "reactance" in the literature on social persuasion (Brehm & Brehm, 1981). Reactant or oppositional behaviors reflect the patient's attempt to restore his/her sense of freedom or self-control, which is threatened by an external demand to acquiesce to another person's influence.

Psychological reactance is aroused in an individual when the individual believes that his/her freedom is being challenged or threatened. However, individuals are not equally sensitive to these threats. When initial assessment indicates that an individual is particularly prone to perceive a threat to his/her sense of freedom, the treatment plan should avoid recommending procedures that require the direction of a clinician. Paradoxical or nondirective interventions are indicated in such instances, whereas clinician-directed interventions are reserved for use with individuals who are more tolerant of or less sensitive to external control.

While reactance level defines the likelihood of a patient's exhibiting resistant and oppositional behavior when confronted with interpersonal demands, patients also differ in their ways of managing anxiety arising from internal conflicts. Accordingly, one's "coping style" refers to how an individual manages anxiety arising from intrapersonal or internal conflict (Beutler, Machado, Engle, & Mohr, 1993). Coping styles have been conceptualized in numerous ways in the psychological literature; these include the traditional, unconscious ego defenses of Freud and other psychoanalysts, as well as consciously driven efforts to escape the anticipation of harm.

The most frequently used definitions of coping style represent efforts to protect oneself from anxiety as either a continuum or a series of points along a dimension ranging from acting out against others ("externalizing") to withdrawing and criticizing oneself ("internalizing"). Specific defense mechanisms are clustered at various points along this continuum, as are consciously driven efforts to cope with stress. These coping styles serve as useful markers for identifying a nominal grouping of enduring and preferred strategies on which a patient relies.

The clusters of coping patterns representing the ends of the continuum of coping have proven themselves to be useful in planning treatment. A preference for "internalizing" coping patterns defines patients who tend to repress, avoid, deny, and compartmentalize sources of anxiety. These individuals tend to be excessively self-critical, introspective, introverted, overcontrolled, and avoidant, and to have a limited range of emotional expressions or feelings. In contrast, those who prefer and rely on "externalizing" coping patterns tend to deal with anxiety by direct avoidance, acting out, rationalizing, and projecting their anxiety onto their surroundings. They typically manifest a degree of disregard for others' feelings, as well as an insensitivity to their own. Thus, they tend to be extraverted, impulsive, spontaneous, and sometimes manipulative as they fail to modulate their feelings and behavior.

Effective interventions differ for individuals of these two types. Specifically, the more patients prefer externalizing coping styles, the less able they are to use insight to facilitate change. However, these "externalizers" do respond to interventions that directly modify and alter behavioral contingencies, as well as to those that place external limits on disruptive behaviors. Conversely, patients who rely on internalizing coping styles tend to be sensitive to and able to respond to interventions that exert their influence through the mechanisms of insight and awareness.

Figure 9.1 provides an overview of the dimensions and decisions discussed in this chapter. This figure serves as a point of focus for our ensuing discussion of psychological assessment and treatment planning.

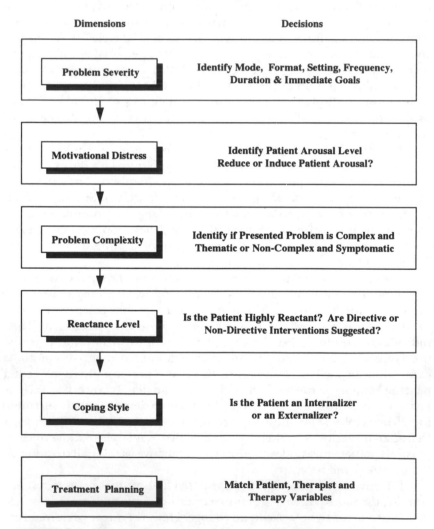

FIGURE 9.1. Systematic treatment selection: Dimensions and decisions.

Patient Assessment on the Five Dimensions

As we have repeatedly emphasized, when a clinician relies on an approach to personality assessment that is founded in a single theory of psychopathology, he/she introduces the possibility that those who adhere to other viewpoints will discount the results. Likewise, viewing patients through a single theory can introduce bias that colors the interpretation. Material that relies heavily on clinician interpretation, in the absence of evidence that these observations are reliable, valid, and normatively related, is especially subject to the clinician's theoretical bias, as well as to the unnoticed influence of peculiar situational and environmental factors. Thus, we recommend that treatment recommendations be relatively free from theory-driven concepts. This section of the report should be quite practical and useful to professionals with widely varied backgrounds.

In order to avoid interpretations that rely too heavily on theoretical jargon, we offer two additional recommendations. First, it is helpful to select and use at least some psychological assessment devices (tests) and methods that are relatively theory-free. Comparing the interpretations of theory-driven devices against empirically driven methods provides some check on the freedom of the interpretations from theoretical jargon and bias. The faith that is justified in these interpretations is proportional to the degree to which the interpretations arising from different sources of information are consistent with one another.

Second, it is useful to develop interpretations based on an internal model that is closely tied to empirical findings related to treatment rather than to a theory of psychopathology. That is, if a clinician employs constructs in his/her formulation that have been empirically related to treatment decisions, it affords a degree of protection from bias that is not obtained if the formulation is based primarily on theoretical concepts of psychopathology.

Each of the five patient dimensions discussed in the preceding section can be assessed both with formal tests and with clinical judgments based upon history and direct observations. They are also relatively theory-neutral, being selected primarily because of their empirically defined utility. This section describes the application of the integrated assessment model presented throughout this book to the problem of planning and designing a treatment program. We highlight the treatment implications for each of the five dimensions. Our decision to give special consideration to the psychotherapeutic aspects of treatment planning reflects our belief that since these are the least consistently applied of all interventions in clinical practice, standardizing and organizing their application are urgently needed.

Table 9.1 is adapted from Beutler, Wakefield, and Williams (1994) and summarizes the use of formal assessment procedures for identifying the dimensions used in the systematic treatment selection process. The reader

TABLE 9.1. Selected Assessments Used to Evaluate Dimensions of Systematic Treatment Selection

	Dimensions				
Instrument	Problem severity	Motivational distress	Problem complexity	Reactance level	Coping style
BDI*	×	×			
BHS*	×	×			
BSI*	×	×	×		
DSM					
Mini-SCID	×		×		
SCID-II	×		×		
MMPI-2*	×	×	×		×
MSE	×				
STAI*	×	×			
TRS*				×	
SSQ*	×				
Clinical indicators	×	×	×	×	×

Note. Instruments identified with an asterisk (*) are self-report measures. Adapted from Beutler, L. E., Wakefield, P., & Williams, R. E. (1994). Use of psychological tests/instruments for treatment planning. In M. Maruish (Ed.), *Use of psychological testing for treatment planning and outcome assessment.* Hillsdale, NJ: Erlbaum. Copyright by Lawrence Erlbaum Associates. Adapted by permission.

is referred to earlier chapters and to the manuals of the various instruments presented for specific guidelines in administering, scoring, and interpreting these instruments.

Problem Severity

Since problem severity represents the degree to which the patient's problems interfere with and disrupt his/her daily social, occupational, and intrapersonal functioning, it is measured as a dimensional variable. Related concepts include coping ability, ego strength, some aspects of cognitive ability, and problem chronicity. It is also related to the availability of environmental support (social and familial), since these are forces that increase the ability to cope. Coupled with an assessment of subjective or "motivational" distress, estimates of severity provide indicators for the mode (i.e., medical/somatic or psychosocial), format (e.g., drug and electroconvulsive therapies on the one hand, and individual, group, marital, or family interventions on the other), treatment intensity (e.g., duration and frequency of treatment), and the immediate goals (e.g., symptom reduction and stabilization) to which treatment should be addressed (Beutler & Clarkin, 1990; Beutler & Consoli, 1992). Armed with a diagnostic description, an assessment of the patient's social support network, and an index of social impairment, the clinician can make an initial decision regarding the type and restrictiveness of treatment immediately required (e.g., hospitalization, crisis intervention, maintenance, outpatient treatment).

Many measures of problem severity can easily be incorporated into the assessment protocol (Beutler, Wakefield, & Williams, 1994). Since it is a multidimensional construct, we recommend that several different means be used to evaluate different facets of its presentation. At a minimum, an indication of DSM-IV Axis I and Axis II status should be obtained; an index of social/environmental functioning and resources should be available; and a measure of interpersonal disturbance should be obtained. In the following paragraphs, we briefly review some of the instruments that we believe are useful for these purposes, and present some treatment guidelines that are associated with this dimension.

The DSM multiaxial evaluation system (American Psychiatric Association, 1994) allows the clinician to generate an abbreviated descriptive set of clinical judgments and observations, which are grouped into psychiatric diagnoses. The value of these diagnoses is threefold. First, the clinician can determine whether the patient requires a specific degree of confinement, given the severity of the disorder (e.g., schizophrenia, disorganized type, episodic with interepisode residual symptoms). Second, diagnoses of severe pathology often also indicates the need for medical intervention, such as the use of psychotropic medications (e.g., antipsychotics, antidepressants, etc.). Finally, the symptoms described by the diagnosis allow the clinician to assess the progress of treatment (e.g., remission). As has been noted (Beutler & Clarkin, 1990; Beutler, Consoli, & Williams, 1994), the value of psychiatric diagnoses rarely extends into the planning of psychotherapy, however. Hence, other dimensions are necessary as supplements to diagnosis for the purposes of planning and selecting among different treatment settings, treatment formats, modes, durations, frequencies, and goals.

Chapter 4 has described the use of standard interview techniques that yield diagnostic and cognitive information; Chapter 5 has described the use of the WAIS-R; and Chapter 8 has described the use of the MCMI as a diagnostic measure for many disorders. The self-report format of the MCMI, along with its correspondence with DSM diagnostic criteria, provides a useful cross-validation on interview- and clinician-based diagnostic procedures. The reader is encouraged to become familiar with the WAIS-R, with the MCMI, and with the various forms of the SCID (e.g., the Mini-SCID, the SCID-II) in order to generate sound psychiatric diagnoses.

In addition to Axis I and Axis II information, however, measures that are not specifically wedded to DSM nosology also provide information of use in assessing severity. For example, the GAF scale is designed to provide a measure of severity of impairment, which is coded on Axis V of the DSM multiaxial diagnostic system (American Psychiatric Association, 1994). The GAF scale offers a clinical assessment of the patient's psychological, social, and occupational functioning. It allows separate assessments of the patient's current and past level of functioning, the latter estimate representing the highest level of functioning within the past year. Inspecting these levels and their relationship to each other provides the data for judging problem chronicity. The rating of maximal level of functioning over the previous year provides a baseline by which to judge outcomes of treatment. Specifically, a judged low level of functioning within the past year suggests the presence of a chronic and persistent problem with a poor prognosis for more than baseline functioning in the future (American Psychiatric Association, 1994).

The GAF scale ranges from 0 (usually reserved for patients on whom there is inadequate information) to 100 (indicating that symptoms are absent and functioning is superior); the higher the score, the higher the functioning. The GAF is anchored with descriptions to assist the clinician in assigning a score (see American Psychiatric Association, 1994, p. 32), and these scores can be treated as a continuous measure of degree of impairment in social and interpersonal relationships.

The BSI (Derogatis, 1992) offers a relatively efficient (a 10-minute administration time) assessment of aspects of patient self-defined severity. It should be noted that this and other self-report measures confound concepts of distress with those of severity by combining indices of frequency of occurrence with the stress associated with them. Nonetheless, it can be used to supplement more objective measures of functional impairment. The 53-item BSI indexes symptom patterns on nine primary dimensions of distress and three global indices. Interpretation of the BSI profile begins with the global indices. For the purposes of treatment planning, the Global Severity Index (GSI) is most often used as an estimate of subjective or motivational distress and represents an average of all 53 symptom-oriented items, whether rated as being a problem or not. We return to this measure in our discussion of motivational distress.

The Positive Symptom Distress Index (PSDI) provides a more refined estimate of distress than the GSI when the patient's symptoms are quite restricted or confined to a limited number of related areas (Derogatis, 1992). The PSDI is computed as an average of intensity ratings, based only on those symptoms that are acknowledged. It complements the third global index, the Positive Symptom Total (PST), which is a simple count of the number of symptoms among the 53 items that the patient reports experiencing (Derogatis, 1992), regardless of intensity.

The BSI can also alert the clinician to both depression and suicidality by means of item and subscale responses. The Depression subscale includes items reflecting dysphoric mood and affect, vegetative signs, withdrawal, hopelessness, and anhedonia. The Psychoticism dimension represents a continuum ranging from "mild interpersonal alienation to dramatic evidence of psychosis" (Derogatis, 1992, p. 15) and can easily alert the clinician to possible psychoticism. The other dimensions of the BSI also serve as important indicators of the patient's current psychological state, and can complement the diagnostic indicators from the clinical interview. The clinician is encouraged to read the BSI manual for further information.

If, during the evaluation, the patient presents with moderate levels of depression on the BSI, additional assessment of suicidality is recommended. The BDI (Beck et al., 1961; Beck & Steer, 1987) and the BHS (Beck, Weissman, Lester, & Trexler, 1974; Beck & Steer, 1988) are examples of procedures that may be useful for this purpose (see Chapter 3) and can assist the clinician in deciding whether the patient requires immediate hospitalization for protection. In addition, vegetative signs that may be documented with the BDI may serve as indicators for the use of antidepressant medications. As a rule of thumb, when items 2 (hopelessness) and 9 (suicidal ideation) receive intensity ratings of 3 or 4, medication or hospitalization should be considered in detail (Beck & Steer, 1987). Notably, hopelessness has been found to be a better predictor of suicidal behavior than depression, and patients who score in the moderate to severe range on the BHS (scores above 9) should be considered to be at risk (Beck & Steer, 1988).

The MMPI and MCMI (see Chapters 7 and 8) can also provide information regarding the patient's problem severity. When several scales on either of these instruments extend into the clinical range, or when the average clinical scale elevations are in the clinical range, relatively severe problems are indicated. Moreover, the more the slope of one of these test profiles favors (i.e., is higher for) the scales on the right-hand side of the summary sheet, the more severe and serious the impairment of function is likely to be. On the MMPI, the most pronounced indicators of severity include the Paranoia, Schizophrenia, and Hypomania scales. On the MCMI, the three "severe personality pathology" subscales (Schizotypal, Borderline, Paranoid) and the three "severe syndrome" subscales (Thought Disorder, Major Depression, Delusional Disorder) are indicative of severely impaired functioning.

In the case of either the MMPI or the MCMI, a visual inspection of the profile sheet serves as a check and cross-validation of clinical information, psychiatric history, and diagnostic evaluation. This information is used in recommending the setting, intensity, and modality of the interventions to be applied. The more severe the dysfunction, the more likely the need for a restrictive setting, for medical intervention, and for long-term and intensive treatment.

An intellectual evaluation (e.g., the WAIS-R; see Chapter 5) and a mental status exam (e.g., the MSE; see Chapter 4) can also provide indications of level of problem severity (Beutler & Clarkin, 1990; Beutler & Consoli, 1992). Whether applied via a formal interview schedule or an informal clinical interview, together a mental status examination and intellectual assessment together provide an indication of the patient's orientation to person, time, and place; immediate, recent, and remote memories; capacity for exercising insight and social judgment; and aspects of spatial perception and cognitive organization (Sattler, 1988). The clinician can observe impairments in these areas and can make an informed judgment of the degree to which the manifest problems are interfering with the patient's functioning across several domains (Sattler, 1988): appearance and behavior; speech and communications; content of thought; sensory and motor functioning; intellectual level; cognitive efficiency; insight and judgment; and emotional functioning.

As with the other indicators of severity, when a patient reveals a high degree of incapacitation in several or all of these domains, medical interventions and restrictive environments are indicated. Intellectual levels below the borderline range (IQ ≤ 75), lack of personal orientation, marked confusion, loss of short-term memory, and severely inappropriate mood or affect all contraindicate the use of psychosocial interventions oriented toward insight. Sattler (1988), Folstein, Folstein, and McHugh (1975), and Shea (1990) provide further information that may be of value to the clinician in making complex judgments when the information available is contradictory.

In studying correlates of social support, Sarason et al. (1983) suggest the following:

1. Individuals with low social support are more emotionally and socially labile than those with adequate support systems.
2. Individuals with low social support are more pessimistic than individuals with high social support.
3. Individuals with high social support experience more rewarding relationships than those with lower social support.
4. Individuals with high social support have higher levels of self-esteem, better self-concepts, lower levels of anxiety, and a stronger perception of control than those with less strong social support systems.

The SSQ, developed by Sarason et al. (1983), represents a method of efficiently deriving information in the domain of social satisfaction. This questionnaire provides information about the number of available sources of support (quantity) and yields a rating of the patient's level of satisfaction with this support system (quality). The SSQ-N score indicates the degree to which support objects are available; it is an index of the size of the support network, and can be separated to differentiate between the extent of family and nonfamily support systems. The SSQ-S provides an index of the quality of support received, indexed by a rating of patient satisfaction. Scores on each of these scales are derived by dividing the domain total for each index by the number of items on the SSQ. Although Sarason et al. (1983) do not provide normative cutoff scores, their studies of college students yielded a combined mean of approximately 4.0 for each of the two scales.

An indication of the nature and extent of the patient's social support system is particularly helpful in assigning the patient to various treatment formats (e.g., individual, family, marital, or group therapy). External support systems buffer patients from the effects of stress (Sarason et al., 1983); thus, social support availability has been found to be related to maintenance of good psychological adjustment and to the patient's ability to manage the stress of social changes (Sarason et al., 1983). A group format of treatment, because it facilitates the development of emotional ties to other individuals, often gives the isolated or socially inappropriate patient an environment in which to develop his/her interpersonal relationships (Beutler, Consoli, & Williams, 1994). Group therapy, for example, allows the patient to identify with and practice new behaviors with other patients who also offer advice, external structure, social control, and feedback (Beutler & Clarkin, 1990). Individual therapy formats, in contrast, allow the patient to focus specifically on himself/herself and the therapist; it is assumed either that support systems are in place or that the patient already has access to the skills needed to develop them.

In the planning of treatment, a low level of social support suggests the need for a family or group treatment format to strengthen social networks, and may indicate the absence of protective controls in the environments of suicidal patients. More adequate levels of social support suggest that the resources are there to support changes made in individual treatment formats. Low levels of satisfaction with the quality of family support may suggest a particular need for family-oriented interventions, especially if historical and current status information suggest a high level of family disruption. As a rule of thumb, a median normative score (4.0) on the SSQ-N can be used as a rough demarcation point for differentiating adequate from inadequate support networks. Patients who earn SSQ-N scores above 4.0 probably have adequate levels of social support to support individual therapy.

Trait or generalized anxiety levels can also be indicators of the need for treatment. The STAI Trait Anxiety scale (Spielberger et al., 1983) has been particularly useful for assessing these dimensions. Spielberger et al. (1983) point out that trait anxiety reflects a stable expression of a personality quality and reflects the level of anxiety that cuts across situations. Hence, high STAI Trait Anxiety scores represent the typical or usual level of disturbance that is likely to arise when an anxious patient faces a new situation. The generality or pervasiveness of this anxiety across situations differentiates trait anxiety from state-like responses, which are situation-specific and temporary. We discuss state anxiety more thoroughly in our description of motivational distress.

Although Spielberger et al. (1983) do not provide a normative definition or cutoff for what constitutes a "high" Trait Anxiety score, the mean scores and T scores of the various normative samples provide some indication of working values. As a general rule, Trait Anxiety scores above 40 indicate at least mild problems, and those above 55 indicate relatively severe problems. These rough indicators should be considered along with other test and clinical indicators in recommending treatment settings, formats, and modalities.

After inspecting the tests and clinical patterns, and compiling a summary judgment of the patient's problem severity, the clinician is in a position to select a variety of options regarding treatment setting, intensity, and modality. Figure 9.2 presents a worksheet designed to assist the clinician in making these clinical judgments. Information from the patient's history is used to complement formal test scores. The duration of the problem, the nature of the impairments, changes in functioning, and alterations of perceptions and problem-solving efficiency as reported by the patient and his/her family are all clinical indicators that can be used to cross-validate formal test results. The form provided in Figure 9.2 provides a scale for deriving a summary rating of problem severity, and is used in the development of treatment strategies.

To summarize, the purposes of assessing problem severity are to measure the degree of disruption to the patient's life and to use this information in selecting from among a variety of treatment modes, formats, frequencies, durations, and immediate goals. For instance, it is important to determine whether the problem is so disruptive and impairing that the patient requires hospitalization to stabilize him/her; to judge the balance among psychosocial and medical interventions that should be applied; to select the intervention format that complements the patient's level of social support; to offer the most efficient blend of individual, group, and family therapy; and to make an initial estimate as to the probable length and intensity of treatment required.

If the clinical interview and mental status evaluation suggest the presence of a depressive syndrome, the clinician should employ a depressive symptom scale (e.g., the BDI) and a measure of social support (e.g., the SSQ). If suicidality is suggested, then the BHS is helpful as well. Low levels of social support and problem chronicity are further risk factors that should be considered as indicators for using a restraining environment when hopelessness and suicidal ideation are present.

Motivational Distress

Arousal of emotions is an important motivational construct in understanding human behavior. Up to a point, increasing arousal is associated with heightened motivation, improved memory, enhanced cognitive efficiency, and faster motor performance. However, as arousal continues to increase, it reaches a point beyond which further arousal is associated with deteriorating cognitive and motor efficiency. Very high arousal impairs a person's ability to focus his/her attention; as a result, both motivation and problem-

Directions: Enter values and clinical observations as appropriate.   Use the check boxes provided.
Refer to the instrument manuals for administration, scoring and interpretation guidelines.

**Check if
Administered**

☐ **Dx**   Axis I:_____   Axis II::_____

☐ **BSI**   Scales of T≥ 63:_____

☐ **GAF**   Current GAF:_____   Highest GAF Past Year:_____

☐ **MMPI-2**   Mean T-Score of Clinical Scales:_____   ☐ High   ☐ Average ☐ Low

☐ **STAI**   Trait Anxiety Score:_____   ☐ High (> 55) ☐ Average   ☐ Low (< 40)

☐ **MSE**   ☐ No Impairment   ☐ Mild Impairment   ☐ Moderate/Severe Impairment

☐ **SSQ**   SSQ-N:____   If above 4.0, then "high" in social support.   ☐ High SS   ☐ Low SS

☐ **Clinical
   Indicators** ☐ Problem interferes with patient's functioning during interview
                 ☐ Patient cannot concentrate on interview tasks
                 ☐ Patient is distracted even by minor events
                 ☐ Patient appears incapacitated by problem and has difficulty in functioning
                 ☐ Patient has difficulty in interacting with the interviewer as a result of problem severity
                 ☐ Multiple areas of performance are impaired in daily life

Suicide Potential   ☐ **Check if at risk**

☐ **BDI**   Item 2 Score:_____   Item 9 Score:_____   BDI Total Score:_____

☐ **BHS**   BHS Total Score:_____   (A score ≥ 9 strongly suggests the patient is at suicidal risk.)

                 ☐ Anti-suicide contract made?

Based on the above assessment results and clinical observations, rate the patient's problem severity in terms of impairment by placing an 'X' on the scale below.

```
 |————————————————————|————————————————————|
 No Impairment       Mild Impairment      Moderate/Severe
                                          Impairment
```

FIGURE 9.2. Problem severity: Summary worksheet.

solving efficiency decline. In psychological treatment, for example, where a patient's personal distress is the form of arousal that serves this motivational role, the patient's level of distress must not be so high as to impair the ability to concentrate and process information. But neither should it be so low as to prevent the patient from being motivated to engage in treatment (Beutler, Wakefield, & Williams, 1994; Beutler, Consoli, & Williams, 1994; Graham, 1990).

Because people are motivated to avoid discomfort, it is commonly assumed (Frank & Frank, 1991) that there is a window of subjective distress within which treatment strategies will exert the most pronounced effect among patients. To reach this window, some patients will benefit most from interventions that increase their level of arousal, whereas others will benefit from those that reduce their arousal levels to the "optimal" range.

At first glance, the definition of motivational distress sounds similar to that of problem severity, and indeed the two concepts are related. But they have somewhat different treatment implications. Distress reflects the level of subjective discomfort rather than objective impairment. Whereas the degree of a patient's impairment (i.e., severity) influences the selection of initial treatment modes, formats, and settings, the level of a patient's motivational distress suggests the degree to which the patient will benefit from structure and support on the one hand, and confrontation on the other. Through careful assessment of motivational distress, the clinician can determine whether the patient's level of discomfort should be increased or reduced. Certain treatment techniques seem particularly well suited to each of these tasks, and these can be assigned discriminatively when the clinician is sensitive to the degree to which the patient's distress is within motivational limits.

Another difference between motivational distress and problem severity is that distress is more changeable and situationally responsive. That is, distress is a state-like quality rather than a slowly changing trait, and is expected to vary from session to session or even within a single session (Beutler, Consoli, & Williams, 1994). Thus, the clinician should be prepared to match his/her treatment strategies to the patient's rather fluid window of arousal. Frequent assessment is particularly needed in this ever-changing domain.

Motivational distress can be assessed by means of a multitude of formal instruments, as well as a number of clinical indicators. Some of the formal tests utilized are the same as those used for assessing problem severity, but when they are used to assess motivational arousal, attention is focused on the state-responsive subscales rather than the subscales that assess traits. For example, as previously described, the PSDI and PST summary scores from the BSI are valuable complements to clinical judgments of severity of impairment; however, the GSI from this instrument offers the single best indicator of overall distress level (Derogatis, 1992). Derogatis suggests that when the GSI value exceeds a T score of 63, a treatment that is designed to reduce subjective distress levels is indicated. Conversely, Beutler, Consoli, and Williams (1994) point out that if distress levels are low, even though the patient exhibits at least moderate levels of social and interpersonal impairment, the clinician is faced with the task of identifying interventions that will safely confront the patient with how his/her behavior may be maintaining the impairment. Confrontation like this is frequently used in an effort to induce the distress needed to motivate change.

The GAF scale also provides an index of current distress, in addition to its use as a measure of problem severity. The clinician impressions that serve as the basis for this assessment complement the self-report format of the BSI and other measures. To assess motivational distress from the GAF, the clinician inspects current functioning, paying relatively less attention to past functioning level than when assessing severity of impairment. For example, a patient who seeks treatment but who receives a rating of 80 (a high rating) is generally experiencing transient and mild symptoms (American Psychiatric Association, 1994). Such a patient may benefit from confrontational procedures that increase levels of arousal (discomfort) and motivation for treatment. Alternatively, a patient who earns a lower GAF rating is probably experiencing distress that can potentially interfere with effective treatment; in this case, the clinician may be advised to choose strategies that are designed to reduce patient discomfort.

The MMPI provides yet another approach to assessing motivational distress. Two major indicator scales can identify the type of psychological distress that motivates change. Explicitly, the Pt subscale (scale 7) represents "a good index of psychological turmoil and discomfort" (Graham, 1990, p. 74). Those who score in the clinical range on this scale tend to be very anxious, high-strung, jumpy, tense, and agitated. They tend to worry excessively and often have diffuse aches and pains, fatigue, and sleeping disturbances that interfere with effective functioning (Graham, 1990). These symptoms indicate the use of procedures that are designed to reduce psychological turmoil.

In a complementary fashion, scores above 70 on the F subscale may suggest good motivation for treatment, because scores at this elevation occur among patients who are quite uncomfortable and feel that something is wrong with them. Thus, patients who score moderately high on both of these subscales may be particularly well motivated for treatment. However, Graham (1990) observes that there are certain other MMPI scales whose elevations may attenuate the motivational properties of these distress indicators and can be used to identify individuals whose distress is not a source of motivation for treatment. Patients whose high scores on the F scale are accompanied by equally high elevations on the L and K scales tend to disown their discomfort and to be resistant, hostile, and reactant to authority figures. Graham (1990) points out that, unlike those whose F scores are substantially higher than their L and K scores, these reactant patients are not open to change in treatment. Thus, high Pt and F scores may be good indicators that the patient has both arousal and openness to treatment only when the L and K scores are relatively lower (10 points or more).

In a related way, if a patient's Pt score is very low in relation to the objective severity of the problems, it may indicate an unrealistic level of self-confidence and indifference to real and personal problems (Graham, 1990). In this case, the clinician may need to induce arousal through confrontation and corrective feedback before the patient will be motivated for change.

The STAI State Anxiety subscale also serves as a measure of motivational distress, complementing the Trait Anxiety subscale, which is an indicator of enduring problem severity (Beutler, Consoli, & Williams, 1994; Spielberger et al., 1983). It is important to observe that individuals with high Trait Anxiety scores also tend to have elevated State Anxiety scores; this suggests that they have both distressing and severe problems, which leave them experiencing the world as threatening and dangerous. In using the STAI for assessing motivational distress, therefore, the clinician should inspect both Trait Anxiety and State Anxiety scores in light of both normative data and his/her own clinical judgment to decide whether inducing or reducing arousal levels is warranted. Although no formal limits have been established, as a rule of thumb, we are cautious about using confrontational techniques with patients whose State Anxiety scores are within the top normative quartile. These individuals may have sufficient distress as to impede attentional focus, concentration, and other aspects of motivation.

In addition to formal tests, motivational distress can be assessed through clinical observations of behavior and historical information, although these are of uncertain reliability. Some of these clinical indicators are presented in Figure 9.3, along with the indicators provided by formal tests. Excessively high levels of distress are indicated clinically by intense emotional arousal, excited affect, nervousness/agitation, and inability to concentrate, as well as by an excited, unsteady voice. Conversely, excessively low levels of distress are indicated by lack of emotional variability, blunted or constricted affect, lethargy, and low symptomatic distress. The indicators presented, though not an exhaustive list, highlight the extremes of this continuum of distress.

Together, formal tests and clinical indicators provide the basis for making a single integrated judgment of the patient's level of motivational distress. For simplicity, and because of the insensitivity of many of the measures, this final judgment is expressed in Figure 9.3 as a simple dimension ranging from excessive to insufficient distress to maintain treatment efforts. A rating between these extremes is reserved for those whose distress and ability to focus seems to foster sufficient motivation for change.

Beutler, Consoli, and Williams (1994) suggest that patients with a low level of motivational distress can be matched to experiential strategies that challenge patients to face and accept their problems and that effectively raise the patients' level of sensitivity to distress. Experiential therapists have developed many treatments that serve this purpose, and these procedures complement the interpretative and confrontational strategies of dynamic therapies to provide quite an extensive armamentarium. For high-distress patients, on the other hand, the use of supportive, structured, and relaxation strategies drawn from the behavioral and cognitive therapy approaches can reduce their distress and can thereby enhance their treatment motivation.

Directions: Enter values and clinical observations as appropriate.   Use the check boxes provided.
Refer to the instrument manuals for administration, scoring and interpretation guidelines.

**Check if
Administered**

☐ **BSI**   GSI:_____

☐ **GAF**   Current GAF:_____   Highest GAF Past Year:_____

☐ **MMPI-2**   Scale 7 (Pt) T-Score:_____   ☐ High ☐ Average ☐ Low

              F T-Score:_____   Is F ≥ L and K by 10 T-Score units? ☐ Yes ☐ No

☐ **STAI**   State Anxiety Score:_____   ☐ High ☐ Low

☐ **Clinical   High Distress   Low Distress
    Indicators**
              ☐ High emotional arousal   ☐ Low emotional arousal
              ☐ High symptomatic distress   ☐ Low symptomatic distress
              ☐ Motor agitation   ☐ Reduced motor activity
              ☐ Difficulty in maintaining concentration ☐ Low investment in treatment
              ☐ Unsteady/faltering voice   ☐ Low energy level
              ☐ Autonomic symptoms   ☐ Blunted or constricted affect
              ☐ Hyperventilation   ☐ Unmodulated verbalizations
              ☐ Hypervigilance   ☐ Slow verbalizations
              ☐ Excited affect
              ☐ Intense feelings

Based on the above assessment results and clinical observations, rate the patient's motivational distress by placing an 'X' on the scale below.

Motivational   Motivational
distress is Low   distress is High

├─────────────────────────┼─────────────────────────┤

Patient's
motivational distress
is Adequate

Notes:

FIGURE 9.3. Motivational distress: Summary worksheet.

Problem Complexity

The complexity of the presenting problem(s) represents another aspect of
patient functioning that is related to problem severity. Though it was initially considered to be indistinguishable from problem severity (Beutler,
1986, 1987), experience has suggested that problem complexity is best considered as an independent construct. A complex problem is defined as one
that is pervasive and enduring; it is chronic and transsituational rather than

situation-specific and acute (Beutler & Clarkin, 1990; Beutler & Consoli, 1992). The operative question is this: "Are these problems simply habits that are maintained by the environment or are they symbolized expressions of unresolved conflictual experiences?" (Beutler & Clarkin, 1990, pp. 225–226). This question captures the essence of the difference between complex and noncomplex problems. That is, the symptoms associated with complex problems are indirect or symbolic expressions of the initiating or provoking stimuli, and these stimuli are unseen internal events rather than circumstances of the environment; the problems recur in somewhat different but related forms whenever the conflict is activated; and they spread across a variety of symptoms and situations. On the other hand, noncomplex problems are situationally evoked, infrequently recurrent unless the same situation is encountered again, and reflected in complexes of common symptoms (Beutler & Consoli, 1992).

The assessment of problem complexity, as with problem severity and motivational distress, can be accomplished with both formal tests and impressions from historical and observational data. For example, tests like the BSI offer insight into the degree to which the problem spreads across symptom domains—one aspect of complexity. Beutler and Consoli (1992) point out that noncomplex problem presentations are often represented on the BSI as spikes on overlapping scales (little or no symptom spread), whereas complex problems are represented as elevations across a variety of conceptually unrelated symptom dimensions. This determination can be made, at least tentatively, by inspecting the symptom subscale elevations: Somatization, Obsessive–Compulsive, Interpersonal Sensitivity, Depression, Anxiety, Hostility, Phobic Anxiety, Paranoid Ideation, and Psychoticism (Derogatis, 1992). If patient achieves peaks (T scores ≥ 63) on several of these symptom dimensions, the patient's problem can be characterized as complex (Beutler, Consoli, & Williams, 1994). Although one would expect Somatization, Anxiety, and Depression to be highly correlated, if these scales are elevated along with less highly correlated ones such as Paranoid Ideation, Psychoticism, and Hostility, there is reason to believe that the problem is complex and is affecting a variety of response domains.

The global indices of the BSI provide a shorthand method for inspecting the level of symptom spread. For example, if all three summary indices are elevated to the clinical range, a complex pattern is suspected. Alternatively, if the GSI is low (low overall intensity) but the PSDI is high, a constricted range of intensely disturbing symptoms is indicated, suggesting a narrow band of symptom spread.

The MCMI and MMPI provide a gateway into another aspect of symptom complexity, the chronicity of the problem. MMPI two-point code types (see Graham, 1990, pp. 87–89, for an instructive discussion) and Axis II indicators from the MCMI (or SCID-II) both shed light on this dimension. Specifically, on the MMPI, if Hs is lower than D and the latter scale is within the clinical range, then the patient is likely to be presenting with acute symptoms. Likewise, if Pt is higher than Sc, acuteness is indicated and the patient often reports anxiousness, tension, and nervousness (Graham, 1990). If both Pt and Sc are among the highest in the profile, the patient may be experiencing significant inner turmoil; have self doubts; feel insecure, inferior, and inadequate; and have difficulty in making decisions (Graham, 1990). Such a patient has inadequate defenses to cope with problems, and is often depressed, worried, tense, and confused.

If either Hs is higher than D or Sc is higher than Pt and any or all of these scales are elevated into the clinical range, both chronic and complex problems are indicated. This interpretation is further enhanced in the presence of indications of a personality disorder from either the MCMI or the clinical interview.

The most important aspect of problem complexity, from the standpoint of treatment planning, cannot be easily determined by the foregoing methods. Assessment of this dimension requires a determination as to whether a presenting problem reflects a recurring internal conflict or a simple response to externally evoking events. Although the presence of internal and continuing conflicts can be inferred both from the presence of chronic (recurrent) symptoms and from symptom spread, clinical judgments based upon the patient's history are also necessary. Complex problems are seen as recurrent patterns or themes arising within objectively different but symbolically related relationships. From a review of the patient's history of interpersonal relationships, the clinician attempts to determine the degree to which the patient re-enacts certain patterns with individuals who occupy distinctive evoking roles. Objects of authority and intimacy are particularly provocative of ritualized patterns. If similar patterns of disturbance arise whenever the patient encounters an object of authority, even when this behavior is inconsistent with the evoking behaviors and expectations of the authority himself/herself, a thematic or systemic conflict is suspected.

Thematic presentations are ritualized attempts to resolve past interpersonal conflicts in current, different, and now inappropriate interpersonal relationships. For a problem to qualify as complex or thematic, the clinician must judge the historical nature of the problems that arise in different forms and at different times to have underlying similarities that are unrealistic for the present situation, and to be occurring in situations that are objectively dissimilar to the originally evoking one. Since the patient's current relationships do not require the enactment of anachronistic themes, the recurrent behaviors that were originally designed to avoid discomfort are frequently met with disapproval and other negative consequences. Thus, one characteristic of thematic problems is that they often result in further suffering rather than gratification in current relationships.

Figure 9.4 presents a list of clinical indicators to guide and assist the clinician in making a judgment of problem complexity. Once again, a final

Directions: Enter values and clinical observations as appropriate. Use the check boxes provided.
Refer to the instrument manuals for administration, scoring and interpretation guidelines.

**Check if
Administered**

☐ **BSI**   How many of the nine symptom dimension scales are T≥63?:_____

GSI:_____   PST:_____   PSDI:_____

☐ Multisymptomatic   or   ☐ Monosymptomatic

☐ **Dx**   Axis II Dx?   ☐ Yes   or   ☐ No   Identify Axis II Cluster   ☐ Cluster A
                                                                                 ☐ Cluster B
                                                                                 ☐ Cluster C

☐ **MMPI-2**   Are Scales 1 (Hs) or 2 (D) above 65? If so, is Scale 1 > Scale 2?   ☐ yes   ☐ no
                                                                        • If yes, chronicity is suggested.

Are Scales 7 (Pt) or 8 (Sc) above 65? If so, is Scale 7 < Scale 8?   ☐ yes   ☐ no
                                                                        • If yes, chronicity is suggested.

☐ **Clinical
Indicators**   Non-Complex Problem Indicators   Complex Problem Indicators

Non-Complex Problem Indicators	Complex Problem Indicators
☐ Chronic habits and transient responses	☐ Behaviors are repeated as themes across unrelated and dissimilar situations
☐ Behavior repetition is maintained by inadequate knowledge or by ongoing situational rewards (positive reinforcement)	☐ Behaviors are ritualized (yet self-defeating) attempts to resolve dynamic and/or interpersonal conflicts
☐ Behaviors have a direct relationship to initiating events	☐ Current conflicts are expressions of the patient's past rather than present relationships
☐ Behaviors are situation-specific	☐ Repetitive behavior results in suffering (rather than gratification)
	☐ Symptoms have a symbolic relationship to initiating events
	☐ Problems are enduring, repetitive and symbolic manifestations of characterological conflicts

Based on the above assessment results and the clinical indicators, identify the patient's problem complexity.

Non-Complex   ☐   Complex   ☐
(Constricted/Situational)

Notes:

FIGURE 9.4. Problem complexity: Summary worksheet.

determination or rating of problem complexity should combine and integrate information from formal assessment instruments with those deriving from clinical impressions and historical events. From this summary judgment evolves a recommendation that treatment be evaluated in terms of its success at altering either symptomatic presentations (noncomplex problems) or systemic and interpersonal themes (complex problems).

Once the clinician makes a determination of the level of problem complexity presented by the patient, he/she must then move to identify a set of focal objectives by which the outcome of treatment can be measured. On the one hand, noncomplex problems can be treated by directly addressing the symptoms, their antecedent cognitive and environmental events, and their maintaining consequences. Complex problems, on the other hand, may be best treated by altering the patterns, networks, and underlying processes through which the symptoms occur. These patterns are frequently interpersonal in nature and indicate the presence of dynamic conflicts or systemically maintained roles. Thus, the identification of the intermediate goals through which complex problems are to be corrected requires a different, more abstract, and more clinician-dependent process than that needed for defining the intermediate and long-term goals for treating noncomplex problems.

Specifically, a complex problem suggests that the overt symptoms are interrelated and caused by some common but unseen process. The objective of treatment is to change this process; relatively little attention is given to the evoking environments and external contingencies. However, because the nature of this underlying process can only be defined at a theoretical level (since it cannot otherwise be observed), the goals of treatment for complex problems are defined by the theory of personality and psychopathology that is held by the clinician providing the treatment. In a psychological report, the consulting psychologist must define the themes underlying complex problems in terms that either cut across theoretical lines are or easily translatable from one theory to another. Chapters 6 and 8 of this volume have presented two methods of assessing thematic processes, varying in level of abstraction and in theoretical transportability. A major advantage of both of these approaches is that the theoretical constructs are directly tied to a system of measuring them, permitting the mediating change processes to be measured as a means of assessing treatment efficacy.

On the one hand, the Rorschach (Chapter 6) considers perceptual recurrences and patterns as examples of enduring and cross-situational themes, which in turn embody an interplay of needs and defenses. The themes that are assessed by this means reflect an underlying psychodynamic framework. Presenting these themes may be most appropriate when the consultant is assured that those who utilize the report will understand and be sympathetic to this viewpoint.

The MCMI (Chapter 8), in contrast, offers a very pragmatic theory for assessing underlying themes and patterns. The MCMI is particularly useful for the consultant who is attempting to define the short- and long-term objectives of treatment for an audience whose theoretical preferences are diverse. As pointed out in Chapter 2, this model also represents a reasonably good balance between the complexity of a psychodynamic model and the concreteness of purely empirical models, thus allowing easy translation among theoretical models.

Defining a theme, however, does not tell us how to modify or treat it.

To say that a problem is a complex representation of a lingering conflict and is manifested in a recurrent systemic theme is not to say that a therapist is to utilize procedures to elicit insights. Many systemic and structural therapies, for example, are quite successful at modifying themes without attempting or initiating insight into a patient's problems. The mechanisms used to meet the symptomatic or thematic change goals are more logically selected from an understanding of the patient's reactance potential and coping style.

Reactance Level

"Interpersonal reactance" describes an indwelling tendency to respond oppositionally to external demands (Beutler & Consoli, 1992). Reactance is a trait-like quality that propels an individual to resist or defend against control and intrusion from outside forces. It can occur in a variety of patterns, however, and varies considerably in how directly it is manifested. For example, a highly reactant but socially sensitive and self-critical patient may respond paradoxically to a clinical intervention while seeming to make an effort to comply; he/she may become tense when directed to relax, or may consistently misunderstand or forget the homework assignment. Reactance level, therefore, indicates the level of potential resistance to the therapist's interventions, suggestions, and/or interpretations, not the form that this resistance will take (Beutler, Consoli, & Williams, 1994; Beutler & Gaw, 1993). Treatment recommendations attempt to match the patient's reactance level with the degree to which the therapist utilizes procedures that require therapist direction or that draw attention to the therapist's role as an expert and authority.

For the purposes of treatment planning, it is helpful to consider reactance level as existing along a three-point continuum—high, medium, or low. This dimension of patient behavior may be assessed in numerous ways. Clinical interpretations of certain patterns of response on the MMPI and MCMI bear a descriptive similarity to empirically based descriptions of reactance potential. For example, Graham (1990) describes patients who score high on the MMPI L, F, and K validity scales to be so guarded that they are unable to accept the therapist's authority or influence. Empirically derived indices from the MMPI research scales (Beutler et al., 1991) have also yielded promising results as predictors both of oppositional responses when patients are provided with directive interventions and positive responses when patients are given self-directed interventions. However, these empirically derived indices are still premature for clinical use.

One of the more promising instruments for assessing reactance is the TRS (Dowd et al., 1991; Dowd & Wallbrown, 1993), a brief (28-item) self-report assessment instrument. The TRS produces a single score, ranging from 28 to 112. In two previous normative studies using the TRS, Dowd et al. (1991) obtained means of 66.68 and 68.87. The combined mean of 68 can be used as a rough cutoff score to identify those who are prone to be excessively reactant. A score above this level suggests a patient who is likely to resist therapist control and direction. For such a patient, non-directive or self-directed interventions may be indicated in order to stimulate change and improvement. In the extreme, if reactance potential is very high, even nondirective interventions may be counterproductive. In these instances, paradoxical interventions (prescribing "no change" or increased symptoms) may be indicated. As a working rule, we suggest that patients with scores above 84 (75%) on the TRS should be considered for the use of paradoxical interventions. Homework assignments that prescribe "no change," prescriptions for symptom exaggeration, reframing of problem behaviors in positive terms, and warnings against making rapid changes are among the strategies that have been used successfully. Beutler and Consoli (1992) warn of possible symptom exaggeration (worsening) if such a patient is treated by an authoritative, directive therapist—a situation that may not only destabilize the relationship, but even endanger the patient.

A score below 68 on the TRS suggests a compliant and open patient. If a patient is compliant, the use of therapist-initiated directives (instructions, homework, guided discussions, etc.) may help the patient move toward therapeutic change and improvement. Low scores provide the therapist with more flexibility in designing treatment than is true for high scores, since low-scoring individuals can probably respond well to either directive or nondirective interventions.

There are also a variety of clinical indicators, derived from history and observed interactions with the therapist, that can be used to identify the reactant patient. Some of the more pronounced indicators are presented in Figure 9.5 and can be used to complement formal test scores in deriving a summary judgment of patient reactance. The clinical indicators presented in the figure derive from empirical evidence that the reactant individual is dominant, aggressive, defensive, and quick to take offense, and is frequently also a loner. These descriptions include positive qualities as well: Reactant persons tend to be interpersonally autonomous and individualistic, and are effective (yet forceful) leaders (Dowd & Wallbrown, 1993).

By integrating the results of the TRS or other reactance indices with impressions drawn from the patient's interpersonal history, the clinician can provide recommendations regarding the use of directive, nondirective, self-directed, and paradoxical interventions. The nature of homework assignments that will be most effective can also be specified, with attention given to the degree to which these are self-monitored or directed by the therapist. The report can also note the expected prognosis and level of cooperation that can be expected of the patient, along with recommendations for the selected interventions.

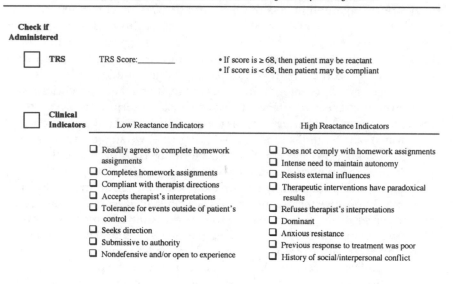

Directions: Enter values and clinical observations as appropriate. Use the check boxes provided.
Refer to the instrument manuals for administration, scoring and interpretation guidelines.

Check if Administered

☐ **TRS**   TRS Score:_____   • If score is ≥ 68, then patient may be reactant
                                            • If score is < 68, then patient may be compliant

☐ **Clinical Indicators**

Low Reactance Indicators	High Reactance Indicators
☐ Readily agrees to complete homework assignments	☐ Does not comply with homework assignments
☐ Completes homework assignments	☐ Intense need to maintain autonomy
☐ Compliant with therapist directions	☐ Resists external influences
☐ Accepts therapist's interpretations	☐ Therapeutic interventions have paradoxical results
☐ Tolerance for events outside of patient's control	☐ Refuses therapist's interpretations
☐ Seeks direction	☐ Dominant
☐ Submissive to authority	☐ Anxious resistance
☐ Nondefensive and/or open to experience	☐ Previous response to treatment was poor
	☐ History of social/interpersonal conflict

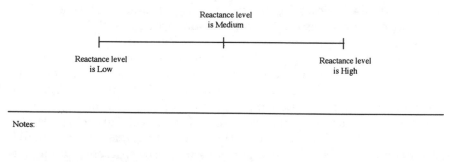

Based on the above assessment results and clinical observations, rate the patient's reactance level by placing an 'X' on the scale below.

Reactance level
is Medium

Reactance level   Reactance level
is Low   is High

Notes:

FIGURE 9.5. Reactance level: Summary worksheet.

Coping Style

The final patient dimension to be considered in treatment planning is the patient's style of coping with distressing experiences. Although various points along the externalization–internalization continuum may characterize distinctive personality styles, a twofold classification fits the current developmental level of knowledge about the distinctive demand characteristics of different psychotherapies. However, even at this current early level of knowledge, we can see a direct correspondence between the externalizing–internalizing continuum and the behavioral-to-insight dimension that distinguishes among psychotherapies.

Externalizing patients blame others for their problems, attribute the cause and responsibility for their discomfort to fate, are relatively unresponsive to insight, and lack psychological-mindedness (Beutler & Consoli, 1992). Thus, they may act impulsively to escape and avoid even minor discomfort arising from interpersonal relationships, and are more likely to respond to efforts to change their behavior through contingency management and cognitive practice than to strategies that are designed to facilitate insight, self-responsibility, and awareness (Beutler et al., 1991).

Internalizing patients cope with distress in a very different manner. They tend to direct their coping efforts inward, being acutely sensitive to discomfort, blaming themselves for lacking skills or abilities, and overcontrolling their impulses and feelings. That is, internalizers tend to "act in" rather than "acting out," and consequently are more prone to suffer than are externalizers.

The MMPI is useful in defining patient coping styles along the internalizing–externalizing dimension. Virtually all of the clinical scales have been identified as reflecting dispositions toward either internalizing or externalizing. Moreover, selective combinations of clinical scales reliably define enduring tendencies toward either internalization or externalization (Beutler & Consoli, 1992). The most reliable indices are comprised of ratios, with two or more "externalizing" scales being weighted against two or more "internalizing" scales as an index of preference for one or the other of these coping styles. The MMPI scales that are most frequently used to indicate externalizing patterns are the Hy, Pd, Pa, and Ma scales. Alternatively, the scales that are most frequently used to indicate internalizing coping styles are the Hs, D, Pt, and Si scales.

The first internalization ratio was constructed by Welsh (1952; see Dahlstrom, Welsh, & Dahlstrom, 1972). Variations on this original ratio have been successful in predicting differential response rates to insight-oriented and cognitive–behavioral treatment (Beutler et al., 1991). Indeed, we believe that the following procedure can be used to identify a patient's coping style in a way that has treatment relevance: If the sum of the Pd, Pa, and Ma scales is greater than the sum of the D, Pt, and Si scales, the patient can be classified as an externalizer. However, if the patient has a diagnosable depressive disorder, this internalization ratio is not sufficiently sensitive to differentiate meaningfully between the two coping styles. For this type of patient, the following formula is suggested: If the sum of scales 4 and 6 is greater than or equal to 140 (T score), then the depressed patient can be classified as an externalizer. These classification rules are included in Figure 9.6.

To supplement the index of coping style, clinical indicators are again useful; some are included in Figure 9.6. Although patients will often have

Directions: Enter values and clinical observations as appropriate. Use the check boxes provided.
Refer to the instrument manuals for administration, scoring and interpretation guidelines.

Check if Administered	List T-Scores for the following Scales. Then total each column.	Pd(4): ____ D(2): ____
☐ MMPI-2		Pa(6): ____ Pt(7): ____
		Ma(9): ____ Si(0): ____
		Total: ____ Total: ____

• If (Pd + Pa + Ma) > (D + Pt + Si), then the patient is an externalizer
• If (Pd + Pa + Ma) < (D + Pt + Si), then the patient is an internalizer

Note: When the patient is clinically depressed, use the following decision rule:
If the T-Score sum of Scales 4 + 6 ≥ 140, then consider the patient an externalizer

---

☐ **Clinical Indicators**

Internalization Indicators	Externalization Indicators
☐ Undoing	☐ Ambivalence
☐ Self-punishment	☐ Acting out
☐ Intellectualization	☐ Blaming others and self
☐ Isolation of affect	☐ Low tolerance for frustration
☐ Emotional overcontrol or constriction	☐ Difficulty in differentiating emotions
☐ Low tolerance for feelings or sensations	☐ Avoidance and/or escape
☐ High resistance for feelings and sensations	☐ Projection
☐ Denial	☐ Conversion symptoms
☐ Reversal	☐ Paranoid reactions
☐ Reaction formation	☐ Unsocialized aggression
☐ Repression	☐ Manipulation of others
☐ Minimization	☐ Ego-syntonic behaviors
☐ Unrecognized wishes or desires	☐ Stimulation seeking
☐ Introverted	☐ Extraverted
☐ Social withdrawal	☐ Somatization (seeks secondary gain from physical symptoms)
☐ Somatization (autonomic nervous system symptoms)	

Based on the above assessment results and clinical indicators, identify the patient's coping style.

Internalization ☐   Externalization ☐
Coping Style   Coping Style

Notes:

FIGURE 9.6. Coping style: Summary worksheet.

behavioral patterns that incorporate both internalizing and externalizing indicators, the clinician will usually observe a pattern that favors one or the other of these styles most of the time. This pattern can be used to cross-validate formal indicators from the MMPI in order to derive a final, reliable judgment.

When the information derived from Figure 9.6 is being used to plan treatment, the guiding rule reflects the belief that externalizing and internalizing patients are sensitive and responsive to interventions aimed at different levels of functioning. Empirical research suggests that, indeed, externalizing patients are most responsive to treatment procedures directed at facilitating behavioral and symptom change, and are quite unresponsive to interventions directed at fostering insight. In contrast, internalizing patients are sensitive to and able to respond to treatments that enhance insight, emotional awareness, or emotional discrimination, but appear to be much less responsive to interventions that focus directly on symptoms and behaviors (Beutler & Clarkin, 1990; Beutler & Consoli, 1992).

Coping style considerations add to treatment strategy by directing the therapist to select the level of intervention (behavioral vs. insight). To provide a complex and patient-responsive treatment plan, this dimension is combined with indicators for directive, nondirective, self-directive, or paradoxical procedures; indicators for objectives of symptom change or systemic theme change; indicators for procedures that either raise or lower the patient's level of discomfort; and indicators for various settings and levels of treatment intensity. Just as it is necessary to integrate information from a variety of sources, it is also necessary to integrate the recommendations and occasional disagreements from among the various dimensions to present a comprehensive picture of the planned treatment program.

The Integrated Treatment Plan

Generating a treatment plan or a set of treatment recommendations is a complex task; it incorporates all of the qualities and characteristics that the patient brings to the treatment environment, as well as the resources of the therapist and the therapist's own personal and interpersonal environment. In developing a treatment plan, the therapist must initially attend to such concerns as treatment setting, format, mode, frequency, duration, and immediate goals. The therapist then proceeds to outline recommended interventions, using the dimensions of motivational distress, problem complexity, reactance level, and coping style to construct a strategy for psychotherapy. By gathering sufficient information before the initiation of treatment, the clinician can develop a plan to match the patient on his/her characteristics of interest. We can see how this process comes together through a closer examination of the treatment planning process.

We have already seen how Figures 9.2 through 9.6 separately permit a clinician to assess a patient's problem severity, motivational distress, problem complexity, reactance level, and coping style. We have also seen how each of these dimensions relates to a separate aspect of an overall treatment strategy. At this point, the clinician can review these strategic decisions and integrate the separate decisions into a single strategy that will guide treatment. To do this, the clinician uses the prescriptive therapy planning form and summary sheet, presented in Figure 9.7. This figure presents a sum-

Directions: Complete this summary sheet <u>after</u> completing the attached worksheets that assess problem severity, motivational distress, problem complexity, reactance level and coping style. Transfer the ratings generated on the worksheets to Part One of this sheet. Then, based on the ratings of the patient's characteristics, identify in Part Two the matching treatment plan. Once a treatment plan has been established, use the treatment planner worksheets to identify interventions that match the plan.

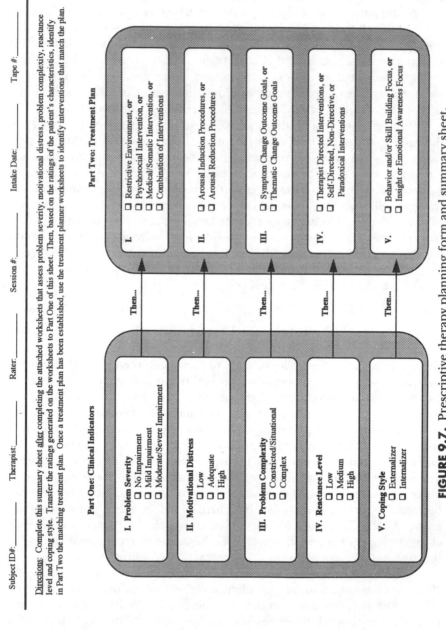

Part One: Clinical Indicators

I. Problem Severity
☐ No Impairment
☐ Mild Impairment
☐ Moderate/Severe Impairment

II. Motivational Distress
☐ Low
☐ Adequate
☐ High

III. Problem Complexity
☐ Constricted/Situational
☐ Complex

IV. Reactance Level
☐ Low
☐ Medium
☐ High

V. Coping Style
☐ Externalizer
☐ Internalizer

Part Two: Treatment Plan

I. ☐ Restrictive Environment, or
☐ Psychosocial Intervention, or
☐ Medical/Somatic Intervention, or
☐ Combination of Interventions

II. ☐ Arousal Induction Procedures, or
☐ Arousal Reduction Procedures

III. ☐ Symptom Change Outcome Goals, or
☐ Thematic Change Outcome Goals

IV. ☐ Therapist Directed Interventions, or
☐ Self-Directed, Non-Directive, or
☐ Paradoxical Interventions

V. ☐ Behavior and/or Skill Building Focus, or
☐ Insight or Emotional Awareness Focus

Then...

FIGURE 9.7. Prescriptive therapy planning form and summary sheet.

310

mary of decisions based upon Figures 9.2–9.6. Figure 9.7 is divided into two sections; the left-hand side summarizes the results of the assessment, and the right-hand side identifies the decisions comprising the treatment strategy.

The clinician attempts to match the data summarized in the first section of the form with the treatment plan components in the second section. For example, consider a patient who is identified with the following dimensional characteristics: motivational distress, high; problem complexity, indicative of thematic patterns; reactance level, low; and coping style, internalizing. The treatment strategy will include the following features: thematic change outcome goals, arousal reduction, focus on facilitating insight and emotional awareness, and use of therapist-directed interventions. The level of problem severity does not require a restrictive environment, and the patient presents himself/herself as a viable candidate for psychosocial therapy. This strategy is derived completely from an assessment of the patient's standing on the five dimensions.

Thus, by placing the various patient variables side by side with their treatment implications, Figure 9.7 allows the clinician to outline an overall *strategy* of treatment. However, missing from this process is a delineation of the techniques through which the strategy may best be implemented. With the general strategy in mind, the clinician can now proceed to the final two steps of treatment planning: (1) the construction and selection of procedures through which to implement the strategic plan, and (2) the implementation of these procedures with some assurance that the planned program is being applied faithfully and skillfully.

The treatment planner worksheets presented in Figures 9.8 and 9.9 translate these general strategies into menus of recommended procedures for patients with complex problems. It should be noted that specific procedures are quite flexible and often can be used in very different ways to adapt to a multitude of treatment needs. Hence, the ones listed in these two figures are suggested only because they appear to be particularly suitable for the purposes indicated. We believe that they have a relatively high probability of effecting change in patients of the types indicated. The specific treatment procedures presented are drawn from various therapeutic approaches. By virtue of the philosophies of different therapy models, the procedures have varying characteristics that make them specifically useful in either raising or lowering arousal, facilitating either insight or behavior change, and adapting to either high or low reactance levels in order to accommodate individual patients' treatment needs. Relaxation procedures, for example, are quite good at changing behavior and lowering distress, having been constructed to do so in compliance with the theory underlying the behavioral model from which they arose. Likewise, transference interpretations have been developed within a theo-

<u>Directions:</u> The following sets of treatment menus have been organized by the variables previously assessed. Use this worksheet when the patient's problem is complex and arousal reduction is needed. Locate the group of treatment interventions that match the patient's predisposing variables. Compliance raters are to use the check boxes beside each intervention.

Behavior Focus

Arousal Reduction & "Fits" Resistant Patient	Arousal Reduction & "Fits" Low Resistant Patient
❑ Emotional support	❑ Thought stopping
❑ Reassurance	❑ Counter conditioning
❑ Relaxation	❑ Covert practice
❑ Hypnosis	❑ Identify automatic thoughts
❑ Structuring	❑ Self instruction
❑ Cathartic discharge	❑ Relaxation
❑ Behavior contracting	
❑ Teaching contingencies	
❑ Graded exposure	
❑ Prescribe "no change"	
❑ Role rehearsal	
❑ Apply stimulus control	
❑ Identify automatic thoughts	
❑ Identify alternative assumptions	
❑ Self monitoring	

Insight Focus

Arousal Reduction & "Fits" Resistant Patient	Arousal Reduction & "Fits" Low Resistant Patient
❑ Reflection/feeling	❑ Focusing
❑ Restatement	❑ Therapist directed imagery
❑ Hypnosis	❑ Supportive interpretation
❑ Question schema & assumptions	❑ Associative imagery
❑ Genograms	❑ Dream interpretation
❑ Dream work	❑ Self statement practice
❑ Supportive transference	❑ Direct instruction
❑ Supportive interpretation	❑ Confront "schematic" assumptions
❑ Redecision work	
❑ Explore themes & schemata	
❑ Symptom or "no change" prescription	

FIGURE 9.8. Treatment planner worksheet: Arousal reduction.

retical model in which therapists are authorities and low arousal is seen as denial. Thus, they may be especially effective in facilitating insight and in increasing arousal.

In selecting procedures to accommodate the needs of the particular patient with complex problems described above, the reader is directed to inspect the lower right-hand menu within Figure 9.8. The patient's characteristics suggest a treatment strategy that is insight-oriented, reduces arousal,

Directions: The following sets of treatment menus have been organized by the variables previously assessed. Use this worksheet when the patient's problem is complex and arousal induction is needed. Locate the group of treatment interventions that match the patient's predisposing variables. Compliance raters are to use the check boxes beside each intervention.

Behavior Focus

Arousal Induction & "Fits" Resistant Patient

☐ Behavior contracting
☐ Teaching contingencies
☐ Overt practice
☐ Prescribe "no change"
☐ Symptom exaggeration
☐ Identify alternative assumptions
☐ Self monitoring
☐ Predict symptom occurrence

Arousal Induction & "Fits" Low Resistant Patient

☐ Closed questions
☐ Directed imagery
☐ Thought stopping
☐ Covert practice

Insight Focus

Arousal Induction & "Fits" Resistant Patient

☐ Silence
☐ Two chair work
☐ Physical movement
☐ Question schema & assumptions
☐ Discuss painful memories
☐ Free association
☐ Free fantasy
☐ Dream work
☐ Predict symptom occurrence

Arousal Induction & "Fits" Low Resistant Patient

☐ Closed questions
☐ Interpretation
☐ Exaggerate sensory state
☐ Directed imagery
☐ Enacting opposites
☐ Confrontation
☐ Interpret transference
☐ Interpret resistance
☐ Analyze unconscious

FIGURE 9.9. Treatment planner worksheet: Arousal induction.

and is adapted to a low-resistant patient. The specific procedures recommended for implementing this strategy include focusing, therapist-directed imagery, supportive interpretation, and directive instruction, all of which are directed as thematic change. In all, eight different menu sets are represented in these two figures, representing the eight basic treatment strategies for addressing complex problems within the systematic treatment selection model.

Directions: The following sets of treatment menus have been organized by the variables previously assessed. Use this worksheet when the patient's problem is non-complex and a pure symptomatic presentation. Locate the group of treatment interventions that match the patient's predisposing variables. Compliance raters are to use the check boxes beside each intervention.

Symptom-Based Behavior Focus

- ☐ Social skill training
- ☐ *In Vivo* or *in vitro* exposure to avoided events
- ☐ Graded practice
- ☐ Reinforcement

Symptom-Based Cognitive-Behavioral Focus

- ☐ Identification of cognitive errors
- ☐ Evaluation of risk
- ☐ Evaluation of distortion
- ☐ Question dysfunctional beliefs
- ☐ Question dysfunctional assumptions
- ☐ Self monitoring
- ☐ Self instruction
- ☐ Practice of alternative thinking
- ☐ Test and evaluate new assumptions

Additional Therapist Tasks for Symptom-Based Problems

- ☐ Therapist's interventions are focused on patient's identified symptoms
- ☐ Therapist presents the proposed interrelationship of events and symptoms
- ☐ Therapist identifies the order of priority for treating the symptoms
- ☐ Therapists engages the patient to collaborate in the procedures of behavioral and cognitive-behavioral change
- ☐ Therapist provides the patient practice opportunities in problem-solving and problem resolution

FIGURE 9.10. Treatment planner worksheet: Symptom-based and noncomplex problems.

Corresponding sets of menus are presented in Figure 9.10 for patients with noncomplex problems. These problems, it will be recalled, are considered to warrant treatments that are largely behavioral or cognitive–behavioral in nature (Beutler & Clarkin, 1990). Foci of these types are designed to initiate symptomatic changes through the alteration of distorted cognitive patterns and disruptive (excessive or insufficient) social or interpersonal behavior. Beutler and Clarkin (1990) offer two sets of generic treatment menus to meet the needs of the two basic types of "simple" symptomatic presentations. The first, designed for a patient with low reactance, includes procedures such as social skills training, *in vivo* or *in vitro* exposure to avoided events, graded practice, and reinforcement, all of which require high levels of therapist direction. Alternatively, when the symptom-based problem is associated with high levels of reactance, a less therapist-directed set of interventions are implemented. Cognitive–behavioral interventions are suggested as the model in this case. Beutler and Clarkin (1990) suggest the following steps in the latter situation: identification of cognitive errors, evaluation of risk or degree of distortion, questioning dysfunctional beliefs and/or assumptions, self-monitoring, self-instruction, the practice of alternative thinking, and testing and evaluating new assumptions. Although treating a symptomatic presentation is not limited to these menus, they do provide useful starting points for treatment.

The final component of treatment planning within the systematic treatment selection model is the assessment of how accurately and skillfully the treatment plan is implemented. To assist in this process, Figure 9.11 presents a series of rating scales that can be applied by supervisors and colleagues to assist in skill development.

These ratings should be based upon observations of entire sessions, and should be completed after a review of the patient characteristics and patterns that emerged in the initial evaluation. The therapist can also complete the form after reviewing his/her own taped sessions, as a means of self-evaluation and self-reflection.

The form presented in Figure 9.11 has two functions: (1) to identify what procedures were used after their prescription, and (2) to rate the therapist's skill in implementing the procedures. The need for such evaluation is indicated by the observation (e.g., Orlinsky & Howard, 1986; Schaffer, 1983) that therapists often exaggerate the degree to which they are able to modify their procedures to fit patients' needs. Furthermore, research suggests that therapist skill is significantly (and positively) related to treatment outcome (Orlinsky & Howard, 1986). Figure 9.11 helps the therapist to observe himself/herself in order to preserve treatment integrity and to enhance the development of therapeutic skill.

In summary, attending systematically to characteristics of the patient that are relevant for treatment planning, and to the skill of the therapist in designing and implementing the treatment, should result in improved and enhanced therapeutic effects. It is imperative that therapists continue to seek new knowledge about the important parameters of effective treatment, basing this knowledge upon sound empirical demonstrations of the clinical efficacy of these interventions. They must then continually seek to increase their skill in applying these effective procedures.

1A Indicate on the following scale, the degree to which the therapist focused upon symptoms or conflictual themes that relate to the patient's condition.

Totally on Symptoms	Mainly on Symptoms	About Equally on Each	Mainly on Conflicts	Totally on Conflicts

├──────────┼──────────┼──────────┼──────────┤

1B. Rate how appropriately matched this focus was to the complexity of the patient's problems.

Consistently Inappropriate	Often Inappropriate	Often Appropriate	Consistently Appropriate

├──────────────┼──────────────┼──────────────┤

1C. Rate the therapist's skillfulness in applying this focus.

Highly Skilled	Moderately Skilled	Inconsistently Skilled	Unskilled

├──────────────┼──────────────┼──────────────┤

2A. Indicate on the following scale, the degree to which the therapist focused upon achieving behavioral/cognitive change versus insight and awareness.

Totally on Insight	Mainly on Insight	About Equally on Each	Mainly on Behavior	Totally on Behavior

├──────────┼──────────┼──────────┼──────────┤

2B. Rate how appropriately matched this level of intervention was to the coping style of the patient.

Consistently Matched	Often Matched	Often Mismatched	Consistently Mismatched

├──────────────┼──────────────┼──────────────┤

2C. Rate the therapist's skillfulness in applying cognitive/behavioral and/or insight interventions.

Highly Skilled	Moderately Skilled	Inconsistentiy Skilled	Unskilled

├──────────────┼──────────────┼──────────────┤

3A. Indicate on the following scale, the degree to which the therapist worked to increase patient's in-session motivational arousal level as opposed to decreasing in-session arousal level.

Totally on Increase	Mainly on Increase	About Equally on Each	Mainly on Decrease	Totally on Decrease

├──────────┼──────────┼──────────┼──────────┤

3B. Rate how appropriately matched this effort to increase or decrease arousal levels was to the patient's level of motivational arousal.

Consistently Inappropriate	Often Inappropriate	Often Appropriate	Consistently Appropriate

├──────────────┼──────────────┼──────────────┤

FIGURE 9.11. Compliance and skill ratings.

3C. Rate the therapist's skillfulness in applying techniques for either increasing or decreasing patient motivational arousal levels.

Highly Skilled	Moderately Skilled	Inconsistently Skilled	Unskilled

├─────────────────┼─────────────────┼─────────────────┤

4A. Indicate on the following scale, the degree to which the therapist applied either non-directive or directive interventions during the therapy session.

Totally on Directive	Mainly on Directive	About Equally on Each	Mainly on Non-directive	Totally on Non-directive

├──────────┼──────────┼──────────┼──────────┤

4A$_1$. If directive in nature, how frequently were these interventions paradoxical in nature?

Very	Sometimes	Rarely	Never

├─────────────────┼─────────────────┼─────────────────┤

4B. Rate how appropriately matched the therapist's use of directive and non-directive interventions were to patient's level of resistance.

Consistently Matched	Often Matched	Often Mismatched	Consistently Mismatched

├─────────────────┼─────────────────┼─────────────────┤

4C. Rate the therapist's skillfulness in applying directive and/or non-directive techniques.

Highly Skilled	Moderately Skilled	Inconsistently Skilled	Unskilled

├─────────────────┼─────────────────┼─────────────────┤

5. Overall, how well do you think this therapist adjusted his/her treatment to fit the patient and situation?

Very Well	Moderately Well	Quite Poorly	Very Poorly

├─────────────────┼─────────────────┼─────────────────┤

Comments:

References

Amchin, J. (1991). *Psychiatric diagnosis: A biopsychosocial approach using DSM-III-R.* Washington, DC: American Psychiatric Press.

American Psychiatric Association. (1994). *Diagnostic and statistical manual of mental disorders* (4th ed.). Washington, DC: Author.

Beck, A. T., & Steer, R. A. (1987). *Beck Depression Inventory: Manual.* San Antonio, TX: Psychological Corporation.

Beck, A. T., & Steer, R. A. (1988). *Beck Hopelessness Scale: Manual.* San Antonio, TX: Psychological Corporation.

Beck, A. T., Ward, C. H., Mendelson, M., Mock, J., & Erbaugh, J. (1961). An inventory for measuring depression. *Archives of General Psychiatry, 4,* 561–571.

Beck, A. T., Weissman, A., Lester, D., & Trexler, L. (1974). The measurement of pessimism: The Hopelessness Scale. *Journal of Consulting and Clinical Psychology, 42,* 861–865.

Beutler, L. E. (1986). Systematic eclectic psychotherapy. In J. C. Norcross (Ed.), *Handbook of eclectic psychotherapy* (pp. 94–131). New York: Brunner/Mazel.

Beutler, L. E. (1987). Systematic eclectic psychotherapy: Growing into separation. In J. C. Norcross (Ed.), *Casebook of eclectic psychotherapy* (pp. 53–90). New York: Brunner/Mazel.

Beutler, L. E., & Clarkin, J. F. (1990). *Systematic treatment selection: Toward targeted therapeutic interventions.* New York: Brunner/Mazel.

Beutler, L. E., & Consoli, A. J. (1992). Systemic eclectic psychotherapy. In J. C. Norcross & M. R. Goldfried (Eds.), *Handbook of psychotherapy integration* (pp. 268–299). New York: Basic Books.

Beutler, L. E., Consoli, A. J., & Williams, R. E. (1994). Integrative and eclectic therapies in practice. In B. Bonger & L. E. Beutler (Eds.), *Foundations of psychotherapy: Theory, research, and practice* (pp. 264–299). New York: Oxford University Press.

Beutler, L. E., Engle, D., Mohr, D., Daldrup, R. J., Bergan, J., Meredith, K., & Merry, W. (1991). Predictors of differential and self-directed psychotherapeutic procedures. *Journal of Consulting and Clinical Psychology, 59,* 333–340.

Beutler, L. E. (Producer), & Gaw, K. F. (Associate Producer). (1993). *Systematic treatment selection: Improving efficacy* [Video]. Santa Barbara: Regents, University of California.

Beutler, L. E., Machado, P. P. P., Engle, D., & Mohr, D. (1993). Differential patient × treatment maintenance among cognitive, experiential, and self-directed psychotherapies. *Journal of Psychotherapy Integration, 3,* 15–31.

Beutler, L. E., Wakefield, P., & Williams, R. E. (1994). Use of psychological tests/ instruments for treatment planning. In M. Maruish (Ed.), *Use of psychological testing for treatment planning and outcome assessment* (pp. 55–74). Hillsdale, NJ: Erlbaum.

Brehm, S. S., & Brehm, J. W. (1981). *Psychological reactance: A theory of freedom and control.* New York: Academic Press.

Butcher, J. N., Dahlstrom, W. G., Graham, J. R., Tellegen, A. M., & Kaemmer, B. (1989). *Manual for the restandardized Minnesota Multiphasic Personality Inventory: MMPI-2. An administrative and interpretive guide.* Minneapolis: University of Minnesota Press.

Dahlstrom, W. G., Welsh, G. S., & Dahlstrom, L. E. (1972). *An MMPI handbook: Vol. 1. Clinical interpretation*. Minneapolis: University of Minnesota Press.

Derogatis, L. R. (1992). *BSI: Administration, scoring and procedures manual—II* (2nd ed.). Baltimore: Clinical Psychometric Research.

Dowd, E. T., Milne, C. R., & Wise, S. L. (1991). The Therapeutic Reactance Scale: A measure of psychological reactance. *Journal of Counseling and Development, 69*, 541–545.

Dowd, E. T., & Wallbrown, F. (1993). Motivational components of client reactance. *Journal of Counseling and Development, 71*, 533–538.

Folstein, M. F., Folstein, S. E., & McHugh, P. R. (1975). "Mini-mental state": A practical method for grading the cognitive state of patients for the clinician. *Journal of Psychiatric Research, 12*, 189–198.

Frank, J. D., & Frank, J. B. (1991). *Persuasion and healing* (3rd ed.). Baltimore: Johns Hopkins University Press.

Graham, J. R. (1990). *MMPI-2: Assessing personality and psychopathology*. New York: Oxford University Press.

Millon, T. (1987). *Millon Clinical Multiaxial Inventory—II (MCMI-II) manual*. Minneapolis: National Computer Systems.

Norcross, J. C. (Ed.). (1986). *Handbook of eclectic psychotherapy*. New York: Brunner/Mazel.

Orlinsky, D. E., & Howard, K. I. (1986). Process and outcome in psychotherapy. In S. L. Garfield & A. E. Bergin (Eds.), *Handbook of psychotherapy and behavior change* (3rd ed., pp. 311–381). New York: Wiley.

Sarason, I. G., Levine, H. M., Basham, R. B., & Sarason, B. R. (1983). Assessing social support: The Social Support Questionnaire. *Journal of Personality and Social Psychology, 44*, 127–139.

Sattler, J. M. (1988). *Assessment of children* (3rd ed.). San Diego, CA: Author.

Schaffer, N. D. (1983). The utility of measuring the skillfulness of therapeutic techniques. *Psychotherapy: Theory, Research, and Practice, 20*, 330–336.

Shea, S. C. (1990). Contemporary psychiatric interviewing: Integration of DSM-III-R, psychodynamic concerns, and mental status. In G. Goldstein & M. Hersen (Eds.), *Handbook of psychological assessment* (2nd ed., pp. 283–307). Elmsford, NY: Pergamon Press.

Spielberger, C. D., Gorsuch, R. L., Lushene, R., Vagg, P. R., & Jacobs, G. A. (1983). *Manual for the State–Trait Anxiety Inventory (Form Y)*. Palo Alto, CA: Consulting Psychologists Press.

Spitzer, R. L., Williams, J. B. W., & Gibbon, M. (1986). *The Structured Clinical Interview for DSM-III-R—Patient version*. New York: Biometrics Research Department, New York State Psychiatric Institute.

Wechsler, D. (1981). *Manual for the Wechsler Adult Intelligence Scale—Revised*. New York: Psychological Corporation.

Welsh, G. S. (1952). An anxiety index and an internalization ratio for the MMPI. *Journal of Consulting Psychology, 16*, 65–72.

10

Integrative Assessment:
A Workbook

M. Anne Corbishley
Elizabeth B. Yost

The purpose of this chapter is to illustrate how the worksheet described in Chapter 2 is used in the integrated approach to assessment. Four cases have been selected to include different levels of pathology and a variety of assessment questions, procedures, diagnoses, and special considerations. To facilitate use of the worksheet, the material has been arranged in the form of a workbook, so that you, the reader, can participate in the process of evaluating and summarizing information from the different procedures. Each case is presented separately and includes results of procedures, blank worksheets for you to complete, sample worksheets as completed by us, and a sample assessment report based on the information provided.

One purpose of the worksheet is to decrease the difficulty of evaluating complex assessment results by focusing on highlights of the patient and on the most relevant or unusual material, without the distraction of facing a mass of detail and irrelevant information. The worksheet is intended to assist *you*: It will be most useful if you keep your comments brief and use the information to stimulate your memory when you write the report. Sometimes only one or two words may be sufficient to direct your thoughts when you are writing the report. Yet care must be taken to evaluate and summarize each procedure within the context of the referral question and of the client's unique characteristics and circumstances.

A second purpose of the worksheet is to encourage you to consider each assessment procedure separately from all others, as far as that is possible, in order to allow the different procedures to make their own unique and uncontaminated contribution to the overall picture. It is therefore important to complete the column for each procedure without reference to preceding information, and without any effort to reconcile possibly conflicting material from different procedures. The "Summary" column, by contrast, views the assessment procedures in comparison to one another, and is the point at which discrepancies are resolved. As you complete the "Summary" column, bear in mind the focus and scope of each procedure, and highlight the interplay among the demand characteristics of the various procedures. Thus, the "Summary" column captures the hypotheses that are common to all or most procedures, and develops new hypotheses that attempt to reconcile differences among procedures. Chapter 2 provides a more detailed discussion of the development of the "Summary" column.

Instructions for Using the Workbook

Work through one case at a time, utilizing and drawing from the forms provided. Before the presentation of each case, a blank summary worksheet is provided. You may make notes on this form in order to help you organize the material. Next, information is provided regarding the patient's history. This information is written as it would be in the first part of a psychological report; it includes demographic/identifying information, the referral question, and the assessment procedures used. Following this material, we provide a brief explanation of the reasons these assessment materials were selected. (This explanation is not ordinarily included as part of the report and is for your information only.) After this comes a description of the case background.

Next, we present a series of materials to help you develop an interpretation of each separate assessment procedure. We proceed through the instruments one at a time, including worksheets for the reader's use, assessment results or test profiles, and a completed worksheet section that describes some of the conclusions we believe are warranted from the assessment instrument. We do not elaborate on how we derived our interpretation; this allows you, the reader, to go back to the relevant chapter, construct your own interpretation, and check this interpretation against ours.

For each case, begin by reading the information provided in the case description: (1) the first part of the sample assessment report, including the referral question and assessment procedures; (2) our explanation for the selection of these procedures, together with other pertinent considerations; and (3) the second part of the sample assessment report, which contains information from the clinical interviews. Then complete the blank interview worksheet and compare your entries with ours on the completed sheet we have provided. Repeat this latter sequence for each of the additional procedures presented: That is, review the results, complete the blank worksheet, and compare your worksheet with the example. Where the results of a procedure would be too limited to be informative or too lengthy to present, the blank worksheet for your completion has been omitted, and only the cells as completed by us have been provided.

Once you have completed the worksheets for all of the procedures used in a given case example, go back and review your worksheets, and summarize the results by completing the blank summary worksheet. Once again, compare your responses with ours, and read the section of the sample assessment report that contains the conclusions, diagnosis, and recommendations.

Case 1: Antonio Ramirez—Sample Report

Identifying Information

Name: Antonio Ramirez
Date of birth: 7/4/62
Sex: Male
Dates of examination: 8/22/94, 8/23/94

Referral Question (Sample Narrative)

Antonio Ramirez, a 32-year-old Latino male, is a sergeant with the Detroit, Michigan, Police Department, currently working as a narcotics officer. In the past few weeks, he has exhibited signs of stress but has refused to take sick leave, claiming that there is nothing wrong. He was referred by his commanding officer for psychological assessment to determine the extent to which recent events in Mr. Ramirez's life may have affected his ability to continue with his present duties.

Assessment Procedures (Sample Narrative)

Mr. Ramirez's personnel file and the referring physician's report were reviewed, and Mr. Ramirez reluctantly agreed to allow his wife, Donna, to be interviewed. On August 22, 1994, Mrs. Ramirez was interviewed for 1 hour while her husband took the Minnesota Multiphasic Personality Inventory—2 (MMPI-2). He complained of headache and blurred vision, which he claimed prevented further assessment that day. He returned the next day for a 1-hour interview, after which he completed the Rorschach and the Wechsler Adult Intelligence Scale—Revised (WAIS-R).

Explanation of Assessment Procedures (Note to Reader)

The referral indicates that this client is in crisis. Since the client's continuation in his present work may be at stake, and he has already denied having

	Interview	Pers. File	Wife/M.D.	MMPI-2	Rorschach	WAIS-R	Summary
Approach and Reliability/Validity							
Cognitive Functioning and Ideation							
Affect/Mood/ Emotional Control							
Conflict Areas							
Intra- and Interpersonal Coping Strategies							
Diagnostic Impression							
Recommendations							

Procedures

FIGURE 10.1. Blank summary worksheet for Antonio Ramirez (Case 1).

problems, assessment must be conducted on the assumption that the client will attempt to conceal pathology. Given this assumption, and the potential for public harm that is presented by an unstable member of the police force, assessment should include procedures that are both structured and unstructured and that also involve a variety of stressors. Input from the client's spouse and personnel file should also be sought in an effort to counteract possible concealment, to provide a fuller picture of the extent of his current impairment, and to identify any previous similar occurrences. The WAIS-R is required to assess possible job-related cognitive difficulties. The MMPI-2 and Rorschach appear appropriate for use with this client, to assess pathology and to present the client with different types of testing demands.

Background (Sample Narrative)

Information Relevant to Referral Question (Sample Narrative)

Mr. Ramirez is currently living with his wife of 8 years, a 6-year-old daughter, and a 4-year-old son. He has been employed by the Detroit Police Department since 1984 and has a satisfactory record. In general his health is good, and he expresses satisfaction with his job and marriage. His social life is limited, which he attributes to the fact that as a police officer he is viewed with unease by potential friends, and also to the unpredictable hours he must work.

He has good relationships with his siblings but sees them rarely, as they all live in distant parts of the country. He has no hobbies and spends his limited spare time at home, occasionally playing with his children, but primarily maintaining his house and yard. His relationship with his wife is by his report close, but he says they rarely discuss feelings and he would not burden her with his worries. His wife describes him as a good husband, faithful, even-tempered, and a loving father, but she says he takes life too seriously, and would like him to learn to have more fun.

Mr. Ramirez was raised by his mother in considerable poverty, his father having died in an industrial accident when Antonio was 8 years old. He remembers his father as "stern, but you knew he loved you." He describes his mother as "always worn out, always sad." At the time of his father's death, there were three younger children, ages 5 years, 3 years, and 6 months. Mr. Ramirez early took on the role of family supporter, working after school and on weekends to add to the family income, and helping to discipline his younger siblings. He remembers his developmental years as "not much fun, a lot of struggling to survive."

At school he was an isolate because of his work schedule and also because he was determined to complete his education, and thus had no time for "fooling with the guys." He learned to fight in self-defense when necessary, to pursue his own course, and to persist at whatever he tried. His sexual development was unremarkable. Since his mother seemed already to be burdened and since he had no close friends, he learned to keep problems and feelings to himself. After 2 years of college he entered the police academy, attracted by the discipline and structure of the organization and the opportunity to defend the public. On the police force he acquired a reputation for being fair, even-tempered, tough, and completely dependable, but not an easy person to get close to—indeed, almost frightening in his self-sufficiency.

In the last 3 months, he has experienced a number of disturbing events. His partner was wounded during a raid; Mr. Ramirez himself was shot at, though not injured, while making a routine traffic check; his wife was attacked, though not raped or physically harmed, on the way home from work one evening; and he was the first on the scene to discover two children under the age of 5 beaten to death in a "crack" house.

This accumulation of violence appears to have affected Mr. Ramirez in several ways. He has had several uncharacteristic outbursts of temper at minor frustrations; on one occasion, to the distress of his fellow officers, he fired his police weapon with insufficient provocation. Somatic symptoms include a 15-pound weight loss over the past 2 months, and (according to his wife) restless sleep and nightmares several times a week. In addition, he has become irrationally overprotective of his family, refusing to let the children visit friends' houses, and angrily demanding that his wife stop work. At work he appears jumpy and distractible, to an extent that has become a concern to his fellow officers. When doing work requiring close attention, he has, on several occasions, developed a headache. Several of his written reports, usually meticulously completed, have contained careless errors and omissions. He has refused to discuss any of these incidents or their impact with his partner, his immediate supervisor, or the police-appointed physician.

When asked about these unusual behaviors, Mr. Ramirez denied that he had changed and claimed that people were exaggerating. On probing, he admitted that sometimes, when he is involved in unrelated daily activities, he gets flashbacks (especially to the scene with the dead children), but claimed that they neither upset him nor made him lose concentration. He attributed his weight loss and restless sleep to the hot summer weather, and insisted throughout the assessment process that he is "fine," that the events of the past months are just part of his job and of life, and that he is capable of continuing to work as before.

Reliability and Validity of Conclusions (Sample Narrative)

At various points in the evaluation, Mr. Ramirez became agitated and appeared irritated; he jokingly accused the examiner of trying to make him remember "things best forgotten." In unstructured situations (i.e., the

TABLE 10.1. Clinical Interview with Antonio Ramirez (Case 1): Blank Cells

Approach and
Reliability/
Validity

Cognitive
Functioning
and Ideation

Affect/Mood/
Emotional Control

Conflict Areas

Intra- and
Interpersonal
Coping Strategies

Diagnostic
Impression

Recommendations

Note. As far as possible from the information provided, fill in the cells by capturing the highlights of the assessment interview.

TABLE 10.2. Clinical Interview with Antonio Ramirez (Case 1):
Cells as Completed by Authors

Approach and Reliability/ Validity	*Denial. Evasive.*
Cognitive Functioning and Ideation	*Distracted, lost thread. Intrusive images.*
Affect/Mood/ Emotional Control	*Frustrated with need for assessment. Flat, distant. Restless, denies dysphoria.*
Conflict Areas	*Difficulty admitting weakness.*
Intra- and Interpersonal Coping Strategies	*Confident, driving, polite, wanting structure. Competent, organized, planful, watchful, defensive.*
Diagnostic Impression	*Severe–extreme psychosocial stress, adjustment disorder, or PTSD.*
Recommendations	*Therapy to deal with avoidant stress management style; remove from immediate stress.*

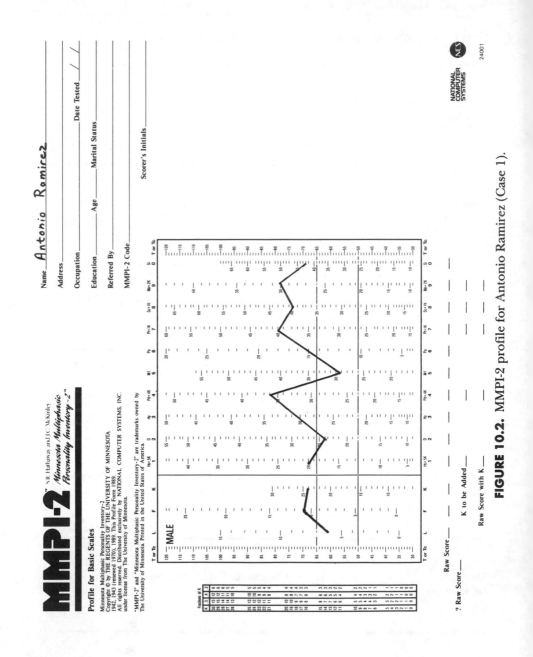

FIGURE 10.2. MMPI-2 profile for Antonio Ramirez (Case 1).

TABLE 10.3. MMPI-2 Profile for Antonio Ramirez (Case 1): Blank Cells

Approach and
Reliability/
Validity

Cognitive
Functioning
and Ideation

Affect/Mood/
Emotional Control

Conflict Areas

Intra- and
Interpersonal
Coping Strategies

Diagnostic
Impression

Recommendations

Note. As far as possible from the information provided, fill in the cells by capturing the highlights of the MMPI-2 profile.

TABLE 10.4. MMPI-2 Profile for Antonio Ramirez (Case 1): Cells as Completed by Authors

Approach and Reliability/ Validity	*Valid. Emotionally distant from own feelings; minimizes conflicts and problems.*
Cognitive Functioning and Ideation	*Able to understand and interpret material; conventional views and perceptions; rigid cognitive processes.*
Affect/Mood/ Emotional Control	*Depressed, insecure mood; overcontrolled hostility; denies emotional problems.*
Conflict Areas	*Impulse control; lacks sense of personal security.*
Intra- and Interpersonal Coping Strategies	*Social discomfort. Suspicious. Judgmental, high social responsibility. Dominant. Self-confident, dogmatic.*
Diagnostic Impression	*Constricted, disturbed mood. No psychosis. No personality disorder. Potential increase in aggression/loss of control unless treated. PTSD.*
Recommendations	*Remove from stressful situations. Psychotherapy re: actual threat and amount of control needed.*

TABLE 10.5. Sample of Rorschach Scores for Antonio Ramirez (Case 1)

Scoring type	Score
R (total responses)	18
F (form, pure)	5
M (movement, pure)	5
FM (form, movement)	4.5
FC (form, color)	3.5
W (whole blot)	8.5
m	3.5

Note. The scoring was based on the Exner system.

TABLE 10.6. Rorschach Profile for Antonio Ramirez (Case 1): Blank Cells

Approach and
Reliability/
Validity

Cognitive
Functioning
and Ideation

Affect/Mood/
Emotional Control

Conflict Areas

Intra- and
Interpersonal
Coping Strategies

Diagnostic
Impression

Recommendations

Note. As far as possible from the information provided, fill in the cells by capturing
the highlights of the Rorschach profile.

TABLE 10.7. Rorschach Profile for Antonio Ramirez (Case 1): Cells as Completed by Authors

Approach and Reliability/ Validity	*High arousal–anger, anxiety. Reduced production. High resistance.*
Cognitive Functioning and Ideation	*Poor reality testing. Not creative.*
Affect/Mood/ Emotional Control	*Blocks strong affect; affective lability; feels threatened; self and life out of control. Aggressive.*
Conflict Areas	*Preoccupation with violence, anger.*
Intra- and Interpersonal Coping Strategies	*Swings from overcontrol to loss of control. Reacts aggressively when frustrated.*
Diagnostic Impression	*Serious disturbance. Critical.*
Recommendations	*Remove from stress. Control hostility. Immediate therapy.*

TABLE 10.8. WAIS-R Results for Antonio Ramirez (Case 1)

Subscale	Raw score	Scaled score	Age-corrected scaled score
Information	28	16	16
Digit Span	12	8	8
Vocabulary	61	13	13
Arithmetic	11	9	9
Comprehension	30	16	16
Similarities	16	8	8
Picture Completion	18	12	12
Picture Arrangement	18	13	13
Block Design	49	16	16
Object Assembly	38	14	14
Digit Symbol	38	6	6

Note. FSIQ = 110; VIQ = 105; PIQ = 115. Total scaled scores = 129; Total Verbal scaled score = 68; Total Perfomance scaled score = 61. Factors: Verbal Comprehension = 118.2; Perceptual Organization = 124; Freedom from Distractibility = 91.6.

TABLE 10.9. WAIS-R Profile for Antonio Ramirez (Case 1): Blank Cells

Approach and
Reliability/
Validity

Cognitive
Functioning
and Ideation

Affect/Mood/
Emotional Control

Conflict Areas

Intra- and
Interpersonal
Coping Strategies

Diagnostic
Impression

Recommendations

Note. As far as possible from the information provided, fill in the cells by capturing
the highlights of the WAIS-R profile.

TABLE 10.10. WAIS-R Profile for Antonio Ramirez (Case 1): Cells as Completed by Authors

Approach and Reliability/ Validity	*Worked hard. Obvious difficulty concentrating.*
Cognitive Functioning and Ideation	*FSIQ = 110, VIQ = 105, PIQ = 115. Memory problems.*
Affect/Mood/ Emotional Control	*Confident. Occasional impatience; clenched fists, deep breath to control self.*
Conflict Areas	*Conformity to authority vs. resentment at being forced to undergo assessment.*
Intra- and Interpersonal Coping Strategies	*Rigid, task-oriented; strict adherence to roles; minimal politeness. Conventional.*
Diagnostic Impression	*Reduced cognitive efficiency, probably stress-related.*
Recommendations	*Work on being less concerned about making mistakes.*

TABLE 10.11. Personnel File for Antonio Ramirez (Case 1): Cells as Completed by Authors

Approach and Reliability/ Validity	*Cumulative over 10 years–different authors.*
Cognitive Functioning and Ideation	*FSIQ = 118.*
Affect/Mood/ Emotional Control	*Stable, controlled, calm.*
Conflict Areas	*Need to be in control.*
Intra- and Interpersonal Coping Strategies	*Inflexible, rather distant, respected but not popular; trustworthy.*
Diagnostic Impression	*No evident pathology; generally functions well; mild social phobia?*
Recommendations	*None indicated.*

TABLE 10.12. Interviews with Wife and Physician Regarding Antonio Ramirez (Case 1): Cells as Completed by Authors

Approach and Reliability/ Validity	*Objective, detailed. Wife worried, may be exaggerating.*
Cognitive Functioning and Ideation	*Forgets routine tasks.*
Affect/Mood/ Emotional Control	*Usually predictable; now wound up tight. Flies off handle— time bomb.*
Conflict Areas	*Won't share feelings.*
Intra- and Interpersonal Coping Strategies	*Kind, reliable, strong. Likes things to go smoothly; can be bossy. Withdrawn. Somaticizes.*
Diagnostic Impression	*Depression?*
Recommendations	*Expand social/recreational life. Express feelings to wife. Couples therapy.*

TABLE 10.13. Summaries across Categories for Antonio Ramirez (Case 1): Blank Cells

Approach and
Reliability/
Validity

Cognitive
Functioning
and Ideation

Affect/Mood/
Emotional Control

Conflict Areas

Intra- and
Interpersonal
Coping Strategies

Diagnostic
Impression

Recommendations

Note. In the cells, summarize the highlights for all assessment procedures. Focus on commonalities and important differences across the cells.

TABLE 10.14. Summaries across Categories for Antonio Ramirez (Case 1): Cells as Completed by Authors

Approach and Reliability/ Validity	*Denial; faking good; temper internal with external information.*
Cognitive Functioning and Ideation	*Reduced efficiency; impaired concentration, memory, reality testing; no thought disorder.*
Affect/Mood/ Emotional Control	*Changed from easygoing to tense, dysphoric. Increased aggression; decreased control over emotions.*
Conflict Areas	*Need to control through autonomy and being strong. Feels obligated to protect others completely.*
Intra- and Interpersonal Coping Strategies	*Conventional, responsible, controlled, reserved; somaticizes; self-confident except socially.*
Diagnostic Impression	*Social phobia; generally effective. No personality disorder. PTSD, multiple stressors.*
Recommendations	*Remove from stressors. Therapy to reduce need to control.*

Rorschach), he produced fewer responses as the test proceeded. It is likely that his high level of arousal affected the validity of his responses to unstructured materials. He had fewer complaints regarding structured materials (i.e., the MMPI-2), but indices of validity indicate an effort to present himself in a favorable light and to deny pathology. During intellectually challenging tasks (i.e., the WAIS-R), he appeared to try hard and was minimally distracted.

All external evidence indicates that Mr. Ramirez's behavior over the past few weeks represents a considerable departure from premorbid levels of functioning, despite his denials. The results of procedures should therefore be interpreted in the light of objective information from external sources.

Summary of Impressions and Findings (Sample Narrative)

On both days of assessment, Mr. Ramirez arrived punctually, in full uniform and meticulously groomed. Whether standing or sitting, he held himself rigidly and made little movement, as if at attention. He made eye contact infrequently and briefly, and spoke in a clear, quite loud, monotone voice, often pausing before speaking, and rarely expanding upon his answers without prompting. Even when he spoke of his inner experiences, he gave the impression of a person making a formal report to a superior. Only while he was responding to unstructured material was there a sense that his responses were spontaneous.

Intellectually, this man is functioning within the "bright normal" range of intelligence, but at a considerably lower level than previous assessment has indicated. In normal circumstances, he thinks carefully and logically (though unimaginatively), and is capable of sustained intellectual efforts. At the present time, he is easily distracted by intense inner experiences. Strong affect and mental images of unpleasant recent events appear to intrude on his problem-solving efforts and reduce his cognitive efficiency. Thus, his concentration and memory are somewhat impaired; recognizing this, he makes halting and ineffective efforts to overcome and compensate. These efforts produce increased physical tension, which may account for his somatic symptoms. It is likely that his reality testing is somewhat impaired under conditions of high stress, especially the stress of perceived threats to his sense of competence or to the welfare of others; under these conditions, his cognitive controls may be insufficient to prevent his becoming overwhelmed by internal or external stimuli. There is no evidence of a thought disorder, and it is likely that he can return to premorbid levels of functioning if he receives appropriate treatment.

Mr. Ramirez's mood is normally bland, almost stoic, with mild expression of emotions appropriate to the situation. He rarely exhibits anger, and, indeed, generally manages his affective experiences so as to avoid arousing strong feelings in himself. He is, however, capable of great emotional intensity, the expression of which he views as weakness, both in himself and in others. His greatest fear is the loss of self-control, since he believes such control to be the prime means of attaining satisfaction in life. Typically, he maintains control over his emotions by avoidance, withdrawal, and denial—even at home, where he feels less need to protect himself. He attempts to prevent both his wife and his children from expressing intense or prolonged affect, both positive and negative. He is experienced by others as emotionally insulated, but not cold or threatening.

Currently, he is reacting with unusual intensity to mild stimuli, and there are indications that he is experiencing acute dysphoria, with barely suppressed rage and frustration. It is apparent that his normal controls over affect are becoming less effective, though he continues to deny either the existence of strong emotion or his own inability to contain it. Since, as a police officer, he must work in daily contact with situations that are bound to elicit unpleasant emotions, and since he will never be able to completely protect his family from all harm, it is likely that his emotions will intensify and that his control will weaken further. A breakdown of control may manifest itself in more severe somatic complaints or in hostile and aggressive action, or in both. It is clear that Mr. Ramirez's current method of dealing with recently encountered stresses is increasingly ineffective.

Mr. Ramirez is generally conforming and conventional, with a need for structure and a strong sense of morality, loyalty, and responsibility to others. He performs best, and experiences a strong sense of competence and self-confidence, in situations where both role and task are clear. He has a need to be—and to be seen as—strong, effective, and in control. To this end, he is planful, vigilant, persistent, and determined, setting goals for himself and pursuing them in an organized manner. When difficulties arise, he tackles them immediately, directly, and actively, and is impatient with ambiguous resolutions to problems. On the other hand, he demonstrates a lack of flexibility and a tendency to be dogmatic and domineering, especially with those he views as inferior or in need of his protection. Because of his confidence and competence, others tend to trust, rely on, and respect him, but they find him emotionally distant and hard to know. Because of these attitudes and behaviors, Mr. Ramirez is, in general, a highly competent police officer.

In his personal life, both his single-minded pursuit of goals and his refusal to acknowledge intense affect make for a rather joyless and dogged existence. His need to avoid appearing vulnerable and his tendency to enjoy solitary pursuits keep him from an active social life, and he experiences considerable discomfort in what appear to him to be purposeless social occasions. Only in his most intimate relationships is he able to relax to some degree—for example, when playing with his children. He has a strong sense of the importance of family, and generally adheres to a traditional view of the male's role as provider and protector. Thus, the recent attack on his wife was experienced by Mr. Ramirez as a severe and multifaceted threat, calling for immediate action. Because he had no control over the situation and has no way to control future, similar situations, Mr. Ramirez feels helpless and vulnerable to a degree that is extremely difficult for him to tolerate.

Diagnostic Impressions (Sample Narrative)

This man's premorbid functioning is likely to have been characterized by mild social phobia, a tendency to restrict affective experiences and expression, and a somewhat rigid personality structure. However, it is likely that he was generally effective in daily living, with stable work and personal relationships. Recent changes in his affect, behavior, and cognitive functioning appear directly related to several severe psychosocial stressors. He reexperiences these events; avoids stimuli associated with the events; and suffers from loss of interest in significant activities, poor concentration, exaggerated startle response, and intense irritability. These symptoms having persisted for at least 1 month, a diagnosis of Post-Traumatic Stress Disorder is warranted.

> Axis I   309.89, Post-Traumatic Stress Disorder
> Axis II   No diagnosis on Axis II
> Axis III   None
> Axis IV   Psychosocial stressors: Injury of partner; wife attacked; discovery of dead children in "crack" house
>   Severity: 4–5 (acute events)
> Axis V   Global Assessment of Functioning (GAF): Current, 53; highest past year, 75

Recommendations (Sample Narrative)

Mr. Ramirez's responses to his environment are increasingly atypical and therefore unpredictable. His current assignment requires self-discipline and cool judgment, which he may no longer be able to produce reliably at premorbid levels. Furthermore, he has apparently almost no insight into his condition, is experiencing anger, and is capable of acting aggressively. It is recommended, therefore, that he be relieved of those duties that involve direct confrontation with violence or danger to himself or to others, with return to active duty contingent upon psychological change.

It is further recommended that Mr. Ramirez seek behavioral psychotherapy—in a group, if possible—that takes a self-management approach. His defensiveness, self-sufficiency, assumption of a conventional male role, and resistance to psychological material indicate that he is unlikely to be a good candidate for insight-oriented psychotherapy, which he would be likely to see as evidence of personal failure. However, it is essential that he learn to modify his need to control every aspect of life, especially if he wishes to continue his present career path. The behavioral/self-management approach seems most likely to present the process of self-examination and change in an acceptable light.

Case 2: Martha Safranek—Sample Report

Identifying Information

> *Name*: Martha Safranek
> *Sex*: Female
> *Age*: 71
> *Date of birth*: 6/13/23
> *Marital status*: Widowed
> *Dates of examination*: 5/14/94, 5/15/94, 5/16/94, 5/18/94, 5/19/94, 5/21/94, 5/23/94
> *Examining psychologist*: Rodney Ranzetta, Ph.D.

Referral Question (Sample Narrative)

This 71-year-old white female, reported to be experiencing confusion, memory loss, and personality change, was admitted to the hospital with malnutrition, dehydration, and exhaustion. Psychological assessment was requested by her physician in order to discover the nature and cause of her current mental condition and to provide guidelines for her future care.

Assessment Procedures (Sample Narrative)

Three 30-minute clinical interviews in the patient's hospital room (May 14, 15, 16) were followed by a 1-hour observation and interview in the patient's home on May 23, 2 days after her discharge. She completed the MMPI-2 on May 18; the Rorschach was administered on May 19; and on the morning of her discharge, May 21, when she was thought to have been restored to physical health, the Folstein Mini-Mental State Examination (MMSE) and the Wechsler Memory Scale (WMS) were administered. The Beck Depression Inventory (BDI, short form) was administered on May 14 and again 1 week later at the patient's home. Hospital Subjective/Objective/Assess-

	Procedures							Summary
	Interview	BDI	MMPI-2	MMSE	WMS	SOAP	Son	Summary
Approach and Reliability/Validity								
Cognitive Functioning and Ideation								
Affect/Mood/ Emotional Control								
Conflict Areas								
Intra- and Interpersonal Coping Strategies								
Diagnostic Impression								
Recommendations								

FIGURE 10.3. Blank summary worksheet for Martha Safranek (Case 2).

342

ment/Plan (SOAP) records were also examined, and her older son was briefly interviewed by telephone.

Explanation of Assessment Procedures (Note to Reader)

In interpreting results from assessment procedures used with older adults, age-related factors that may affect the validity and reliability of results must be taken into account. For instance, healthy nondepressed and physically ill older adults may all present with unusually high depression scale scores. A fatigue factor must also be considered in such a long instrument as the MMPI-2. Furthermore, older adults may be less psychological-minded than younger people, and less inclined to notice or report psychological material, without any intent to misrepresent themselves. Older adults also tend to be more cautious in offering private information and less inclined to endorse extreme or risky alternatives.

In the case of this client, the most important consideration affecting assessment is her physical health status. The conditions mentioned in the referral (dehydration, etc.) can have a severe effect on mental and psychological functioning, especially in older clients, and are likely to render the results of most psychological procedures invalid as measures of typical performance. Furthermore, because of her condition upon admission to the hospital and the likelihood that medications have been administered, it is almost certain that the client would be unable to complete any procedures requiring alertness, energy, and concentration. For these reasons, assessment should take place on several occasions and should not commence until her health has stabilized. The MMPI-2 and Rorschach provide an excellent opportunity for the assessor to evaluate not only current pathology, but, perhaps more important, her cognitive and affective responses to the testing situation. A second important consideration is the likely unreliability of self-report about her daily functioning, because of confusion and memory loss. Information from her family members is therefore essential to evaluating this woman's condition. The hospital SOAP records provide not only an objective record of her behavior, but also an indication of her responsiveness to treatment and her functioning in a new environment. Since the question of long-standing personality traits is not at issue at this point, the Millon Clinical Multiaxial Inventory (MCMI) is not considered necessary. The BDI, administered on two different occasions and in both unfamiliar and familiar environments, indicates intensity and stability of mood. The Folstein MMSE is clearly indicated as a first step in assessing cognitive impairment. It is assumed in cases such as this that assessment conducted in an acute crisis situation is preliminary and will be followed by more intensive investigation as needed, once the client has been allowed to experience the effects of environmental, social, nutritional, and medical changes.

Background (Sample Narrative)

Information Relevant to Referral Question (Sample Narrative)

The patient was the youngest of seven children raised on a farm outside a small prairie town in Alberta, Canada. She remembers her father as "jolly, strong, a rock" and her mother as organized, hard-working, and affectionate. Her parents' marriage was good, with little conflict. Her father was "head of the household," whose family role was to make major decisions and discipline the children. The patient was several years younger than the rest of her siblings, who alternately babied and ignored her. Her parents treated her with more lenience than they had the other children, but still she learned to be obedient and responsible.

Her parents, who were French Canadians and devout Roman Catholics, were somewhat isolated from the largely Presbyterian town; however, this isolation was not felt as a burden, as the family members became their own social network. There were no remarkable aspects to her social, scholastic, sexual, or physical development, and the patient appeared in all respects to be an average child. She completed 10th grade, then went to work in a local feed store. She grew up expecting a life similar to that of her mother, and was, in fact, being courted by a local farmer's son when she met and married Jack Safranek during a visit to a cousin in Montana.

Once she moved with her husband to Heppner, Oregon, Mrs. Safranek gradually lost contact with her family of origin. As far as she knows, her parents and siblings are all deceased. The patient was active in her local church and community women's organization, and once her two boys were in school she occasionally worked part-time as a bookkeeper. However, her primary concern was always her family, where she and her husband played out their traditional roles. Because of her husband's business, the couple had a position of some social importance in the town. Never fully at ease in social settings, the patient learned to adapt to her role by assuming a formal and rather distant demeanor. The patient and her husband moved to Portland when he retired at the age of 70, turning over the business to his older son. The move frightened the patient because of the loss of familiar acquaintances and lifestyle, but it was her husband's dream to live in the city and she did not wish to spoil it for him. In any case, she felt she could rely on him to establish a satisfactory life for them both in their new home.

Before they could get settled in their new community, however, the patient's husband fell ill with cancer. Over the next 2 years, the patient devoted her complete resources to managing his illness, through multiple surgeries, chemotherapy, and his final protracted death at home. During this time, she was completely isolated socially and took up none of her former home craft activities. After his death, she continued to be reclusive, resisting well-meant efforts by church members and others to include her in the community. Her only contacts were weekly telephone calls to her sons, who vainly attempted to persuade her to go out more, or even to move back to Heppner.

With increasing frequency, Mrs. Safranek complained to her physician about her health, but a number of diagnostic procedures failed to discover either the heart problems or the cancer she was convinced she had. When she stopped making frequent requests for medical attention, her physician assumed that she was feeling better. In mid-May, almost a year after her husband's death, the patient telephoned her younger son in Evanston, Illinois, at 3 A.M. *her* time. She sounded confused—unable to say why she was calling, and not sure where she was calling from. She became angry at her son's questions and accused him of not caring about her. He managed to persuade her to visit her physician the next day, arranged for someone local to accompany his mother to the office, and apprised the physician of his mother's condition.

Upon examination, Mrs. Safranek was found to be mildly dehydrated, malnourished, exhausted, and suffering from confusion about why she was visiting her doctor. She had lost 18% of her body weight in the previous 2 months. She agreed to be hospitalized for observation, and, at both sons' insistence, also agreed to psychological evaluation.

Observation of the patient in her home indicated that she was extremely neat, with a large display around the house of mementos from her long marriage. Although things were carefully arranged, the house was quite dirty and the yard untended. The patient explained that she could find no one she trusted to clean or do yard work. She worried excessively and repetitively about small details, such as a noise in the air conditioning unit. The contents of her refrigerator and kitchen cupboards revealed that she subsisted on poor-quality frozen dinners and high-sugar/low-nutrient cereals. Her bathroom cabinet contained multiple half-empty bottles of over-the-counter remedies for constipation, insomnia, heartburn, and "nerves."

Reliability and Validity of Conclusions (Sample Narrative)

The patient took an excessively long time to complete assessment materials. For example, she completed the MMPI-2 in two 1-hour segments, with a 30-minute "rest" period in between. She spent a long time on many of the items, and often changed her answers. However, she eventually completed all items, though it is unclear what effect the 30-minute pause might have had on the results. Likewise, during the interview she was often distracted and rambling in her responses, but she was sufficiently attentive and aware to understand and answer questions. She complained that the BDI made her feel depressed; although her scores were almost identical on the two occasions she took this instrument, she endorsed a very different set of items each time. The Rorschach was terminated by mutual agreement after only four cards, with the patient complaining that her eyes were not good enough to see the pic-

TABLE 10.15. Clinical Interviews with Martha Safranek (Case 2): Blank Cells

Approach and
Reliability/
Validity

Cognitive
Functioning
and Ideation

Affect/Mood/
Emotional Control

Conflict Areas

Intra- and
Interpersonal
Coping Strategies

Diagnostic
Impression

Recommendations

Note. As far as possible from the information provided, fill in the cells by capturing
the highlights of the assessment interviews.

TABLE 10.16. Clinical Interviews with Martha Safranek (Case 2): Cells as Completed by Authors

Approach and Reliability/ Validity	*"Social" demeanor.*
Cognitive Functioning and Ideation	*Sudden onset of memory, concentration problems; mild paranoia; poor problem solving.*
Affect/Mood/ Emotional Control	*Depressed, sad, frightened; frantic pleas for help. Unrealistic, black picture of future and present functioning levels. Focuses entirely on affect.*
Conflict Areas	*Loneliness, not wanting to be a burden. Fear of illness.*
Intra- and Interpersonal Coping Strategies	*Cooperative, sociable, suspicious, impatient; very tidy, yet clothes soiled. Rambles, esp. re: painful material. Talks herself into feeling worse. Exaggerates negatives, glorifies the past. Presents self as a "lady."*
Diagnostic Impression	*Major Depressive Disorder—reactive.*
Recommendations	*Antidepressants, psychotherapy.*

A. (Sadness)
3 I am so sad or unhappy that I can't stand it.
2 I am blue or sad all the time and I can't snap out of it.
1 I feel sad or blue.
⓪I do not feel sad.

B. (Pessimism)
3 I feel that the future is hopeless and that things cannot improve.
2 I feel I have nothing to look forward to.
①I feel discouraged about the future.
0 I am not particularly pessimistic or discouraged about the future.

C. (Sense of Failure)
③I feel I am a complete failure as a person (parent, husband, wife).
2 As I look back on my life, all I can see is a lot of failures.
1 I feel I have failed more than the average person.
0 I do not feel like a failure.

D. (Dissatisfaction)
3 I am dissatisfied with everything.
②I don't get satisfaction out of anything anymore.
1 I don't enjoy things the way I used to.
0 I am not particularly dissatisfied.

E. (Guilt)
③I feel as though I am very bad or worthless.
2 I feel quite guilty.
1 I feel bad or unworthy a good part of the time.
0 I don't feel particularly guilty.

F. (Self-Dislike)
③I hate myself.
2 I am disgusted with myself.
1 I am disappointed in myself.
0 I don't feel disappointed in myself.

G. (Self-Harm)
3 I would kill myself if I had the chance.
2 I have definite plans about committing suicide.
1 I feel I would be better off dead.
⓪I don't have any thoughts of harming myself.

H. (Social Withdrawal)
3 I have lost all of my interest in other people and don't care about them at all.
2 I have lost most of my interest in other people and have little feeling for them.
1 I am less interested in other people than I used to be.
⓪I have not lost interest in other people.

I. (Indecisiveness)
③I can't make any decisions at all anymore.
2 I have great difficulty in making decisions.
1 I try to put off making decisions.
0 I make decisions about as well as ever.

J. (Self-Image Change)
3 I feel that I am ugly or repulsive-looking.
②I feel that there are permanent changes in my appearance and they make me look unattractive.
1 I am worried that I am looking old or unattractive.
0 I don't feel that I look any worse than I used to.

K. (Work Difficulty)
3 I can't do any work at all.
2 I have to push myself very hard to do anything.
1 It takes extra effort to get started at doing something.
⓪I can work about as well as before.

L. (Fatigability)
③I get too tired to do anything.
2 I get tired from doing anything.
1 I get tired more easily than I used to.
0 I don't get any more tired than usual.

M. (Anorexia)
3 I have no appetite at all anymore.
2 My appetite is much worse now.
①My appetite is not as good as it used to be.
0 My appetite is no worse than usual.

FIGURE 10.4. BDI results (first administration, May 14, 1994) for Martha Safranek (Case 2). Total score: 21.

A. (Sadness)
  3 I am so sad or unhappy that I can't stand it.
  ②I am blue or sad all the time and I can't snap out of it.
  1 I feel sad or blue.
  0 I do not feel sad.

B. (Pessimism)
  3 I feel that the future is hopeless and that things cannot improve.
  2 I feel I have nothing to look forward to.
  1 I feel discouraged about the future.
  ⓪I am not particularly pessimistic or discouraged about the future.

C. (Sense of Failure)
  3 I feel I am a complete failure as a person (parent, husband, wife).
  2 As I look back on my life, all I can see is a lot of failures.
  1 I feel I have failed more than the average person.
  ⓪I do not feel like a failure.

D. (Dissatisfaction)
  ③I am dissatisfied with everything.
  2 I don't get satisfaction out of anything anymore.
  1 I don't enjoy things the way I used to.
  0 I am not particularly dissatisfied.

E. (Guilt)
  3 I feel as though I am very bad or worthless.
  ②I feel quite guilty.
  1 I feel bad or unworthy a good part of the time.
  0 I don't feel particularly guilty.

F. (Self-Dislike)
  3 I hate myself.
  2 I am disgusted with myself.
  ①I am disappointed in myself.
  0 I don't feel disappointed in myself.

G. (Self-Harm)
  3 I would kill myself if I had the chance.
  2 I have definite plans about committing suicide.
  1 I feel I would be better off dead.
  ⓪I don't have any thoughts of harming myself.

H. (Social Withdrawal)
  3 I have lost all of my interest in other people and don't care about them at all.
  ②I have lost most of my interest in other people and have little feeling for them.
  1 I am less interested in other people than I used to be.
  0 I have not lost interest in other people.

I. (Indecisiveness)
  3 I can't make any decisions at all anymore.
  2 I have great difficulty in making decisions.
  ①I try to put off making decisions.
  0 I make decisions about as well as ever.

J. (Self-Image Change)
  3 I feel that I am ugly or repulsive-looking.
  2 I feel that there are permanent changes in my appearance and they make me look unattractive.
  1 I am worried that I am looking old or unattractive.
  ⓪I don't feel that I look any worse than I used to.

K. (Work Difficulty)
  ③I can't do any work at all.
  2 I have to push myself very hard to do anything.
  1 It takes extra effort to get started at doing something.
  0 I can work about as well as before.

L. (Fatigability)
  ③I get too tired to do anything.
  2 I get tired from doing anything.
  1 I get tired more easily than I used to.
  0 I don't get any more tired than usual.

M. (Anorexia)
  ③I have no appetite at all anymore.
  2 My appetite is much worse now.
  1 My appetite is not as good as it used to be.
  0 My appetite is no worse than usual.

FIGURE 10.5. BDI results (second administration, May 21, 1994) for Martha Safranek (Case 2). Total score: 20.

TABLE 10.17. BDI Profile for Martha Safranek (Case 2): Blank Cells

Approach and
Reliability/
Validity

Cognitive
Functioning
and Ideation

Affect/Mood/
Emotional Control

Conflict Areas

Intra- and
Interpersonal
Coping Strategies

Diagnostic
Impression

Recommendations

Note. As far as possible from the information provided, fill in the cells by capturing
the highlights of the BDI profile.

TABLE 10.18. BDI Profile for Martha Safranek (Case 2): Cells as Completed by Authors

Approach and Reliability/ Validity	*Endorsed different items each time. Possible exaggeration—she said test "made" her depressed.*
Cognitive Functioning and Ideation	*Unclear about own feelings; indecision.*
Affect/Mood/ Emotional Control	*Severe range of depression on both occasions. Rejects suicide as option. Very reactive to negative stimuli.*
Conflict Areas	*Guilt.*
Intra- and Interpersonal Coping Strategies	*Provided examples, details, as evidence of severity of her feelings.*
Diagnostic Impression	*Depression.*
Recommendations	*Psychotherapy—group.*

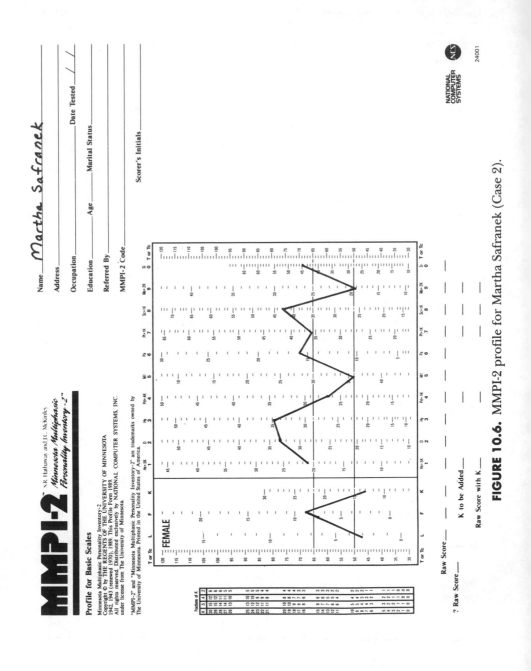

FIGURE 10.6. MMPI-2 profile for Martha Safranek (Case 2).

TABLE 10.19. MMPI-2 Profile for Martha Safranek (Case 2): Blank Cells

Approach and
Reliability/
Validity

Cognitive
Functioning
and Ideation

Affect/Mood/
Emotional Control

Conflict Areas

Intra- and
Interpersonal
Coping Strategies

Diagnostic
Impression

Recommendations

Note. As far as possible from the information provided, fill in the cells by capturing
the highlights of the MMPI-2 profile.

TABLE 10.20. MMPI-2 Profile for Martha Safranek (Case 2): Cells as Completed by Authors

Approach and Reliability/ Validity	*Took her a long time. Made frequent changes in her answers. Inconsistent concentration. Unable to remain objective.*
Cognitive Functioning and Ideation	*Indecisive, confused, unconventional. Unusual ideation.*
Affect/Mood/ Emotional Control	*Depressed, anxious, labile, mildly suspicious. Insecure, rejected, tense. Avoids facing emotional difficulties.*
Conflict Areas	*Excessive bodily concerns.*
Intra- and Interpersonal Coping Strategies	*Obsessive, compulsive, reserved, compliant, modest, sincere; converts psych. distress into somatic complaints. Whines, complains.*
Diagnostic Impression	*Depression, social phobia.*
Recommendations	*Antidepressants. Group psychotherapy. Needs structured interventions—symptom focus.*

TABLE 10.21. Folstein MMSE Results for Martha Safranek (Case 2): Cells as Completed by Authors

Approach and Reliability/ Validity	*Wanted to give up. Distracted by worries about her poor performance.*
Cognitive Functioning and Ideation	*Below age norms. In range of mild dementia.*
Affect/Mood/ Emotional Control	*Anxious, frustrated.*
Conflict Areas	*Desire to give perfect answers.*
Intra- and Interpersonal Coping Strategies	*Self-deprecating, blaming.*
Diagnostic Impression	*Depressed. Rule out dementia.*
Recommendations	*Neuropsych. battery. CAT scan if measures don't work.*

Note. MMSE total score: 24 out of 30.

TABLE 10.22. WMS Results for Martha Safranek (Case 2): Cells as Completed by Authors

Approach and Reliability/ Validity	*Frequent complaints of memory loss; agitated; has less educa-tion than norms for WMS.*
Cognitive Functioning and Ideation	*Below age norms; concerned with own accuracy; unable to decide; many "Don't know's."*
Affect/Mood/ Emotional Control	*Agitation, which increased under pressure.*
Conflict Areas	*Not accepting of age-related changes.*
Intra- and Interpersonal Coping Strategies	*Defensive, hostile.*
Diagnostic Impression	*Depression.*
Recommendations	*Neuropsych. battery; CAT scan if other measures ineffective.*

Note. WMS total score = 80; WMS memory quotient = 74.

TABLE 10.23. Hospital SOAP Records for Martha Safranek (Case 2): Cells as Completed by Authors

Approach and Reliability/ Validity	*Notes recorded by four different staff members are consistent.*
Cognitive Functioning and Ideation	*Observed helping other patient with (easy) crossword; annoyed with self at doing it too slowly.*
Affect/Mood/ Emotional Control	*Frequent complaints about appearance. Self-hatred; self-pity, easily hurt. Withdraws to room, refuses food when very depressed.*
Conflict Areas	*Asking for help before she is desperate.*
Intra- and Interpersonal Coping Strategies	*Reasonably friendly, finicky, doesn't want to be a trouble but demands service. Distracted from personal questions with social trivia. Wanted special attention.*
Diagnostic Impression	*Depression.*
Recommendations	*Socialization.*

TABLE 10.24. Son's Report on Martha Safranek (Case 2): Cells as
Completed by Authors

Approach and Reliability/ Validity	*Information from phone calls confirmed by personal visits in last year.*
Cognitive Functioning and Ideation	*Marked change from premorbid condition: She used to be precise; now indecisive, vague, forgetful, ruminative.*
Affect/Mood/ Emotional Control	*Agitated, tearful, unusually stubborn when depressed; disgusted with self; wishing she could die; fear of illness and being alone; obsessive.*
Conflict Areas	*Can't make up her mind or take action.*
Intra- and Interpersonal Coping Strategies	*Shuts people out; very self-absorbed. Used to be interested in others; has lost usual control over feelings; alternates between clinging and withdrawal.*
Diagnostic Impression	*Major Depressive Disorder—reactive.*
Recommendations	*Antidepressants, psychotherapy.*

TABLE 10.25. Summaries across Categories for Martha Safranek (Case 2): Blank Cells

Approach and
Reliability/
Validity

Cognitive
Functioning
and Ideation

Affect/Mood/
Emotional Control

Conflict Areas

Intra- and
Interpersonal
Coping Strategies

Diagnostic
Impression

Recommendations

Note. In the cells, summarize the highlights for all assessment procedures. Focus on commonalities and important differences across the cells.

TABLE 10.26. Summaries across Categories for Martha Safranek (Case 2): Cells as Completed by Authors

Approach and Reliability/ Validity	*Individual problems; cross-validate carefully.*
Cognitive Functioning and Ideation	*Below normal; memory problems, perseveration, rumination, mild paranoid ideation; aware of and concerned about deficits.*
Affect/Mood/ Emotional Control	*Labile; severe depression, ameliorated by structured social environment; cognitive triad; obsesses, focuses on affect, reduced problem solving; stubborn, approach–withdraw.*
Conflict Areas	*Fears of illness vs. wish to join husband; need to keep up good appearances; excessive bodily concern.*
Intra- and Interpersonal Coping Strategies	*Normally pleasant, compliant, modest, contented, reserved, looks to be taken care of, limited decision making; recent changes to complaining, blaming, suspicious, impatient, self-absorbed, defensive, obsessive–compulsive tendencies.*
Diagnostic Impression	*Major Depressive Disorder.*
Recommendations	*Enhanced environment, nutrition, antidepressant meds, group psychotherapy. Follow by more intensive neuropsych. eval. if deterioration or no remission in 3 months.*

tures clearly, and with the examiner believing that her verbose and irrelevant answers indicated almost total failure to orient to the task.

In spite of her slowness and difficulty, Mrs. Safranek's overall performance was sufficiently consistent to suggest that the assessment represents a fair and adequate estimate of her current functioning. Although each individual assessment procedure can be considered to be somewhat unreliable on its own, it is likely that the cumulative picture that emerges is a fairly reliable and valid one. Because of the consistency that appeared across a wide variety of assessment situations, it is apparent that the difficulties reflect areas of impaired functioning rather than lack of validity of assessment.

Summary of Impressions and Findings (Sample Narrative)

The patient presented as a rather frail elderly woman, neatly dressed in appropriate though not stylish clothes, which hung loosely on her and were somewhat soiled. She was wearing several layers of garments (including a woollen cardigan), despite the warm temperature of the room. She continually plucked at her hair and clothing as if to assure herself that it was all in order, and complained frequently about "their" (unspecified) refusal to let her bring more clothes with her to the hospital. For much of the time, she sat immobile, head bowed, speaking almost inaudibly; at intervals she became restless, wringing her hands, chewing her lips, and speaking in an agitated fashion.

By self-report and the observation of family members, this patient's cognitive functioning has deteriorated considerably in the past year, with sudden onset after the death of her spouse. Assessment procedures indicate that she is functioning below normal for her age in the areas of memory, concentration, problem solving, and decision making. She is aware of and is distressed by her deterioration, tending to focus her attention almost exclusively on this and on other negative aspects of her life, comparing herself unfavorably to others of her age and to her own former levels of functioning. She has an active imagination over which she apparently has little cognitive control at this time. In addition, she tends to perseverate and experiences occasional paranoid ideation, which she inconsistently recognizes as unreasonable, but makes no effort to control. She is generally oriented to time, place, and person, and had little difficulty understanding and remembering hospital routines, indicating a somewhat fluctuating course to her deficits. Her cognitive difficulties are in the mild to moderate range, and a multifaceted treatment approach should have some success in ameliorating these.

At present, the patient's dominant mood is that of severe depression, occasionally reactive to the environment (in particular, to social contact). She is consistently negative about herself, life, and the future, and tends to focus primarily on affect, retreating from planfulness and activity when she is feeling worst. She also reports fear of becoming ill, of being alone, and of dying alone, though she states that she wishes she would die soon so that she can join her husband and be at peace. She is adamant that her religious views prevent even the thought of suicide, so she feels trapped and helpless in her life. She also alternately blames herself, others (especially her sons), and God for her condition, but then experiences guilt that she has done so.

Reportedly, she has always had intense emotional reactions to even minor events; however, her affect has typically been appropriate, and her sons have (up until the present) been able to manage her somewhat exaggerated expression of emotions with relative ease. When she is under acute stress, her general pattern throughout life has been to overemote, give up easily, rely heavily on others' guidance and help, and withdraw if the situation is not speedily resolved. These tendencies are exacerbated in her present state, and complicated by high suspiciousness of others' motives. Thus she alternates between cries for help (which she then refuses) and a stubborn retreat into pseudoindependence.

The patient tends in general to reflect little on psychological matters, preferring a somatic or external explanation for her problems. She has little confidence in her own problem-solving and coping abilities, and tends to belittle or fail to recognize her positive characteristics and achievements. Typically, she is friendly and compliant, modest, and reliable, and makes few demands on others (apart from their continued support). In general, she takes life seriously but is capable of deep enjoyment as long as her safety needs are ensured. She is concerned to follow the conventions of society and to fulfill her role diligently. Within a restrictive but supportive social sphere (such as she has experienced for most of her life), she functions well; she is able to make independent decisions on matters she considers her realm, and can establish satisfactory intimate relationships. In these close relationships, she is warm and expresses affection easily, but she is slow to establish relationships that allow her to relax and be emotionally expansive. Although she may appear overly dependent on intimates for security and satisfaction, it should be noted that she has always taken a fairly active part in community life and has shown no tendency to isolate herself because of acute social discomfort. Her basic common sense is evidenced by the fact that she experienced no adverse emotional effects when her sons grew up and left home; this was what she had anticipated and what she felt was appropriate.

With acquaintances, she tends to be helpful but reserved, taking a leadership role only when required to do so by social convention. She usually experiences others as friendly and accepting. Thus, her current mistrustful, self-absorbed, blaming, and complaining behaviors are a marked departure from her usual approach to people. Similarly, she typically used to exhibit an energetic and organized approach to activities, in contrast to her present apathy, lack of motivation, and comprehensive indecisiveness.

Diagnostic Impressions (Sample Narrative)

The patient's symptomatology is consistent with a diagnosis of Major Depressive Disorder. Although it is possible that a dementing condition underlies her present mood disorder, there is no substantive evidence of such at this time, and the prognosis for recovery with aggressive treatment is good.

Axis I   296.24, Major Depression, single episode, with psychotic features
Axis II   No diagnosis
Axis III Malnutrition; poor hygiene and personal care; dehydration
Axis IV   Psychosocial stressor: Death of spouse
          Severity: Extreme (acute event)
Axis V   GAF: Current, 38; highest past year, 52

Recommendations (Sample Narrative)

Because it is clear that the patient is presently unable to care for her physical and emotional needs while living alone, it is recommended that she be persuaded to move to an environment where nutritionally enhanced meals will be furnished on a regular basis and where social support will be provided. If she refuses this move, the next option would be the combination of a live-in housekeeper and attendance at a geriatric day care and partial care program.

A course of antidepressant medication may also be appropriate, and, if possible, attendance at group therapy designed for her own age group and aimed at combating depression. Her relative lack of psychological sophistication and insight, together with her current cognitive difficulties, would suggest that therapy be supportive, highly focused, and reasonably directive.

If deterioration in her condition is noted or if noticeable progress does not occur within 3 months, the possibility of dementia should be reconsidered, with more extensive medical and neuropsychological assessment.

Case 3: Carson Whitter—Sample Report

Identifying Information

Name: Carson Montgomery Whitter
Sex: Male
Age: 23
Date of birth: 3/11/71
Marital status: Single
Date of examination: 9/10/94

	Procedures					Summary
	Interview	MMPI-2	MCMI-II	WAIS-R	Rorschach	
Approach and Reliability/Validity						
Cognitive Functioning and Ideation						
Affect/Mood/ Emotional Control						
Conflict Areas						
Intra- and Interpersonal Coping Strategies						
Diagnostic Impression						
Recommendations						

FIGURE 10.7. Blank summary worksheet for Carson Whitter (Case 3).

Referral Question (Sample Narrative)

The subject is a 23-year-old white male referred by the Cook County District Attorney's Office for psychological evaluation. The subject was arrested for the attempted robbery of a jewelry store, during which a night watchman was seriously injured. The purpose of the evaluation was to assist in determining the subject's legal sanity and his ability to participate in his own defense.

Assessment Procedures (Sample Narrative)

MCMI-II
WAIS-R
MMPI-2
Rorschach
Clinical interview

Explanation of Assessment Procedures (Note to Reader)

This is a serious but relatively straightforward assessment situation, requiring a well-rounded battery of procedures that will provide the necessary information to answer the single question of legal sanity. Since there is a strong possibility in these circumstances that the subject will attempt to influence the assessment process, an instrument such as the Rorschach is important, as is the WAIS-R to assess intellectual capacity and functioning.

Background (Sample Narrative)

Information Relevant to Referral Question (Sample Narrative)

The subject was interviewed while he was in jail awaiting trial for attempted armed robbery and assault. He was a charming, exceptionally good-looking young man, stylishly dressed, with a warm handshake and ready smile. He was very convincing in the sincerity of his desire to reform, yet appeared not to be concerned about his possible fate.

Mr. Whitter grew up in an upper-middle-class suburb of Chicago, the fourth of five children. His parents still work at a family-owned, relatively successful heating and air-conditioning company, which affords them a good living. When the subject was growing up, his parents drank heavily, with the father routinely beating up his wife and children when he was drunk. The subject relates disliking his father and doing his best to avoid all contact with him. His mother tried, unsuccessfully, to protect herself and her children from violence. The subject remembers her with some contempt, since she would inevitably make the first effort to restore the relationship with her husband after a beating.

From an early age, the subject was in trouble at home for lying, stealing, or bullying his younger brother. At the age of 8, he began charging items at the local store to his father's account, and later stole small appliances from home and sold them. Discipline for these offenses was inconsistent: At times he was punished with a beating; at other times his parents, the father especially, seemed to regard the son's exploits as "cute"; if covering up his misdeeds with elaborate lies did not work, the subject was almost always able to convince his parents how sorry he was, promising that it would not happen again. His siblings learned early not to trust him, but found him a useful scapegoat, because their parents would readily believe any accusations made against the subject. As he grew more daring and aggressive, his brothers and sisters came to fear him and generally kept out of his way. Since he felt no comradeship or kinship with any of his family, he was content to be left alone, and consequently had a great deal of unstructured and unsupervised time in which he could turn to troublemaking.

At school, he was restless and bored, although he would perform well for a while in subjects that caught his interest. In the second grade he was tested for Attention-Deficit Hyperactivity Disorder, but did not quite meet criteria for the diagnosis. Throughout his early school years, his teachers saw his potential and were misled by his facile manner; consequently, he was assigned to various individual and small-group programs designed to increase his motivation and improve his work habits and social skills. At first, these efforts would appear to be successful, until undermined by the boy's preference for making trouble and avoiding work.

Although he never had a steady group of friends or any close friends, he was often in the company of other children who, although somewhat afraid of him, tended also to enjoy his bravado and willingness to defy authority. For his part, he enjoyed being the center of attention, and would tell exaggerated tales of his exploits and ambitions. He was sexually precocious and promiscuous, first experiencing intercourse at age 12, then moving through a series of brief and always self-centered sexual encounters. He has never concerned himself about the possibility of sexually transmitted disease and considers pregnancy the woman's problem.

In his adolescence, the subject did well in auto mechanics, sporadically played football, and acted in school plays, but otherwise had little investment in school. Although he was often truant and was expelled for one semester for hitting a teacher, he might have graduated with minimal requirements, except that at age 17 he was arrested for sexually molesting an 8-year-old girl and was sentenced to 3 years in a juvenile detention center. There, he participated in several educational and rehabilitation courses with apparent enthusiasm and a sincere desire to reform, but soon found reasons to drop out.

After early release for good conduct, he talked his way into a variety of jobs and even received promotions, despite his lack of qualifications. Employers usually had to let him go, however, when they became disenchanted with his unreliability and frequent use of his work position to commit criminal acts of varying severity. He had numerous encounters with the law, but somehow always managed to evade prosecution.

Reliability and Validity of Conclusions (Sample Narrative)

This man's response to the evaluation was colored throughout by his need for self-aggrandizement and his limited capacity for sustained attention. He was superficially cooperative with the procedures, expressing an interest in their purpose and a convincing willingness to present himself honestly. However, as his initial interest waned, he became more extravagant in his approach—laughing at the "stupidity" of some questions, and expanding on the details of his misdeeds in an apparent attempt to shock the interviewer. He tended to be overconfident and careless, regarding the assessment on the whole as a sort of game, which he assumed he would win.

He approached intellectual and factual tasks carelessly and was easily distracted; it is possible that results from these types of questions underestimate his true capability. The unstructured tasks seemed to induce minimal investment, and as these tasks became longer, he gave fewer and fewer responses, reviving briefly when emotionally laden material was introduced (i.e., the color cards on the Rorschach). Again, this procedure may not have adequately captured a picture of more complex aspects of his functioning. When he was provided with structured materials toward the end of the assessment period (i.e., the MCMI-II), he was quite sullen and resentful at having to continue his performance beyond what he had anticipated.

Despite this less than conscientious approach to the assessment, this patient was undoubtedly aware of its purpose and gave no evidence of trying to evade or deceive. Furthermore he did complete all the procedures, and any questions he asked were relevant to the process. It is possible that his demeanor was a form of habitual bravado, beneath which he was actually performing reasonably well. On the whole, it is likely that the results are quite representative of this man's personality and functioning.

Summary of Impressions and Findings (Sample Narrative)

This man is functioning in the "high average" range of intelligence. He perceives and thinks quickly, is mentally alert, has the capacity to organize his

TABLE 10.27. Clinical Interview with Carson Whitter (Case 3): Blank Cells

Approach and
Reliability/
Validity

Cognitive
Functioning
and Ideation

Affect/Mood/
Emotional Control

Conflict Areas

Intra- and
Interpersonal
Coping Strategies

Diagnostic
Impression

Recommendations

Note. As far as possible from the information provided, fill in the cells by capturing
the highlights of the assessment interview.

TABLE 10.28. Clinical Interview with Carson Whitter (Case 3): Cells as Completed by Authors

Approach and Reliability/ Validity	*Flippant, exaggerates strengths; boasts of misdeeds, not defensive; charming, overtly cooperative.*
Cognitive Functioning and Ideation	*Rapid rate of thinking; occasionally tangential, distractible, grandiose; lies to make impressions; doesn't learn from exper.*
Affect/Mood/ Emotional Control	*Cheerful, unaffected by situation; contempt for testing and examiner; no remorse or empathy; sudden loss of charm when criticized. Angry.*
Conflict Areas	*Manipulating interviewer without too much loss of self-indulgence.*
Intra- and Interpersonal Coping Strategies	*Self-centered, self-deceptive. No sense of how others react to him or to his behavior; socially competent when convenient; some difficulty maintaining facade; enjoys attention.*
Diagnostic Impression	*Untrustworthy, amoral, potentially dangerous.*
Recommendations	*Needs impulse control, self-regulation to anticipate consequences of behavior.*

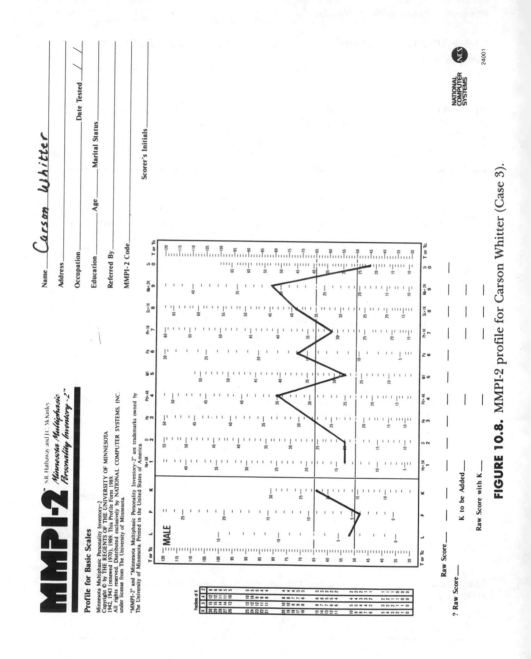

FIGURE 10.8. MMPI-2 profile for Carson Whitter (Case 3).

TABLE 10.29. MMPI-2 Profile for Carson Whitter (Case 3): Blank Cells

Approach and
Reliability/
Validity

Cognitive
Functioning
and Ideation

Affect/Mood/
Emotional Control

Conflict Areas

Intra- and
Interpersonal
Coping Strategies

Diagnostic
Impression

Recommendations

Note. As far as possible from the information provided, fill in the cells by capturing
the highlights of the MMPI-2 profile.

TABLE 10.30. MMPI-2 Profile for Carson Whitter (Case 3): Cells as Completed by Authors

Approach and Reliability/ Validity	*Finished fast; not invested—a game. Incomplete—25 items omitted.*
Cognitive Functioning and Ideation	*Grandiose, poor judgment, little insight; loses control of thought processes. Not manic or psychotic.*
Affect/Mood/ Emotional Control	*Expansive mood; euphoric to bored/restless; fluctuating control; lacks empathy; inappropriate, shallow.*
Conflict Areas	*Authority. No consequences.*
Intra- and Interpersonal Coping Strategies	*Reckless, thrill-seeking; manipulative, self-indulgent; superficial relationships; gregarious, charming; unrealistic view of own abilities. Amoral, immature.*
Diagnostic Impression	*Antisocial, Narcissistic.*
Recommendations	*Therapy unlikely to be effective; control interpersonal behavior; provide alternative outlet for thrill-seeking impulses.*

MILLON CLINICAL MULTIAXIAL INVENTORY-II
FOR PROFESSIONAL USE ONLY

```
ID NUMBER = 11918954          VALID REPORT
PERSONALITY CODE = 6A 5 ** 6B * 1 8A 7 + 4 2 8B " 3    // - ** - *
SYNDROME CODE = - ** - * // - ** - * //
DEMOGRAPHIC = 00130653/ON/M/26/W/N/H12/P/AL/MA/30390/07/06/-----/  334 0028
```

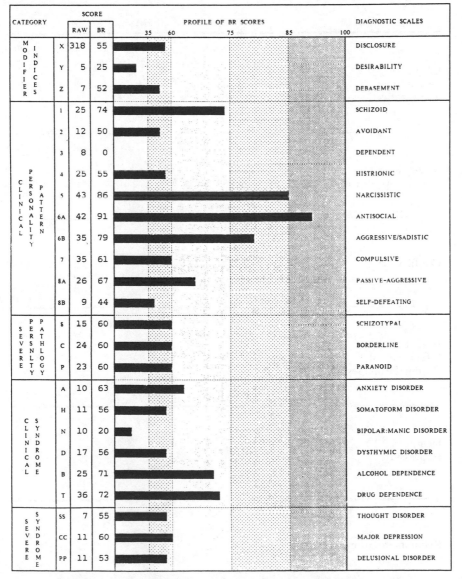

FIGURE 10.9. MCMI-II profile for Carson Whitter (Case 3).

TABLE 10.31. MCMI-II Profile for Carson Whitter (Case 3): Blank Cells

Approach and
Reliability/
Validity

Cognitive
Functioning
and Ideation

Affect/Mood/
Emotional Control

Conflict Areas

Intra- and
Interpersonal
Coping Strategies

Diagnostic
Impression

Recommendations

Note. As far as possible from the information provided, fill in the cells by capturing the highlights of the MCMI-II profile.

TABLE 10.32. MCMI-II Profile for Carson Whitter (Case 3): Cells as Completed by Authors

Approach and Reliability/ Validity	*Sullen, laughed, critical, but completed test. Last procedure.*
Cognitive Functioning and Ideation	*Undisciplined imagination; plausible self-justification.*
Affect/Mood/ Emotional Control	*Lacks guilt or anxiety; optimistic, callous, easily frustrated; no efforts to control mood.*
Conflict Areas	*Maintaining unrealistic self-image.*
Intra- and Interpersonal Coping Strategies	*Irresponsible, exploits. Feels entitled. Flaunts conventions; arrogant; high self-image. Feels special. Acts out.*
Diagnostic Impression	*Antisocial Personality Disorder; Narcissistic Personality Disorder.*
Recommendations	*Needs impulse control, self-regulation, empathy training; needs to learn to anticipate consequences of behavior.*

TABLE 10.33. WAIS-R Results for Carson Whitter (Case 3)

Subscale	Raw score	Scaled score	Age-corrected scaled score
Information	26	15	14
Digit Span	22	11	14
Vocabulary	63	14	15
Arithmetic	10	8	8
Comprehension	15	7	7
Similarities	24	13	13
Picture Completion	19	14	14
Picture Arrangement	9	7	7
Block Design	51	19	19
Object Assembly	41	18	18
Digit Symbol	59	10	10

Note. FSIQ = 120; VIQ = 110; PIQ = 127. Total scaled scores = 136; Total Verbal scaled score = 68; Total Perfomance scaled score = 68. Factors: Verbal Comprehension = 122.4; Perceptual Organization = 142; Freedom from Distractibility = 105.6.

TABLE 10.34. WAIS-R Profile for Carson Whitter (Case 3): Blank Cells

Approach and
Reliability/
Validity

Cognitive
Functioning
and Ideation

Affect/Mood/
Emotional Control

Conflict Areas

Intra- and
Interpersonal
Coping Strategies

Diagnostic
Impression

Recommendations

Note. As far as possible from the information provided, fill in the cells by capturing the highlights of the WAIS-R profile.

TABLE 10.35. WAIS-R Profile for Carson Whitter (Case 3): Cells as Completed by Authors

Approach and Reliability/ Validity	*Careless, confident; results probably underestimate ability.*
Cognitive Functioning and Ideation	*FSIQ = 120, PIQ = 127, VIQ = 110. Good resources, but somewhat distractible, loses concentration. Poor interpersonal judgment.*
Affect/Mood/ Emotional Control	*Appeared to develop buoyant self-confidence that carried him along. Exaggerated mood. Lacks foresight; affect may be inappropriate.*
Conflict Areas	*Appearing "brilliant" without obeying the rules.*
Intra- and Interpersonal Coping Strategies	*Impulsive; makes light of errors; when frustrated, dismisses, belittles, gets angry at source.*
Diagnostic Impression	*Immature. Rule out Bipolar, Antisocial, and Cyclothymic Disorders.*
Recommendations	*Needs impulse control, self-regulation, empathy training; needs to learn to anticipate consequences of behavior.*

TABLE 10.36. Sample of Rorschach Scores for Carson Whitter (Case 3)

Scoring type	Score
R (total responses)	23
Average response time	26 seconds
F (form, pure)	7
M (movement, pure)	2.5
FM (form, movement)	5.5
FC (form, color)	1.5
W (whole blot)	8.5
m	1

Note. The scoring was based on the Exner system.

TABLE 10.37. Rorschach Profile for Carson Whitter (Case 3): Blank Cells

Approach and
Reliability/
Validity

Cognitive
Functioning
and Ideation

Affect/Mood/
Emotional Control

Conflict Areas

Intra- and
Interpersonal
Coping Strategies

Diagnostic
Impression

Recommendations

Note. As far as possible from the information provided, fill in the cells by capturing the highlights of the Rorschach profile.

TABLE 10.38. Rorschach Profile for Carson Whitter (Case 3): Cells as Completed by Authors

Approach and Reliability/ Validity	*Initial interest waned fast, revived for color cards. Decreased productivity as boredom grew.*
Cognitive Functioning and Ideation	*Quick perception; able to organize thoughts, moderately creative; alert, fast responses; fantasy life? Capable of abstraction.*
Affect/Mood/ Emotional Control	*Poor control. Affect labile; moods urgent. Easily angered. Unrestrained emotions.*
Conflict Areas	*Meeting need for stimulus.*
Intra- and Interpersonal Coping Strategies	*Poor ego control; no goals, no planning; impulsive, assaultive, self-centered.*
Diagnostic Impression	*Uncontrolled, alienated.*
Recommendations	*Provide external or internal means to control cognitive, behavioral, affective impulsivity.*

TABLE 10.39. Summaries across Categories for Carson Whitter (Case 3): Blank Cells

Approach and
Reliability/
Validity

Cognitive
Functioning
and Ideation

Affect/Mood/
Emotional Control

Conflict Areas

Intra- and
Interpersonal
Coping Strategies

Diagnostic
Impression

Recommendations

Note. In the cells, summarize the highlights for all assessment procedures. Focus on commonalities and important differences across the cells.

TABLE 10.40. Summaries across Categories for Carson Whitter (Case 3): Cells as Completed by Authors

Approach and Reliability/ Validity	*Colored by self-aggrandizement and boredom; careless, hasty, no effort to deceive.*
Cognitive Functioning and Ideation	*IQ above average; undisciplined thought processes; fantasy life. No insight. Capable of more than he produces. Understands right and wrong.*
Affect/Mood/ Emotional Control	*Lacks empathy, remorse, anxiety; euphoric. Self-confident or bored. Unrestrained, easily frustrated. Shallow.*
Conflict Areas	*Defies rules; needs stimulus; needs attention; cannot foresee consequences or understand others.*
Intra- and Interpersonal Coping Strategies	*Entitled. Exploits. Impulsive, reckless. Superficial relationships, charms; no plans/goals, no self-control.*
Diagnostic Impression	*Antisocial, alienated, narcissistic.*
Recommendations	*Stand trial.*

thoughts, and can think abstractly. He is moderately creative and has a good imagination, which he directs mainly toward unrealistic and exaggerated visions of his own importance and of past or future achievements. He also uses his powers of invention to manipulate others, to justify his own behavior, or to create a favorable impression of himself, usually in order to avoid responsibility or retribution. His perception of reality is not, however, impaired.

His cognitive efficiency is limited by his failure to exercise control over his thought processes. He tends to be distractible, is occasionally grandiose in his thinking, and often shows poor judgment. He does not learn well from experience, in the sense that he repeats behaviors that lead to similar aversive consequences. There is no evidence of psychosis or mania in the content or process of his mentation, but under stress he is likely to let go of cognitive control and allow himself to be carried along on a wave of emotion and imagination. That he is, in fact, capable of controlling his thinking is indicated by his ability to "turn on the charm" when he wishes to; he can select socially appropriate subjects to discuss, in the style and vocabulary most likely to meet his manipulative ends. Although he generally does not plan or set goals (or, indeed, organize his thinking beyond what is needed to provide gratification of immediate needs), he is capable of the planning necessary to, for example, devise a fairly elaborate confidence game. He does not consider the consequences of actions before initiating them, but this appears to be the result of a belief that they will not apply to him, rather than of an inability to understand the concept of consequences. He can, for example, anticipate which of his behaviors will be more or less effective in exploiting a situation for gain.

This man also understands the concept of right and wrong, and can articulate that many of his actions are wrong according to the standards of others. He quite simply does not find the concept of morality important, and prefers to discount conventional mores and laws as long as he can get away without punishment. He has, however, only a feeble understanding of others' emotional reactions to him. He has no sense of their feelings or of the negative impact he has on their lives, though he certainly understands other people and social situations well enough to be able to manage them to his advantage.

The subject's dominant mood is an expansive and optimistic self-confidence. This alternates with a restless boredom and a need for excitement, or with sharp descents into frustration and anger when his immediate desires are not satisfied or when he believes that he is being criticized or laughed at. His affect is typically shallow, constrained, and entirely self-focused. He rarely experiences anxiety, guilt, remorse, sadness, pity, or warmth, and so tends to be unaffected to any great degree by the situation in which he finds himself. His affect may be inappropriate, in that his lack of empathy allows him to laugh at or ignore suffering. If he occasionally experiences a sense of isolation and alienation, he is unable to acknowledge that to himself or to others, and is likely to cope with it by seeking attention from the nearest person or by distracting himself with acting-out behavior or dreaming of personal glory. He has no personal experience or understanding of intimacy; although he can recognize that others appear to need and desire close relationships, he regards this "weakness" simply as a convenient and effective tool for manipulation. In his relationships with women, he is particularly prone to play on their desire both to nurture and to reform him, but quickly abandons them if their emotional demands become stifling.

He experiences his moods as urgent and in general makes little effort to control them, instead allowing his emotions to direct his behavior, which then functions to discharge his needs. Efforts at control are usually made only in the service of a selfish goal, such as sexual gratification; even here, however, his control is limited, and he easily and quickly reverts to acting out in the form of aggression against whoever is thwarting him.

Although self-deceptive, the subject's self-image is good. He views himself as important, as gifted, and as entitled to special treatment because he is different from (i.e., better than) "average" people. He therefore feels justified in exploiting others for his own ends and is enraged if he is required to follow rules laid down for everyone else, or if anyone criticizes him or challenges his high self-esteem. He believes that he has the capacity to be or do anything he wishes, without the sustained efforts that most people would need to invest. Thus, he embarks on ventures without planning but with every expectation of success. Frequently, his high energy, self-confidence, and ability to charm and attract others actually do make for success, at least temporarily. He does not sustain endeavors, partly because he becomes bored and partly because that would require effort and a delay in gratification. In keeping with his self-image, he denies or dismisses mistakes he might make, and becomes angry and frustrated when he is finally brought to task for his crimes or misdemeanors. His behavior is impulsive, reckless, and self-indulgent, with a disregard for damage to person or property. He is capable of assaultive and violent actions, either when these are an incidental part of a venture or when he is frustrated in the attainment of an immediate goal.

His interpersonal relationships are shallow, insincere, and usually quite short, since he loses interest fast. He exploits others callously and is irresponsible in all spheres of life: He makes elaborate and convincing promises but does not keep them; he fails to fulfill responsibilities at work or in his interpersonal roles. He is able to make friends easily, having the intelligence and perception to recognize what will be most effective in bringing someone under his influence. Socially he can be very skilled, and enjoys the limelight, which is where he usually takes care to stand. Others initially find him daring, fun, and exciting, and are attracted by his confidence and his sense of adventure; however, most eventually realize his coldness, arrogance, and utter self-absorption. He has no intimates with whom he shares feelings or mutual plans—only people who are subservient to him and either will fill basic needs (such as providing a home and sexual favors) or will accompany him admiringly on reckless adventures. Although he has no loyalty or devotion toward others, he demands that he be of prime importance in their lives for as long as is convenient to him.

Diagnostic Impressions (Sample Narrative)

All indications are that this man suffers primarily from Antisocial Personality Disorder, with a secondary diagnosis of Narcissistic Personality Disorder; both disorders appear to be well entrenched and are likely to be highly resistant to change. However, neither of these disorders significantly affects this subject's ability to reason or to know the nature and quality of his actions. He also seems to have an awareness of the nature of right and wrong, and is capable of understanding the nature and consequences of his behavior.

Recommendations (Sample Narrative)

It appears that this man has the mental capacity and orientation to reality to be able to contribute to his own defense, and that he otherwise meets the criteria for legal sanity.

Case 4: Petra Stanhope—Sample Report

Identifying Information

> *Name*: Petra Peterson Stanhope
> *Sex*: Female
> *Date of birth*: 3/9/52
> *Dates of examination*: 8/12/94, 8/19/94
> *Referring professional*: The Rev. Tom Blenkinsop, St. Andrew's Church,
>   1734 Whitney St., Chicago, IL 60680

Referral Question (Sample Narrative)

Ms. Stanhope, a 42-year-old African-American female, was referred by the Commission on Ministry of the Episcopal Diocese of Lakewood for psychological assessment and evaluation in connection with her application for holy orders. Specifically, the evaluation was requested to address (1) the presence of psychological problems that could lead to decompensation

	Interview	MMPI-2	MCMI-II	WAIS-R	Rorschach	Summary
Approach and Reliability/Validity						
Cognitive Functioning and Ideation						
Affect/Mood/ Emotional Control						
Conflict Areas						
Intra- and Interpersonal Coping Strategies						
Diagnostic Impression						
Recommendations						

Procedures

FIGURE 10.10. Blank summary worksheet for Petra Stanhope (Case 4).

under the stresses of ministry in the Episcopal Church; (2) her propensity for abuse of the power associated with the role and function of a priest; and (3) her leadership potential.

Assessment Procedures (Sample Narrative)

Assessment took place on two separate occasions. On August 12, 1994, a 1-hour clinical interview was followed by the administration of the MMPI-2 and WAIS-R. In the afternoon of the same day, Ms. Stanhope completed the MCMI-II and the Rorschach protocol. On August 19, after test results had been obtained, she was seen for a further 30-minute clinical interview, in order to follow up on material emerging from assessment measures.

Explanation of Assessment Procedures (Note to Reader)

Two main considerations affect the choice and interpretation of assessment procedures for this client. First, this is not a client presenting herself with problems for therapy, but a normally well-functioning woman whose assessment is required for advancement in her chosen career. She is likely to be concerned to present herself in the best possible light; therefore, such overt procedures as an interview are inadequate to fully assess the possibility of pathological aspects in her personality or functioning. At the same time, the fact that she is not experiencing subjective distress and functions well in her normal environment indicates that assessment procedures focusing on pathology must be interpreted with great caution.

A second major consideration in the assessment of this client is the need for a comprehensive approach. The Episcopal Church is concerned, especially in light of recent disclosures of abuse of power by the clergy of all denominations, to screen new applicants for the priesthood as thoroughly as possible. Since the assessment decision will strongly affect this woman's acceptance into an enduring position of power over others, it is evident that the use of multiple assessment procedures is warranted in order to fully answer the referral questions. The procedures chosen in this case (interview, MMPI-2, MCMI-II, WAIS-R, Rorschach) are designed to assess both Axis I and Axis II pathology, and to provide a balance of objective and subjective approaches.

Background (Sample Narrative)
Information Relevant to Referral Question (Sample Narrative)

Ms. Stanhope has been married for 16 years to a 47-year-old physician. This is her first marriage, and she has no children. Until her marriage, she was employed as an assistant curator at a museum, but is now in a financial position to leave employment to pursue her "call" to the ministry and begin the process of working toward ordination. She has been active in her local congregation since the age of 6, and an "unofficial director of Christian education" since she was 25. On the advice of a friend and with the support of her husband, she has felt encouraged to pursue her lifelong commitment to religious service by applying to study for the priesthood. She experiences this decision as both important and somewhat intimidating, and presented as both anxious about the assessment procedures and relieved that they have been mandated by the church, since she does not wish to make a mistake in such a grave matter. She expressed herself as eager to accept recommendations that might arise from the psychological evaluation.

Ms. Stanhope is the only child of older parents. Her mother, described as "sweet, a model mother," was not employed outside the home, but was the organist and choirmaster in the local Episcopal parish. Her father, a physician, was also active in the church as chairman of several committees. He was "strong, quiet, always careful to do the right thing, and beloved by his patients." Her uncle, whom she idolized when she was a child, is a minister in the church. Ms. Stanhope was raised to be obedient, honest, and helpful to others, and reports having little or no conflict with her parents on these issues. Family disagreements were rare, but when they did occur, Ms. Stanhope reported feeling distress and tended to absent herself from the scene. She loved school, was a conscientious student, and participated in extracurricular activities; however, she tended to avoid leadership positions in favor of service tasks, such as working in the school library or helping induct new students into the school. She describes herself in her adolescence as "a bit shy with strangers, but confident with people I knew well."

She holds an undergraduate degree in art history, and has used this training in several jobs, which she has enjoyed and at which she has been successful. These jobs have all involved a high level of task responsibility but little involvement in personnel management. On two occasions, when she directed a museum project, she enjoyed the organizational and interrelational aspects of the team approach, but found that conflict with colleagues whom she was required to "manage" produced high anxiety with concomitant psychosomatic involvement. Her sexual development appears to have been unremarkable. Prior to her marriage, she had two brief adult romantic relationships, which were not sexual in nature. She reportedly enjoys sexual intimacy; she has conventional attitudes to sexuality and a restricted libido. She believes that she did not date much until her marriage because of her extensive involvement in multiple charitable and church activities, which left her little time for dating and provided her with adequate social contacts.

TABLE 10.41. Clinical Interview with Petra Stanhope (Case 4): Blank Cells

Approach and
Reliability/
Validity

Cognitive
Functioning
and Ideation

Affect/Mood/
Emotional Control

Conflict Areas

Intra- and
Interpersonal
Coping Strategies

Diagnostic
Impression

Recommendations

Note. As far as possible from the information provided, fill in the cells by capturing
the highlights of the assessment interview.

TABLE 10.42. Clinical Interview with Petra Stanhope (Case 4): Cells as Completed by Authors

Approach and Reliability/ Validity	*Anxious to please. Responded somewhat rigidly.*
Cognitive Functioning and Ideation	*Clear thinking, organized, detailed.*
Affect/Mood/ Emotional Control	*Calm, controlled; constricted affect; euthymic mood.*
Conflict Areas	*Directing others' behavior, especially if they resist.*
Intra- and Interpersonal Coping Strategies	*Reserved, affectionate, generous, kind, sensitive. Concerned about how others will react. Friendly; shy with strangers. Generally effective in daily life. Sensitive, good-natured.*
Diagnostic Impression	*Functions well in daily life. Productive and sociable except under conditions of stress, especially interpersonal conflict.*
Recommendations	*Minimal distress to support need for treatment.*

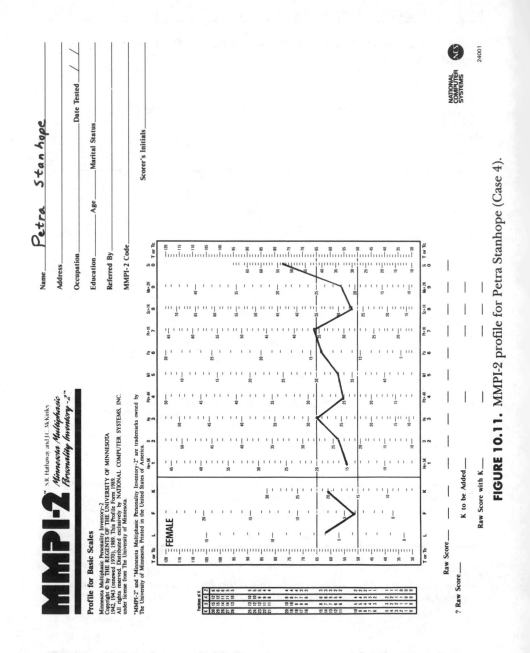

FIGURE 10.11. MMPI-2 profile for Petra Stanhope (Case 4).

TABLE 10.43. MMPI-2 Profile for Petra Stanhope (Case 4): Blank Cells

Approach and
Reliability/
Validity

Cognitive
Functioning
and Ideation

Affect/Mood/
Emotional Control

Conflict Areas

Intra- and
Interpersonal
Coping Strategies

Diagnostic
Impression

Recommendations

Note. As far as possible from the information provided, fill in the cells by capturing
the highlights of the MMPI-2 profile.

TABLE 10.44. MMPI-2 Profile for Petra Stanhope (Case 4): Cells as Completed by Authors

Approach and Reliability/ Validity	*Completed in timely and careful manner. Compliant, not self-inspective, guarded.*
Cognitive Functioning and Ideation	*Practical, concrete thinking. Conservative. Intelligent, rational, clear-thinking. Unimaginative in approach to problems.*
Affect/Mood/ Emotional Control	*Prone to worry. Overcontrolled. Slow personal tempo. Little evidence of depression or disturbed affect.*
Conflict Areas	*Concerned about success and power.*
Intra- and Interpersonal Coping Strategies	*Sincere, conventional, trusting, restrained in relationships. Responsible, cooperative. Accepting of advice and suggestion. Self-critical, cautious, moralistic. Rigid. Accepting of authority.*
Diagnostic Impression	*No diagnosis indicated. Social introversion, especially after encountering interpersonal conflict.*
Recommendations	*Counseling/therapy for overcontrol and nonassertion.*

MILLON CLINICAL MULTIAXIAL INVENTORY-II
FOR PROFESSIONAL USE ONLY

```
ID NUMBER = 000139293        VALID REPORT
PERSONALITY CODE = 3 7 ** 4 * 5 1 6B + 6A 8B " 8A 2   // - ** - *
SYNDROME CODE = - ** - * // - ** - * //
DEMOGRAPHIC = 00139293/ON/F/40/W/F/ G1/C/MA/LO/-----/01/02/-----/  332 0030
```

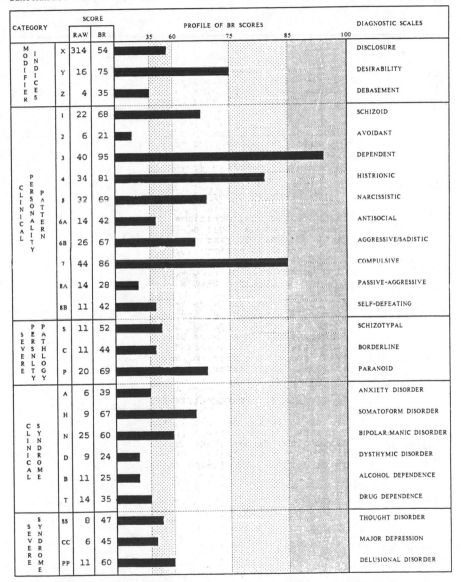

CATEGORY			SCORE		PROFILE OF BR SCORES	DIAGNOSTIC SCALES
			RAW	BR	35 60 75 85 100	
MODIFIER INDICES		X	314	54		DISCLOSURE
		Y	16	75		DESIRABILITY
		Z	4	35		DEBASEMENT
CLINICAL PERSONALITY	PATTERN	1	22	68		SCHIZOID
		2	6	21		AVOIDANT
		3	40	95		DEPENDENT
		4	34	81		HISTRIONIC
		5	32	69		NARCISSISTIC
		6A	14	42		ANTISOCIAL
		6B	26	67		AGGRESSIVE/SADISTIC
		7	44	86		COMPULSIVE
		8A	14	28		PASSIVE-AGGRESSIVE
		8B	11	42		SELF-DEFEATING
SEVERE PERSNLTY	PATHLOGY	S	11	52		SCHIZOTYPAL
		C	11	44		BORDERLINE
		P	20	69		PARANOID
CLINICAL	SYNDROME	A	6	39		ANXIETY DISORDER
		H	9	67		SOMATOFORM DISORDER
		N	25	60		BIPOLAR:MANIC DISORDER
		D	9	24		DYSTHYMIC DISORDER
		B	11	25		ALCOHOL DEPENDENCE
		T	14	35		DRUG DEPENDENCE
SEVERE	SYNDROME	SS	8	47		THOUGHT DISORDER
		CC	6	45		MAJOR DEPRESSION
		PP	11	60		DELUSIONAL DISORDER

FIGURE 10.12. MCMI-II profile for Petra Stanhope (Case 4).

TABLE 10.45. MCMI-II Profile for Petra Stanhope (Case 4): Blank Cells

Approach and
Reliability/
Validity

Cognitive
Functioning
and Ideation

Affect/Mood/
Emotional Control

Conflict Areas

Intra- and
Interpersonal
Coping Strategies

Diagnostic
Impression

Recommendations

Note. As far as possible from the information provided, fill in the cells by capturing
the highlights of the MCMI-II profile.

TABLE 10.46. MCMI-II Profile for Petra Stanhope (Case 4): Cells as Completed by Authors

Approach and Reliability/ Validity	*Completed in timely and careful manner.*
Cognitive Functioning and Ideation	*Able to read and comprehend. At least average intelligence. No cognitive impairment.*
Affect/Mood/ Emotional Control	*Pollyanna attitude to control negative emotions. Helpless, guilty when doesn't live up to others' expectations. Expresses attitudes contrary to feelings. Cognitively inconsistent.*
Conflict Areas	*Problems with assertion. Problems with anger.*
Intra- and Interpersonal Coping Strategies	*Interpersonally submissive. Subordinates needs to stronger, nurturing figure. Cognitively naive, easily persuaded, gullible. Compliant, self-sacrificing. Avoids conflict; docile, passive, warm.*
Diagnostic Impression	*Some symptoms of Dependent Personality Disorder.*
Recommendations	*Work on interpersonal skills.*

TABLE 10.47. WAIS-R Results for Petra Stanhope (Case 4)

Subscale	Raw score	Scaled score	Age-corrected scaled score
Information	28	16	16
Digit Span	17	11	11
Vocabulary	63	14	15
Arithmetic	15	12	12
Comprehension	31	18	18
Similarities	24	13	13
Picture Completion	19	14	15
Picture Arrangement	18	13	14
Block Design	33	10	10
Object Assembly	32	10	10
Digit Symbol	67	12	13

Note. FSIQ = 128; VIQ = 127; PIQ = 117. Total scaled scores = 144; Total Verbal scaled score = 84; Total Performance scaled score = 60. Factors: Verbal Comprehension = 129.4; Perceptual Organization = 112; Freedom from Distractibility = 108.4.

TABLE 10.48. WAIS-R Profile for Petra Stanhope (Case 4): Blank Cells

Approach and
Reliability/
Validity

Cognitive
Functioning
and Ideation

Affect/Mood/
Emotional Control

Conflict Areas

Intra- and
Interpersonal
Coping Strategies

Diagnostic
Impression

Recommendations

Note. As far as possible from the information provided, fill in the cells by capturing the highlights of the WAIS-R profile.

TABLE 10.49. WAIS-R Profile for Petra Stanhope (Case 4): Cells as Completed by Authors

Approach and Reliability/ Validity	*Completed answer sheet confidently and carefully.*
Cognitive Functioning and Ideation	*FSIQ = 128, VIQ = 130, PIQ = 126. Capable of abstract reasoning. Good conceptual skills. Doesn't risk in solving problems.*
Affect/Mood/ Emotional Control	*Unimpaired. No evidence of slow or exaggerated thinking.*
Conflict Areas	*Hesitant on Picture Arrangement—some concern with being observed and judged. Afraid of assertion.*
Intra- and Interpersonal Coping Strategies	*Somewhat reticent and prone to withdraw in case wrong. Unassertive.*
Diagnostic Impression	*Above average intelligence. No evidence of Axis I disorder.*
Recommendations	*Work on self-assertion and acceptance of intellectual strength.*

TABLE 10.50. Sample of Rorschach Scores for Petra Stanhope (Case 4)

Scoring type	Score
R (total responses)	25
F (form, pure)	10
M (movement, pure)	5
FM (form, movement)	2.5
FC (form, color)	4.5
W (whole blot)	9.5
m	0

Note. The scoring was based on the Exner system.

TABLE 10.51. Rorschach Profile for Petra Stanhope (Case 4): Blank Cells

Approach and
Reliability/
Validity

Cognitive
Functioning
and Ideation

Affect/Mood/
Emotional Control

Conflict Areas

Intra- and
Interpersonal
Coping Strategies

Diagnostic
Impression

Recommendations

Note. As far as possible from the information provided, fill in the cells by capturing
the highlights of the Rorschach profile.

TABLE 10.52. Rorschach Profile for Petra Stanhope (Case 4): Cells as Completed by Authors

Approach and Reliability/ Validity	*Tried hard. Anxious with ambiguity. Asked questions re: "right" answer.*
Cognitive Functioning and Ideation	*Deductive, methodical; lacks creativity; impoverished imagination.*
Affect/Mood/ Emotional Control	*Cautious. Tends to overcontrol emotions.*
Conflict Areas	*Dependence needs.*
Intra- and Interpersonal Coping Strategies	*Repression, denial.*
Diagnostic Impression	*Overcontrolled, dependent, anxious to please. No Axis I disorder.*
Recommendations	*Possible group treatment—learn to relax with others and be disclosing.*

TABLE 10.53. Summaries across Categories for Petra Stanhope (Case 4):
Blank Cells

Approach and
Reliability/
Validity

Cognitive
Functioning
and Ideation

Affect/Mood/
Emotional Control

Conflict Areas

Intra- and
Interpersonal
Coping Strategies

Diagnostic
Impression

Recommendations

Note. In the cells, summarize the highlights for all assessment procedures. Focus on commonalities and important differences across the cells.

TABLE 10.54. Summaries across Categories for Petra Stanhope (Case 4): Cells as Completed by Authors

Approach and Reliability/ Validity	*No evidence of factors seriously affecting validity or reliability.*
Cognitive Functioning and Ideation	*Superior IQ. No problems. Cognitive efficiency high. No thought disorder. Concrete, methodical, lacks imagination. Poor problem solving in unstructured environment?*
Affect/Mood/ Emotional Control	*Deliberately appropriate; usually calm, contented, euthymic, vigilant. Avoids/suppresses negative emotions. With interpersonal stress, anxious, overcontrolled, and rigid.*
Conflict Areas	*Major difficulty would be in leadership role. Avoidance of negative affect.*
Intra- and Interpersonal Coping Strategies	*Self-critical, trusting. Needs support, to please others, to submit to authority. Conflict: success vs. self-abnegation; responds with guilt and overcompensation. Limited personal autonomy?*
Diagnostic Impression	*No Axis I, III, or IV. Axis V: GAF 72. Axis II: Some features of Dependent Pers. Dis., but diagnosis not warranted. Impairment noted in leadership roles only.*
Recommendations	*Deny application. Individual treatment for grief over loss.*

Reliability and Validity of Conclusions (Sample Narrative)

Ms. Stanhope appeared concerned to present herself as sincere and open, and had no difficulty in providing negative information, though it was noticeably more difficult for her to respond positively in describing her strengths and achievements. Her manner throughout the procedures was reserved, somewhat rigid, and anxious. She appeared most confident with the structured intellectual assessment material (i.e., the WAIS-R), and most anxious when asked to respond to ambiguous and unstructured material (i.e., the Rorschach), where she asked several questions related to the "accuracy" and appropriateness of her responses. Presumably, ambiguous situations are more threatening to her desire to meet with others' approval than are more familiar and easily structured situations. Despite this slight difficulty, however, she persisted with all the procedures, was able to organize her responses in an appropriate way, and provided detailed and comprehensive information. It appears that the results reported here can be relied on as representative of this woman's usual functioning.

Summary of Impressions and Findings (Sample Narrative)

Ms. Stanhope is functioning in the "above average" range of intelligence, with good cognitive efficiency. She evidences no memory or concentration deficits, thought disorder, or other abnormalities of cognitive functioning. She tends to think in a rational, methodical, and concrete fashion, and is somewhat lacking in imagination—characteristics that should enhance her ability to perform in a structured environment, but may impair the flexibility and creativity of her responses to unpredictable situations and problems.

Ms. Stanhope has no history of emotional problems. Under most circumstances, her mood is calm, mildly cheerful, and contented, and others experience her as comforting and pleasant to be with. In general, her emotions are somewhat limited in range and intensity. She tries to organize her environment and activities so as to prevent or circumvent problems and thus avoid disturbance of her usual mood. She is careful to demonstrate socially appropriate affect, even if that does not always represent her inner experience. She may, for example, express more enthusiasm or interest than she feels, but her strong moral beliefs will in all likelihood prevent her from expressing an emotion she does not actually feel. When problems arise in her life, she tends to intensify her cheerfulness and to deny the extent or importance of negative aspects, thus avoiding the necessity of feeling deep sadness or anger.

In social situations where she is a key player, especially situations with unfamiliar or ambiguous aspects, she displays increased vigilance for negative or intense emotions in herself or in others—in particular, interpersonal conflict and lack of cooperation—and responds by increasing her cognitive control to the point of rigid and stereotypical responses of a practical problem-solving nature, or by physically escaping the situation if possible. She typically experiences mild heightened social anxiety, except when she is with people she knows well and with whom she can take the role of helper or colleague. After a disturbing experience, she regains her equanimity with relative ease, again using strong cognitive controls to rationalize what has happened. She responds empathically to emotions in others, as long as she is not personally involved in the problem, and she is successful in using her desire to be helpful to control her preference for avoiding strong negative affect. By increasing the formality of her behavior and maintaining an objective helping role, she enables herself to respond effectively even in difficult situations.

Ms. Stanhope's strong moral values, pleasant manner, and desire to help others make her a valued friend and colleague. She has maintained stable and satisfactory relationships with family and friends over long periods of time. She discharges her duties willingly and effectively and performs well in teamwork situations when she is not the leader. In her circle of intimates whom she has known for many years, she functions very well and experiences no major problems or conflicts—only a mild tendency to be self-critical and withdrawn. She is able to receive and express affection, to manage her time well, and to work toward goals with a minimum of direction.

Her dominant need appears to be to please and serve others; a secondary need is that of submission to a strong, moral, nurturing figure, usually male. In conflict with these needs is the fact that her academic achievements and successful history of helping others have given her a desire for personal success and authority. She is ambivalent toward this desire, regarding it on the one hand as a legitimate use of God-given talents, and the other as a wavering from what she perceives to be the more moral position of self-sacrifice. To this point, she has tended to cope with this conflict by pursuing success and reputation in areas that she believes meet her higher goal of service, such as becoming an expert at organizing religious conferences. She is somewhat naive in her expectation that others outside her intimate circle will not abuse the power that she gives them, and will respond to her sincerity and conscientiousness with equal cooperation and self-control. In consequence of these needs and perceptions, she tends to be friendly, compliant, and trusting until she meets with unexpected reactions, whereupon she becomes somewhat rigid and cautious, retreating into formalized or avoidance behavior patterns. In a position where she is required to exercise authority over others, she may experience difficulty in asserting herself, especially if those others are also ministers, are male, or resist her authority.

Diagnostic Impressions (Sample Narrative)

Ms. Stanhope is a relatively stable woman who is experiencing no current stressors and has no history of mental illness. She manages most aspects of life well, maintains good community and personal relationships, and is able to pursue a productive and satisfying lifestyle. Since adolescence she has displayed features of Dependent Personality Disorder, but her symptoms do not warrant this diagnosis because of the limited impact of her dependence and her apparent ability to organize her life so as to minimize her impairment without unduly constricting her effectiveness. Difficulties are noted only when she is placed in leadership positions that require her to perform such functions as managing intra- and intergroup dissent, confronting and dealing with negative affect, and making decisions that may be unpopular or that she may have to persuade others to implement. In such a role, she tends to withdraw and look for guidance from someone with more authority.

Recommendations (Sample Narrative)

Ms. Stanhope is unlikely to abuse power to dominate others; on the contrary, she is more likely to fail to make full and effective use of the authority with which she is invested. Although in a relatively calm and circumscribed environment Ms. Stanhope functions well, it would appear that at this time she is unlikely to respond effectively to the interpersonal and leadership demands that would be made of her in the position of a parish priest. For this reason, it is recommended that she withdraw her application to study for the priesthood.

There is a possibility that psychotherapy to address both insight and behavior change issues related to avoidance of conflict and negative affect may help Ms. Stanhope. However, her dependence, especially on authority figures, represents such a long-standing pattern of behavior that she may not be able to overcome these tendencies to a degree sufficient to allow her to fill a strong leadership role.

It is further recommended that Ms. Stanhope immediately undertake individual, supportive psychotherapy to help her through the grief she will doubtless experience at the loss of her long-hoped-for vocation, and that contact be maintained with Ms. Stanhope for some time to monitor the possible development of acute withdrawal or a depressive illness in response to the failure of her ambition.

Index